House Rules

Law and Society Series
W. Wesley Pue, Founding Editor

We pay tribute to the late Wes Pue, under whose broad vision, extraordinary leadership, and unwavering commitment to socio-legal studies our Law and Society Series was established and rose to prominence.

The Law and Society Series explores law as a socially embedded phenomenon. It is premised on the understanding that the conventional division of law from society creates false dichotomies in thinking, scholarship, educational practice, and social life. Books in the series treat law and society as mutually constitutive and seek to bridge scholarship emerging from interdisciplinary engagement of law with disciplines such as politics, social theory, history, political economy, and gender studies.

Recent books in the series

Florence Ashley, *Banning Transgender Conversion Practices: A Legal and Policy Analysis* (2022)

Dia Dabby, *Religious Diversity in Canadian Public Schools: Rethinking the Role of Law* (2022)

Kim Stanton, *Reconciling Truths: Reimagining Public Inquiries in Canada* (2022)

Daniel Rück, *The Laws and the Land: The Settler Colonial Invasion of Kahnawà:ke in Nineteenth-Century Canada* (2021)

Suzanne Bouclin, *Women, Film, and Law: Cinematic Representations of Female Incarceration* (2021)

Amanda Nelund, *A Better Justice? Community Programs for Criminalized Women* (2020)

Trevor C.W. Farrow and Lesley A. Jacobs, eds., *The Justice Crisis: The Cost and Value of Accessing Law* (2020)

Jamie Baxter, *Inalienable Properties: The Political Economy of Indigenous Land Reform* (2020)

Jeremy Patrick, *Faith or Fraud: Fortune-Telling, Spirituality, and the Law* (2020)

Obiora Chinedu Okafor, *Refugee Law after 9/11: Sanctuary and Security in Canada and the United States* (2020)

For a complete list of the titles in the series, see the UBC Press website, www.ubcpress.ca.

House Rules

Changing Families, Evolving Norms, and the Role of Law

EDITED BY EREZ ALONI AND RÉGINE TREMBLAY

UBCPress · Vancouver · Toronto

31 30 29 28 27 26 25 24 23 22   5 4 3 2 1

Printed in Canada on FSC-certified ancient-forest-free paper (100% post-consumer recycled) that is processed chlorine- and acid-free.

Library and Archives Canada Cataloguing in Publication

Title: House rules : changing families, evolving norms, and the role of law / edited by Erez Aloni and Régine Tremblay.
Other titles: House rules (UBC Press)
Names: Aloni, Erez, editor. | Tremblay, Régine, editor.
Description: Series statement: Law and society, ISSN (print) 1496–4953, ISSN (ebook) 1925–0215 | Includes bibliographical references and index.
Identifiers: Canadiana (print) 20220177244 | Canadiana (ebook) 20220177279 | ISBN 9780774867399 (hardcover) | ISBN 9780774867412 (PDF) | ISBN 9780774867429 (EPUB)
Subjects: LCSH: Domestic relations—Canada.
Classification: LCC KE539 .H66 2022 | LCC KF505.ZA2 .H68 2022 | DDC 346.7101/5—dc23

Canadä

UBC Press gratefully acknowledges the financial support for our publishing program of the Government of Canada (through the Canada Book Fund), the Canada Council for the Arts, and the British Columbia Arts Council.

UBC Press
The University of British Columbia
2029 West Mall
Vancouver, BC V6T 1Z2
www.ubcpress.ca

To my parents, Marius and Jenny, for their unstinting generosity and love.
– Erez Aloni

To Susan B. Boyd, FRSC.
– Régine Tremblay

Contents

Preface

This book is one of the research outputs of an international and interdisciplinary workshop – held on 9–10 May 2019 in Vancouver – celebrating the work of Professor Emerita Susan B. Boyd, FRSC. During those two days, scholars from different backgrounds, disciplines, and jurisdictions engaged creatively and rigorously with themes that have animated Susan B. Boyd's scholarship during her career: the public/private divide, autonomy, ideology, privatization, empirical work, and family law reform. These themes are prevalent in our book and informed the contributors' engagements with the fundamental question that our book asks, namely, how do we overcome the gap between rapidly changing familial norms and norm-setting institutions that do not deliver just outcomes?

Since we held that workshop and the presenters revised their papers for inclusion in this book, the world has changed in unprecedented ways, and the impacts of these transformations have yet to be measured. When we met, in person, on those gorgeous spring days in Vancouver, little did we know about what the near future held in store. None of us could have foreseen a global pandemic that would transform our lives, relationships, and families. Some of us were only too aware of the simmering racial tensions in the United States – and in Canada. But again, there was a sense of hope that the best was yet to come and that we were in a moment of positive change. Time has proven us wrong.[1]

The global COVID-19 pandemic has further entrenched many of the stubborn norms that our book highlights, and has underscored the need to unsettle certain norms along with the laws that sustain them. The pandemic has put enormous pressures on relationships and families, and its consequences are still to be measured. At this early stage, we can say confidently that the pandemic has underscored the stickiness of dated norms that reinforce the gendered division of care work and has had unequal effects on women and primary care providers. A United Nations brief states that, "[a]cross every sphere, from health to the economy, security to social protection, the impacts of COVID-19 are exacerbated for women and girls simply by virtue of their sex."[2] One study that surveyed two thousand adults in the United States found that people have adopted more traditional gender norms and roles during the pandemic.[3] A report from British Columbia, Canada, states that women in that province are most likely to work in one of the four industries that have been most affected by public health measures designed to limit the spread of COVID-19. Their concentration in these industries, the report details, led to women in British Columbia losing 60 percent more jobs than men in March 2020.[4] In addition, women, as this book documents, have remained the main channel for the privatization of child care. The impact of no child care and/or the temporary closure of schools fell mainly on women, who have stayed home with their children, worked shorter hours, and spent more time on housework chores during the pandemic.[5] The "private" labour of women has had an enormous effect on public issues, calling further attention to the extent to which the private/public divide persists. Finally, the harm to women has had a disproportional impact on racialized and Indigenous women, as they often work as care providers and in part-time, unstable jobs.[6] Further, severe outbreaks have been common in areas populated by families with low income, where racialized and Indigenous women have a greater chance of getting infected and less access to good health care.[7] The need for intersectional analyses of gender, like the one provided in the chapters by Wanda Wiegers and Chao-ju Chen in this book, is acute.

Other issues that contributors discuss in this book are even more relevant today than when they were written. The pandemic has accentuated access-to-justice problems discussed by a few contributors – and reinforced the necessity of thinking innovatively about solutions. Separated parents have faced various challenges related to raising their children, but courts have mostly been closed to non-urgent issues.[8] The increased use of technology – Zoom trials, for example – might serve as an opening, allowing the legal community to deepen our thinking about how to make courts more accessible.[9] Finally, we need to consider the increased prevalence of family violence and child abuse that has accompanied the pandemic. Again, we have yet to measure the impacts – and prevalence – of this pervasive phenomenon and how it exposes norms and inherent tensions, and highlights the need to unsettle laws and policies in order to assist and protect vulnerable parties in relationships and families.

In essence, the pandemic has underlined the main point that this book advances: the plea to understand family law broadly, as a discipline comprising a vast array of mechanisms affecting family lives and contributing to the structuring of households. Failures of the family law system were evident before March 2020. The pandemic has entrenched existing inequalities and displayed law's dereliction of duty when it comes to fulfilling people's needs. In the next decade, engaging meaningfully with the themes of our book – the necessity to take an empirical turn; creeping privatization; reforming law reform; and employing intersectional analyses, including with respect to patriarchy, racism, colonialism, and class – will be crucial for the development of family laws and, will, we hope, lead to a complete and necessary overhaul of family justice.

Notes

1 We note that one positive change is the amendment to the Canadian *Divorce Act* that came into force on 1 March 2021 with the key objectives of "promot[ing] the best interests of the child; address[ing] family violence; help[ing] to reduce child poverty; [and] mak[ing] Canada's family justice system more accessible and efficient." Whether these objectives will actually be met is a question worth asking. See *An Act to amend the Divorce Act, the Family Orders and Agreements Enforcement Assistance Act and the Garnishment, Attachment and Pension Diversion Act and to make consequential amendments to another Act*, SC 2019, c 16.

2 UN, *Policy Brief: The Impact of COVID-19 on Women* (9 April 2020), online (PDF): <https://www.unwomen.org/-/media/headquarters/attachments/sections/library/publications/2020/policy-brief-the-impact-of-covid-19-on-women-en.pdf?la=en&vs=1406>.

3 Daniel L Rosenfeld & A Janet Tomiyama, "Can a Pandemic Make People More Socially Conservative? Political Ideology, Gender Roles, and the Case of COVID-19" [2021] J Applied Social Psychology, online: National Center for Biotechnological Information, <https://www.ncbi.nlm.nih.gov/pmc/articles/PMC8014651/>.

4 BC Women's Health Foundation, *Unmasking Gender Inequity: Revealing the Socio-economic Impacts of COVID-19 on Women's Health* (November 2020), online (PDF): <https://assets.bcwomensfoundation.org/2020/11/20122829/BCWHF-Unmasking-Gender-Inequity-Report-2020-1.pdf>.

5 Caitlyn Collins et al, "COVID-19 and the Gender Gap in Work Hours" (2020) 28 Gender, Work & Organization 1, online: Wiley Online Library, <https://onlinelibrary.wiley.com/doi/abs/10.1111/gwao.12506>; Matt Krentz et al, "Easing the COVID-19 Burden on Working Parents" (21 May 2020), online: Boston Consulting Group, <https://www.bcg.com/publications/2020/helping-working-parents-ease-the-burden-of-covid-19>.

6 As the United Nations observes, "[t]he situation of indigenous women, who are often the main providers of food and nutrition to their families," is especially grave; UN, Department of Economic and Social Affairs, Indigenous Peoples, "COVID-19 and Indigenous Peoples," online: United Nations, <https://www.un.org/development/desa/indigenouspeoples/covid-19.html>. SG Berkhout & L Richardson, "Identity, Politics, and the Pandemic: Why Is COVID-19 a Disaster for Feminism(s)?" (2020) 42:49 History and Philosophy of the Life Sciences, online: Springer Link, <https://doi.org/10.1007/s40656-020-00346-7> [Berkhout & Richardson].

7 Berkhout & Richardson, *supra* note 6.

8 Graham Slaughter, "COVID-19 Custody Battles Present Tricky Challenge for Overwhelmed Courts" *CTV News* (11 September 2020), online: <https://www.ctvnews.ca/canada/covid-19-custody-battles-present-tricky-challenge-for-overwhelmed-courts-1.5102015>.

9 T Sourdin, B Li & DM McNamara. "Court Innovations and Access to Justice in Times of Crisis" (2020) 9:4 Health Policy & Technology 447–53, online: ScienceDirect, <doi:10.1016/j.hlpt.2020.08.020>.

Acknowledgments

This project was funded by the Social Sciences and Humanities Research Council (SSHRC) through its Connection program, the Centre for Feminist Legal Studies, the Franklin Lew Innovation Fund, and the Peter A. Allard School of Law.

We would like to extend our thanks to the many groups of people who made this collection of essays possible. We could not have published this book without their help. We are extremely grateful to our contributors for working with us to share their important, insightful scholarship on a range of critical issues. Additionally, we are especially grateful to our former Dean, Catherine Dauvergne, and to Natasha Affolder, Doug Harris, Debra Parkes, Susan B. Boyd, Claire Young, Sancho McCann, Crystal Choi, Sara Ghebremusse, Emma Cunliffe, Justice Donna Martinson, Asha Kaushal, Janine Benedet, Michelle Burchill, Simmi Puri, Aki Nishida, Elizabeth Janzen, Nazanin Panah, Leslie Cohen, Gillian Calder, Melissa "MJ" Durkee, and Maira Hassan. As well, we are very indebted to the thoughtful feedback from Michael Boucai. We also owe a great debt to our research assistants, Sophia M. Matthew, Lauren Marshall, and Diana Dahae Kim, who provided invaluable work in different stages of this book's production. We would also like to thank the team at UBC Press: our acquisitions editor, Randy Schmidt; our production editor, Katrina Petrik; and our copy editor, Barbara Tessman. Finally, we are thankful to the three anonymous reviewers for their constructive feedback.

We hope you will enjoy this book.

House Rules

Introduction

Erez Aloni and Régine Tremblay

This book addresses a fundamental question in family law: how to overcome the gap between rapidly changing social norms, both statistical and ideological, and legal policies and practices that so often fail to deliver just outcomes. Even in jurisdictions where legislative and judicial reforms have been instituted to address some of the many problems facing contemporary families, fair and adequate legal solutions remain elusive. Responsive reforms tend to be too limited and often come too late, while more proactive innovations, intended as much to shape as to reflect transformations in family life, often underestimate conventional norms' resistance to change. Either way, the attempt falls short of its object, in many instances entrenching or exacerbating inequality.

Why should a book on family law focus so decidedly on *norms*? To explain, we must first define and clarify the term. Among the meanings supplied by the *Merriam-Webster Dictionary,* the ones that come closest to our usage here define a norm as "an authoritative standard," "a principle of right action binding upon the members of a group and serving to guide, control, or regulate proper and acceptable behavior."[1] Social norms, then, are informal yet authoritative and widespread standards that guide the conduct of members of a specific community. Although they may be expressed in law, social norms "retain a distinctive profile" by representing patterns of behaviour "as peculiarly desirable or obligatory."[2]

Our focus on norms stems from the special status that norms have in family lives and their particular influence on family laws.[3] Social norms relate to almost every aspect of relationships and household management: from decisions about reproduction to parenting, surname to wedding, money management to estate planning. At the same time, norms play a significant role in the institutional design of public policies. Indeed, laws and norms are situated in a complex, intertwined relationship. Because norms have widespread areas of overlap with laws, we adopt an expansive definition of laws and regulations. Laws and regulations are here used interchangeably to mean any legal directives or policies promulgated by state actors.[4] Likewise, institutions and non-state organizations also create, disseminate, and enforce centralized norms in ways that guide patterns of behaviours and therefore are an integral part of inquiry within this book.[5]

Representing four countries (Canada, the United Kingdom, the United States, and Taiwan), the contributors to this book undertake three crucial projects at the juncture of social norms and family law. Some of our authors focus primarily on discovery and description: uncovering and elaborating the norms that actually prevail in the families and households of particular contemporary societies. Others are interested mainly in evaluation and improvement – in critiquing, revising, and offering new tools to critique and transform some of the well-intentioned law reform efforts that have tried to keep up with changing social norms. And still other authors are chiefly concerned with documenting and analyzing some of the effects that resilient norms and inadequate reforms have wrought on diverse types of families and relationships. All three projects are in some sense unsettling, either by questioning and destabilizing norms that lie beneath, adjacent to, or well outside of family law, or by exposing how certain norms are themselves disturbing or are being disturbed.

The name of this collection, *House Rules*, means to capture how diverse norms operate among various communities and households and play a vital role in organizing everyday lives. House rules can be the idiosyncratic norms that govern each and every household, as well as the rules pertaining to economic management of the household, division of chores, and guidelines reflecting what parents expect from their children. At the same time, house rules can solidify norms. *Merriam-Webster* defines a house rule as "a rule (as in a game) that applies only among a certain group or in a certain place."[6] It follows that norms that guide behaviours can also appear formalized and centralized, like those of card games in a casino or the norms of a member of a legislative branch.[7] Understanding the dominant house rules and their relation to regulations is one main topic we address in this book.

Norms, Laws, Scholarship: Playing Catch-Up

How have legal systems and scholarship responded to changes in familial social norms? There is no question that modifications in social norms have posed daunting challenges to regulators. Over the past few decades, lawmakers have struggled to adjust normative content in the face of dramatic shifts in norms, practices, and structures that govern households and relationships.[8] Consider that, in many households, both partners have now joined the paid labour force, prompting adjustment of laws – custody rules, for example – designed under the assumption that households are composed of a breadwinner and a homemaker.[9] At the same time, the norm of marriage as a lifelong commitment has declined, and an expectation of easily available divorce has grown. When laws failed to keep pace with these new norms, some people manufactured "fault" as a way to get a divorce; whereas others suffered a great deal until legislatures implemented no-fault divorce. Then, after no-fault divorce became widespread and dissolution of marriage more common and readily available, the nuclear family lost some of its dominance. The norm of getting married at all has lost its prominence; lawmakers still struggle with formulating a policy that will effectively address the skyrocketing numbers of unmarried cohabitants. More recently, laws have had to engage with changing norms with respect to same-sex relationships and sole parenting. Finally, in a new set of challenges, laws need to respond to the increased trendiness of polyamory and other family arrangements that involve more than two adults, whether as parents or partners. As laws and policy have striven to keep up with these evolutions, new norms have continued to arise and disrupt legal systems' ability to effectively address the realities of families' lives.

Simultaneously, lawmakers have occasionally struggled with norms that have not altered fast enough and with the adverse outcomes that these now-outdated or undesirable norms have produced for families. Consider, as an example, the allocation of unpaid care work within the household. On average, across the Global North, women remain responsible for a larger share of domestic work and care, an imbalance that contributes to gender-based differences in career progress and to gaps in income and wealth holding.[10] These discrepancies can create major economic effects during and after the end of relationships. Laws in many common law jurisdictions, and various other jurisdictions, were amended to help correct the unequal consequences that divorce had on primary caregivers, by compensating them for economic losses that resulted from their domestic responsibilities and interdependency. Yet, as some chapters in this book show, despite reforms, legal systems have failed to produce just results.[11] The norm of care work being performed unequally has been particularly sticky. Indeed, sometimes, as some of our contributors demonstrate, family laws are at least partly responsible for this reinforcement.

Along with changing norms and some attempts at reforming laws, family law scholarship has metamorphosed.[12] This transformation is expressed by the topics that scholars explore, the methods they use, and by their interdisciplinary, comparative, and intersectional approaches. In terms of topics, from a field focused primarily on spouses/state relationships and the financial consequences of divorce, scholarship is now reaching into, and advancing in, new spheres. Unashamedly, family law scholarship probes a wide variety of issues related to the internal and external operations and functions of households, ranging from wealth inequality to urban design, from privatization to dispute resolution and to what constitutes a family in the first place. Laura Kessler calls this expanded version of family law "the law of intimate relations." She envisions that this version "will not be centered on marriage; it will erase the market/family and public/private distinctions; and it will include a multitude of human connections involving sex, reproduction, and care."[13] In correlation with the evolution of scholarship, the breadth of the fields from which scholars draw their analytical tools is larger than ever.

Complementing this shift in scholarship is a renewed interest in comparative family law and in exploring globalization's effects on families and their regulations.[14] Ideas flow easily and quickly across jurisdictions, inspiring and influencing reforms – and sometimes backlash – elsewhere.[15] One particular theoretical framework that has had global influence in family law scholarship is intersectionality.[16] A pivotal exploration by four scholars – including Kimberlé Crenshaw, who first introduced the theory – mapped intersectionality as an interdisciplinary analytical tool and as a social movement, one that "moves across national boundaries."[17] Growing literature begins with the view that intersectional harms characterize inequalities in family law.

Reflecting those changes in scholarship, particularly vis-à-vis the exploration of social norms, this book grows out of our belief that comparative perspectives are fruitful in inspiring scholarship, policymaking, and discourse, especially in the area of family studies.[18] Likewise, two chapters emphasize intersectionality as a fundamental paradigm in regulating family life, and many chapters incorporate feminist, queer, and critical perspectives. In adopting this wide-ranging approach, we recognize that contemporary family law must be data-driven, conceptual, and culturally sensitive. Embracing an integrative approach – in terms of methods and scope of interventions – helps underscore this point.

The Book's Central Themes

Five central themes emerge from and structure the arrangement of the chapters. Each part of the book introduces the two chapters most representative of the theme, but nothing prevents other chapters from engaging with other themes. Part 1, "Locating Norms," explores unconventional areas of law in which novel family law scholarship looks for social norms, and it gives reasons for an expanded vision about what constitute meaningful norms for family law. Part 2, "Law's Norms," uncovers certain important social norms that family law upholds and promulgates, particularly the traditional division of house and care work. Part 3, "Norms' Stickiness," addresses how different manifestations of the private/public divide are particularly resistant to change. Part 4, "Measuring Norms," considers how empirical methods can uncover norms, and how such methods can and should be used to inform policy. Part 5, "Reforming Norms," contemplates how to reform the reform process itself, both concretely in legislative attempts, and in more theoretical and conceptual levels.

Locating Norms

Traditionally, family law scholarship confined itself to areas governing entrance into and exit from marriage – including rules concerning financial obligations following the breakdown of marriage – as well as some parent/child/state relationships. Janet Halley and Kerry Rittich call these areas

"Family Law 1," or, for short, "FL1."[19] They claim that, typically, to identify which topics constitute core areas in the FL1 field, one should look to contemporary family law textbooks, treatises, and law codes. Following their advice, Laura Kessler recently studied eighty-six family law casebooks published in the United States from 1960 to 2019. She found that "the core of the academic field of family law has remained relatively stable in the past 60 years."[20] By ascertaining what FL1 focuses on, we learn implicitly what topics it excludes and we can begin to inquire into the consequences of those exclusions.

According to Halley and Rittich, "Family Law 2" (FL2) refers to the laws that govern the family but are not part of distinct family law statutes. This category includes definitions of "family" and references to family members in legal rules concerning, for example, immigration, taxation, and welfare assistance. Put differently, FL2 regulations are those that quite clearly define and shape the family even as they lie outside of FL1's core.

"Family Law 3" (FL3) ventures into even more remote territory, encompassing various legal directives – from ordinances to definitions of family in human resources regulations – that affect the household's governance and composition more generally.[21] Consider, as examples, zoning laws that restrict the types of families that can live in an area, and condominium bylaws that disallow children.[22] Finally, "Family Law 4" (FL4) consists of myriad social and familial norms that shape FL1, FL2, and FL3. Although FL4 norms have no legal status, their content strongly influences the other three types of family law.

Probing family laws and family lives in the context of diverse legal regimes – a shift from a predominant focus on FL1 to a combination of all four areas – is part of an analytical move that contests the "exceptionalism" of family law: a tendency among scholars, judges, policymakers, and even laypeople to treat family law as distinct from other legal fields and as isolated from influences and values that guide other areas of law. Exceptionalism thus refers to doctrinal and normative characterizations of the family as a special object of moral or cultural concern and a special repository of values. The exceptionalism is achieved by a set of dichotomies where family is an entity positioned in opposition to the market, as a site of altruism instead of individualism, and as the site of status as opposed to contract.[23]

Doctrinally, according to conventional exceptionalist perspective, the foundational doctrines and theories of private laws should not constitute part of the corpus of family law (in the singular, as this is a unique type of law; we sometimes use "family laws" in the plural to reflect a set of regulations that reach far beyond the laws that constitute FL1).[24] This doctrinal isolation is supposed to reflect a view that families – and the laws that apply to them – represent the local, private, vulnerable, and altruistic.[25] Family law is understood as safeguarding the family from the influences of the market, including the perils of individualism and globalization.

Casting aside these foundational oppositions unveils a nuanced and complex body of family laws. Several contributors to this book turned their focus to how FL4 (social norms) interacts with the other types of legal directives that affect family life, be they within FL1, FL2, or, mainly, FL3. Escaping the traditional silos of family law brings new insights to light, in which regulations of family have a distributional impact on the market and society at large.

In Chapter 1, for example, Allison Tait explores the long-lived norm of financial privacy among elite families, showing how this norm has persisted, albeit in newer forms. The chapter unsettles deep-rooted norms of financial privacy among the ultra-rich. To locate the norm in its current manifestations, Tait draws on a wide variety of unconventional sources, far from FL1: from financial regulations that privilege the "family office" to the advertisements used by trust companies and wealth managers. Tait shows how various laws, related mainly to tax, trust, and estate planning, create a special regime that provides a distinctive and exclusive kind of financial privacy to wealthy families. Although these uber-rich families seek to shield their "private" information, she contends that they are *not* outside the market, rather, connected to the market and manipulate the market to their needs. And the outcomes are far from private: market behaviour creates negative externalities for most other families. Indeed, the privacy norm that elites are free from government scrutiny stands in contradiction to the norms governing everyone else's lives, especially people with low incomes. For the latter, privacy from government intrusion cannot be purchased. The result of norms that allow ultra-rich families to escape the scrutiny of the law is the increase in wealth inequality.

In Chapter 2, Chao-ju Chen tackles the legal challenges experienced by Taiwanese Indigenous women who transmit their Indigenous status to their children. Patronymic naming has been a particularly ingrained norm in that country; 98 percent of all newborns are given their father's name, and over 80 percent of non-marital children are given their father's surname after paternal acknowledgment. Indigenous mothers who intermarry with non-Indigenous partners must choose between giving Indigenous status to their child or having the child receive their spouse's name, a choice that reflects norms associated with both gender and racial hierarchies. Chen's research leaves FL1 altogether and moves freely between FL2 (administrative laws that govern name change) and FL3 (rules regarding the transfer of Indigenous status) to expose the work that FL4 does in shaping the law – namely, preserving patrilineal normativity.

Chen's chapter deals with denying Indigenous mothers the ability to pass on Indigenous status to their children, which is a form of discrimination at the intersection of patriarchy and colonialism. The rules enabling this denial often involve discrimination based on various combinations of gender, marital status, age, and race. Informed by scholarship on multiculturalism and feminism, her chapter contends that "the intersection of private and public laws produces a unique situation where gender-neutral law perpetrates gender inequality through *private choice*." Chen contends that paternal bloodlines were privileged in order to sustain racial hierarchy – a goal that has survived several legal reforms through the imposition of the gendered and racialized duty of naming. She theorizes that group self-determination does not facilitate the dual goals of gender and Indigenous justice if Indigenous sovereignty is established as a private sphere that tolerates internal domination. Her work marks an assessment of a failed reform – a theme we discuss later in detail – and uses intersectionality as a major analytical lens to illuminate the roles that gender and Indigeneity play in creating the problem and the role they must play in solving the inequality.

Several other chapters seek the norms that influence family lives outside standard family law codes. In our view, what is most important is the conclusion: family laws cannot be found only in the core statutes and legal directives where the word "family" appears. Family law is, and ought to include, the vast array of legal mechanisms that affect family lives and contribute to the structuring of households and personal relationships.

Law's Norms

Laws and social norms have complex relations. Sometimes, laws incorporate and express existing norms. At other times, laws are responsible for the creation and/or the maintenance of norms. Often, norms are attendant to specific *roles*. Classic examples include doctor, friend, teacher, and student. Each role entails a web of social norms that almost everyone understands and internalizes. Laws and norms that constitute a role are interconnected in many ways. As Cass Sunstein puts it, "prevailing roles and norms can be fortified by legal requirements; they may even owe their existence to law. Law is frequently an effort to prescribe roles ... In fact, many roles are so deeply internalized that they seem 'natural,' even though they owe their origin to social and even legal conventions."[26]

In our book, the role of *spouse* has loomed large as a central element at the intersection of law and familial norms. Historically, gendered spousal roles were upheld by laws, for example, by the doctrine of coverture, or by duties of obedience and protection. Although rules that directly prescribe gendered roles are no longer in effect – and indeed same-sex marriage is now legal in all jurisdictions discussed in this book – traditional spousal norms of unequal allocation of care remain ingrained. What is the function of laws in sustaining the gendered dimensions of spousal roles? Does law have a role in dismantling them?

Uncovering the norms that laws promote is an arduous task. Gender-neutral language in legal directives and court opinions often eclipses the gendered effects of legal rules. To ascertain the responsibility of legal rules to the maintenance of traditional spousal roles, scholars need to dig deep and examine distributional consequences of various laws from diverse fields, as well as how they affect norms. Further, the fact that diversity of spousal relationships exists – with different or similar patterns of division of labour, with same-sex marriage, and with different class and racial dimensions – makes it harder to elucidate the norms without falling into an essentialist perspective as if most women are housemakers and most men are breadwinners.

Notwithstanding the difficulties, contributors in this book derive norms that show prominence in different legal systems, and expose the mechanisms used to promote them. The authors of Chapters 3 and 4 conduct their work in FL1 – rules pertaining to divorce, parenting, and property – but from their analysis, they learn what norms and roles the systems advance. The rhetoric that courts adopt purports to hide the stubbornness of traditional gendered norms, making their entrenchment more difficult to identify. The authors find that laws sometimes establish or support norms that help shape and structure households; at other times, a change in laws does no more than camouflage the continuation of previous outcomes.

In Chapter 3, Alison Diduck takes up the connection between familial norms and the functions of relevant laws by analyzing "[l]egal statements – judicial and legislative statements of the law" – in England and Wales. Her case study of rules pertaining to property division finds that older doctrines were designed under the norm of a breadwinner/homemaker household. Scholars and judges have characterized recent changes in rules governing division of assets as reflecting a shift from protecting societal institutions like marriage to creating policies that aim to protect the individual. That is, nowadays cases purport to reflect the new social norms that dominate relationships: those of independence, autonomy, and personal responsibility. Diduck doubts whether norms of individualism – such as clean break in divorce, in which each spouse is assumed or encouraged to reach self-sufficiency right after divorce – have taken prominence and replaced older norms. She points out that the substantive rules about division of property always have "said as much about the way society and the state organize and value economic, reproductive, and caring responsibilities as about the way family members do." Upon scrutiny, she contends, new doctrines still contain much of the previous laws' underpinnings. The expressive role of English law that praises independence is not in line with gendered norms and structures (like employment) that guide individuals in the role they adopt in their marriages. Both the old and new doctrines, despite the different norms they purport to promote, deliver the same outcome: they maintain a social order structured around traditional spousal roles of effectively a temporary breadwinner and a primary care provider.

In Chapter 4, Rachel Treloar shows how spousal roles transcend dimensions of relationships, before and after divorce. Her chapter uncovers the entrenchment of gendered norms related to parenting, based on a qualitative study conducted with twenty-five parents in British Columbia who at one time experienced a high-conflict separation or divorce. The chapter illustrates how a gendered division of labour is dynamic, generational, and related to class. Even those women who worked full time outside home during the marriage took a larger share of the care work than their former partners. Treloar finds that "most participants described men's work as prioritized within their marriage, whereas women's work inside the family was often invisible outside of it." The dynamics in division of labour, however, shifted after the divorce, where some of the ex-husbands asked to take a larger role in the care of the children. Some of these changes were conceptualized as part of a litigation strategy; at other times, when men took more responsibility for care, it opened their eyes to the complexity of the caregiving role, reminding us that gender-based norms harm all those who do not conform to the traditional construction of gender.

Treloar illuminates the massive part that gender roles and gendered expectations play during marriage and after divorce. Interviewees show that inequalities in division of labour persisted after divorce, in various manifestations. Their divorce proceedings heavily influenced the gender dynamics after the relationships, and most mothers felt disappointed by the legal system. Many believed that their ex-husbands were able to abuse the system by demanding to pay less child support while asking for more decision-making responsibilities and control over the children. Many mothers expressed the view that relevant laws diminished their roles as caregivers during the marriage, while forcing them afterwards to start being financially self-sufficient. Each parent deals with these inequities differently – some accept them, some fight them – but what is clear is how salient gender norms are in the lives of people who have gone through high-conflict divorce. The interplay of gender and roles, then, is multifaceted, with personal and legal aspects.

Norms' Stickiness

Beyond the chapters showing how the inegalitarian allocation of domestic labour persists and is sometimes advanced by legal systems, some contributors also contextualize conventional norms as part of the private/public divide. The function of family laws as vehicles to privatize care work – essentially, to roll the responsibility of caregiving onto families rather than the state – has long stood at the centre of family law scholarship. In her canonical 2002 work on privatization and family law, Brenda Cossman argues that, in the era of neoliberalism, privatization has acquired "a newfound importance."[27] American scholars have also analyzed how privatization gradually becomes the gold standard for family law.[28] Accordingly, one of the primary functions of family law is to free the state from the burden of supporting dependent members of society. The state "recognizes and bestows benefits on families so that they will serve a private welfare function, minimizing reliance on state and federal coffers."[29] The state shifts responsibilities for care onto families, forgoing its obligation to remedy structural causes of dependency. Often, this is done by increased enforcement of private support obligations, such as between unmarried partners. Simultaneously, as they have classically been construed, various laws often continue to shield the "private" domain from state scrutiny, a situation that maintains inequality, most often harming the primary caregiver (still commonly a woman) in the household.

Several chapters contribute to our understanding of how privatization works and how embedded it is within family law systems in different countries. In Chapter 5, Wanda Wiegers tracks the prevalence of gendered-care norms across a few fields of family laws: from regulation governing child support and custody to laws concerning child protection. In these contexts, the stereotypical norms of care do not merely survive legal reforms but, upon scrutiny, are promoted by various state policies. Across these different legal regimes, the cost of care is, yet again, trundled from the state onto families. In the area of child protection, for example, foster parents in British Columbia must meet stringent requirements of care for their foster children, including residential space, educational support, and health care. In the area of custody, the obligation of non-parents to pay child support is limited and rarely arises, thus concentrating the responsibility for care and support on parents and their post-divorce conjugal partners, and rarely on non-parents such as extended family. In any event, in all these arenas, women disproportionately bear the costs of privatizing care. Furthermore, foster care and kinship care, both of which have been under-compensated in the past, have increasingly recruited Indigenous and racialized women as care providers. The outcome is that the costs of privatization of care are not distributed evenly but are disproportionally borne by working-class, impoverished, and Indigenous women. One particularly sticky manifestation of the public/private divide is expressed by the "unremunerated nature of labour performed (usually by women) in the home, in contrast to the remunerated labour performed (traditionally more by men than women) in the market."[30] Wiegers's chapter rectifies how regulations replicate long-standing assumptions that care work in a family setting is or will be in some measure provided altruistically – further confirming care work as a domain that belongs to the privacy of the household, distinct from the market, and one that does not warrant adequate compensation.

Another aspect of the private/public divide relates to the distinction between state regulation and the market. One manifestation of this distinction, as underscored by Susan B. Boyd, has been the difficulty "to introduce regulatory measures that promote women's equality into non-government workplaces."[31] In Chapter 6, Nicola Barker complicates this idea by offering a fresh analysis of the private/public divide in the context of human rights legislation in the United Kingdom. She critiques the application of the *Human Rights Act of 1998* (*HRA*)[32] and its failure to improve women's lives, especially for those who work in what has traditionally been considered "private domains." Accordingly, despite the *HRA*'s potential to advance equality, courts have rendered it ineffective through their narrow interpretation. As but one example, courts have refused to recognize private contractors who perform services that traditionally were considered public (for example, providing health care services) as liable for human rights violations under the *HRA*. This narrow interpretation, Barker argues, has a particular impact on women, not only as service users but also as service workers. She concludes that the *HRA* has not sufficiently advanced access to justice for women in family matters and that it "largely falls short ... in its utter failure to move beyond, or even shift the borders of, the public/private divide." Further, Barker's contribution demonstrates how the *HRA* has had limited impact in reducing the effects of reforms that greatly curtail access to justice for family law litigants. The reforms, she suggests, privatized family law conflicts by encouraging alternative dispute resolutions and private settlements and by virtually eliminating legal aid in "private" family law matters. The reforms' outcome is further privatization, and the *HRA*'s power to prevent this process has been inadequate.

Finally, in what we deem a new articulation of the private/public divide, one that is possible only when scholarship explores areas outside FL1,

Chapter 1 by Allison Tait offers several examples of the methods by which some financial activities continue to enjoy exemption from regulatory insight primarily because they are deemed private, notwithstanding their impact on the economy and society at large. For instance, by using sophisticated trusts, high-wealth families shield their money from creditors, tax authorities, and even from ex-spouses. By doing so, rich families "not only reshape household economies, but they also, once again, potentially recalibrate the relationship between public and private markets."

Measuring Norms

In a 2018 essay, Clare Huntington documented the "empirical turn in family law"[33] – that is, the increased reliance on empirical data in family law advocacy and policy design. While she celebrates this growing use of empirics, she also warns that outcomes and data are not everything: there are various "competing, and often contested, values also at play in family law," and these values should be taken into consideration.[34] We contend that it is imperative to take an empirical approach to uncover prevalent norms as a means to understanding better how they affect the content of FL1, FL2, and FL3.

To clarify, when we discuss empirical research, we mean both qualitative and quantitative approaches. As defined by John Baldwin and Gwynn Davis, a qualitative approach "involves an attempted in-depth exploration of legal processes, typically focusing on a modest number of interactions but viewing these from a variety of perspectives and perhaps over time. The strength of this approach lies in its capacity to reflect the complexity of legal processes, and the complexity of the relationship between process and outcome."[35]

Chapter 7 is particularly significant in creating and using empirical data in the search for norms – and their impact on schema of legal policies. In it, Hélène Belleau contributes to our knowledge of cohabitants' lives in Canada and shows how data should guide policymaking. Belleau is primarily concerned with whether unmarried cohabitants know about the laws governing their mutual obligations (which, in most jurisdictions, do not automatically create financial obligations among the partners) when they make decisions about their family form (married or unmarried). For example, she reports on a study she conducted in 2015 that surveyed 3,250

Quebec residents who live as unmarried cohabitants.[36] Forty-five percent of respondents believed they had the same legal protections as married people regarding mutual financial obligations – a crucial mistake. Belleau's chapter is replete with key findings, from the reasons that unmarried partners chose not to get married to the over-optimism exhibited by most cohabitants when evaluating their chances of not breaking up. Belleau calls on legislatures, when crafting regulations in this area, to abandon the myth that unmarried couples make an informed choice not to marry, and to design a policy that is in line with reality. She concludes that "the gap between social norms and values, on the one hand, and those enacted by the law, on the other, risks compromising the effectiveness of laws." Belleau's chapter, then, is an example of using empirical data to uncover the norms that underlie a decision to live as de facto spouses, with the goal of using these data to reform laws fairly and effectively. It also challenges the norms the state uses to guide regulation of families.

In Chapter 8, Erez Aloni and Adam Vanzella-Yang seek norms that motivate couples to share residency. In interviewing couples who cohabit informally, they find that norms around love and commitment are secondary to norms and economics of the housing rental market in terms of catalyzing couples to move in together. The authors argue that understanding the norms that trigger cohabitation is essential to improving the design of policies in a wide range of areas, from housing to governmental benefits. If inaccurate perceptions of which norms animate decisions to live together are used to shape laws about financial obligations among unmarried couples, they are likely to create injustice. Moving between FL1 (rules about when cohabitation begins for purposes of division of property), FL4 (norms of commitment and love), and FL2 (rules concerning the definition of "spouse" for the purpose of qualification and disqualification of public assistance), this chapter provides an example of family studies that moves between the layers of family laws and norms to expose the complex ways in which norms – including a wrong perception of norms – inform laws.

Aloni and Vanzella-Yang's chapter advocates collecting further data on the lives of unmarried cohabitants in general and on the process of relationship development specifically and engaging further with the data in policymaking. They argue that norms related to people's reasons for not getting married, and policies designed to address their lives, must rely on data and not hunches. For instance, they note that the decision to move in together – a decision that has legal meaning both for recognition of a relationship as spouse-like and for commencing the time during which gains in property are dividable – often stems not so much from a relationship's progression as from housing market and other socio-economic considerations.

Reforming Norms

How can we reduce the weight of some norms in creating inequality and promoting privatization? And what can be done about regulations that cultivate unequal norms? Our contributors make it clear that effectively reforming family laws to reflect changes to or entrenchment of norms is a daunting task. One challenging aspect in the field of family law is that, in some jurisdictions and some areas, laws have constantly been reformed and transformed. The consequences, as some chapters show, are unsettling laws that deliver unstable and unpredictable outcomes. Contributors examine reform processes from top to bottom. They analyze different reform strategies, the reasons for reforms, and the effects of reforms.

In Chapter 3, discussed above, Alison Diduck offers a cautionary tale of reform failure in the United Kingdom. She presents a genealogy of a botched attempt to reform laws that govern property disputes among divorcing couples. Her chapter explores how contemporary doctrines that control division of assets upon divorce have contended with historical "chaos" in family law doctrine and values. Located within the narrative of progress, family law is seen as having worked out its conflicting philosophies and discarded its debris from earlier centuries. Yet, the narratives of progress and chaos are not always straightforward and can have significant material and symbolic implications for intimate partners. Diduck teaches that, when examining the success of reform, looking at the rhetoric is insufficient: investigating the outcomes is equally important. Her caselaw analysis focuses on FL1, but the analysis is aimed primarily at FL4, for Diduck cares mainly about the laws' expressive function – the norms upheld and delivered by the set of rules. Her point is that evaluating what norms play key role in adjudication can only be measured by results, not by rhetoric.

Two chapters systematically illuminate the particular challenges of confronting organizational norms in the context of courts and of legislative reforms. In Chapter 9, Julianna Ivanyi and Régine Tremblay examine how to reform law reforms. They analyze not simply one reform but, more generally, the process of reforming. Their point of departure is the interplay between changing norms and changing legal contexts: changes in norms influence reform; hence, to evaluate the success of reform, we must examine how the norms are implemented and reflected within the new regulations. Because family laws have been, as the authors put it, "subject to the winds of change," they contend that it is imperative to learn how to assess the outcomes of law reforms systematically and to determine what makes a reform successful. Their all-inclusive exploration begins with defining "reform" – a task more complicated than it sounds – and ends with creating a framework to evaluate reforms. They argue that law reform assessment includes treatment of "process," "content," and "effects." Careful to avoid the trap of family law exceptionalism, they state, "[p]arsing family law out as exceptional ignores the reality that family law does not exist in a vacuum – instead, it touches and interweaves with many different areas of the law." With that in mind, they propose that, in the family law context, policy-makers and other stakeholders might pay particular attention to two areas: public consultation and education/resource allocation. Ultimately, they advise that law reform is only one tool to effect change for families, and that it may or may not lead to progressive change. Either way, more thinking is required to make better family law reform. Ivanyi and Tremblay's chapter also contributes to the argument about the importance of empirical work to reforms. One of their arguments is that "reform must ... be empirically based." At the same time, they warn that "empirical data on specific aspects of a law reform can provide for good assessments of success, but we have to be careful with these numbers."

Closing the book, in Chapter 10, Brenda Cossman suggests that contemporary family law in Ontario does not work for many. The problem is access to justice: the changes in norms and law – for example, ease of getting divorced – have overwhelmed the courts. As a result, the system is unequipped to meet the needs of many, thus preventing individuals from relying on what is otherwise an exemplary law (in terms of its substantive content). According to Cossman, the substantive rules governing obligations upon dissolution of relationships are judicious; however, enforcing the rules is difficult, especially with an increasing number of unrepresented litigants and in the absence of a well-functioning court system. The problems within this system, she maintains, are deeply entrenched and difficult to repair. Cossman is pessimistic about the opportunity for effective reform, arguing that "path dependency" – how future reform has been dependent on how we have gotten certain outcomes to date – will make serviceable reform nearly impossible. She thus questions the premise that an incremental fixing of particular shortcomings will change the structures that prevent family laws from functioning adequately.

The chapter contests family law exceptionalism directly. Cossman suggests that we should restructure the family law system so that it is "disarticulated from its private, civil law moorings." To overcome the structural barriers, Cossman proposes that we change the framework altogether, not merely tweak the rules. A possible new system might increase reliance on novel digital technologies to facilitate disputes resolutions. But it must go further: for technology to work, she maintains, we have to consider reducing court discretion, because it undercuts consistency and predictability. Innovatively, she imagines marriage insurance as a method of allocating the risk of dependency among many individuals, as insurance typically operates. The idea is to try to envision an apparatus removed from the private and exceptional elements of traditional family laws as a means of overcoming the endless process of small and unsuccessful reforms. Abolishing family law is a thought experiment only, but it allows us to imagine what family laws that are detached from the influence of core areas could look like.

***

Multiple stakeholders have expressed the view that there is a shortage of sustained family law scholarship at a time when such research is essential.[37] Responding to this challenge, and particularly to the need to keep thinking about the disconnect between social norms and family laws, this book assesses norms that are situated at the centre of family law matters, and methods of affecting substantive reforms. Together, the chapters provide an insight about the breadth of norms that are at play in the intersection of family laws and social norms: moving in together, living in marriage or informally, dividing house and care work, understanding societal meaning of marriage, purchasing financial privacy, privatizing care, naming offspring, parenting post-divorce, to name just a few. Contesting exceptionalism to different extents, the chapters find the operation of norms in conventional and unconventional domains: courts, housing market, administrative law, trusts, reform process, as well as in the unwritten norms of care among divorced and between unmarried couples. The results of unequal norms and inadequate laws, the chapters discover, are cultural, gender, racial, and economic inequalities. The chapters ask that we think harder and more creatively about the challenges posed by the changing norms and by attempts to transform or adjust those norms. The interdisciplinary and contextual approach taken in this book, we hope, will provide tools to analyze and help resolve some of the difficulties in designing apt laws that respond both to ongoing, sometimes radical, shifts in norms and, other times, to the entrenchment of norms of inequality.

Notes

1 "Norm," online: *Merriam-Webster.com Dictionary* <www.merriam-webster.com/dictionary/norm> [perma.cc/FQ8C-W8QC].

The second of these formulations recalls Philip Pettit's observation that almost all scholarly uses of "norm" carry two necessary meanings. First, a norm is a regularity to which people in a given society conform; and second, members of the society generally approve of the regularity and abhor deviance from it. Philip Pettit, "Virtus Normativa: Rational Choice Perspectives." (1990) 100:4 Ethics 725, <http://www.jstor.org/stable/2381776>.

2 Pettit, *supra* note 1 at 725.

3 Although social norms have immense influence on different fields of laws and diverse areas of life, "norms particularly shape the relationships and intimate decisions that fall within the ambit of family law." Clare Huntington, "Familial Norms and Normality" (2009–10) 59 Emory LJ 1103 at 1105.

4 See Colin Scott, "Analysing Regulatory Space: Fragmented Resources and Institutional Design" (2001) Public L 283 at 283 (defining "regulation" as "any process or set of processes by which norms are established, the behavior of those subject to the norms monitored or fed back into the regime, and for which there are mechanisms for holding the behavior of regulated actors within acceptable limits of the regime").

5 Richard H McAdams & Eric B Rasmusen, "Norms and the Law" in A Mitchell Polinsky & Steven M Shavell, eds, *The Handbook of Law and Economics* (Amsterdam: Elsevier, 2007) 1573.

6 "House rule," online: *Merriam-Webster Dictionary* <https://www.merriam-webster.com/dictionary/house%20rule>.

7 "House rule," online: *Dictionary.com* <https://www.dictionary.com/browse/house-rule>.

8 Action Committee on Access to Justice in Civil and Family Matters, *Access to Civil and Family Justice: A Roadmap for Change* (October 2013), online (PDF): <www.cfcj-fcjc.org/sites/default/files/docs/2013/AC_Report_English_Final.pdf> [perma.cc/2B9U-JB8B] [Action Committee]; Elizabeth S Scott, "Social Norms and the Legal Regulation of Marriage" (2000) 86:8 Va L Rev 1901; Fiona Kelly, "Multiple-Parent Families under British Columbia's New *Family Law Act*: A Challenge to the Supremacy of the Nuclear Family or a Method by which to Preserve Biological Ties and Opposite-Sex Parenting" (2014) 47:2 UBC L Rev 565; Li-Ju Lee, "Law and Social Norms in a Changing Society: A Case Study of Taiwanese Family Law" (1998) 8 S Cal Rev L & Women's Stud 413; Nancy E Dowd, "Law, Culture, and Family: The Transformative Power of Culture and the Limits of Law" (2003) 78:2 Chicago-Kent L Rev 785.

9 Susan B Boyd, ed, *Challenging the Public/Private Divide: Feminism, Law, and Public Policy* (Toronto: University of Toronto Press, 1997) at 5–6.

10 Sophie Ponthieux & Dominique Meurs, "Gender Inequality" in Anthony B Atkinson & François Bourguignon, eds, *The Handbook of Law and Economics* (Amsterdam: Elsevier, 2015) vol 2A 981.

11 See Chapter 3 by Alison Diduck and Chapter 4 by Rachel Treloar in this book.

12 The change occurred in many places; however, we restrict our claim to the four jurisdictions that contributors represent in this book.

13 Laura T Kessler, "Family Law by the Numbers: The Story That Casebooks Tell" (2020) 62 Ariz L Rev 903 at 907.

14 See, generally, Daphna Hacker, *Legalized Families in the Era of Bordered Globalization* (Cambridge: Cambridge University Press, 2017).

15 See e.g. Kelly Kollman, "Same-Sex Unions: The Globalization of an Idea" (2007) 51:2 Intl Studies Q 329.

16 See generally Ange-Marie Hancock, *Intersectionality: An Intellectual History* (Oxford: Oxford University Press, 2016) at 26 (discussing "the global reach of intersectionality").

17 Devon W Carbado et al, "Intersectionality: Mapping the Movements of a Theory" (2013) 10:2 Du Bois Rev Social Science Research on Race 303 at 307.

18 This book is cross-disciplinary, composed of chapters written by legal scholars and sociologists. It is more accurate, then, to characterize it as part of "family studies," a term we use to delineate the broad scope of issues and methodologies reflected here. Two chapters in particular – Chapter 7 by Hélène Belleau and Chapter 8 by Erez Aloni and Adam Vanzella-Yang – fall more into the sociology of the family than into legal analysis per se; but the other authors in the book have also adopted a broad and interdisciplinary perspective. We use "family

studies" as an umbrella term that encompasses family law scholarship and scholarship concerning the household generally.

19 Janet Halley & Kerry Rittich, "Critical Directions in Comparative Family Law: Genealogies and Contemporary Studies of Family Law Exceptionalism" (2010) 58:4 Am J Comp L 753 at 761–62.

20 Kessler, *supra* note 13 at 933.

21 See Halley & Rittich, *supra* note 19 at 762–64.

22 See e.g. Kate Redburn, "Zoned Out: How Zoning Law Undermines Family Law's Functional Turn" (2019) 128:8 Yale LJ 2412, discussing the discrepancy between functional family law and definitions of "family" in zoning laws.

23 Halley & Rittich, *supra* note 19 at 755, 758.

24 See e.g. Frances E Olsen, "The Family and the Market: A Study of Ideology and Legal Reform" (1983) 96:7 Harv L Rev 1497.

25 As Halley and Rittich note, colonial order has often imported the colonizer's rules about contracts from the mother's country, whereas personal laws (rules applicable to family matters like marriage and divorce) were left to be governed by the local orders. Halley & Rittich, *supra* note 19 at 771–772.

26 Cass R Sunstein, *Free Markets and Social Justice* (New York: Oxford University Press, 1997) at 43.

27 Brenda Cossman, "Family Feuds: Neo-Liberal and Neo-Conservative Visions of the Reprivatization Project" in Brenda Cossman & Judy Fudge, eds, *Privatization, Law, and the Challenge to Feminism* (Toronto: University of Toronto Press, 2002) 169 at 169.

28 See e.g. Laura A Rosenbury, "Federal Visions of Private Family Support" (2014) 67 Vand L Rev 1835.

29 *Ibid* at 1866–67.

30 Boyd, *supra* note 9 at 9.

31 Boyd, *ibid* at 8.

32 *Human Rights Act 1998* (UK), 1998, Sched 1.

33 Clare Huntington, "The Empirical Turn in Family Law" (2018) 118:1 Colum L Rev 227.

34 *Ibid* at 232.

35 John Baldwin & Gwynn Davis, "Empirical Research in Law" in Mark Tushnet & Peter Cane, eds, *The Oxford Handbook of Legal Studies* (Oxford: Oxford University Press, 2005) 880 at 891.

36 See also Hélène Belleau, Carmen Lavallée & Annabelle Seery, *Unions et désunions conjugales au Québec: rapport de recherche. Première partie: le couple, l'argent et le droit* (June 2017), INRS Centre – Urbanisation Culture Société, online (PDF): <espace.inrs.ca/5763/1/belleau-2017-unionsA.pdf> [perma.cc/38K4-A9T6].

37 Alice Woolley, "Law Schools' Dirty Little Secret" (26 April 2018), online: *Slaw* <www.slaw.ca/2018/04/26/law-schools-dirty-little-secret/> [perma.cc/976S-D2L9]; Action Committee, *supra* note 8. See also Laura Robertson & Karen Broadhurst, "Introducing Social Science Evidence in Family Court Decision-Making and Adjudication: Evidence from England and Wales" (2019) 33:2 Intl JL Pol'y & Fam 181 at 182–84.

PART 1

Locating Norms

1

The Private Lives of High-Wealth Families

Allison Anna Tait

> We were not as rich as the Rockefellers or Mellons, but we were rich enough to know how rich they were.
>
> – Louis Auchincloss[1]

> Everyone knows you should never divulge your income unless you're speaking with a headhunter or spouse. The same guidelines apply to your bonus. And under no circumstances should you ever brag about your compensation package, even if you don't mention an exact number. Sometimes, however, you may be put in the uncomfortable position of someone asking you how much you earn. The only appropriate response is "I make enough to get by," says Post.
>
> – Stacey Bradford[2]

Never discuss money. And never, ever divulge how much of it you have or you earn. This is, narrators and novelists tell us, a standard rule of etiquette in upper-middle-class and elite social circles.[3] This social rule originated, one manners consultant suggests, in Britain at a time when society was smaller and more insular than it is currently: "People who were wealthy didn't need to talk about it because they knew – from how many houses you had, what cars you drove, how many servants you had, the yachts that you had, where you vacationed. They could figure out what your net worth was."[4] Or, as Blaise Pascal commented enigmatically yet satirically in one of well-known *Pensées*: "Il a quatre laquais" ("He has four footmen").[5] Historical circumstances have changed, and social norms have evolved since Pascal or the days of Edwardian aristocrats. Nevertheless, this particular elite norm of viewing personal and financial privacy as a highly desirable good still has a strong hold, not least in the domain of wealth preservation and management.

This chapter is a brief attempt at unravelling the various ways in which high-wealth families can purchase personal privacy, especially as it relates to financial privacy, and the ways in which this financial privacy both produces cascading results of complex inequality and complicates conventional notions of where the family, writ large, is situated along the public/private divide. The first part of this chapter begins with a description of the ways in which high-wealth families can manage their privacy, offering an examination of family offices and other investment mechanisms that provide various forms of privacy before turning to the ubiquitous family trust and how it is used as a vehicle to protect not only the identities but also the assets of high-wealth families. A description of these legal mechanisms for creating and preserving both family wealth and privacy lays the groundwork for our understanding of how exceptionalism works on various levels and the acute degree to which high-wealth and low-wealth family rules are distorted, almost phantasmagoric reflections of one another.

Building on this descriptive material, the second part of this chapter takes up some of the larger questions posed by this volume. It illustrates that social norms and legal rules about family money vary across wealth and income lines. Additionally, the analysis reveals how this asymmetry of both expectations and governance systems unsettles conventional notions of the public/private divide, establishing some families as separate and apart from the public sphere of state while others are subject to state scrutiny. What high-wealth rules – especially in comparison with the treatment of low-wealth families – bring into focus is that, as Nicola Barker points out in her chapter (citing Susan B. Boyd), the public/private divide is aptly described as "an ideological marker that shifts in relation to the role of the state at particular historical moments, in particular contexts, and in relation to particular issues."[6] This second part also seeks to disturb the public/private boundary in another way, by undermining the exceptionalist framing of families as existing apart from the market. As the legal rules for high-wealth families reveal, despite a covering discourse of privacy and isolation, high-wealth family privacy is intimately and intricately connected to market participation and market manipulation. That is to say, privacy for and the successful privatization of certain families strongly reinforce the connection between families more generally and the market and demonstrate how the market actions of privileged families at the top of the wealth chain severely endanger those at the bottom. Finally, this part briefly explores the question of what family justice looks like when both traditional and emerging norms as well as rules around family money are themselves drivers of family inequality.

Family Privacy, Family Investments, and the Family Trust

Citibank's Global Family Office Group released a report on private family wealth protection in 2018.[7] In the report, the authors reminded their high-wealth clients[8] that privacy is a "fundamental right" and quoted former US Supreme Court Justice William O. Douglas, who stated that "the right to be let alone is indeed the beginning of all freedom."[9] The report authors admit that "[s]uch lofty concepts can seem almost irrelevant when downloading an app to control your heating. However, it is important to understand these abstract concepts and their concrete consequences."[10]

Privacy, the authors state, benefits family members on a personal level because it allows them to "change and grow without being shackled by their past."[11] In this sense, "[p]rivacy fosters the ability to reinvent, develop, and mature."[12] Moreover, the authors acknowledge that "[e]veryone has something they would like to remain private and no-one should be made to feel self-conscious about it."[13] Privacy also benefits family members on a collective and reputational level. Privacy measures protect against reputational damage to the family office or larger family business, "[f]or example, leaked emails could have detrimental effects on the professional reputation of a family business by revealing confidential proposed business transactions or family information that should remain private."[14]

The report authors suggest that high-wealth families protect their privacy in very immediate, security-minded ways. High-wealth families can hire security teams for their families, take "anti-drone measures," ensure the "encryption of files and digital watermarking," and even engage in the "social media monitoring and gatekeeping of all guests."[15] Privacy, for these families and through these mechanisms, is easily purchased, installed, and adjusted. In fact, entire industries exist that cater to ultra-wealthy families and their privacy needs, providing personal security guards, threat-response teams, and cyber-intelligence monitoring.[16] Even wealth mangers, whose primary task is asset management, have a role in protecting the personal privacy of their clients and safeguarding family secrets:

> Wealth managers need to know ... intimate details of their clients' lives because so many of the factors that affect high-net-worth individuals also affect their fortunes. As a fiduciary, the wealth manager is bound to protect clients' wealth from risk: This includes not just financial risk but the threat of spendthrift heirs dissipating the family assets or of family members with embarrassing secrets who might be targeted for blackmail.[17]

Privacy for high-wealth families is paramount in the arena of financial management. High-wealth families are eager not only to protect their financial information but also to protect their investment strategies (for proprietary or political reasons) and obscure the extent of their asset ownership (in order to avoid regulation, taxation, or even publicity). Here again, high-wealth families are able to purchase privacy every day, in multiple ways that ordinary- and low-wealth families are not. The high-wealth family has access to multiple financial products and investment mechanisms designed specifically to enable privacy while also reducing taxation and controlling all possible consequences of wealth transfer. Because the stakes are high for these families, and the work lucrative for the banks and trust companies, the wealth-management landscape is highly creative and ever evolving. The wealth management profession is staffed by money managers and investment advisers dedicated to maximizing the benefits that high-wealth families get from various wealth modules. Moreover, trust companies and financial institutions regularly invent new products catering to this high-wealth clientele and their desire to protect their family fortunes. The result is that "wealthy people are constantly coming up with new and ever more sophisticated legal structures to house their fortunes."[18]

There are, nevertheless, certain high-use vehicles that have been proven through time and experience to provide benefits. High-wealth families often invest in private equity or hedge funds, which, in the United States, are relatively unregulated by the US Securities and Exchange Commission (SEC). Because of this light regulation, there may be more transactional privacy and investment confidentiality. Another popular "trend"[19] is the creation of private label funds that, "similar to a mutual fund,"[20] consist of the pooled assets of a family.[21] Private label funds can be designed in any way to meet the specific investment and legal needs of the family, and "[t]hey are seen by many as ideal for private wealth structuring, not least because their existence may not be a matter of public record."[22] Investment in privately held companies offers many of the same advantages, and not only are "a substantial percentage of single-family offices ... investing in privately held companies[, but] a small but growing number of them are doing so secretly – at least to start."[23]

One of the most popular ways in which ultra-wealthy families, from Canada and the United Kingdom to India, maintain their financial privacy is through the use of a family office.[24] The family office is a multi-purpose and flexible entity that may look different for each family. As Morven McMillan has noted, "[f]or some, the phrase [family office] conjures up a discreet presence located in Zurich or Boston for example; for others, a visit to the family office could easily mean a visit to a castle and estate in Scotland or a high-tech operation in Silicon Valley."[25] Wherever it is located, however, the family office can "be designed to do anything [the family] wants,"[26] from event and travel planning to household management. Some family offices may also provide more comprehensive services, including tax and estate planning, and coordination with trust companies and private bankers.[27]

The family office can also specifically handle all family investment and financial management, and these offices are widely used by high-wealth families globally to invest, trade, and sell on the New York Stock Exchange (NYSE) because federal law in the United States offer privacy benefits to family offices as investors. This investment privacy stems from the fact that family offices are exempt from the definition of "investment adviser" under the *Dodd-Frank Wallstreet Reform and Protection Act,*[28] and therefore also exempt from registering with the SEC. A report from the Senate Committee on Banking, Housing, and Urban Affairs, circulated at the time the exemption was being considered, endorsed the exemption, stated that SEC registration "[was] not designed to regulate the interactions of family members, and registration would unnecessarily intrude on the privacy of the family involved."[29] Accordingly, family offices are not required to disclose information about family operations, office staffing, the amount of assets under management, or the office's trading history.[30] Underscoring the importance of this exclusion, after it was enacted, George Soros transitioned his US$24.5 billion hedge fund into a family office to gain privacy and avoid compliance costs. Steven Cohen likewise started a family office, Point72 Asset Management, worth about US$11 billion, and, since then, numerous ultra-wealthy investors, including Bill Gates, Leslie Wexner, Sergey Brin, and the Koch brothers, have all created family offices.[31]

In addition to these elite investment vehicles, one of the most common ways for high-wealth families to obtain enhanced privacy in the financial arena is through the use of trusts. Trusts are a ubiquitous planning mechanism for high-wealth families because they provide financial privacy in a variety of ways. At the most basic level, trust creation and details are not on the public record and are not generally available, even to family members. Wills, the primary competitor to trusts in estate planning, are a matter of public record and "[t]he decedent who chooses the will [gets] public knowledge of her assets, beneficiaries, and disposition – both testamentary and personal." Using just one example, "the day after Jacqueline Kennedy Onassis' will was filed in the New York Surrogate's Court, the media reported in detail the disposition of her real and personal property."[32] Trusts, on the other hand, allow those who establish them to keep their estate plans private and avoid both family and media scrutiny.

Trust law, however, "has placed such a premium on privacy that it has denied trust beneficiaries as well as the general public access to the trust instrument."[33] More commonly, new rules have given trust beneficiaries increased rights of access to the trust documents that govern their distribution.[34] Certain US states, however, still market their jurisdictions as favourable sites for trust creation because of their secrecy laws. One trust company operating in South Dakota advertises that the state "is universally considered by advisors and academics to have the most comprehensive and flexible quiet trust statute in the nation, granting the settlor, trust protector, and the investment/distribution advisor the power to expand, restrict, eliminate, or modify the rights of the beneficiaries to discover information about a trust."[35] Elsewhere, companies mention that "Delaware provides a maximum amount of privacy for the details of a family's fortune because it does not require any court supervision or filings during the life of the trust" and because "Delaware law allows a settlor to proscribe which beneficiaries should receive notice about the existence and assets of a trust."[36] One common use for trust secrecy is when the trust settlor wants to provide support for an individual with whom the settlor is having an extramarital relationship.[37] The secrecy feature is also useful for parents who give their children different amounts of money.[38]

More generally, trusts provide not just personal but also financial privacy because they obscure the actual ownership of assets. The settlor, whose assets form the trust corpus, has no real role to play and can remain almost entirely private. Legal ownership of the assets resides in the trustee, who has no real rights to the assets. Accordingly, trusts allow "the true owners, beneficiaries or controllers of trust assets to keep hidden, especially from public scrutiny."[39] Put differently, trusts "provide a firewall between an asset and its owner,"[40] sometimes to the degree that "the very legal basis of ownership becomes muddied."[41] Trust companies routinely advertise their competitive advantages in providing this form of financial privacy. Taking a direct approach, several estate-planning firms actually market a "privacy trust." One firm states: "The Privacy Trust successfully conceals ownership of bank and brokerage accounts, the family home, rental properties, and interests in other entities ... [T]he Privacy Trust adds a desirable level of confidentiality to your personal affairs."[42] Nevis, one of the smallest of the Caribbean islands, prides itself on offering the most privacy and protection possible for trust settlors. Nevis, according to one financial reporter, "specialises in letting its clients create corporations with greater anonymity than almost anywhere else on earth."[43] Justifying this strong stance on financial privacy, Nevis's premier, Mark Brantley, has told a reporter that "[w]e feel very strongly that people are entitled to some semblance of financial privacy ... Why shouldn't you be entitled to a secret?"[44]

If a private trust (or *the* privacy trust), created and managed by a conventional trust company or bank, does not provide sufficient privacy, ultra-rich families can also form their own private trust company (in select US states as well as offshore jurisdictions). With a private trust company, the family staffs and manages the trust that holds the family fortune, employing either family members or carefully chosen financial advisers. *Forbes* explains the phenomenon quite simply: "Given the risks, some wealthy families aren't playing the banks' game anymore. They're playing their own game on their own terms. They've formed private family trust companies and they own the game."[45] Private trust companies offer unmatched financial privacy because the founding family is exempt from state reporting requirements about their holdings, transactions, or investments. The families are not required to disclose public annual reports or meeting minutes, list directors and officers, or share financial reports that have gone out to shareholders.[46] Private trust companies also compound identity privacy because "their complex control structures often confuse authorities about who really controls or benefits from the assets."[47] Trust companies advertise accordingly. The Frontier Administrative Services LLC's marketing tag line is: "Keep It in the Family. Consider a Wyoming Private Family Trust Company."[48]

Finally, layered on top of – and working in tandem with – identity privacy, trusts also offer asset "privacy," or asset protection. One Wyoming trust company has explained the asset-protection benefits of the trust this way:

> Beyond tax benefits, the dynasty trust also protects assets from a future generation's creditors. For example, teen age automobile accidents or divorces. These are called unintended beneficiaries. They are called unintended because when you set everything up your intent was not to pay for an automobile accident or for half the funds to go to your child's ex-spouse. With proper planning you can "lock out" unintended beneficiaries.[49]

Trusts safeguard a beneficiary's interest by separating legal and beneficial ownership, vesting the trustee with legal title and the beneficiary with equitable rights. Because of this partitioning, it is hard for creditors to attach assets. The trustee, who has no real rights to the property, holds legal title, and the beneficiary, who owes the debt to the creditor, does not legally own any assets (the beneficiary is an equitable owner). By avoiding the indices of ownership, a beneficiary can avoid any number of debts and obligations, including taxes, equitable distribution and spousal support at divorce, and any other legal judgments.

In Canada, the family trust is widely marketed and commonly used for asset protection and estate-planning purposes.[50] Moreover, it is worth noting that wealth management for high-wealth families is a global industry and enterprise; therefore, elite families in Canada – and around the world – are targets of massive marketing campaigns created by various jurisdictions competing for trust business and offering new and exceptionally strong forms of asset protection. The leading competitors for this global wealth are top financial secrecy jurisdictions including the United States, the United Kingdom, Switzerland, Singapore, and "offshore" jurisdictions in the Caribbean such as the Cayman Islands and British Virgin Islands.[51] All of these jurisdictions attract a global clientele by offering the strongest asset protection available for traditional trusts and regularly pioneering new forms of asset-protection trusts.[52]

Ultimately, then, the trust is one of the most useful vehicles available to high-wealth families in their collective quest to preserve family wealth and protect it from both public scrutiny and various kinds of creditor claims. The trust offers both personal and financial privacy to high-wealth families, affording them privacy privileges that routinely are not available to other families. More generally, as even this brief overview demonstrates, high-wealth families have a multitude of legal mechanisms at their disposal, all designed to enhance both personal and financial privacy. These wealth preservation mechanisms are not – as the next part of this chapter takes up – available to ordinary-wealth families and certainly not to those living in poverty; those families have few assets to protect and, even if they do have assets they would like to protect, they cannot access or afford the legal protections available to high-wealth families.

Private Families and Public Outcomes

The privacy that trusts and other high-wealth financial vehicles enable for ultra-rich families is striking in its depth and power, even viewed on its own terms and without comparison. Nevertheless, when this system of financial governance is placed in the larger socio-economic context, the unequal treatment of families across the wealth spectrum truly crystallizes. As the preceding part of this chapter detailed, high-wealth families have the ability and capacity to purchase privacy for themselves. The situation is quite the opposite for low-wealth families and families living in poverty.

Pairing the financial privacy rights that high-wealth families possess with the privacy risks that low-wealth families encounter daily helps us to understand the disparate treatment of the two groups on the same grounds. Charles Tilly, in his foundational work on "durable inequality," suggested the value of this kind of "pairing" approach, exploring "paired and unequal categories, consisting of asymmetrical relations across a socially recognized (and usually incomplete) dividing line."[53] Michèle Lamont and her colleagues have similarly described the usefulness of a paired approach because "processes do not solely depend on the actions of dominant actors … [S]ubordinates often participate in the elaboration of cultural processes as much as dominant agents do … from intentional actions or as an unintended consequence."[54] The same can be said of legal processes.

This pairing, then, of high- and low-wealth rules enables a clear view of how an expansive legal matrix allows certain families to conceal the details of their household economies while it oppresses and surveils other families. The comparison between high- and low-wealth rules also uncovers the reflective distortions that define their pairing and troubles the conventional notion of which families are public and which private. Moreover, placing high-wealth privacy in a larger context also helps disrupt the conventional categorization of the family as a private and insulated economy that exists outside of and apart from the public market. High-wealth privacy rules uncover the degree to which all family fortunes are interconnected and the ways in which the actions of high-wealth families as market actors create negative effects and vulnerabilities across wealth lines.

Private Families, Public Families, and the Fine Line of Difference

A first example of how this pairing operates, designed to unearth reflective identities between high- and low-wealth families, is around the relationship between benefiting from governmental funds and suffering governmental intrusion into the daily life of the family. High-wealth families, as the preceding part of this chapter described, are almost immune to certain forms of surveillance and intrusion. They can employ security details, encrypt family information, and avoid the disclosure of intimate family details (including wealth holdings and investments) by using highly selective private services. High-wealth families can create walls, both literally and figuratively, around themselves, their family histories, and their family money, thereby avoiding the prying eyes of outsiders, including governmental agencies. Through the purchase of privacy and the receipt of legal privilege, then, high-wealth families constitute themselves as isolated and insulated entities, existing on their own private islands of wealth and control far from regulatory demands and governmental intrusion.

Low-wealth families, on the other hand, are often subject on a daily basis to monitoring, particularly through governmental programs that dispense both thin benefits along with moralizing discourses about the state of their poverty.[55] Professor Khiara Bridges frames the "poverty of privacy rights" that afflicts poor women this way:

> If we understand certain information about ourselves as private – like details about our marriages or romantic relationships, the healthiness of our eating habits, the frequency with which we exercise (or not), and our success at remaining gainfully employed (or not) – then these programs invade poor women's privacy inasmuch as they require women to divulge that information and inasmuch as they share that information, once collected, with third parties.[56]

Low-wealth families – women and mothers, in particular – are often, according to this and other such analyses, subject to gross invasions of privacy and various kinds of monitoring by the state, just as they are subject to critique and public scrutiny for their spending, their leisure, and their labour. The details of the private lives of these women and families are gathered, compiled, and deployed in various ways by the state. These families have little personal privacy, and their financial lives are sometimes even a matter of public record, visible in collection notices, bankruptcy filings and proceedings, and public assistance records.[57]

This contrasting view of privacy rights and public obligation, which turns on wealth, tells us something quite direct and evident about how inequality works and how it grows in various ways in the landscape of a highly capitalist political economy. The contrast also tells us something about how we understand the public/private divide in family law. From the outset, this paired contrast undermines the "classic liberal notion" of the family that, as Nicola Barker reminds us in her chapter, construed the family as "'unproblematically private and as a barely visible appendage to society."'[58] Barker states that, "[w]ith the growth of the welfare state and increasing regulation of family through the twentieth century, the emphasis, where it was on the family at all, was on preserving family privacy." Nevertheless, an alternate narrative, illustrated by our pairing, speaks to an emergent family privacy framework in which some families, usually of high wealth, are granted status as private families, while low-wealth families are forced into public spotlights and in governmental and judicial theatres of poverty and morality.

The dualism of this construct – high-wealth families as private entities and low-wealth ones as subject to public scrutiny – evokes descriptions of the "dual" system of family law, in which scholars have demonstrated how different rules govern low-wealth and high-wealth families. This phenomenon was identified and analyzed by Jacobus tenBroek, who asserted, in a leading family law article, that "we have two systems of family law," and subsequently described the two systems in this way:

> [The systems are] different in origin, different in history, different in substantive provisions, different in administration, different in orientation and outlook. One is public, the other private. One deals with expenditure and conservation of public funds and is heavily political and measurably penal. The other deals with the distribution of family funds, focuses on the rights and responsibilities of family members, and is civil, nonpolitical, and less penal. One is for under-privileged and deprived families; the other for the more comfortable and fortunate.[59]

Switching from a "dual" system to the "triple" system that June Carbone and Naomi Cahn suggest makes little difference to this socio-legal fabrication of public and private families.[60] Carbone and Cahn explain that, in between tenBroek's two groups, there is a large "middle" class that exists in shades of grey on the financial privacy spectrum, somewhere in between the highly private and public families. The real public-private binary, however, continues to apply most particularly to the polar ends of the wealth spectrum. While only the top fraction of households benefits from true financial privacy, achieved through the use of financial instruments like trusts, only the bottom fraction is subject to extreme governmental intrusion and disciplinary technologies. And, once again, low-wealth families are constructed as "public" families who exist within a "public" system of family law because of their use of public funds, while high-wealth families are conceptualized as private, allowed to engage in private ordering, familiar with a standard set of private processes that they use to manage their legal lives.

While the work done by tenBroek, Carbone, and Cahn to describe these variegations is descriptive, done to underscore the inequalities of the legal system, the unequal treatment of high- and low-wealth families with respect to personal privacy is often justified by others on the grounds that low-wealth families invite the state into their personal lives once they apply for governmental assistance. Low-wealth families, from this perspective, merit surveillance and inquiry into the corners of their lives because they are requesting and taking money from the public fisc. Public assistance moves a family from the shadows of anonymity and into the light of scrutiny, making the private family public. High-wealth families, on the other hand, are allowed to remain apart from public exposition and inquiry because they do not, as the story goes, make demands on the public fisc.

The narratives that undergird this characterization of low-wealth families as public and high-wealth ones as private are, however, intrinsically flawed, because they are tied to a biased understanding of whose actions implicate public money and therefore deserve public scrutiny. First, the ways in which wealth laws allow high-wealth families to manage their wealth have potentially enormous effects on the public fisc. High-wealth families, just like some low-wealth ones, are the recipients of governmental benefits; it is just that they are packaged and distributed differently, often in the form of tax exemptions or other tax benefits. In addition, Bridges points out that monitoring and privacy invasions occur whether low-income parents actually receive governmental benefits or not: "[P]oor parents will find that the families they create [are] supervised, regulated, interfered with, and managed without regard to whether they receive a welfare benefit."[61] In other words, the state polices and disciplines family actors who seek financial assistance from the state – as well as those who do not. In this way, low-wealth families are subject to state supervision and discipline based solely on their poverty. Which families are public and which private, then, shifts along the scale of income and wealth, with some families benefiting from privacy and others not. What is worth noting is that the instability of the public/private divide and the way it is bifurcated along economic axes reinforce the notion that the family, as a category of social actor, is never fully private. And, as Alison Diduck mentions in Chapter 3 in this volume, the narrative of "progress in family law" premised on privatization over paternalism is more complex and textured than it may seem at first glance.

Privatized Families, Market Families, and Public Effects

Understanding how high-wealth families purchase financial privacy rights – and pairing that ability with the inability of low-wealth families to do the same – helps to unravel another iteration of the public/private concept as applied to families: namely, that the family exists separate and apart from the market as a site of non-market values and vocations. Moreover, the pairing helps us see the ways in which all families are interconnected economically such that the actions of high-wealth families as market actors have effects that ripple out and touch all families.

An example that is useful here is the high-wealth/low-wealth differential in financial privacy as it touches on the ability of families to protect assets from creditors. High-wealth families have various mechanisms at their disposal to help them safeguard assets from creditor claims, a tangible benefit of certain forms of financial privacy. More specifically, using trusts, high-wealth families can not only obscure their financial footprints, but they also have the ability to shield money from creditors, including tax authorities, credit card companies, judgment creditors, ex-spouses with divorce orders, and even children with child support orders.

For a number of reasons, these benefits are not available to families of low or even ordinary wealth. Not only do low-wealth families not know about these financial management strategies or have access to wealth management and estate-planning services; they also have neither the assets to put in trust nor the wealth to pay for such financial services. Low-wealth families do not therefore have the ability to pick and choose among their financial obligations. They do not benefit from "[preemptive] asset shielding … [which] is one of the most powerful tools for coding capital" and preserving wealth.[62] Consequently, low-wealth families must operate transparently with their finances and pay their creditors and their tax bills, paying high interest rates on credit if they have to borrow to pay these debts or steep fines for failure to pay. Indeed, criminalized debt, at least in the United States, is a leading cause of imprisonment.[63]

This difference in financial privacy rights between families – and the right to "preemptive asset shielding" – created through trusts is meaningful in several ways for the insights it provides. As with the previous example, the unequal legal privilege and treatment is stark and relatively obvious. What is less obvious is how this difference speaks to the situatedness and participation – intentional or not – of all families in the market. Despite the layers of privacy that enshroud high-wealth families, what becomes clear upon investigation is how significantly these families have a role in moving markets and producing negative externalities for all other families. For example, high-wealth families reshape credit markets and raise the price of credit for everyone else in the market solely by exempting themselves from conventional credits relationships and being exempt from paying what they owe. When high-wealth families engage in tax avoidance, they harm and diminish the public fisc, producing subsequent effects on private markets. When high-wealth family members fail to pay money owed to ex-spouses and to children in the form of child support, they not only reshape household economies, but they also, once again, potentially recalibrate the relationship between public and private markets.

From one perspective, then, high-wealth families are the epitome of private, as they embody a political economy based on privatization. In an economic world order controlled by markets and governed by neoliberal philosophies of economic rationality, high-wealth families are those that most skilfully and dexterously manipulate private resources. And, to a certain degree, the extent to which certain high-wealth families succeed at gaining wealth more than others is "dictated by how well the adults within them negotiate market forces … [and] how much bargaining power and skill these adults have."[64] High-wealth families negotiate through a field of private institutions with ease and use private markets both to increase their wealth and to wrap their family wealth in multiple layers of protective legal coverings. Within the framework of privatization, the high-wealth family is the success story, relying on markets to facilitate the purchase of opportunity, privilege, and prosperity. To varying degrees, most other families fail to flourish under the privatization logic as they compete "to ensure their hard-fought place in the economic hierarchy."[65]

And, "[w]hile most families have lost as a result of this competition, poor families have lost the most."[66] The privatized state is fertile grounds for high-wealth families but toxic to many other families who do not possess the same purchasing power or personal credit.

Nevertheless, while the privatized family may seem to be the epitome of private, in the sense that it relies on private ordering and privatization of resources, the privatized family is distinctly public on account of its ability to move markets, shape economies, and influence public finances. The tremendous impact that high-wealth families have on myriad markets underscores the falsity of the notion that, as Julianna Ivanyi and Régine Tremblay remark in Chapter 9 in this volume, "normative aspects of society, such as the market, are viewed as incompatible with, or inapplicable to, family law." As Ivanyi and Tremblay further observe, "conceptions that family law lies outside of certain norms are shifting – the idea that family law is incompatible with the market, for example, ignores the fact that family law routinely allows spouses to engage in market-like behaviour." Adding to this correction about how families and family members engage in market-like activity, it is also important to further complexify our understanding of how high-wealth families actually engage in markets and contour them to replicate the forms of inequality visible in legal governance.

Recognizing Public Families and Creating Family Justice

The privacy that high-wealth families purchase camouflages the extremely public nature of these families: they benefit from the government in numerous and extensive way, and their market behaviour creates negative externalities for most other families. High-wealth privacy is, in this way, a mechanism for shielding from view the levers that have created and continue to create the monumental wealth inequality that is coming to define the current global economic landscape.[67]

In the United States, wealth inequality is such that, from 1983 to 2016, the top 1 percent "saw their average wealth ... rise by over $15 million or by 150 percent ... while the middle quintile showed no change and the average wealth of the poorest 40 percent fell by $15,800."[68] The phenomenon is not limited to the United States. The UBS Group AG's *Billionaire's Report* for 2018 announced that, globally, billionaires increased their wealth by

$1.4 trillion or 20 percent and that the past thirty years "have seen far greater wealth creation than the Gilded Age of the late nineteenth century."[69] Furthermore, while wealth inequality harms most parts of the population other than the highest-wealth families, it harms certain groups and demographics within low-wealth communities more than others. A look at where wealth lives shows that the most likely sites of wealth accumulation are families headed by married, white men who are the primary, if not sole, earner.[70] The sedimentation of wealth through the use of trusts and other financial privacy mechanisms compounds the racial wealth gap by preserving the wealth of those with historical wealth advantages. From the outset, white families are more likely than their Black counterparts to inherit – five times more likely:[71] "28% of whites received bequests, compared to just 7.7% of black families."[72] Even among those families receiving inheritances, Black families receive less: "Blacks received 8 cents of inheritance for every dollar inherited by whites."[73] Black families, as a result, hold less wealth than white families do, even in the upper echelons of wealth: "The 99th percentile black family is worth a mere $1,574,000 while the 99th percentile white family is worth over 12 million dollars."[74] The trust-based wealth management and transfer practices of high-wealth families crystallize these wealth- and race-based differences and embed various forms of inequality.

Financial privacy in wealth management and wealth transfer laws has played a large part in creating the wealth inequality that now plagues countries and communities. As one commentator has remarked, "Trusts are one of the primary vehicles used to create and perpetuate wealth concentration, enabling wealthy elites [to] escape tax, regulation and creditors – and they must lie at the centre of debates about inequality."[75] More broadly, wealth management, investment, and transfer tools – the very tools that enable family financial privacy – are implicated in the creation of and increase in wealth inequality and should consequently be a focus of conversations relating to economic equality between families. Creating family justice – a goal this volume encourages us to think about – means addressing this severe wealth inequality, which harms the collective community and the democratic populace, by dismantling the architecture of financial privacy in order to enable inclusive financial opportunities and economic justice for all families.

Conclusion

The private lives of high-wealth families are, as this brief inquiry underscores, consequential. The privacy that they enjoy based on purchasing power and legal privilege allows them to circumvent governmental regulation and exploit market forces as they order their families according to private desires and through private means. High-wealth privacy, as a result, yields measurable benefits to elite families, but it also impacts the lives of ordinary- and low-wealth families through a consolidation of wealth that intensifies unequal levels of wealth and opportunity. In so doing, high-wealth privacy reconfigures the social and economic fabric of communities and states. Etiquette may demand privacy around money matters for the ultra-rich; equality, however, may demand the opposite.

Notes

1 Louis Auchincloss, *The Book Class* (Boston: Houghton Mifflin, 1984) at 15.

2 Stacey Bradford, "Money and Manners: Are You Offensive?" *CBS News* (13 September 2010), online: <www.cbsnews.com/news/money-and-manners-are-you-offensive/>.

3 See Laura Shin, "The Money Taboo: Why It Exists, Who It Benefits, and How to Navigate It," *Forbes* (14 April 2015), online: <www.forbes.com/sites/laurashin/2015/04/14/the-money-taboo-why-it-exists-who-it-benefits-and-how-to-navigate-it/#57f1b8b82f62>.

4 *Ibid.*

5 Pascal, *Pensées* (Paris: GF Flammarion, 1976) at 140 (art V, 318–19) [translated by author].

6 Susan B Boyd, ed, *Challenging the Public/Private Divide: Feminism, Law, and Public Policy* (Toronto: University of Toronto Press, 1997) at 4.

7 See Global Family Office Group, "Protecting the Privacy of the World's Wealthiest Families" (30 October 2018), online (PDF): Citi <www.privatebank.citibank.com/ivc/docs/Protectingtheprivacy.pdf>.

8 In the wealth-management field, high-net-worth (HNW) families have a minimum of $5 million in investable assets, and ultra-high-net-worth (UHNW) families are defined as those with at least $30 million in investable assets. As to numbers of families in these categories, "[a] 2015 study found that nearly 70,000 individuals living in North America have assets of $30 million or more – a huge jump from a decade ago. It found that some 5,000 households had assets of over $100 million. These figures include just liquid, investable assets (not real estate)." See David Callahan, *The Givers: Wealth, Power and Philanthropy in a New Gilded*

Age (New York: Penguin Random House, 2017) at 18. See also Brooke Harrington, *Capital without Borders: Wealth Management and the One Percent* (Cambridge, MA: Harvard University Press, 2016) at 11.

9 Global Family Office Group, *supra* note 7 at 13 citing *Public Utilities Commission of District of Columbia v Pollak,* 343 US 451 (1952) at 343. The report authors also stated that high-wealth families and their wealth managers may have an innate understanding of the importance of privacy: "family offices tend to view privacy as a fundamental right ... that does not require any justification for protection" (at 4).

10 *Ibid* at 13.

11 *Ibid* at 5.

12 *Ibid.*

13 *Ibid.*

14 *Ibid* at 3.

15 *Ibid* at 9–10.

16 See "Private Client and Family Office Services" (2019), online: Kroll, <www.kroll.com/en/services/security-risk-management/operational-security-services/private-client-family-office-services>; Hillard Heintze, a risk management company, stated that "[t]he headlines – at least when something goes wrong – tell part of the story. A housepainter working for a leading talk show host crafts a plan to abduct the host's son. Angry protesters track the CEO of a Wall Street investment bank back to his residence. A mentally unstable employee is charged with stalking the wife of a high net worth executive." See also Hillard Heintze, "Protecting High Net Worth Individuals and Families" (2013) at 2, online (PDF): <www.hillardheintze.com/wp-content/up-loads/2017/03/HH-360-Insight-Protecting-High-Net-Worth-Individuals-and-Families.pdf>.

17 Brooke Harrington, "The Extraordinary Intimacy between the Ultra-Rich and Their Wealth Managers," *The Atlantic* (12 September 2016), online: <www.theatlantic.com/business/archive/2016/09/wealth-managers/499064/>.

18 Thomas Piketty, *Capital in the Twenty-First Century,* translated by Arthur Goldhammer (Cambridge, MA: Belknap Press of Harvard University Press, 2014) at 451.

19 See Ishika Mookerjee, "Private Label Funds Gaining Prominence: UBS Family Advisory Head" *Citywire* (24 January 2017), online: <citywireasia.com/news/private-label-funds-gaining-prominence-ubs-family-advisory-head/a986466>. See also "Amicorp Offers Private Label Fund Solutions for Families" (March 2017), online: Amicorp, <www.amicorp.com/AmiNews/2017/march/amicorp-offers-private-label-fund-solutions-for-families.php> [Amicorp].

20 See Mookerjee, *supra* note 19.

21 See Amicorp, *supra* note 19. A piece by Amicorp Group stated that "[t]he fund can hold a family's assets including companies, real estate, as well as liquid financial assets."

22 *Ibid.*

23 Russ Alan Prince, "Billions of Dollars from the Super-Rich Are Looking for Direct Investment Opportunities," *Forbes* (11 June 2018), online: <www.forbes.com/sites/russalanprince/2018/06/11/billions-of-dollars-from-the-super-rich-are-looking-for-direct-investment-opportunities/#73e932614d72>.

24 Family offices are on the rise in Canada, the United Kingdom, and India as well as many other jurisdictions. See e.g. Jeff Beer, "The Rise of the Family Office," *Advisor's Edge* (21 October 2011), online: <www.advisor.ca/news/industry-news/the-rise-of-the-family-office/>; "UK Family Office," online: Family Office Club, <familyoffices.com/uk-family-office/>; Mayur Shetty, "Family Office Gains Ground among India's Super Rich," *Times of India* (4 December 2018), online: <timesofindia.indiatimes.com/business/india-business/family-office-gains-ground-among-indias-super-rich/articleshow/66928907.cms>.

25 Morven McMillan, "The Various Roles of the Successful Family Office," *Cayman Financial Review* (18 July 2017), online: <https://web.archive.org/web/20180925221917/http:/www.caymanfinancialreview.com/2017/07/18/the-various-roles-of-the-successful-family-office//>.

26 See Adam Hayes, "Family Offices" (25 June 2019), online: Investopedia, <www.investopedia.com/terms/f/family-offices.asp>. See also Stephen Martiros & Todd Millay, "A Framework for Understanding Family Office Trends," online (PDF): <https://www.martiros.com/guides/family-office-trends/download>.

27 See Martiros & Millay, *supra* note 26 at 2. See also Allison Tait, "The Law of High-Wealth Exceptionalism," (2020) 71 Ala L Rev 981.

28 *Dodd-Frank Wallstreet Reform and Protection Act,* Pub L No 111–203, 124 Stat 1376 (2010), para 409(A).

29 Robert Frank, Gregory Zuckerman & Steve Eder, "Soros Fund All in the Family," *Wall Street Journal* (27 July 2011), online: <www.wsj.com/articles/SB10001424053111903999904576469761599552864>.

30 See Family Office Services, "EY Family Office Guide" (2017), online (PDF): Global Family Business Center of Excellence <https://www.fintrx.com/hubfs/1006031-family-office-guide-hr.pdf>. A family office may still be subject to various forms of securities reporting such as beneficial ownership reporting.

31 See Frank, Zuckerman & Eder, *supra* note 29.

32 See Frances H Foster, "Trust Privacy" (2008) 93 Cornell L Rev 555 at 560.

33 *Ibid* at 566.

34 This is particularly true of US states that have adopted the *Uniform Trust Code* (*UTC*), s 813(b)(1), which provides that that a trustee must promptly furnish a copy of the trust instrument to any beneficiary who requests a copy. Nevertheless, "[t]he tension between the concept that information and reporting is a fundamental duty of the trustee and the desire of some settlors to limit or eliminate information and reporting has led to controversy over the information and reporting provisions in the *UTC*. See Kevin D Millard, "The Trustee's Duty to Inform and Report under the Uniform Trust Code" (2005) 40:2 Real Property, Probate and Trust J 373 at 375.

35 "Privacy" (2019), online: Bridgeford Trust Company, <bridgefordtrust.com/south-dakota-advantage/privacy-trust-laws/>.

36 Richard P Trumpler, "Delaware Advantages for International Wealth Planning" (February 2012), online (PDF): New York Private Trust, <https://www.nyptrust.com/wp-content/uploads/2012/02/Delaware-Advantages-for-International-Wealth-Planning.pdf>.

37 See Harrington, *supra* note 8 at 124–25.

38 See Foster, *supra* note 32 at 577.

39 *Ibid*. For these reasons, trusts, including private trust companies, are the most commonly used vehicle for providing tax advantage and avoidance. "Trusts, they said, prove such a hurdle to investigation, prosecution (or civil judgment), and asset recovery that they are seldom prioritized in corruption investigations." See Emile van der Does de Willebois et al, "The Puppet Masters: How the Corrupt Use Legal Structures to Hide Stolen Assets and What to Do About It" (Stolen Assets Recovery Initiative, the World Bank, and UNODC, 2011) at 45, online (PDF): <star.worldbank.org/sites/star/files/puppetmastersv1.pdf>.

40 "What Is Financial Secrecy?" (2019), online: Tax Justice Network, <www.financialsecrecyin-dex.com/faq/what-is-financial-secrecy>.

41 *Ibid*.

42 "Privacy Trust" (2019), online: Law Office of Robert J Mintz <www.rjmintz.com/types-of-trusts/the-privacy-trust>.

43 Oliver Bullough, "Nevis: How the World's Most Secretive Offshore Haven Refuses to Clean Up," *The Guardian* (12 July 2018), online: <www.theguardian.com/news/2018/jul/12/nevis-how-the-worlds-most-secretive-offshore-haven-refuses-to-clean-up>.

44 *Ibid*.

45 See Todd Ganos, "Wealthy Families Create Private Trust Companies for Privacy, Protection, Tax Savings, and Control," *Forbes* (28 October 2015), online: <www.forbes.com/sites/toddganos/2015/10/28/wealthy-families-create-private-trust-companies-for-privacy-protection-tax-savings-and-control/#368945e63713>.

See also See Matt Tobin & Tom Cota, "Nine Reasons to Start a Private Family Trust Company" (9 January 2018), online: Family Office Exchange, <www.familyoffice.com/insights/nine-reasons-start-private-family-trust-company>.

46 See Iris J Goodwin, "How the Rich Stay Rich: Using a Family Trust Company to Secure a Family Fortune" (2010) 40 Seton Hall L Rev 467 at 475. See also Christopher C Weeg, "The Private Trust Company: A DIY for the Uber Wealthy" (2017) 52 Real Property, Trust and Estate LJ 121 at 137.

47 See Goodwin, *supra* note 46 at 477. See also Ganos, *supra* note 45.

48 "Why Establish a Private Trust Company?" (2019), online: Frontier Administrative Services LLC, <wyoprivatetrust.com/about-us/why-establish-private-trust>.

49 "Wyoming Asset Protection Trust: Anonymous Creditor Protection" (2019), online: Wyoming Trust & LLC Attorney, <wyomingllcattorney.com/Wyoming-Asset-Protection-Trust>.

50 See Bryan Hubbell, "Benefits of Family Trust Planning in Canada" (17 August 2017), online: Manning Elliot, <manningelliott.com/blog/benefits-of-family-trust-planning-in-Canada>; see also "Family Trusts in Canada" (2019), online: INC Business Lawyers, <www.incorporate.ca/family-trusts-canada>.

51 See e.g. Stewart Sterk, "Asset Protection Trusts: Trust Law's Race to the Bottom?" (2000) 85 Cornell L Rev 1035; Robert H Sitkoff & Max M Schanzenbach, "Jurisdictional Competition for Trust Funds: An Empirical Analysis of Perpetuities and Taxes" (2005) 115 Yale LJ 356 at 376, n 66.

52 See Katharina Pistor, *The Code of Capital: How the Law Creates Wealth Inequality* (Princeton, NJ: Princeton University Press, 2019) at 8. See also *The Deloitte International Wealth Management Centre Ranking 2018*, 3rd ed (Deliotte Consulting, 2018), online (PDF): <www2.deloitte.com/content/dam/Deloitte/ch/Documents/financial-services/ch-fs-1800914_Deloitte-wealth-managemnet-Ranking-2018.pdf>.

53 Charles Tilly, *Durable Inequality* (Los Angeles: University of California Press, 1998).

54 Michèle Lamont, Stefan Beljean & Matthew Clair, "What Is Missing? Cultural Processes and Causal Pathways to Inequality" (2014) 12:3 Socio-Economic Rev 573.

55 See e.g. Khiara M Bridges, *The Poverty of Privacy Rights* (Stanford, CA: Stanford University Press, 2018).

56 *Ibid* at 5.

57 *Ibid.*

58 Citing Margaret Thornton, ed, *Public and Private: Feminist Legal Debates* (Oxford: Oxford University Press, 1995) at 5.

59 Jacobus tenBroek, "California's Dual System of Family Law: Its Origin, Development, and Present Status: Part I" (1964) 16:2 Stan L Rev 257 at 257–58.

60 June Carbone & Naomi Cahn, "The Triple System of Family Law" (2013) Mich St L Rev 1185 at 1189.

61 See Bridges, *supra* note 55 at 132.

62 See Pistor, *supra* note 52 at 50.

63 See e.g. Neil Sobol, "Charging the Poor: Criminal Justice Debt and Modern-Day Debtors' Prisons" (2015–16) 75 Md L Rev 486.

64 See Maxine Eichner, "The Privatized American Family" (2017) 93:1 Notre Dame L Rev 213 at 214.

65 *Ibid* at 229.

66 *Ibid.*

67 See Josh Eidelson, "U.S. Income Inequality Hits a Disturbing New Threshold," *Bloomberg* (1 March 2018), online: Bloomberg, <www.bloomberg.com/news/articles/2018-03-01/america-s-wage-growth-remains-slow-and-uneven>. See also Paul Krugman, "Why We're in a New Gilded Age," *New York Review of Books* (8 May 2014), online: <www.nybooks.com/articles/2014/05/08/thomas-piketty-new-gilded-age/>; Robert M Solow, "Thomas Piketty Is Right: Everything You Need to Know about 'Capital in the Twenty-First Century,'" *New Republic* (22 April 2014), online: <newrepublic.com/article/117429/capital-twenty-first-century-thomas-piketty-reviewed>; Piketty, *supra* note 18; Ganesh Sitaraman, *The Crisis of the Middle-Class Constitution* (New York: Penguin Random House, 2017); Lawrence H Summers, "The Inequality Puzzle" (2014) 33 Democracy: A Journal of Ideas, online: <https://democracyjournal.org/magazine/33/the-inequality-puzzle/>.

68 See US, National Bureau of Economic Research, *Household Wealth Trends in the United States, 1962 to 2016: Has the Middle Class Recovered?* (Working Paper No 24085), by Edward N Wolff (November 2017), online (PDF): <www.nber.org/papers/w24085.pdf>. See also US, National Bureau of Economic Research, *Global Wealth Inequality* (Working Paper No 25462), by Gabriel Zucman (January 2019) at 14, online: NBER, <www.nber.org/papers/w25462>.

69 Switzerland, UBS Group AG, *Billionaires Report 2018: New Visionaries and the Chinese Century* (2018), online: UBS, <www.ubs.com/global/en/wealth-management/uhnw/billionaires-report.html> at 24.

70 To begin, "[m]arried households are significantly wealthier than non-married households ... Never-married women's median net worth is just $2,500 compared to the $148,700 median net worth of married individuals." Karuna Jaggar, "The Race and Gender Wealth Gap" (2008) 15 Race & Regionalism 79. The fact that never-married women have the least wealth of all household types has particular implications for single Black and Hispanic women. Insight Center for Community Economic Development, *Lifting as We Climb: Women of Color, Wealth, and America's*

Future (Spring 2010), online (PDF): <https://static1.squarespace.com/static/5c50b84131d4df5265e7392d/t/5c5c7801ec212d4fd499ba39/1549563907681/Lifting_As_We_Climb_InsightCCED_2010.pdf>. The median wealth for single white women is $41,500; the median wealth for single Black and Hispanic women is $100 and $120 respectively. *Ibid* at 10.

71 Jaggar, *supra* note 70.

72 Cedric Herring & Loren Henderson, "Wealth Inequality in Black and White: Cultural and Structural Sources of the Racial Wealth Gap," (2016) 8 Race & Social Problems 4 at 8 ("[T]hrough inheritance, the children of whites and blacks chart very different economic courses"). Most private wealth in the United States is inherited, which perpetuates the racial wealth gap. Approximately 80 percent of assets come from transfers from prior generations.

73 *Ibid.* One-quarter of white families received an inheritance averaging almost $145,000, but only one in twenty African American families inherited, with an average inheritance of approximately $42,000. Jaggar, *supra* note 70.

74 William Darity Jr et al, *What We Get Wrong about Closing the Racial Wealth Gap* (Samuel DuBois Cook Center on Social Inequality and Insight Center for Community Economic Development, 2018), online (PDF): <https://socialequity.duke.edu/sites/socialequity.duke.edu/files/site-images/FINAL%20COMPLETE%20REPORT_.pdf>. Looking at it from the perspective of educational attainment, "[i]t takes a postgraduate education for a black family to have comparable levels of wealth to a white household with some college education or an associate degree" (at 6).

75 See Andres Knobel, "Trusts: Weapons of Mass Injustice?" (February 2017) Financial Transparency Coalition 1 at 5, online (PDF): <https://www.taxjustice.net/wp-content/uploads/2017/02/Trusts-Weapons-of-Mass-Injustice-Final-12-FEB-2017.pdf>.

2

Identity Choices at the Intersections

The Inequality of Cross-Border Motherhood and What to Do about It

Chao-ju Chen

In Canada, Sharon McIvor could not transmit her Indian status to her grandchildren under the (now-repealed) *Indian Act* 1951's double-mother rule[1] because she traced her ancestry through her maternal side. In the United States, Julia Martinez could not make her daughter a member of her tribe according to the Santa Clara Pueblo's tribal ordinance because she had married outside the tribe. Denying Indigenous mothers the ability to transmit Indigenous status to their children (and grandchildren) is a common, if not universal, form of motherhood discrimination. Indigenous legal status is regulated by state public laws and/ or non-state Indigenous laws, and often involves various combinations of discrimination based on sex, marital status, age, and race.[2] Historically and transnationally, settler-state Indigenous membership laws were designed and functioned to facilitate the supremacy of the dominant race and/or the paternal line, resulting in maternal amnesia as well as the decline of the Indigenous population. That a woman who mothered across racialized boundaries produced members of the race of the father was probably one of the most familiar aspects of the inequality of cross-border motherhood.[3]

Around the world, legal efforts have been made to change this inequality, resulting in both failures and limited successes. Julia Martinez was turned down both by her tribal council, which did not see it as sex discrimination to give tribal membership to children of out-marrying Pueblo men but not to children of out-marrying Pueblo women, and also by the Supreme Court of the United States, which considered mainly procedural justice and deemed it a matter of tribal sovereignty and self-government in which the federal judiciary had no jurisdiction to interfere.[4] Sharon McIvor won in the British Columbia Supreme Court,[5] and the United Nations Human Rights Committee also found in her favour.[6] Subsequent amendments to the (Canadian) *Indian Act* 1985 in 2011 and 2017 have provided significant but incomplete remedies to First Nations women and children who have been unable to obtain Indian status due to past legal sex discrimination.

Taiwan is no exception to this inequality against Indigenous women. In Taiwan, however, the legal regulation of Indigenous women's capacity to pass down their status to their children takes a somewhat different form – one in which family law and administrative law intersect, and that permits identity choices at the intersections of race and sex. Cheng Chuan-ju's case is an illustration of how the intersection of private and public laws produces a unique situation where gender-neutral law perpetrates gender inequality through *private choice*.[7] Cheng (an Indigenous woman) and Wu (a Han[8] man), both lawyers, decided to give their daughter a Han-Chinese[9] name and Wu's surname while also passing on Cheng's Indigenous status to her. This was a socially understandable but legally impermissible decision. Parents are legally entitled to give their child either the father's or the mother's surname,[10] but over 98 percent of all parents of newborns in Taiwan are given their fathers' surnames.[11] However, a child born to the intermarriage of an Indigenous person and a non-Indigenous person can obtain Indigenous status only when they are given the Indigenous parent's surname or the tribe's traditional name.[12] The choice is in the parents' hands, but their choice of name must coincide with that of ethnic status. Predictably, Cheng and Wu's application to register their daughter's status as an Indigenous person was denied. The couple appealed on their daughter's behalf, arguing that the law establishes an unreasonable association of a child's name and Indigenous status, which constitutes discrimination against women and Indigenous peoples and also infringes on Indigenous peoples' right to self-determination.[13] Cheng explicitly protested that the law, ignorant of but operating in the context of patronymic hegemony, has created an awkward situation where an Indigenous mother is incapable of producing an Indigenous child, and she demanded that Indigenous status be determined by Indigenous peoples' own membership rule.[14]

In terms of the Indigenous status or tribe membership of mixed-descent children, the US model respects tribal governments' self-determination with regard to tribe membership, whereas the Canadian model regulates Indian status by constitutional and federal law. Taiwan adopts a middle ground approach in which state law makes status a matter of parental autonomy, albeit with limited options. Cheng's case exemplifies the equality concerns resulting from this approach: Does parental autonomy promote or undermine mothers' equality? Will the model of self-determination (Indigenous peoples' autonomy) with respect to Indigenous identity/status/membership – which Cheng, Taiwan's Indigenous movement, and the *United Nations Declaration on the Rights of Indigenous Peoples* [*UNDRIP*][15] all demand – provide a proper approach for gender equality? How does the intersectionality of race, sex, and marital status play out in the determination of the Indigenous status of mixed-race children? What can and should be done to address this intersectional inequality of cross-border motherhood and to promote mothers' autonomy?

My deliberation begins with the concepts of autonomy and equality. Susan B. Boyd has argued against individualized autonomy and for relational autonomy in the parenting context, and has advocated for a strong presumption in favour of the mother's position being adopted, with a simultaneous acknowledgment of a genetic father's entitlement to a parental relationship if he has developed a significant and constructive relational tie to the child (and the mother).[16] Boyd's approach has been applied in the context of children's surnaming to criticize the sharing of decision-making authority and cultural markers of biological relatedness.[17]

As much as I am sympathetic to Boyd's relational autonomy approach and endorse the substantive equality theory, I do find it challenging to respond to the intersectional inequality of cross-border motherhood in support of mothers' autonomy. This approach refuses to establish parenthood solely based on biological terms, but it neither necessarily objects to Indigenous peoples' self-determination to determine tribal membership by blood (if they choose to do so) nor inevitably endorses the legal rule of determining a mixed-race child's racial status by both blood and culture (for example, by naming), which, as the case of Taiwan demonstrates, can function to jeopardize rather than facilitate the mother's autonomy. The relational autonomy approach can justify Cheng's claim to pass on her Indigenous status to her child both in the current situation where her Han husband is an engaged father committed to fostering the child's Indigenous identity and in the hypothetical situation where her Han husband could be a disengaged father who disapproved of the child obtaining Indigenous status. It does not, however, provide obvious or comfortable answers for cases of intersectionality[18] involving various combinations of privilege and oppression. In a nutshell, can identity choices at the crossroads bring about equality – and, if so, whose equality?

My way out of this conundrum is to bring in Iris M. Young's proposal of defining Indigenous self-determination as nondomination, which emphasizes relational autonomy,[19] as well as the Indigenous feminist critique of Indigenous justice, which argues that "the quest of Indigenous self-determination for justice and freedom must include gender justice."[20] Building on the theories of Boyd and Young, I will elucidate that the self-determination model is the preferred model and that it is more capable of dealing with both mothers' autonomy and Indigenous peoples' autonomy. Valuing both Indigenous justice and gender justice, I will argue for a revised principle of *jus sanguinis* for the state law model, one that places the primary caretaker mother at the centre. My discussion begins with a critique of the racial duty of naming, followed by an assessment of the self-determination model and the state law model in terms of their implications for cross-border motherhood and Indigenous peoples. I will demonstrate that the intersection of family law and Indigenous status law has operated to deteriorate mothers' disadvantaged situation by imposing the racial duty of naming, but that it can also be reformulated to pursue balance between mothers' and Indigenous peoples' equality by incorporating the primary caretaker doctrine. I will argue that the primary caretaker doctrine's recognition of child-care work can contribute to a balance between a mother's entitlement to establish her child's racial identity and Indigenous peoples' need for their survival as a nation.

Against the Racial Duty of Naming

Intimate relationships between Indigenous peoples and Han-Taiwanese have a long history. The use of a person's name in the determination of Indigenous status for mixed-race children, however, is a relatively recent convention.[21] In 1956, the government enacted a law that established a regime of regulating Indigenous status, which determined mixed-race children's status by paternal blood.[22] The law was revised in 1980 to include a "marry-out clause" (subsequently abolished in 1991) and to impose a surname requirement for mixed-race children (subsequently expanded in 1991). The surname requirement, which granted mixed-race children Indigenous status on the condition that they took their Indigenous mother's surname (and that the mother had no brother) or their Indigenous father's surname (and that the father was married into the mother's household),[23] was not designed to support mothers' autonomy. In the context of Han male hegemony, it served as a mechanism of assimilation (for mixed-race children of Indigenous women) and exclusion (for mixed-race children of Han women). Years of determination on the part of the Indigenous peoples' movement to claim their own identity came to partial fruition in 2001, when the legislature passed the *Status Act for Indigenous Peoples* [*Status Act*].[24] It created a new regime that determines Indigenous status based on blood and name and that permits parental choices. The following discussion will demonstrate that the new regime's combination of blood and name is an improvement made in the name of gender equality and group survival but motivated by a desire to exclude mixed-race children of Indigenous mothers married to Han men. By imposing a racial duty on parents of mixed-race children to perform racialized naming, it enhances a mother's autonomy to a limited extent while it legitimates her lack of autonomy through her consent under constraints.

The Rise of the Gender-Neutral Choice Regime

The *Status Act* explicitly abolishes the old principle of patrilineage in the determination of mixed-race children's status and replaces it with the principle of *unilineality by choice*. A child of intermarriage between Indigenous and non-Indigenous individuals acquires Indigenous status if that child is given the Indigenous father's or mother's surname or their tribe's traditional name.[25] A non-marital child of an Indigenous mother acquires Indigenous status but will forfeit the status once the non-Indigenous father acknowledges the child, unless the parents have an agreement to give the child the mother's surname or her tribe's traditional name.[26] A non-marital child of a non-Indigenous mother acquires Indigenous status provided that the Indigenous father acknowledges the child and that the parents have an agreement to give the child the father's surname or his tribe's traditional name.[27]

Developed into the above standards for mixed-race children's Indigenous status, the unilineality by choice regime combines *jus sanguinis* with parental autonomy (exercised through the choice of name), and grants unwed fathers a constrained right to transmit Indigenous status to their child or to revoke the child's Indigenous status, which requires the mother's permission to change the child's name. A marital child is to inherit the racial status of the parent from whom the child receives the surname, and the child's parents jointly decide which racial status the child shall inherit through the choice of surname, making it a form of co-parenting. The *Status Act* does not specify the way to resolve parental disputes over the choice of a marital child's status through naming, but the *Civil Code* does provide a random solution in the case of parental disagreement over a child's surname: drawing lots at the household registration office.[28] A non-marital child's birth mother is entitled to transmit her racial status to her child, and the biological father's acknowledgment can change the child's status only when the mother permits it by agreeing to change the child's name, or when the court orders a change of name if the father appeals to the court and successfully proves that a change of name is in the child's interest, and that the child is not named after the custodial parent or that the mother is an irresponsible parent.[29]

On its face, the law is gender-neutral and respects autonomy. It abolishes the preference of patrilineage, and an unwed mother is entitled to reject a genetic father's request to change their child's name and status inherited from her. Yet the law demonstrates ignorance of and disrespect for Indigenous peoples' naming culture, and it also discriminates against women. A close look into the legislative records of the *Status Act* reveals that the choice regime was created in the name of gender equality and Indigenous equality but also with suspicions about granting Indigenous status to out-marrying Indigenous women's children.

The legislature reviewed three bills. Explicitly opposing patrilinealism and demanding gender equality, the two bills proposed by male and female Indigenous legislators endorsed the principle of *jus sanguinis* for children of dual descent while also granting parents the right to co-decide: the male Indigenous legislator's bill required *opting in,* whereas the female Indigenous legislator's bill allowed *opting out*.[30] The government's bill, which also indicated its endorsement of gender equality, added a name requirement to combine the principle of *jus sanguinis* with the principle of cultural identity based on the claim that it is crucial for children of dual descent to demonstrate their belonging and identity by name so as to be considered Indigenous people.[31] This legal design was based on the recommendation of a government-commissioned report, which contended that the status of children of intermarriages should be determined by their parents through naming, because there should be no rights without responsibility: it would be unreasonable for children using their non-Indigenous father's surnames to inherit their Indigenous mother's status.[32] After closed-door party negotiations, the government's version prevailed and became law.

During committee review, the female Indigenous legislator Chang Jen-Hiang (章仁香) criticized the opting-in design, contending that it would undermine the continuance of Indigenous peoples, and the male Indigenous legislator Yang Jen-Fu (楊仁福) concurred with her.[33] The Deputy Minister of the Council of Indigenous Affairs (an Indigenous man), however, insisted on the official position that both bloodline and culture matter, explaining that, for the following reasons, some sort of "cultural requirement" is necessary to facilitate the next generation of Indigenous peoples' affirmation of their cultural identity: (1) one-fourth of all married Indigenous people are married to non-Indigenous people, and intermarriages between Indigenous women and non-Indigenous men have accounted for one-fifth of all Indigenous households; (2) Indigenous women married to non-Indigenous men often live in households with a family atmosphere and economic resources better than those of average Indigenous families; and (3) many Indigenous women live the Han way of life after marrying into Han families, and their children, despite having Indigenous blood, are not provided with an environment in which to learn the Indigenous ways of knowing and being, which leads to their lack of Indigenous identity.[34]

On the one hand, legislator Chang's criticism of opting in demonstrates deep skepticism about the choice model in the context of gender and racial hierarchy.[35] On the other hand, the Deputy Minister's defence of the government's bill – the "no rights without responsibility" rationale – reveals a serious distrust of out-marrying Indigenous women's capacity to nurture Indigenous identity and a rejection of their Indigenous authenticity for "marrying out and up," which makes them and their children less qualified for affirmative government protection. Moreover, the choice model with a name requirement did not reflect the majority opinion of Indigenous interviewees in the commissioned report's survey.

An overwhelming majority of interviewees agreed that marital children of intermarriages and non-marital children of Indigenous peoples should be granted Indigenous status, and they were in favour of Indigenous women's non-marital children retaining Indigenous status.[36] Interviewees expressed majority support for retaining an Indigenous woman's non-marital child's Indigenous status after the genetic Han father acknowledged the child, but their support for granting Indigenous status to children of Indigenous men and non-Indigenous women significantly exceeded that for granting Indigenous status to children of Indigenous women and non-Indigenous men.[37] They were also more supportive of Indigenous men's acknowledged non-marital children acquiring Indigenous status than of Indigenous women's non-marital children having Indigenous status after their non-Indigenous fathers acknowledged them.[38]

The government's skeptical attitude toward out-marrying and unmarried Indigenous women's children getting Indigenous status was shared by some Indigenous peoples – whose view, however, was the minority opinion according to the above survey. The result is a gender-neutral law that formally abolishes the "marry-out" clause but, for practical purposes, continues to reproduce the outsider status of Indigenous women and their mixed-race children. It is a formal equality law that reflects, rather than challenges, the dominant arrangement of mixed-race children inheriting Indigenous status along the patrilineal line.[39]

A Choice That Is Not: The Gendered Racial Duty

The choice regime created by the 2001 *Status Act* enforces discrimination based on race, sex, and marital status, and then legitimates it through the notion of consent.[40] First, the law burdens the Indigenous parent of mixed-race children with a "negative racial duty" to avoid using an Indigenous name and to comply with the Han naming rule, or with an "affirmative racial duty"[41] to perform a *naming act* so as to demonstrate a commitment to embracing the Indigenous parent's naming culture. Indigenous peoples in Taiwan have neither a unified naming system nor a surname system. Tribal name practices are as diverse as can be, involving various combinations of the personal name, house name, parent's name, kinship terms, and other terms, and may also be subject to change when a new life comes into the family.[42]

Cheng's tribe, the Truku people, uses a combination of the child's personal name and the father's name. Therefore, neither of the two legal options work for Cheng and Wu in naming their daughter. It is meaningless either to give the child Cheng's surname or to name her in accordance with the Truku people's naming system: Cheng's surname – itself an indication of Han colonial oppression – holds no cultural meaning to her, and Wu, as a Han man, does not have a Truku name to be given to the child.[43] Consequently, performing the affirmative racial duty cannot achieve its proclaimed goal of embracing the Indigenous cultural identity, and performing the negative racial duty would reinforce the colonial oppression of imposing the Han naming system on Indigenous peoples. Operating in Taiwan's society, where the legal and social ban on the use of Indigenous names has resulted in the unfortunate fact that approximately 96 percent of all Indigenous peoples still use Han-Chinese names, despite the legal ban having been lifted for more than two decades,[44] the racial duty is anything but an effective legal means to promote Indigenous naming cultures. It lends more support to Han supremacy than to Indigenous equality, and the racial hierarchy remains intact.

Second, the racial duty is unequally gendered. Cheng's case reveals how an Indigenous mother's choice of passing Indigenous status to her mixed-race child, even with the endorsement of her husband, is constrained by the legal requirement of naming as well as by the social reality shaped by historical and current colonial oppression. Considering the fact that 98.21 percent of all newborns' parents *agree* to give their child the father's surname and that only 0.02 percent of all newborns are given traditional names,[45] it is no surprise that an Indigenous mother does not or cannot "choose" to give her mixed-race child her surname or her tribe's traditional name. This situation makes it more likely that the mixed-race child will not acquire Indigenous status and that the Indigenous mother will be the only racial outsider in the family. Moreover, it is usually only a privileged few women who can secure a name contract with their husbands to name the child after the mother. A study based on regression analysis of two nationwide social surveys indicates that a woman with greater educational and occupational advantages is more likely to prefer matronymic naming and to have a husband supportive of giving the child her surname.[46] Although a small-scale survey study claims that it is more likely for an

Indigenous mother than a non-Indigenous mother to give her child her surname,[47] it also suggests that a non-Indigenous mother is in a relatively disadvantaged position when it comes to negotiating the child's status and name with her Indigenous husband, whose capacity for passing Indigenous status to their child is enhanced by patronymy.

Third, a woman's marital status can act as a double-edged sword: married motherhood is burdened with constraints on decision-making but blessed with the legitimacy of marriage; single motherhood seems to enjoy more autonomy but endures the burden of illegitimacy. The choice regime qualifies discrimination based on marital status and sex because the legal institution of legitimacy systematically disadvantages mothers, albeit differently for married and unmarried mothers. A married father's entitlement to co-decide his child's name and status is based solely on his marital relationship to the mother. Under the hierarchy of gender inequality in which patronymic naming is the norm, *the formal equality of a wife and a husband's right to decide* becomes *the substantive inequality of his power to decide and her right to dissent*. Even though a random solution (drawing lots at the household registration office) is provided for parents who differ in their opinion about assigning the child's name at birth, which therefore allows a dissenting wife to seek the random solution, in practice this option is rarely sought: from 2007 to 2017, only 0.12 percent of all newborns' names were determined by drawing lots, and only one newborn was given a traditional name as a result of drawing lots.[48] The fact that very few wives exercise the right to seek a random solution indicates their constrained autonomy and married men's de facto power. As a result, the institution of legitimacy facilitates the exclusion of Indigenous women's marital children of dual descent, suggesting that *opting in* is a gendered mechanism of exclusion and assimilation.

Compared to its subordinating effects on married Indigenous women, the institution of legitimacy's treatment of an unmarried Indigenous mother seems to privilege her by automatically granting her child Indigenous status without the name requirement. However, the genetic Han father's acknowledgment can undermine the unmarried mother's innate advantage resulting from "the anchoring effects of birth names" (one's birth name tends to stick to one's identity: it shapes the status quo of one's identity and its change is hindered by numerous social and legal costs),[49] despite the legal requirement that the mother's "consent" is needed to change the child's name and status. As of 2020, non-marital children account for only 3.94 percent of all newborns, and approximately two-thirds of them are unacknowledged by their genetic fathers.[50] A total of 81.06 percent of non-marital children take their fathers' surname after their fathers acknowledge them,[51] which demonstrates the power of patrilineal normativity to undo the anchoring effects, and which can result in Indigenous mothers' non-marital children losing Indigenous status and Indigenous fathers' non-marital children acquiring it. An unmarried father's privilege to make the child a member of his group is not without legal constraints. If an unmarried mother refuses the genetic father's request to change the child's name and status after he has acknowledged the child, he is entitled to appeal to the court but has to meet certain legal requirements.[52] Since the courts are receptive to a "status-as-interest argument" (granting Indigenous status to the child is in the child's interest due to the benefits and rights provided for Indigenous peoples) in cases involving widowed or divorced Indigenous mothers, it is possible that an Indigenous custodial father or mother stands a better chance in court. However, court challenges are uncommon, and the questions of whether race matters and whether race trumps gender in courts is subject to verification. It can be argued that the effects of the institution of legitimacy on non-marital cross-border motherhood are a mixture of discrimination and privileges.

In Defence of Self-Determination as Nondomination

Designed to secure the cultural authenticity of Indigenous peoples and operated in the context of Han supremacy, the gender-neutral choice regime with a racial duty updates the preference for the male bloodline in the name of cultural survival and legitimates it by consent. An inquiry into the legislative intent behind the law shows that it is the product of official historical distrust and exclusion of out-marrying Indigenous women, whose marriages to Han men are considered a form of assimilation. These women are presumed to be unqualified to produce Indigenous children unless proven otherwise by having their children named after them. Indigenous men's marriages with Han women, in contrast, do not undermine their qualification to produce Indigenous children, unless they have their children take their mother's surname. In addition, a father's marital relationship with the mother facilitates his advantage to determine the child's racial status, regardless of his commitment to parenthood. The choice regime does little to protect the autonomy of cross-border motherhood, and both Indigenous mothers and Han mothers are constrained in their capacity to choose their mixed-race children's racial status. Given the increasing trend of intermarriages and the fact that intermarriages between Indigenous women and non-Indigenous men consistently outnumber those between Indigenous men and non-Indigenous women,[53] the inequality of cross-border motherhood is likely to deteriorate rather than improve in the future, and Indigenous women's limited choices at the crossroads serve more to confirm rather than challenge their historical exclusion.

In response to the urgent need for reform, Cheng's proposal not only aims to remove the racial duty (abolishing the name requirement) but also seeks to pursue the collective goal of the Indigenous peoples movement: self-determination. Cheng and Wu's brief argues that the *Status Act*'s regulation on children of dual-descent infringes on Indigenous people's right to self-identification and also constitutes a violation of racial and gender equality.[54] In support of this position, the brief cites international human rights documents that endorse the principle of Indigenous peoples' self-identification;[55] the definition of gender discrimination, which includes indirect discrimination, in the *Convention on the Elimination of All Forms of Discrimination against Women* [*CEDAW*];[56] and Taiwan's constitutional protection of equality, freedom of personality, freedom of naming, and multiculturalism. In her scholarly work, Cheng further advocates the establishment of Indigenous self-governance on the grounds that the state is not entitled to define Indigenous membership and to impose Han culture on Indigenous peoples.[57] That is to say that Indigenous peoples should have the sole jurisdiction over its membership.

On top of Indigenous peoples' advocacy for self-determination, various bills to amend the *Status Act* have been proposed in the legislature. Two bills exist on the two ends of the spectrum: one that relies on bloodline/parentage only, and another that requires both bloodline/parentage and cultural identity. Highlighting gender equality and the need to recognize bilineality without discriminatory restrictions, the first bill (Bill A),[58] proposed by a group of Han legislators, adopts *jus sanguinis* descent rule that would automatically grant Indigenous status to a child born to an Indigenous father or mother. It specifically stipulates that a child born to an unmarried Indigenous woman will be granted Indigenous status; so will a child born to an unmarried non-Indigenous woman and acknowledged by the Indigenous father. Consequently, a non-Indigenous father's acknowledgment will not result in the deprivation of an Indigenous mother's non-marital child's Indigenous status. Indigenous status in cases of unmarried women requires neither parental agreement nor proof of cultural identity. By contrast, the bill initiated by a female Indigenous legislator Kolas Yotaka and a group of Han legislators (Bill B) emphasizes the necessity for dual requirements that associate "internal blood connection" (biological belonging) with "external representation of cultural identity" (cultural affiliation) so as to secure the matching of one's legal status and personal identity. It would grant Indigenous status to an Indigenous person's marital child only when the child is given an Indigenous peoples' traditional name using Indigenous peoples' languages.[59] It appears that neither Bill A nor Bill B was drafted in collective consultation with Indigenous peoples' advocacy groups.

The self-determination model creates a new choice regime that substitutes Indigenous peoples' autonomy for parental autonomy and emphasizes state non-intervention. Bills A and B are two instances of what I call the state law model, which affirms state jurisdiction over Indigenous peoples' membership and seeks new ways to define that membership. In light of the discussions on the inequality of cross-border motherhood earlier in this chapter, which model can better serve to correct this inequality and promote both gender and Indigenous justice?

Self-Determination as Nondomination

Self-determination is a right, a principle, and a fundamental value that is considered the core of Indigenous justice. The self-determination model permits and, indeed, requires two levels of identity recognition: the individual level (self-identification) and the group level (group recognition). Since a newborn obviously cannot perform self-identification, this means that someone else must decide for them, making it a decision of the child's parent(s), the tribe, or another recognized subject of decision making. Under this model, the state should respect Indigenous peoples' self-governance over their membership and restrain itself from infringing on Indigenous peoples' autonomy. This model, which is considered a crucial step toward decolonization, is endorsed by Cheng, Taiwan's Indigenous peoples' movement, and international human rights law. Wu and Cheng's argument in their brief for Indigenous peoples' right to self-identification also invokes freedom of association to claim the right of a group to determine its membership so as to pursue its goals, whether with respect to bloodline, language, lifestyle, or world view maintenance. It is Indigenous peoples, and only Indigenous peoples, who can determine the qualifications for members and identify their members.[60]

The above sketch of the self-determination model is a representation of the notion that Iris M. Young called "self-determination as noninterference."[61] The noninterference model of self-determination equates self-determination with sovereignty and presupposes an independent subject of sovereignty free from outside intervention. Young considered this model "a dangerous fiction" because it falsely assumes that people are, or ought to be, independent, and it mistakenly understands freedom as being free from outside interference.[62] Against this dangerous fiction, she has argued that people and groups are embodied in relationships, claiming that "an unfree person may not experience interference" and that "a free person may be interfered with."[63] Noninterference also does not protect insiders from domination by other insiders or by the governing institution.[64] Accordingly, Young has urged a conceptual shift from noninterference to nondomination, which takes account of all agents' interdependence and embeddedness in relationships; does not consider a group to be a unity with a set of common interests, agency, and will of its own; and focuses on the relationships between groups as well as within a group.

The model of "self-determination as nondomination" adopts the *prima facie* principle of noninterference but also requires that "in so far as their activities affect each other, peoples are in relationship and ought to negotiate the terms and effects of the relationship" and that "peoples have the right to participate *as peoples* in designing and implementing intergovernmental institutions aimed at minimizing domination."[65] Young has further claimed that Indigenous peoples' claim to self-determination is "better understood as a quest for an institutional context of nondomination,"[66] and that the *prima facie* principle of noninterference may be suspended so as to enact the common decisions of units to prevent domination by one unit over another as well as to prevent some members of a self-governed people from dominating members internally.[67]

Young's application of relational autonomy in the context of Indigenous peoples' self-determination is supported by a synthetical reading of *UNDRIP*, which requires the principles of self-identification (Article 33), non-discrimination (Article 9), and gender equality (Article 44),[68] as well as a synthetical reading of Taiwan's Constitution, which guarantees both equality and multiculturalism.[69] Her critique of the noninterference model's assumption of a homogeneous group serves as a warning reminder of cultural essentialism, suggesting the need to pay attention to hierarchal differences between groups and within a group, and, in particular, the need to take into consideration vulnerable insiders and cultural dissent from within. Embracing Young's theory (and Jennifer Nedelsky's theory of relational autonomy[70]) in her exploration of Indigenous justice and gender justice, Rauna Kuokkanen has also persuasively argued for a theory of self-determination as a fundamental value aiming at fostering the norm of integrity and at restructuring all relations of domination, including gender.[71] Indeed, the inequality of cross-border motherhood begs for remedies that can address its intersectional nature, which must include both gender and Indigenous justice. Self-determination is, therefore, the preferred model, and we can combine self-determination as nondomination with Boyd's primary caretaker approach[72] and her application of relational autonomy within the context of parenting to evaluate the two models of self-determination.

First, internal domination can be better addressed by the nondomination model, but suspending the *prima facie* principle of noninterference should not be a priority. The noninterference model does not prohibit the adoption of a membership rule that denies or undermines an Indigenous mother's autonomy (such as excluding an out-marrying Indigenous woman's children because she objects to certain cultural practices that she deems discriminatory or requiring a Han father's consent for an Indigenous woman to apply for the child's Indigenous status) so long as it is the Indigenous people's own membership rule. Scholars who defend multiculturalism also justify their support of self-determination by claiming "the right to exit."[73] Yet critics have argued that, by forcing a difficult and unjust choice between culture and equality, to exit may not be a desirable or affordable option, and it does not necessarily improve vulnerable members' situation.[74] An Indigenous woman who disapproves of her tribe's membership rule may not want to or be able to leave, and leaving would further disqualify her child from Indigenous membership. In this respect, Cheng and Wu's claim is a "self-determination as noninterference" argument[75] that overemphasizes the freedom to be let alone and understates the danger of "domination in the form of freedom." Their claim for the respect of a voluntary association's freedom from intervention risks mistaking the right of association for an unfettered right to set whatever goal the association wants and to use whatever means it wishes to pursue its goal.

While there is no convincing evidence that Indigenous peoples will adopt discriminatory approaches for the purpose of self-preservation, it is not unlikely that a discriminatory membership rule will be considered. Indigenous women may bear disproportionate costs for preserving their group's identity, which is what Ayelet Shachar called "the paradox of multicultural vulnerability."[76] In the United States, Julia Martinez's tribe adopted a membership rule that excluded out-marrying tribal women's children, and inside efforts to change the rule have repeatedly failed.[77] In Canada, the Band Council determined that Sandra Lovelace (the plaintiff in *Lovelace v Canada*) had no right to live on the reserve, and many women who were reinstated with Indian status are not automatically granted band membership once Band Councils were entitled to set their own band membership rule.[78] In Taiwan, the Qalang Smangus tribe's self-governance ordinance, for instance, stipulates that "[t]he Tayal traditional Gaga (Indigenous legal norm) does not consider out-marrying daughters members of the tribe, and they are not allowed to bring their husbands back to invest in the tribal economy; the tribal council's approval is required if they need to come back and receive support from parents and other family members due to straitened circumstances."[79] Female Indigenous legislator Kolas Yotaka proposed a bill[80] that includes a racial duty regardless of its disproportionate negative effect on Indigenous women, which effect has been proven by the implementation of the current *Status Act*. The survey documented in the government-commissioned report also reveals that Indigenous peoples were more open to accepting the non-marital mixed-race children of Indigenous men than those of Indigenous women.

The nondomination model may suspend the *prima facie* principle of noninterference because it involves internal domination. The question is, will outside intervention deliver equality? While I agree with Brenda Gunn that "[r]egardless of its origins (pre-contact or resulting from colonialism), sexism exists within communities,"[81] I still find it necessary to note the harms of colonization (and colonization as a gendered process) and what Sarah Song has called "the congruence effect" of majority cultural norms (dominant cultures' own patriarchal norms offer support for patriarchal practices in minority cultures).[82] Regardless of whether or not the Qalang Smangus tribe's Gaga does have a historical tradition of excluding out-marrying women – which could possibly be an invention of tradition and an example of "the paradox of multicultural vulnerability" – the tribe's ordinance receives support from the Han patriarchal cultural tradition (in which married women are considered outsiders of their natal families).[83] A study of the Peiwan people also argues that the adoption of the Han-Chinese name system has resulted in an increased tendency toward male-centredness.[84] If the Han people's record on sex discrimination is any guide, outside intervention does not guarantee equality. More attention should be directed to cultural dissents within a group, and outsiders can play a better role not by direct intervention but by supporting insiders' claims and actions for change. Indeed, as Catharine MacKinnon has argued, "it looks more like *in*equality is the white idea. And what women like Julia Martinez might make equality mean, no white man invented."[85] Kuokkanen has also forcefully claimed that neither individual self-determination nor collective self-determination should be compromised in the name of the other.[86] The nondomination model should first seek to empower women insiders in the shaping of their culture and to increase their representation, which is a deliberate democratic approach to cope with the tensions between multiculturalism and feminism;[87] and, as Sarah Song has proposed, based on her discussions of Canada and the United States, the state should play a role that need not impose a different set of rules but that takes measures to support democratic processes within the tribe.[88]

Second, the nondomination model can provide a better balance between outsiders' legitimate interests and Indigenous peoples' needs. The noninterference model could permit Indigenous peoples to adopt an inclusive membership rule that automatically grants Indigenous status to the newborn of an estranged and uncommitted Indigenous father but against the will of that child's primary caretaker Han mother (an affected outsider), who might have non-discriminatory reasons for her preference (for example, not being willing to fulfill the membership obligation of cultural participation because it would compel her to co-parent with the child's estranged father and failing to do so would make her an irresponsible mother at risk of losing custody). The noninterference model could also permit Indigenous peoples to adopt a membership rule that allows only an Indigenous parent to apply for the child's Indigenous status; thus, a primary caretaker Han mother who is committed to fostering the child's Indigenous or multifaceted identity cannot do so against the will of the Indigenous father who prefers the child to be a Han. The nondomination model would suggest the establishment of an intergovernmental institution, to be designed and implemented by Han and Indigenous peoples as peoples with the aim of minimizing domination. It would also require that Indigenous peoples hear the claim of the affected outsider, and that the affected outsider recognize that her preference for the child's status affects the Indigenous people. Under this model, the guiding principle of nondomination supports Boyd's claim that a racialized parent is not unavoidably best suited for the parental decision[89] and facilitates the primary caretaker mother's autonomy by taking her concerns into account.

A Revised Principle of *Jus Sanguinis* under the State Law Model

Self-determination as nondomination is the preferred model because it can facilitate both gender justice and Indigenous justice by promoting the autonomy of both mothers and Indigenous peoples. The implementation of Indigenous peoples' self-governance in Taiwan is, however, not in the foreseeable future. In the absence of legal recognition of self-determination, how can the state law model correct the inequality of cross-border motherhood? It should be noted that Indigenous peoples have limited political representation at the national and local levels. It is critical for the Han-dominated legislature to consult with Indigenous peoples and to ensure a deliberate democratic process (in particular, the participation of vulnerable minority members) in the remaking of the allocation of Indigenous status under the state law model.

To facilitate the autonomy and equality of cross-border motherhood, a state law regulating Indigenous status should:

(1) recognize the historical injustice toward Indigenous peoples, particularly the denial of Indigenous status to out-marrying Indigenous women and their children by sex-specific law or gender-neutral law, and seek to

empower these women's capacity to transmit Indigenous status to their children;[90]

(2) minimize or diminish a genetic but uncommitted father's privilege to undermine the primary caretaker mother's autonomy; and

(3) aim to foster a child's dual or multiple identity without the presumption that a racialized parent is unavoidably best suited to make the child's identity choice and without placing unreasonable burdens on the primary caretaker mother.

Bills A and B serve as my starting point for discussing application of the above criteria. In the name of gender equality and Indigenous women's equality in particular, Bill A adopts the principle of *jus sanguinis* with no preference for the paternal or maternal bloodline, and leaves no room for a biological parent to decide otherwise or for both biological parents to agree otherwise. Aiming to preserve Indigenous cultural heritage through naming, Bill B cancels the option of performing the negative racial duty and requires a new affirmative racial duty that demands rigid cultural authenticity (using an Indigenous name in the Indigenous language). It is willing to pursue both blood and cultural authenticity at the risk of decreasing the Indigenous population, and it continues the opting-in mechanism that considers a child's Indigenous status a matter of parental choice.

Bill B requires choice, whereas Bill A allows no choice. Bill B values both cultural association and bloodline/parentage, whereas Bill A is concerned only with bloodline/parentage. The fact that Bill B repudiates biological essentialism, however, does not make it a better option than Bill A. Bill B's requirement of cultural authenticity (affirmative racial duty) is ignorant of the harms of Han male supremacy and unequal power relations in an unequal society in which Indigenous women suffer disparate impacts, albeit with the good intention to preserve Indigenous cultures. It authorizes the government to decide the authenticity of a certain cultural practice (i.e., what counts as an Indigenous name in the Indigenous language), and to use this as a proxy for cultural authenticity. Placing the power to define culture in the wrong hands – that is, those of the Han-dominated government – Bill B enforces cultural essentialism and overlooks the somewhat conflicting needs of the Indigenous peoples to *preserve* as well as to *change* their cultures. To burden identity choices at the crossroads with a racial duty derived from state-enforced cultural essentialism fails to take into account the unequal conditions under which choices are made, and can result in gendered exclusion. By replacing the right to use Indigenous names with the duty to use Indigenous names to establish a nexus between Indigenous rights and duties, it is also an ineffective tool to promote Indigenous naming culture in a changing society with a long history of interracial intimacies that continue to grow. Cheng's case has shown how an opting-in mechanism with a racial duty can function to undermine rather than promote a mother's autonomy, and how the option of using an Indigenous name places the parents in an awkward, and sometimes impossible, situation. Cheng's child would ultimately not be granted Indigenous status under Bill B. In this light, Ayelet Shachar's proposal of a new membership principle of "*jus nexi*" – a principle of membership acquisition that emphasizes the actual membership or social fact of connection (connection, union, or linkage) over and above any privilege of inherited entitlement ("soil" under *jus soli* or "blood" under *jus sanguinis*) – in the context of national citizenship[91] does not seem a preferred alternative in the context of Indigenous membership under the state law model. Authorizing the state to determine whether or not a person is substantively connected to the Indigenous community (for example, by using an Indigenous name) will inevitably reinforce the domination of the Han people over Indigenous peoples, on top of the fact that a state law model for Indigenous status unavoidably intervenes in Indigenous peoples' autonomy.

In contrast to Bill B's under-inclusive strategy to advance intergenerational cultural continuity in the reproduction of the collective, Bill A pursues gender equality at the risk of being over-inclusive and undermining a non-Indigenous mother's autonomy. Allotting Indigenous status in accordance to the principle of *jus sanguinis* means that the status is a birthright automatically granted based solely on the incident of birth, and that, in the case of a mixed-race child, the Indigenous parent trumps the non-Indigenous parent in terms of the capacity to pass on racial status because dual-status is not permitted. Bill A assures an Indigenous mother of passing on her Indigenous status, regardless of her marital status and the racial status of the child's father. Cheng's child would no doubt be granted Indigenous status under Bill A. Whereas an Indigenous mother will not be able to "opt out" of her child's Indigenous status, the lack of the right to exit does not confer inequality, given the history of forced exit (including "consented" exit arising from Han domination). In the case of the Han father of an Indigenous child, enduring Han male supremacy will lend support to his preference for a Han identity (if he refuses to provide a nurturing environment for the child's Indigenous status), but the Indigenous mother will likely be empowered by the law to bargain for the child's de facto dual identity.

A primary caretaker Han mother, however, will not be able to transmit her status to her child if the genetic father is an Indigenous man and if his paternity is established by marriage or acknowledgment, regardless of the father's substantive engagement. Once the child has been granted Indigenous status, the Han mother might be expected to perform a mothering role of an Indigenous child, and failing in this duty might result in her being labelled an irresponsible or unfit mother. In the case of a Han mother raising a child with a committed Indigenous father, Han supremacy will probably facilitate the child's dual identity. However, in the case of a Han mother raising an Indigenous child of a disengaged Indigenous father, the mother might be incapable of fostering the child's dual or Indigenous identity, and her autonomy as a mother could be undermined. If the quest for Indigenous justice is to include gender justice, then the differentiated situations of Indigenous mothers and Han mothers should be taken into account: an Indigenous mother is historically and cotemporally prevented from reproducing for her people, whereas a Han mother is assumed to reproduce for the people of her child's father. The former serves the purpose of assimilation and the interests of the Han people; the latter denies a mother's autonomy and facilitates women's subordination to men.

My bold, unsettling, and imperfect proposal is to revise the principle of *jus sanguinis* by placing the primary caretaker mother at the centre to correct the injustice of cross-border motherhood. Under this proposal, *jus sanguinis* is the *prima facie* principle for a child's acquisition of Indigenous status,[92] but the principle should be suspended when an Indigenous biological father lacks a substantive and positive relationship with the mother or/and the child. Under this proposed principle, an Indigenous mother's child will acquire Indigenous status regardless of the father's racial status, and an Indigenous father's child with a non-Indigenous mother will acquire Indigenous status under one of the two conditions: (1) that he is an engaged father; (2) that the non-Indigenous mother consents to it and demonstrates her ability to provide a nurturing environment to foster the child's dual or Indigenous identity despite the fact that the Indigenous father (and his extended family) lacks a substantive ties with her or the child. By permitting a non-Indigenous mother to conditionally opt in with respect to the child's Indigenous status, the proposed principle imposes restrictions on an Indigenous father's entitlement to pass on his status to the child in order to balance Indigenous peoples' need for survival and a non-Indigenous mother's autonomy. Against the symmetric demands of formal equality, it is an asymmetrical principle that sets no limitation on an Indigenous mother's entitlement to pass on her status to her child due to her role as the primary caretaker, but does place restrictions on a non-Indigenous mother's right to opt in for her child conceived with an Indigenous man due to her status as a non-Indigenous person.

Under the current *Status Act,* an Indigenous father's mixed-race child has a much better chance of acquiring Indigenous status than an Indigenous mother's mixed-race child, which means that Indigenous women enjoy lesser entitlement to transmit their Indigenous status while it is easier for non-Indigenous women to produce Indigenous children for Indigenous fathers. Adopting this proposed principle will reverse that scenario: Indigenous mothers' mixed-race children will automatically acquire Indigenous status, whereas non-Indigenous mothers' mixed-race children will conditionally acquire Indigenous status. This is a proposal that aims to enhance a mother's autonomy and entitlement to transmit her status to her child – in particular, an Indigenous woman's entitlement to participate in the collective reproduction of her people. This is also a proposal that denies a non-Indigenous father's unfettered right to pass on his Indigenous status to his mixed-race child, and that places restrictions on an Indigenous father's right to make his mixed-race child a member of his people. How this proposal will be received by Indigenous peoples is in the unknown future, but I expect that challenges and criticism will exceed approval.

Conclusion

Mothering across racial borders has a price for women, and that price varies depending on the combination of sex, race, marital status, and other factors. Indigenous women's inability to transmit Indigenous status to their children receives the most attention from equality scholars and serves as the primary focus of this chapter, which also sheds light on the relatively unattended situation of non-Indigenous women reproducing for Indigenous peoples. This investigation of Taiwan's postwar legal regulation of mixed-race children's status reveals how paternal bloodline has been privileged to sustain racial hierarchy, which survives recent legal reforms through the imposition of the gendered racial duty of naming. The marriage of family law (i.e., children's surname law) and state Indigenous status law has produced a new gender-neutral choice regime that aims to facilitate gender equality and Indigenous equality but fails on both counts. Identity choices at the intersections of sex, race, and marital status reflect neither the autonomy nor the equality of cross-border motherhood. The intertwining hierarchy of sex and race undermines that equality. Consequently, the case of Taiwan exemplifies how cross-border motherhood can be made unequal by gender-neutral law and private choice.

If the individual right to choose fails to deliver justice, can Indigenous peoples' collective right to choose do the job? International human rights laws have established Indigenous peoples' right to self-determination, but tensions between Indigenous self-determination and gender justice have given rise to challenges and criticism. Endorsing self-determination as nondomination rather than as noninterference, this chapter asserts that group self-determination will not facilitate the dual goals of gender and Indigenous justice if Indigenous sovereignty is established as a private sphere that tolerates internal domination. I also argued that, in the situation where self-determination is not realized and state law serves as the primary source of regulation, adapting the primary caretaker doctrine to revise the principle of *jus sanguinis* in the determination of mixed-race children's status empowers mothers (Indigenous and non-Indigenous, married and non-marital) more than enhancing individual choices does, despite tensions that might arise due to the proposed revision's restrictions on Indigenous fathers' ability to transmit Indigenous status to children. This revised principle will also enhance mixed-race children's access to Indigenous status and foster their association with the Indigenous community. To correct the inequality of cross-border motherhood, what we need is not more choice, but less domination.

Notes

1 See *Indian Act*, RSC 1951, c 29, s 12 [*Indian Act* 1951], which has since been repealed. See *Indian Act*, RSC 1985, c I-5 [*Indian Act* 1985] for the most recent legislation.

2 This does not suggest that Indigenous peoples inherently discriminate against women and create their own victimization through self-governance. See the discussions on self-determination as nondomination later in this chapter.

3 I choose the term "cross-border motherhood" rather than "mixed-race motherhood" to emphasize the sovereignty and jurisdictional issues resulting from border crossing. Although the term can include mothering across national borders, which involves national citizenship, this chapter focuses its discussion exclusively on the border crossing between the Indigenous peoples of Taiwan and Han-Taiwanese. The term "mixed race" in this chapter narrowly refers to the mixture of Indigenous and Han people. Due to the limited scope of this chapter, my discussion deals with the status of newborns (and non-marital children) and does not extend to the issue of "naturalization" and a mixed-race adult's right to choose Indigenous status.

4 *Santa Clara Pueblo v Martinez*, 436 US 49 (1978).

5 *McIvor v Canada (Registrar of Indian and Northern Affairs)*, 2009 BCCA 153.

6 *Views adopted by the Committee under article 5 (4) of the Optional Protocol, concerning communication No. 2020/2010*, ICCPR Dec, UN HR Committee, 124 Sess, UN Doc CCPR/C/124/D/2020/2010 (11 January 2019).

7 For Cheng's case, see Taipei Gaodeng Xingzheng Fayuan (臺北高等行政法院) (Taipei High Administrative Court), 106 Niendu Yuan Su Zi Di 2 Hao (106 年度原訴字第 2 號) (106 Yuan Sue Zi Judgment No. 2), 29 June 2017; Zuigao Xingzheng Fayuan (最高行政法院) (Supreme Administrative Court), 106 Niendu Pan Zi Di 752 Hao (106 年度判字第 752 號) (106 Pan Zi Judgment No. 752), 28 December 2017.

8 The Han people are the overwhelming racial majority in Taiwan. Indigenous peoples account for less than 2.5 percent of the population in Taiwan.

9 In this chapter, "Chinese" refers to the Chinese language, not the Chinese race.

10 Article 1059 of *Zhonghua Minguo Minfa* (中華民國民法) (*Civil Code of the Republic of China*) [*Civil Code*].

11 The 2018 Taiwan census shows that 95.33 percent of all newborns adopt their father's surname, and 98.21 percent of these newborns are given the father's surname through parental agreement. See Taiwan, Neizhengbu 內政部 (Ministry of the Interior), Quanguo Xingshi Tongji Fenxi 全國姓氏統計分析 (National Statistics and Analysis of Names) (2018): 236–37 [Neizhengbu].

12 Paragraph 2 and 3, art 6 of *Yuanzhumin Shenfenfa* (原住民身分法) (*Status Act for Indigenous Peoples*) [*Status Act*].

13 See Cheng & Wu's brief for constitutional review. The petition for constitutional review was filed in 2018. Taiwan's Constitutional Court held oral arguments in this case on January 17, 2022, and is scheduled to announce its ruling on April 1, 2022.

14 As a legal and Indigenous law scholar, Cheng has turned her personal experience into scholarly work. See Cheng Chuan-ju (鄭川如), "Yuanzhumin Shenfen Fa zhong 'Xingshi Bang Shenfen' Tiaokuan de Weixian Fenxi" 「原住民身分法」中「姓氏綁身分」條款的違憲分析 (Analysis of the Constitutionality of the Indigenous Status Act), (2013) 40 Guoli Zhongzheng Daxue Faxue Qikan 國立中正大學法學期刊 (National Chung Chen ULJ) Cheng, "Xingshi Bang Shenfen" 1; Cheng Chuan-ju 鄭川如, "Shei YouQuan Jueding Shei Shi Yuanzhumin? Cong Liang Renquan Gongyue Ji Xiangguan Guoji Wenjian Jianshi Yuanzhumin Shenfen Rending Wenti" 誰有權決定誰是原住民?—從兩人權公約及相關國際文件檢視原住民身分認定問題 (Who Has Right to Decide Who Is an Indigenous Person? Analysis of the Issue of Indigenous Membership Identification from the Perspective of Two Human Rights Covenants and Relative International Documents), (2015) 66 Faling Yuekan 法令月刊 (Law Monthly) 81 [Cheng, "Shei YouQuan"].

15 See *United Nations Declaration on the Rights of Indigenous Peoples*, GA Res 295, UNGAOR, 61st Sess, Supp No 49, UN Doc A/RES/61/295, 46 ILM 1013 (2007) at 14 [*UNDRIP*]. Section 1 of art 33 states: "Indigenous peoples have the right to determine their own identity or membership in accordance with their customs and traditions. This does not impair the right of Indigenous individuals to obtain citizenship of the States in which they live."

16 Susan B Boyd, "Autonomy for Mothers? Relational Theory and Parenting Apart" (2010) 18:2 Fem Leg Stud 137 at 154; Susan B Boyd et al, *Autonomous Motherhood? A Socio-Legal Study of Choice and Constraint* (Toronto: University of Toronto Press, 2015) at 224–27.

17 See Hester Lessard, "Mothers, Fathers, and Naming: Reflections on the Law Equality Framework and *Trociuk v British Columbia (Attorney General)*" (2004) 16:1 CJWL 165 at 197–98.

18 As Ann Garry rightly points out, the term "intersectionality," while initially intended to apply to multiple oppressions, is sometimes used more broadly to include axes of privilege and/or oppression. See Ann Garry, "Essences, Intersections, and American Feminism" in Cheryl Misak, ed, *The Oxford Handbook of American Philosophy* (Oxford: Oxford University Press, 2008) 595 at 610–11.

19 Iris Marion Young, *Global Challenges: War, Self-Determination and Responsibility for Justice* (Cambridge: Polity Press, 2007) at 13–76.

20 Rauna Kuokkanen, *Restructuring Relations: Indigenous Self-Determination, Governance and Gender* (New York: Oxford University Press, 2019) at 217.

21 Melissa J Brown has speculated that, from the late seventeenth to the nineteenth century, people of mixed heritage were able to claim Han status and were likely to be considered Han if they had a Han father or grandfather whose surname

they could take with legitimacy in the eyes of other Han, because patrilineally derived surnames had long been markers of Han status. She has also asserted that the mixed population used ancestry (probably through the use of Han surnames), not culture, to claim Han identity. See Melissa J Brown, *Is Taiwanese Chinese? The Impact of Culture, Power, and Migration on Changing Identities* (Berkeley and Los Angeles: University of California Press, 2004) at 16, 134. Brown's proposition is speculation awaiting further examination. During the Japanese colonial period (1895–1945), the racial status of mixed-race children was subject to various administrative orders and determined on a case-by-case basis, which appeared to apply to the tribes' customs. See Wang Tay-sheng (王泰升), "Taiwan Faluishi Shang de Yuanzhumin Zu: Zuowei Teshu de Renqun Diyu yu Fawenhua" 台灣法律史上的原住民族: 作為特殊的人群、地域與法文化 (Indigenous Peoples in the Legal History of Taiwan: Being a Special Ethnic Group, Territory and Legal Culture) (2015) 44 Guoli Taiwan Daxue Faxue Luncong 國立臺灣大學法學論叢 (National Taiwan ULJ) 1639 at 1668.

22 It was an ordinance entitled Taiwansheng Pingdi Shanbao Rending Biaozhun (臺灣省平地山胞認定標準) (The Criteria for Identifying Lowland Mountain People in the Province of Taiwan) and enacted by the Taiwan provincial government in 1956. The ordinance was renamed Taiwansheng Shanbao Rending Biaozhun (臺灣省山胞認定標準) (The Criteria for Identifying Mountain People in the Province of Taiwan) in 1980 and replaced by Shanbao Rending Biaozhun (山胞身分認定標準) (The Criteria for Identifying Mountain People) enacted by the Ministry of Interior in 1991.

23 Article 3 and 6 of the Criteria for Identifying Mountain People, 1991, *supra* note 22.

24 *Status Act, supra* note 12.

25 *Ibid,* para 2, art 4.

26 *Ibid,* paras 1, 2, art 6.

27 *Ibid,* para 3, art 6.

28 *Civil Code, supra* note 10, para 1, art 1059.

29 *Ibid,* para 2, art 1059–1.

30 See Taiwan, Lifayan Gongbao 立法院公報 (*Legislative Yuan Gazette*) (Taipei City: Legislative Yuan, 2000) [*Legislative Yuan Gazette*] vol 89, no 13 at 9; vol 89, no 19 at 3.

31 See *Legislative Yuan Gazette,* vol 89, no 57 at 13.

32 See Lim Siu-theh 林修澈, Yuanzhumin Shenfen Rending de Yanjiu 原住民身分認定的研究 (The Research of the Identity of Aborigine's Status) (Taipei: Council of Indigenous Peoples, 1999) at 247.

33 See *Legislative Yuan Gazette,* vol 89, no 28 at 350, 351.

34 See *ibid* at 334, 339, 341.

35 See *ibid* at 350.

36 All interviewees agreed that Indigenous women's non-marital children should be granted Indigenous status. See Lim Sui-theh, *supra* note 32 at 251.

37 See *ibid* at 243–45.

38 See *ibid* at 251.

39 A qualitative study based on the 2010 census data finds that patrilineal rules still have significant impacts on the choice of surname for children with an Indigenous mother and a Han Taiwanese father. See Liu Chien-chia 劉千嘉 & Chang Ying-hwa 章英華, "Yuan han Tonghun Jiating zhong Shuangyi Zinü de Zuqun Congshu: Zidai Zingbie yu Shuliang de Yingxiang" 原漢通婚家庭中雙裔子女的族群從屬:子代性別O與數量的影響 (Ethnic Status Inheritance in Aboriginal-Han Marriages and Families: Inference of Gender and Quantity of Offspring) (2020) 32 Renwen ji Shehui Kexue Jikan 人文及社會科學集刊 (Journal of Social Sciences and Philosophy) 1.

40 The following critique of the *Status Act for Indigenous Peoples* is an expansion and revision of my argument that Indigenous mothers suffer discrimination based on sex, race, and marital status in terms of names. See Chen Chao-ju, "Becoming 'Outsiders Within': A Feminist Social-Legal Study of Surname Inequality as Sex, Race, and Marital Status Discrimination in Taiwan" (2018) 18:1 J Korean L 1 [Chen].

41 I borrow Devon W Carbado and Mitu Gulati's terminology of "negative racial duty" and "affirmative racial duty" in their study of anti-discrimination employment law but revise the meaning of the second term to apply two terms in the context of the name requirement. "Affirmative racial duty" is defined here as the duty to demonstrate one's association with the Indigenous peoples. Devon W Carbado and Mitu Gulati also distinguish "racial status" from "racial act." See Devon W Carbado & Mitu Gulati, "Working Identity" (2000) 85:5 Cornell L Rev 1259 at 1287.

42 For an introduction to Indigenous people's naming system, see Cheng, "Xingshi Bang Shenfen," *supra* note 14 at 29–31.

43 See Cheng & Wu's brief, *supra* note 13.

44 According to 2018 national statistics, only 0.04 percent of all Indigenous people use "traditional names," and 3.97 percent of them use a combination of Chinese names and romanized "traditional names." See Neizhengbu, *supra* note 11 at 246, 248 (percentages calculated by author).

45 See *ibid*, 236–37 (percentages calculated by author).

46 Chen Chao-ju, Peng Yen-wen & Chang Chin-fen, "Women's (No) Naming Right under the Shadow of Patronymy: Changes of the Public Attitudes in Taiwan between 2002 and 2012" (2017) 38 Diaocha Yanjiu – Fangfa yu Yingyong (調查研究–方法與應用) (Survey Research – Method and Application) 57.

47 Peng Yen-wen 彭渰雯 & Hung Ling-Chun 洪綾君, "Weihe Zong Mu Xing? Fuqi Yueding Zinü Xingshi de Yingxiang Yinsu Diaocha" 爲何從母姓？夫妻約定子女姓氏的影響因素調查 (Why Taking Mother's Surname? Investigating the Factors That Influence Taiwanese Married Couples' Decision on Their Children's Surnames) (2011) 28 Nuxue Xuezhi: Funü Yu Xingbie Yanjiu 女學學誌：婦女與性別研究 (J Women's and Gender Studies) 1.

48 Neizhengbu, *supra* note 11 at 236–37.

49 See Chen, *supra* note 40 at 39.

50 Taiwan, Ministry of the Interior, Department of Statistics, Number and Rates of Birth, Death, Marriage and Divorce, online: Ministry of the Interior <https://ws.moi.gov.tw/001/Upload/OldFile/site_stuff/321/1/month/m1-02.xls > (percentages calculated by author). There are no data on the number of non-marital children born to Indigenous women or men; my discussion is therefore somewhat in the dark in terms of this information.

51 See Neizhengbu, *supra* note 11 at 222. There is no information on the ways these children's surnames are changed (by mutual agreement or by court orders) or on how many of them acquire their Indigenous status as a result of the name change.

52 *Civil Code, supra* note 10, art 1059–1.

53 See Cheng, "Shei YouQuan," *supra* note 14 at 91.

54 Article 7, 22 and paras 6, 11, and 12, Additional Article 10 of the Constitution of the Republic of China [ROC Constitution]. They also argue that the name requirement violates the principle of proportionality (ROC Constitution, art 23).

55 These documents include *UNDRIP, supra* note 15 at 6; *International Covenant on Civil and Political Rights,* 16 December 1966, 2200A UNGA (XXI) at 7 (entered into force 3 January 1976); *Convention on the Rights of the Child,* 20 November 1989, 44 UNGA 25 at 9 (entered into force 2 September 1990); José Martínez Cobo, Commission on Human Rights, *Study of the Problem of Discrimination against Indigenous Populations,* Department of Economic and Social Affairs, UN Doc E/CN.4/Sub.2/1983/2; *Sandra Lovelace v Canada,* Communication No. R. 6/24 (29 December 1977), U.N. Doc. Supp. No. 40 (A/36/40) at 166 (1981). Cheng & Wu's brief cites *Lovelace* for embracing Indigenous peoples' self-identification and omits the fact that *Lovelace* was not determined on equality grounds. See Cheng & Wu's brief, *supra* note 13.

56 *Convention on the Elimination of All Forms of Discrimination against Women,* 1 March 1980, 1249 UNTS 13, Can TS 1982 No 31 (entered into force 3 September 1981) [*CEDAW*].

57 Cheng, "Shei YouQuan," *supra* note 14 at 103–6.

58 Proposal No 19050, Yuan General Directory No 1722, Proceedings of 12th meeting, 1st legislative session, 9th congress of the Legislative Yuan (4 May 2016).

59 Proposal No 21073, Yuan General Directory No 1722, Proceedings of 3rd meeting, 4th legislative session, 9th congress of the Legislative Yuan 4 (4 October 2017). I will not venture into Bill B's many flaws, which include indeterminacy regarding the ways to determine non-marital children's status.

60 See Cheng and Wu's brief, *supra* note 13.

61 Young, *supra* note 19 at 44–48, 63–65.

62 *Ibid* at 46.

63 *Ibid* at 48.

64 See *ibid* at 64.

65 *Ibid* at 51. Emphasis in original.

66 *Ibid* at 50.

67 See *ibid* at 66.

68 *UNDRIP, supra* note 15 at 6, 12, 14.

69 ROC Constitution, *supra* note 54, arts 5, 7, and paras 6, 11, 12, additional art 10.

70 Jennifer Nedelsky, *Law's Relations: A Relational Theory of Self, Autonomy, and Law* (New York: Oxford University Press, 2011).

71 See Kuokkanen, *supra* note 20.

72 See Boyd, *supra* note 16.

73 See e.g. Chandran Kukathas, "Are There Any Cultural Rights?" (1992) 20:1 Political Theory 105. Wu and Cheng's brief does not claim the right to exit but does make an analogy to a ball team's entitlement to expel a team member for violation of its membership rule. See also Cheng & Wu's brief, *supra* note 13. The *Status Act* provides the right to exit, but a discussion of this issue is beyond the scope of this chapter.

74 See e.g. Oonagh Reitman, "On Exit" in Avigail Eisenberg & Jeff Spinner-Halev, eds, *Minorities within Minorities: Equality, Rights and Diversity* (Cambridge: Cambridge University Press, 2004) 189 at 208.

75 See Cheng and Wu's brief, *supra* note 13.

76 Ayelet Shachar, "The Paradox of Multicultural Vulnerability: Individual Rights, Identity Groups, and the State" in Christian Joppke & Steven Lukes, eds, *Multicultural Questions* (New York: Oxford University Press, 1999) at 88.

77 Sara Song, *Justice, Gender and the Politics of Multiculturalism* (New York: Cambridge University Press, 2007) at 114–41. Her discussion of Martinez as a case of "internal minorities" also covers a discussion of the situations and struggles of First Nations women in Canada.

78 Brenda L Gunn, "Self-Determination and Indigenous Women: Increasing Legitimacy through Inclusion" (2014) 26:2 CJWL 241 at 248.

79 Lahuy Icyeh, *Shishei Zaijiang Shenmeyang di Zhishi? Smangus Buluo Zhutixing Jiangou yu Difang Zhishi Shijian* 是誰在講什麼樣的知識? Smangus 部落主體性建構與地方知識實踐 (Who Is Telling What the Knowledge Is About? The

Construction of Smangus Subjectivity and Local Knowledge Practices) (master's thesis, Province University, Taiwan, 2008) [unpublished] at 131–32.

80 See the discussion on Bill B earlier in this chapter.

81 Gunn, *supra* note 78 at 249.

82 Song, *supra* note 77 at 6.

83 *Ibid.*

84 See Ku Kun Hui, "'Who Is Your Name?' Naming Paiwan Identities in Contemporary Taiwan" in Yangwen Zheng & Charles J-H Macdonald, eds, *Personal Names in Asia: History, Culture and Identity* (Singapore: NUS Press, 2010) at 214–15.

85 Catharine A MacKinnon, *Feminism Unmodified: Discourses on Life and Law* (Cambridge, MA: Harvard University Press, 1987) at 69.

86 Rauna Kuokkanen, "Self-Determination and Indigenous Women's Rights at the Intersection of International Human Rights" (2012) 34:1 Hum Rts Q 225 at 247.

87 See e.g. Susan Williams, "Democracy, Gender Equality, and Customary Law: Constitutionalizing Internal Cultural Disruption" (2011) 18:1 Ind J Global Leg Stud 65. Kuokkanen also builds on Nancy Fraser's three-dimensional theory (distribution, recognition, and representation) to pursue gender justice in Indigenous peoples' quest for self-determination. See Kuokkanen, *supra* note 20.

88 Song, *supra* note 77 at 141.

89 See e.g. Susan B Boyd & Krisha Dhaliwal, "Race Is Not a Determinative Factor: Mixed-Race Children and Custody Cases in Canada" (2015) 29:2 Can J Fam L 309.

90 For those Indigenous women who have lost their Indigenous status due to marriage, art 8 of the *Status Act* provides remedies, albeit imperfect ones, for them to reinstate their status. The reinstatement also enables their children to acquire Indigenous status if they meet the name requirement.

91 Ayelet Shachar, *The Birthright Lottery: Citizenship and Global Inequality* (Cambridge, MA: Harvard University Press, 2009) at 164–90.

92 Whether the *jus sanguinis* descent principle triggers discrimination based on race is an issue that extends beyond the scope of this chapter. For relevant discussion, see Kristy Gover, "Indigenous Citizenship in Settler States" in Ayelet Shachar, Rainer Bauböck, Irene Bloemraad & Maarten Vink, eds, *The Oxford Handbook of Citizenship* (New York: Oxford University Press, 2017) at 467–72.

PART 2
Law’s Norms

3

Family Law as Expression

Financial Relief in the English Courts

Alison Diduck

John Eekelaar observed in 2018 that family law in England and Wales before the mid-twentieth century was designed to sustain the existing social structure including marriage, legitimacy, and patriarchy.[1] After the 1960s, however, these social institutions were undermined as the law that reinforced them was replaced by law that recognized "individual self-determination and sought to protect individual well-being"[2] rather than social institutions and structures. Gillian Douglas also sees a change in the law that reflects changing social norms.[3] Drawing on Ulrich Beck and Elisabeth Beck-Gernsheim's idea of individualization, she characterizes this social change as a turn to "a focus on the individual, rather than on a family or other group," which means that the individual becomes the "target and recipient of state attention."[4] This concurrent legal and social emphasis on individual well-being means that it is now acceptable to leave a marriage that fails to provide emotional self-fulfillment, and that the law's role is simply to ensure that parties are able to begin new relationships, unencumbered with the baggage of earlier ones.[5]

Eekelaar observed further that:

> [t]he relaxation of the legal and social structures within which personal relationships are supposed to take place has raised new concerns that the predictability and security those structures created have been threatened. The response has been to try to encourage individuals to exercise their rights responsibly. So the law may seek to *build up* a social norm.[6]

This process is a symbiotic one: "[t]he law draws on social values in formulating legal principles," Eekelaar explained, "which it was hoped would, in turn, further reinforce those values."[7]

Legal statements – judicial and legislative statements of the law – express the social values and practices by which people are to live their lives. In this chapter, I consider this expressive role played by law in the context of family living – specifically, the ways courts exercise their discretion in financial and property matters on divorce. The principles by which the law distributes a family's wealth and financial responsibilities at the end of the marital relationship have always said as much about the way society and the state organize and value economic, reproductive, and caring responsibilities as about the way family members do. These principles make normative statements about the social, political, and legal value of caring and earning, independence and dependence, and the structural conditions that sustain them. Therefore, legal statements about financial matters on divorce draw on complex social values ranging from gender equality and compensation for relationship-generated disadvantage, to support for the "traditional" breadwinner/homemaker family, and to notions of personal responsibility, autonomy, and individual self-fulfillment.[8] Contrary to Eekelaar's view, however, I wonder if these statements may not only be about protecting individual well-being, but may also continue to be about building up and reinforcing a particular social structure thought to be under threat and thus reconfiguring heterosexual marriage and patriarchy for the twenty-first century.

The Legal Context

In England and Wales, discretion lies at the heart of a court's determination about finances and property on divorce. Unlike in many jurisdictions, property and support matters are dealt with as one package. The courts may make a combination of different orders regarding property and support as they exercise a broad statutory discretion to devise a settlement that is meant to be fair to both parties. As Lord Denning noted in 1981:

> The Family Court takes the rights and obligations of the parties all together – and puts the pieces into a mixed bag. Such pieces are the right to occupy the matrimonial home or to have a share in it, the obligation

> to maintain the wife and children and so forth ... The court [then] hands [the pieces] out without paying any too nice a regard to their legal rights or equitable interests but simply according to what is the fairest provision for the future, for mother and father and the children.[9]

Of course, this discretion has never been arbitrary; it was and is still meant to be exercised with reference to the factors enumerated in the *Matrimonial Causes Act 1973* (UK) (*MCA 1973*)[10] and guidelines "derived by the courts from values about family life which it considers would be widely accepted in the community."[11] In the ordinary case, it is usually a matter of finding a way to stretch one or, more often, one and a half incomes across two households, and guidelines often take a back seat to this necessity.[12]

Ordinary cases do not make law, however. It was, and still is, the so-called big-money cases, decided when heterosexual couples divorce, that state the expectations for divorcing properly. These cases create the principles and precedents for those ordinary cases that, more often than not, do not end up in court but are resolved by way of private negotiations, arbitrations, and mediation. In a big-money case, the Court of Appeal reminded us that:

> The applicant's reasonable requirements became the focus of the case, throughout its preparation and its final determination ... The emphasis on the applicant's reasonable requirements as the yardstick of the award satisfied the anxiety of the judges and others that we should not be drawn into the extravagance of some American states, particularly California, where very large awards were commonplace.[13]

Of course, the above-mentioned "values about family life" considered to be "widely accepted in the community" are never static. At one time, courts understood values about family life as "traditional" family values, including protection of collective family welfare and enforcing the bread-winner's obligation to support reasonably his dependants. In 2000, however, when the House of Lords of the United Kingdom introduced the objective of fairness for these decisions and said further that fairness included non-discrimination and equality,[14] it implied that these values had changed.

In the landmark case *White v White*, drawing on what it considered to be community values of equality and non-discrimination, the House of Lords also implied that, in big-money cases, the reasonable requirements ceiling was unfair:

> If a husband and wife by their joint efforts over many years, his directly in his business and hers indirectly at home, have built up a valuable business from scratch, why should the claimant wife be confined to the court's assessment of her reasonable requirements, and the husband left with a much larger share? Or, to put the question differently, in such a case, where the assets exceed the financial needs of both parties, why should the surplus belong solely to the husband?[15]

Yet, as courts have noted, fairness is an "elusive concept."[16] It, "like beauty, lies in the eye of the beholder,"[17] said Lord Nicholls, and it also lies, apparently, in the eyes of society. Six years later, in *Miller v Miller: McFarlane v McFarlane,* Lord Nicholls said that fairness was "an instinctive response to a given set of facts ... [and was] ultimately ... grounded in social and moral values."[18]

Fleshing out this understanding of fairness as grounded in social and moral values, the House of Lords in *Miller: McFarlane* further identified three elements of fairness, or rationales for redistributing family property and finances: needs; sharing and compensation; and confirming *White's* statement that needs, or reasonable requirements, are not the sole element of fairness. But, as Jo Miles has pointed out,[19] identifying these elements may have complicated rather than clarified the search for fairness. They embrace a potentially inharmonious mix of values or norms, ranging from approbation of marriage itself as a form of economic insurance (sharing), to the traditional obligation of the breadwinner to support his dependants (need), to the marginalizing of marriage per se in favour of examining the consequences of the parties' actual family practices (compensation).

What are we to make of this complicated or inharmonious mix? Oliver McGregor in 1981 characterized the family law "legal scene" in England and Wales as "a chaos of overlapping jurisdictions and conflicting philosophies, strewn with ... much debris from earlier centuries."[20] While we would like to think that family law has now resolved this "chaos," we see evidence that McGregor's observation remains as true today as it was in 1981. As family law becomes more firmly fixed within a trend to conceive even intimate relationships in terms of autonomy, economic rationality, and choice, we may see simply a modern version of McGregor's chaotic legal scene rather than its demise.[21]

Family law remains, for example, firmly entrenched within law's property rhetoric. This rhetoric, the principal normative theory of property, is associated with three notions, namely: autonomy as independence from others, which limits obligations to those that can be characterized as voluntarily assumed; property as a reward for economically productive labour in the marketplace; and economic inequality as an inextricable feature of a market system that protects private property rights.[22] The property rhetoric is linked with the labour market desert theory, in which property rights are justified only as a reward for the expenditure of one's labour, and, in the family law context, this rhetoric can be seen either as debris from an earlier time, or as an expression of contemporary values, depending on how one defines labour.[23]

Similarly, family law professes a narrative of progress, from patriarchy – marriage as indissoluble, creating the breadwinner's lifelong obligation to meet his dependant spouse's needs, to equality – marriage as a freely chosen and easily dissolvable partnership of equals. Shahar Lifshitz observes that the narrative of progress in family law contains three elements. The first is privatization, the retreat of the state and its values – or "paternalism" – in favour of the individual. The second element is the move from the family as the unit of concern to the individual, who is viewed not as a family member but as an abstract autonomous entity. The third is the assumption of the achievement of gender equality.[24] Martha Minow regrets this traditional history of family law, which "treats autonomous rights-bearing individualism as the destiny of progress."[25]

This "progress" in family law is said to be the result of changing values or social norms. Sir Mark Potter P, in a postscript to his decision in *Charman v Charman*, one of the leading family property cases, stated that the reliance on "reasonable requirements," which "ruled essentially for a generation from the mid-1970s to the year 2000[,] … suited the society of its day,"[26] but that there may have been a need for its reform as society's view of marriage changed. In his words:

> Was the need for reform met by the decision of the House in *White*? The decision deprived practitioners and judges of the old measure of reasonable requirements, offering instead the cross check of equality to ensure fairness and to banish discrimination. Of course these innovations were well founded on profound social change, particularly in the recognition that marriage is a partnership of equals and that role of man and woman within the marriage are commonly interchangeable.[27]

Finally, we must not ignore the fact that all of these decisions are supported by the law's pursuit of individualized justice. The judiciary defends its broad discretion by claiming that it enables judges to provide *bespoke* justice, to consider the circumstances of each individual family with which they are concerned. In this way, the judiciary downplays the expressive or symbolic function of their statements, whether for other courts, for private dispute resolution, or for families who may not be in dispute at all.[28]

The big-money cases, which proclaim fairness in the law for all cases and at least to some degree proclaim the social values by which all families are meant to live, demonstrate McGregor's conflicting philosophies.[29] As we did in 2010,[30] we continue to see modern norms of gender equality and the importance of individual self-fulfillment and individual responsibility mixed with the "debris" of the property rhetoric and the traditional breadwinner/homemaker allocation of responsibilities.

I will map the direction of judicial travel over the past ten years or so, continuing to explore the courts' negotiation of fairness that I began in 2010, now in the light of the competing norms in the *Miller: McFarlane* and *White* cases and the conflicting social values and assumptions about social and legal "progress" they express. For, as much as family lawyers may have thought in 2006 that non-discrimination and equality (sharing), meeting needs, and compensation were the community and legal norms of fairness by which families lived and separated, the courts may be telling us something different, at least in the way these norms are said to link with twenty-first-century values such as autonomy and personal responsibility. It seems to me that the normative appeal to equality, autonomy, and personal fulfillment may be driving or legitimating a return to the reasonable requirements measure that was so decisively rejected by the House of Lords in *White*.[31]

I will first explore how we may have gotten back to this place, given, first, judicial acknowledgment or proclamation of changes in family values or norms from dependant/breadwinner to the partnership of equals, and second, the House of Lords' assertion that the elements of fairness, based on those community values or norms, are needs, sharing, and compensation (*Miller: McFarlane*) and equality and non-discrimination (*White*). Then I will consider the social consequences of those judicial statements. They have both symbolic and material consequences as expressions about the public and private value attributed to the gendered roles still undertaken, usually in heterosexual marriages, but also in same-sex marriages and civil partnerships.[32] These social consequences form the basis of my disagreement with Eekelaar. As I illustrate below, judicial statements may protect more than simply individual self-determination and well-being in marriage; they may also protect "traditional" gendered family living.

The Law

Let us look first at how the courts have considered compensation as one of the elements of fairness. As Lord Nicholls explained in *Miller*:

> [Compensation] is aimed at redressing any significant prospective economic disparity between the parties arising from the way they conducted their marriage. For instance, the parties may have arranged their affairs in a way which has greatly advantaged the husband in terms of his earning capacity but left the wife severely handicapped so far as her own earning capacity is concerned. Then the wife suffers a double loss: a diminution in her earning capacity and the loss of a share in her husband's enhanced income. This is often the case. Although less marked than in the past, women may still suffer a disproportionate financial loss on the breakdown of a marriage because of their traditional role as home-maker and child-carer.[33]

He contined: "Compensation and financial needs often overlap in practice, so double counting has to be avoided. But they are distinct concepts, and they are far from co-terminus. A claimant may be able to earn her own living but she may still be entitled to a measure of compensation."[34]

And here is Baroness Hale on compensation in this case:

> [S]ome consider that the provision for need is compensation for relationship-generated disadvantage. But the economic disadvantage generated by the relationship may go beyond need, however generously interpreted ... If the other party who has been the beneficiary of the choices made during the marriage, is a high earner with a substantial surplus over what is required to meet both parties' needs, then a premium above needs can reflect that relationship-generated disadvantage.[35]

These statements by the House of Lords are significant. Parties may choose to conduct their family living along traditional lines, but the breadwinner husband's share of responsibility for the financial consequences of those choices is now framed through new norms of equality and entitlement, rather than through any lingering vestige of his traditional duty to support. Responsibility for those choices and for bearing their consequences is now to be shared and no longer falls upon the homemaker wife alone. Finally, compensation is an essential element of fairness; it is different from, and to be considered separate from, needs and sharing.

Yet, despite the normative significance (and precedential value) of this statement, lower courts have been hostile to it, making their own conflicting statements about responsibility for family choices. Awards that include any compensatory element are extremely rare. Courts have interpreted the House of Lords as saying that compensation is not to be made for advantage conferred upon the earner, only for disadvantage incurred by the dependant.[36] They have stated that it is too difficult to speculate about what, if anything, the claimant may have lost, and so it is too difficult to quantify a compensatory award.[37] The courts have stated that, for this reason, and because compensation is not to be treated as a separate "head" of award, it should simply be subsumed within needs measured by assessing contribution to the family.[38]

These statements all confirm the traditional norm of the breadwinner's responsibility to meet the needs of his dependants from *his* wealth, wealth that he has either earned as income or acquired in property. But these statements sustaining law's property rhetoric are explained by reference to new norms. Consistent with the new norms of autonomy, choice, and personal responsibility in marriage, for example, while career sacrifice may create relationship-generated disadvantage, it is said to be a lifestyle choice for which the chooser bears personal and economic responsibility.[39]

In *S v S*,[40] for example, after confirming throughout his judgment that equality was the norm in marriage, the judge commented on the issue of compensation for the wife's alleged relationship-generated employment disadvantage. The judge stated that:

> In this case, I am not persuaded at all that anything has been lost by the seven and one-half year gap in the applicant's employment, or as a result of the mutual agreement between the parties that she would not work: indeed the understanding, and her own desire, as was plainly in evidence, was that this arrangement of her not working would not be limited to the period when she might have to be the carer of the children, but would extend to their joint enjoyment of his retirement at Brudenell, where she would choose to spend her time in sailing and painting … I make no award, or allowance, for compensation under this head.[41]

The judge clearly felt that the applicant was not entitled to be compensated for something she had apparently freely chosen to do. He stated, in conclusion, that an award of 40 percent of the marital assets met both the wife's needs and her entitlement.[42] This language also expresses competing norms. The wife was entitled to a share in the family's wealth (she is not a supplicant), yet her entitlement appears to be only to have her needs met. Further, while the judge accredits the "mutual" traditional family choices these parties made, he sees no problem with the wife bearing the heavier burden for their consequences.[43]

Subsuming compensation within needs also occurred in *VB v JP*, in which the judge stated:

> I am faced in this case with an amalgam of uncertainties to take into account, which in my view need to be approached on a basis generous to the wife in the circumstances of the case, including the element of relationship-generated disadvantage. I propose to deal with the wife's

> entitlement not by seeking to calculate or quantify a specific premium above needs, but to take a generous approach to those needs as they are likely to continue to exist until the children are off the mother's hands which in my judgment is unlikely to be before the end of their tertiary education.[44]

In the Court of Appeal case of *Hvorostovsky v Hvorostovsky*,[45] reference to "relationship-generated disadvantage" was considered to be a "departure from reality." The Court of Appeal reflected on whether "an endeavour to assert a relationship related disadvantage [was] really necessary" before concluding that "[w]hatever she gave to him and to the children is aptly assessed under the heading of 'contribution' [which is one of the statutory factors to guide discretion]. That, rather than relationship-related disadvantage is the language of the statute."[46] In all these cases, compensation is either subsumed within needs or within contribution to the family welfare.

Even the Law Commission has queried the concept of compensation as a separate principle:

> 2.38 ... The concept of compensation may simply make explicit what has always been regarded as an element of needs, that is, making provision, on divorce, for the long-term financial consequences of the marriage. This is not a new concept but the term "compensation" may be useful because it draws attention to financial consequences of divorce that may not be immediately obvious.
>
> 2.39 The recognition that an award focused on this type of disadvantage is a form of compensation may help the courts to focus their attention upon the real value of what has been lost. It is arguable that the introduction of compensation as a separate concept therefore simply teases out the complex notion of "needs generously interpreted," to which the Supreme Court majority in *Radmacher v Granatino* referred.[47] We note that this was not the view of Baroness Hale in *Miller v Miller, McFarlane v McFarlane* who took the view that compensation for relationship-generated disadvantage "goes beyond need, however generously interpreted."
>
> 2.40 But this, at least, appears to be the way that the courts have subsequently applied the concept, as the introduction of compensation as a

distinct concept has made no difference in the level or the nature of the awards made.[48]

In *SA v PA*[49] we see all of the counter-normative statements in play. Here the couple had four children, aged nineteen, seventeen, fifteen, and thirteen at the time of the proceedings. The wife claimed that her overall award should be increased based on the principle of compensation.[50] In response to the claim, Mostyn J outlined what he saw as the problems with compensation claims. First, he did not understand how the parties' choices supplied the rationale for compensation, where compensation denoted to him a payment made by a wrongdoer to a victim to make amends for harm caused by the wrongdoer to the victim. It was not intended where the "victim" was an active, enthusiastic, and voluntary participant in the events that gave rise to the claim.[51] He concluded with an interpretation of the *Miller: McFarlane* case, in which Mrs. McFarlane was awarded compensation for giving up her job as a solicitor: "What cannot be disputed is that the reason Mrs. McFarlane gave up work was because she, an intelligent liberated autonomous adult woman, decided to give up work. I cannot see how that can be characterised as a loss 'suffered' by her entitling her to an award in excess of her reasonable needs."[52]

Second, he thought that the compensation principle required the court to find "extraordinary" counterfactual findings, and that such findings "involve[d] making an award in hard money based on a guess founded on a vision that events that did happen, did not happen, and events that did not happen, did."[53] He said these awards were "highly" arbitrary and difficult to compute "rationally, let alone predictably."[54] Finally, he found that the ultimate award previously made by the House of Lords to Mrs. McFarlane was no more than a conventional needs-based exercise would have produced.

But, of course, Mostyn J could not overrule or ignore the *McFarlane* decision. Instead, he interpreted it so as to declare that the compensation principle is to be applied only in a very rare and exceptional case in which a court could say with almost near certainty that the claimant's lost high-earning career would have led to earnings at least equivalent to the respondent's and where the claimant is able to demonstrate a track record during the marriage of following her career. Even in such a rare case, he found that compensation should be reflected by fixing the periodical payments award toward the top end of the discretionary bracket applicable for a needs assessment on the facts of the case. Disregarding or reinterpreting both Baroness Hale and Lord Nicholls in *McFarlane*, compensation ought not, he said, be reflected by a premium or additional element on top of a needs-based award.[55]

It was not until 2020, in *RC v JC*,[56] that an award to compensate the wife for the consequences of family choices was made. In that case, Moor J awarded the former wife an additional sum over and above her half share of the assets in order to compensate her for the disadvantage she suffered when she gave up her job in a law firm:

> She viewed herself as the parent who would take primary responsibility for the children. The Husband's career took precedence. She therefore rejected any suggestion of trying to establish herself at another magic circle firm, in favour of a move to the legal department of the bank. I am clear that the Husband was fully supportive of this decision.[57]

But, even here, the judge stated that this was an "exceptional" decision and warned future litigants not to take this judgment as any sort of "green light" to make compensation-based claims unless the circumstances are "truly exceptional."[58]

It appears from these cases that there is almost no place for compensation to be accounted for as a separate principle when the family wealth is distributed on divorce; it is simply to be subsumed within an assessment of needs. Not only do these cases marginalize compensation as a principle, they have real consequences for the parties, usually disadvantaging the homemaker and enriching the earner.

We see this disadvantage highlighted when the court is asked to consider compensation-related periodical payments rather than compensation-related property awards. Periodical payments, maintenance, or support, called "financial orders" in the *MCA 1973*, are invariably needs based. Extended or lifelong orders are discouraged according to the clean-break principle, which itself, of course, supports the norms identified by Eekelaar and Douglas. The Family Justice Council endorsed this view in its 2018 guidance for judges on "financial needs on divorce."[59] The guide stated that "[t]he objective of financial orders made to meet needs should be to enable a transition to independence to the extent that is possible ... in the circumstances."[60]

Needs-based financial orders are therefore subject to the clean-break principle. But, compensation-based payments are not. Indeed, as Lord Nicholls noted in *Miller: McFarlane*,

> Section 25A(2) [on clean break] is ... concerned with the termination of one party's "financial dependence" on the other "without undue hardship." These references to financial dependence and hardship are apt when applied to a periodical payments order making provision for the payee's financial needs. They are hardly apt when applied to a periodical payments order whose object is to furnish compensation in respect of future economic disparity arising from the division of functions adopted by the parties during their marriage. If the claimant is owed compensation, and capital assets are not available, it is difficult to see why the social desirability of a clean break should be sufficient reason for depriving the claimant of that compensation.[61]

Here also is Baroness Hale in *Miller: McFarlane*: "In general, it can be assumed that the marital partnership does not stay alive for the purpose of sharing future resources unless this is justified by need or compensation."[62] The House of Lords is here expressing norms of fairness that include clean break and independence but also include equality, non-discrimination, and compensation for relationship-related advantage and disadvantage, which go beyond a simple needs-based assessment. Yet as courts after *Miller: McFarlane* have subsumed compensation within needs; compensation not only loses its value as a distinct principle, but also in practice becomes subject to clean-break.

In *K v K*, the parties agreed in 1998 that the (homemaker) wife would receive an equal share of the family assets in addition to periodical payments, which were ordered as the only means available for her to share in her husband's pension, as there was no pension-splitting legislation in force at the time.[63] The husband applied seven years later to vary that consent order and terminate his periodical payments, one of the grounds for this being that his former wife was in a three-year cohabitation with another man and therefore no longer needed his support. But, if those periodical payments were a means of dividing pension benefits rooted in compensation, it should not have mattered whether or not the former wife remarried or cohabitated with another person, and it should not have mattered whether or not she *needed* those payments. Indeed, the wife's counsel made this argument, but the court disagreed, terminating her payments on the basis that she no longer needed the support and that it was her responsibility to bear the consequences of her *choice* not to remarry.[64]

Indeed, the Family Justice Council guidance for courts also approved the statement made in *SS v NS* that a term-limited award for periodical payments based on needs (as it seems they all are, even when they include a compensatory element) should always be considered by the court unless the payee would be unable to adjust without undue hardship to the ending of the payments.[65] The Council agreed that some degree of hardship for the payee in that adjustment is acceptable.[66] Where compensation is subsumed within needs, therefore, we see again the traditional obligation to support, but it is now tempered for the benefit of the breadwinner by new social norms of independence and clean break, even where the payments include some compensatory element and where only one party is forced to suffer (some, but not undue) hardship to achieve it.

So, as compensation based on sharing equally the consequences of family choices has been marginalized, we have the return to legal dominance of the traditional breadwinner obligation simply to meet needs. But this return has been inspired and reinforced by legal statements proclaiming new norms of independence, autonomy, and personal responsibility.

Miller: McFarlane's other element of fairness, in addition to needs and compensation, is the sharing principle. In this principle, we see acknowledgment of the importance of the *institutions* of marriage and civil partnership and also their changed natures. The family's assets are meant to be equally shared, and the partners' contributions to the welfare of the family are to be equally valued. All of the parties' assets are available for sharing on the basis of fairness. It is said that on this basis, most orders will end up being the *greater* of an equal sharing award and a needs-based award, which usually recognizes that meeting needs may not be achieved by an equal split. However, it is important to recognize the number of ways that courts have found to manoeuvre around equal sharing where assets exceed needs. To protect the wealth of one spouse from a claim by the other, the courts have created a number of exceptions to the sharing principle. The exceptions are said to protect and promote contemporary norms such as autonomy and individual responsibility, and they also appear to reinforce law's still existing property rhetoric.

There is, for example, the exception created by recognizing a "stellar contribution" to the welfare of the family, which has become, in reality, an unequal contribution to the creation of wealth or acquisition of assets. Indeed, how can a homemaker ever evidence such a "stellar contribution" as the wife in *Work v Gray* argued?[67] Yet, finding a "stellar contribution" permits a departure from equality in recognition of that special contribution. There is also the judicial creation of the category "non-matrimonial property."[68] In addition to inherited property, non-matrimonial property includes property acquired before the marriage; property acquired and income earned post-separation; and a new category, simply called unilateral property, which includes assets acquired during the marriage but kept separate from the family's "joint" use.[69] The sharing principle does not apply to assets in these categories if the former spouse's needs can be met without them. In these cases, where needs, however generously assessed, can be met, we end up with an order similar to those so-called traditional marriages litigated prior to *White,* where once the homemaker's needs (or reasonable requirements) are met, all other assets are retained by the breadwinner.

In *Hart v Hart,* the Court of Appeal dismissed the wife's appeal of an order of £3.47 million based on a calculation of her needs, despite a second calculation based up the sharing principle, which would have given her an award of £3.85 million.[70] That calculation sought to remove both parties' non-matrimonial property from the equation before dividing the remaining figure equally. The trial judge thought, however, that this figure was "thoroughly unreliable," due to the husband's litigation misconduct and lack of disclosure, making the calculation of his pre-acquired wealth "little more than a guess."[71]

The Court then dismissed Mrs. Hart's argument that, even if a departure from equality were justified on the basis of non-marital assets and in spite of her husband's litigation misconduct, the decision to ground the award on the basis of her needs was arbitrary and incorrect. In reply to her argument, the Court reminded the parties (and, arguably, the public) that the notion of property being marital or non-marital was in fact a legal construct and that an asset could be both matrimonial and non-matrimonial in its nature. The Court found that, when an asset is a combination of both types of property, it is artificial to seek a sharp division.[72] Therefore, the Court stated that the trial judge was not required to follow a formulaic approach to valuing assets. He had conducted an overview or cross-checked his broad approach to the case to check that the proposed award was fair.[73] The husband's non-disclosure did not matter, and the award did not matter; Mrs. Hart's needs were met, and Mr. Hart kept everything else.

The sharing principle is also marginalized in favour of needs where the question is about periodical payments. As stated above, periodical payments seem always to be about needs. The court in *B v S* was critical of applying the sharing principle to income from which periodical payments are made.[74] It stated that "it [was] problematic, because at the end of the day the only reason there is income after separation is because of work done after separation."[75] After thus impliedly endorsing the market labour desert theory, the judge made a clear statement of principle:

> Save in the exceptional kind of case exemplified by *McFarlane* a periodical payments claim ... should in my opinion be adjudged generally speaking, by reference to the principle of need alone ... To allow consideration of the concept of sharing to intrude in the assessment of a periodical payments award seems to me to be based on a doubtful principle, and is replete with problems of quantification by any sure standard.[76]

Like compensation, therefore, sharing has not been held to be relevant to periodical payments. Periodical payments are purely needs-based and, consistent with the clean-break principle, are meant only to encourage the payee's independence. Here we see the mix of old and new norms again, with the result being that, despite the fact that the ability to generate income may be the result of the parties' decisions about how each was to contribute to the relationship, sharing that income on divorce is subject only to a needs-based assessment rather than one based on either equal sharing or compensation.

The final case I will review is the recent case of *Waggott v Waggott*,[77] which illustrates all of the issues I have highlighted in this chapter. After a twenty-one-year marriage, during which a couple decided to prioritize the husband's career after the wife gave up hers in the finance industry, his estimated income was £3.47 million per year. They had accrued substantial assets during the marriage, and the award from which she appealed was a capital one of £9.76 million. The husband's share was assessed at £7.8 million. Additionally, the judge ordered the husband to pay ongoing maintenance for joint lives at the rate required to meet his former partner's income needs, which he assessed to be £175,000 per year.

Mrs. Waggott appealed on the basis that, first, Mr. Waggott's considerable earning capacity was a matrimonial asset in which she was entitled to share as she would with any other such asset. It was developed during the marriage and was, therefore, the product of marital endeavour. Second, Mrs. Waggott argued that it was not fair that she should have to make use of her capital share, including by the attribution of a notional investment return, to meet her income needs, when Mr. Waggott would be able to meet his through his substantial earned income. Finally, she submitted that she was entitled to a share of her husband's earned income by application of the compensation principle. That principle, she said, applied not only when an applicant has sustained a financial detriment but also when a financial benefit or advantage had accrued to a respondent by reason of the relationship that produced a surplus of resources over needs.[78]

Mr. Waggott cross-appealed, seeking the termination of the periodical payments after two years on the basis that Mrs. Waggott would be able in that time to adjust to independent living without undue hardship.

In dealing with these submissions, Moylan LJ, with whom the two other members of the court agreed, acknowledged that "the first, over-arching, principle is that the court must exercise its discretionary powers in [*sic*] manner which is not discriminatory."[79] After acknowledging the importance of earning capacity, the court found that it was not an asset that was subject to the sharing principle. It stated that "[i]t can make no difference whether the court is proposing to ascribe a capital value to such a capacity or proposing to make an order for periodical payments so that its product is shared between the parties."[80]

On compensation, the court referred to Lord Nicholls' speech in *Miller: McFarlane*, where he described the principle as applying "when one party's earning capacity has been advantaged at the expense of the other."[81] When specifically addressing periodical payments, Lord Nicholls was clear that they could be ordered "for the purpose of affording compensation."[82] He stated:

> It would be extraordinary if this were not so. If one party's earning capacity has been advantaged at the expense of the other party during the marriage it would be extraordinary if, where necessary, the court could not order the advantaged party to pay compensation to the other out of his enhanced earnings when he receives them. It would be most unfair if absence of capital assets were regarded as cancelling his obligation to pay compensation in respect of a continuing economic advantage he has obtained from the marriage.[83]

Yet, despite these apparently clear statements, based on the difficulty of assessing the degree to which the marriage had contributed to the husband's income, the *Waggott* court dismissed the compensation argument as well.[84]

On the overall fairness of the award, the court referred[85] to a case from before *Miller*. In *Lambert v Lambert*,[86] Thorpe LJ could see "no possible reason why the wife alone should be required to amortise"[87] her share of the marital wealth to meet her needs.[88] Likewise, Bodey J considered that, for the wife "to have to amortise capital when the husband himself would not have to do likewise" would not "meet the aim of achieving fairness."[89] Yet again, despite these statements, the *Waggott* court found that the award met Mrs. Waggott's needs and thus was fair.

Finally, and perhaps unsurprisingly, the husband was successful in his cross-appeal. The court ordered Mrs. Waggott's periodical payments to stop in 2021, when she will be fifty-two years old, because, if she were still unemployed then, she would be able to draw on her sharing award for her day-to-day maintenance. The judge stated:

> I appreciate that the husband may well have continued to generate a very substantial income and that his financial position will have been enhanced as a result. But first looking specifically at section 25A(2), it is plain to me

> that the wife would be able "to adjust without undue hardship" to the termination of maintenance. To require her to use the above proportion of her award would not be unfair having regard to all the section 25 factors.[90]

To do otherwise, the court said, would contravene the clean-break principle.

According to one commentator, the overall consequence of this decision is that:

> Mrs. Waggott left a 21 year long relationship with a limited earning capacity and a requirement for her not only to use the income from her "surplus" capital in a way that Mr. Waggott is not required to do, but also to deplete that capital to support her income needs, while Mr Waggott hangs on to his substantial income of approximately £3.7 million net per annum plus his capital share. If this isn't financial discrimination in favour of the "breadwinner," one might ask what is?[91]

One final point raised by the decision bears directly on the relationship between social and legal norms and the expressive role of the law. The court noted that:

> During the course of the hearing, Mr. Turner [the barrister for Mrs. Waggott], was evidently concerned that recent public debate about how the courts determine a spouse's claim for maintenance might somehow intrude into the determination of this case. His particular focus was what he described as the unfair use of the expression "meal ticket for life" which, he suggested, was often deployed without regard to a spouse's fair entitlement which might properly include long-term maintenance … I understand why he suggests that the expression "meal ticket for life" can be used as an unfair trope. However, I would make clear that my determination of this appeal has been based solely on my view of the proper application of the 1973 Act and the principles identified above to the facts of this case.[92]

It is interesting that the Court disclaimed any influence these public statements may have had on its decision. Yet, a quick internet search shows that the *Waggott v Waggott* case has become synonymous with the end of a wife's "meal ticket for life."[93]

Concluding Observations

When we think about or debate the value of new social norms such as independence, emotional self-fulfillment, autonomy, and self-reliance in addition to focusing on them as symbolic statements about marriage, we must also look closely at the degree to which they reflect the reality of family living and the different consequences their legal reinforcement has for homemakers, caregivers, and breadwinners.

Cass Sunstein, similar to Eekelaar, asserts that prevailing norms are not pre-social givens but are products of a complex set of social forces, including law.[94] Sunstein says further, however, that, while a legal statement itself is important,[95] we should judge its rightness or justice at least in part by its consequences. Sunstein explained his assertion as follows: "My basic proposition is that, at least for the purposes of law, any support for 'statements' should be rooted not simply in the intrinsic value of the statement, but also in plausible judgments about its effect on social norms and hence in 'on balance' judgments about its consequences."[96] In other words, the compelling question may not be whether or not we believe that new norms of independence, autonomy, emotional self-fulfillment, and marriage as a partnership of equals are intrinsically progressive or just. Rather, our judgment about them should depend at least in part on their social and legal consequences. And, crucially, if the law is, as Eekelaar has stated, "seeking to build up" social norms, it is important to consider the effects of those norms, particularly when they coexist with competing norms.

The law is expressing those values that are said to be prized in contemporary society generally. Indeed, it is sending out messages about how families should live. But the abilities of real families to live according to these aspirational values are constrained by competing social and gender norms. For some families, the consequences of these conflicting normative conditions are significant. Individual responsibility and self-fulfillment may have intrinsic personal and social value, for example, but they are different lived experiences for women, who continue to take the role of primary caregiver in the family,[97] than they are for men. Clean break and the partnership of equals may also have intrinsic value and be supported in the community, but the gendered roles still undertaken in many relationships create economic differences upon divorce. Earners/men benefit, and caregivers/women lose. Douglas concluded that the effect of the development of the law that valorized these norms "has been to safeguard male interests."[98]

Finally, recall Baroness Hale of Richmond's words in *Miller*: "the ultimate objective is to give each party an equal start on the road to independent living."[99] We have seen how these words have given force to the clean-break principle and the requirement that the payee adjust as soon as possible to independent living, even if it causes her (some, if not undue) hardship. But arguably, Baroness Hale's words may mean more than simply dividing the marital acquest equally[100] and promoting clean break as well as the homemaker's financial independence. If law's ultimate goal is to adjust fairly, or equalize as far as possible, each party's start on the road to independent living, it must acknowledge the choices both parties made in their marriage and the importance of sharing and compensation, as well as needs, in meeting that goal. This means taking seriously and adjusting fairly the consequences of the potentially conflicting social values by which families live and make choices, including equality, non-discrimination, *and* gendered ideas of responsibility for care and independence.[101] It seems, however, that the House of Lords' attempts in *Miller: McFarlane* and *White* to do just this have been curtailed by subsequent decisions.

Moreover, parties' personal choices depend not only on social or community norms about family living. They depend also to some considerable degree on the gendered social norms about employment and the other structural conditions that are a part of those choices. The loss to (primarily) women and the gain to (usually) men consequent upon the way work and care are socially as well as personally organized must also be taken into account when equalizing, as far as possible, their start on the way to independent living.[102] These structural conditions provide normative constraints upon men's and women's choices in organizing their marital living and clearly affect their relative abilities to recover from the end of those living arrangements on divorce. These structural conditions are more than the mere context of a marriage; they, like community and legal norms about the partnership of equals or the breadwinner/homemaker, are part of what a marriage *is* to those involved and to society. Again, statements from the House of Lords and the Supreme Court of the United Kingdom (and from Lady Hale in particular) acknowledge the importance of these gendered structural conditions, but normative support for individual responsibility and formal equality in subsequent lower court decisions has marginalized them.

What does all this mean for family law as expression? Despite the House of Lords' attempts to acknowledge and perhaps reinforce changing values, the earner's obligation only to meet his dependant's reasonable requirements, now called "needs" (however generously assessed), seems to have returned as the dominant principle years after it was rejected as unfair in *White*. However, its new justification lies in norms of autonomy and individual responsibility rather than in traditional patriarchal familialism. Thus, even while explicit recourse to tradition or to patriarchal authority is no longer legitimate, normative statements about family living succeed, as they always have done, and as we saw in 2010, in "allowing 'Family' to remain situated as guarantor of a moral and social order in which women remain primary caregivers and dependants, and men remain the providers who [temporarily] meet their needs."[103] And, ultimately, the social-structural conditions that both promote and rely on that notion of family remain intact.

Notes

1 John Eekelaar, "Family Law and Legal Theory" in Elizabeth Brake & Lucinda Ferguson, eds, *Philosophical Foundations of Children's and Family Law* (Oxford: Oxford University Press, 2018) 41 at 46, 47.

2 *Ibid* at 47.

3 Gillian Douglas, *Obligation and Commitment in Family Law* (Oxford: Hart Publishing, 2018) [Douglas, *Obligation*] at 65 citing Ulrich Beck & Elisabeth Beck-Gernsheim, *Individualization: Institutionalized Individualism and Its Social and Political Consequences* (London: Sage Publications, 2002).

4 Douglas, *Obligation, supra* note 3 at 32.

5 See *ibid* at 130.

6 Eekelaar, *supra* note 1 at 49. Emphasis in original.

7 *Ibid* at 50.

8 For a discussion of the development and implications of these statements to 2010, see Alison Diduck, "What Is Family Law For?" (2011) 64:1 Current Leg Probs 287 [Diduck, "What Is Family Law For?"].

9 *Hanlon v Law Society,* [1981] AC 124 at 147, Denning LJ.

10 *Matrimonial Causes Act 1973* (UK), c 18 [*MCA*].

11 *Piglowska v Piglowski* [1999] 3 All ER 632, at 785, Hoffmann LJ.

12 On the role of discretion in family law, see Chapter 10 by Brenda Cossman in this book.

13 *Charman v Charman (no 4),* [2007] EWCA Civ 503 at para 106, [2007] 1 FLR 1246, Potter P [*Charman* cited to EWCA Civ].

14 See *White v White,* [2000] UKHL 54, [2000] 2 FLR 981 [*White v White* cited to FLR].

15 *Ibid* at 992.

16 See *Miller v Miller: McFarlane v McFarlane,* [2006] UKHL 24 at para 4, [2006] 2 AC 618 [*Miller: McFarlane* cited to UKHL].

17 See *White v White, supra* note 14 at 989.

18 See *Miller: McFarlane, supra* note 16 at para 4.

19 Jo Miles, "Charman v Charman (No 4): Making Sense of Need, Compensation and Equal Sharing after Miller/McFarlane" (2008) 20:3 Child & Fam LQ 378.

20 Oliver Ross McGregor, *Social History and Law* (London: Stevens and Sons, 1981) at 47. See also John Dewar "The Normal Chaos of Family Law" (1998) 61 Modern L Rev 467.

21 See also Alison Diduck, "Sharing Loss on Divorce: A Commentary" (2018) 32:1–2 Austl J Fam L 132 [Diduck, "Sharing Loss"].

22 See Milton C Regan Jr, *Alone Together: Law and the Meanings of Marriage* (Oxford: Oxford University Press, 1999) at 169. See also Thorpe LJ's comments in *Dart v Dart,* [1996] EWCA Civ 1343 at para 16, [1996] 2 FLR 286 at 294. He stated that "[t]he scheme of [*MCA 1973*] must also be set in the wider perspective of history and general civil law. In this jurisdiction rights of property are not invaded or reduced by statutory powers save for specific and confined purposes." See also *MCA, supra* note 10.

23 *Ibid.*

24 See Shahar Lifshitz, "The Liberal Transformation of Spousal Law: Past, Present and Future" (2012) 13:1 Theor Inq L 15 at 54.

25 Martha Minow, "'Forming Underneath Everything That Grows': Toward a History of Family Law" (1985) 4 Wisc L Rev 819 at 893.

26 *Charman, supra* note 13 at para 106.

27 *Ibid* at paras 114–15.

28 See e.g. Alison Diduck, "Autonomy and Family Justice" (2016) 28:1 Child & Fam LQ 133.

29 The problem with big-money cases transcends jurisdictions. See, for example, Chapter 7 by Hélène Belleau in this book.

30 Diduck, "What Is Family Law For?," *supra* note 8.

31 See *White, supra* note 14 at 992.

32 See e.g. *Lawrence v Gallagher,* [2012] EWCA (Civ) 94.

33 *Miller: McFarlane, supra* note 16 at para 13.

34 *Ibid* at para 15.

35 *Ibid* at para 140.

36 See e.g. *Waggott v Waggott,* [2018] EWCA Civ 727, [2018] 2 FLR 406 [*Waggott* cited to EWCA].

37 See e.g. *SA v PA,* [2014] EWHC 392 (Fam) [*SA*].

38 *Hvorostovsky v Hvorostovsky,* [2009] EWCA Civ 791, [2009] 2 FLR 1574 [*Hvorostovsky* cited to EWCA].

39 Diduck, "What Is Family Law For?," *supra* note 8. See e.g. the case of Katriona MacFarlane in 2017, in which Moylan LJ in the Court of Appeal stated that "no-one had twisted her arm when she gave up full-time work." See "Court of Appeal Rejects Ex-Wife's Claim Based on Lost Earnings," *Family Law Week* (17 February 2017), online: <www.familylawweek.co.uk/site.aspx?i=ed176060>. See also Lydia Willgress, "Divorcees Don't Need to Afford Lifestyle They Were Accustomed to in Marriage, Court of Appeal Judge Says as He Rules against Ex-Wife," *Telegraph* (13 February 2017), online: <www.telegraph.co.uk/news/2017/02/13/divorcees-dont-need-afford-lifestyle-accustomed-marriage-court/>. See also the majority in *Radmacher v Granatino,* [2010] UKSC 42 at paras 121, 194, [2011] 1 AC 534 [*Radmacher* cited to UKSC]. The court agreed that there was no question of compensating Mr. Granatino for the economic effects of his career change, on the basis that his was an individual choice, not a family decision. Note, however, Lady Hale's strong dissent, on this particularly.

40 *S v S* [2006] EWHC 2793 (Fam); [2007] 1 FLR 1496. Cited to EWHC. See also *FS v JS,* [2006] EWHC 2793 (Fam).

41 *S v S, supra* note 40 at paras 59–60.

42 See *ibid* at para 68.

43 *Ibid* at para 59. For further discussion of this case, see Diduck, "What Is Family Law For?," *supra* note 8.

44 *VB v JP,* [2008] EWHC 112 (Fam) para 82, [2008] 1 FLR 742.

45 *Hvorostovsky, supra* note 38.

46 *Ibid* at para 38.

47 *Radmacher, supra* note 39 at para 28.

48 UK, The Law Commission, *Matrimonial Property, Needs and Agreements,* Law Com 343 (London: Stationery Office, 2014).

49 *SA, supra* note 37.

50 See *ibid* at para 2.

51 *Ibid* at para 28.

52 *Ibid* at para 28.

53 *Ibid* at para 30.

54 *Ibid* at paras 31, 32.

55 See *ibid* at para 36.

56 *RC v JC*, [2020] EWHC 466 (Fam).

57 *Ibid* at para 52.

58 *Ibid* at para 72.

59 UK, Family Justice Council, *Guidance on "Financial Needs on Divorce"* (2nd ed) (London: Family Justice Council, 2018) [Family Justice Council].

60 *Ibid* at para 12.

61 *Miller: McFarlane*, *supra* note 16 at para 39. See also *MCA*, *supra* note 10, s 25A. This section enshrines the clean break principle. 25A(2) obliges the court to "consider whether it would be appropriate to require those payments to be made or secured only for such term as would in the opinion of the court be sufficient to enable the party in whose favour the order is made to adjust without undue hardship to the termination of his or her financial dependence on the other party."

62 See *Miller: McFarlane*, *supra* note 16 at para 144.

63 *K v K*, [2005] EWHC Fam 2886, [2006] 2 FLR 468.

64 See *ibid* at para 88 and Diduck, "What Is Family Law For?," *supra* note 8. Periodical payments end automatically on the marriage of the recipient, *MCA*, *supra* note 10 at s 28(1)(a).

65 *SS v NS*, [2014] EWHC 4183 (Fam).

66 See Family Justice Council, *supra* note 59 at para 41.

67 *Work v Gray*, [2017] EWCA Civ 270 at para 67, [2018] Fam 35. There, the Court of Appeal dismissed the wife's argument that the concept of special contribution was discriminatory.

68 See *Miller: McFarlane*, *supra* note 16.

69 *Sharp v Sharp*, [2017] EWCA Civ 408 at paras 92, 96, [2018] Fam 317.

70 *Hart v Hart*, [2017] EWCA Civ 1306, [2018] Fam 93. Cited to EWCA.

71 *Ibid* at para 19.

72 See *ibid* at para 85.

73 See *ibid* at para 99.

74 *B v S*, [2012] EWHC 265 (Fam), [2012] 2 FLR 502. Cited to EWHC.

75 *Ibid* at para 76.

76 *Ibid* at para 79.

77 *Waggott*, *supra* note 36.

78 *Ibid* at paras 8–10.

79 *Ibid* at para 69.

80 *Ibid* at para 89.

81 *Miller: McFarlane, supra* note 16 at para 28.
82 *Ibid* at para 32, Lord Nicholls.
83 *Ibid.*
84 *Ibid* at para 139.
85 *Waggott, supra* note 36 at para 112.
86 *Lambert v Lambert,* [2002] EWCA Civ 1685, [2003] Fam 103. Cited to EWCA.
87 *Ibid* at para 60.
88 *Ibid.*
89 *Ibid* at para 75.
90 *Waggott, supra* note 36 at para 153.
91 Phoebe Turner, "Discrimination in the Courts? Waggott v Waggott" (18 April 2018), *Stowe Family Law,* online (blog): <www.stowefamilylaw.co.uk/blog/2018/04/18/discrimination-in-the-courts-waggott-v-waggott-by-phoebe-turner/>.
92 *Waggott, supra* note 36 at para 156.
93 Of the twenty hits on the first two pages of Google at the time of writing this chapter, the case is referred to as the "meal ticket for life" case. See e.g. Patrick Sawer, "'Meal Ticket for Life' Bid Backfires as Divorcee Loses £175,000 a Year from Ex-Husband," *Telegraph* (11 April 2018), online: <www.telegraph.co.uk/news/2018/04/11/divorcees-meal-ticket-life-bid-backfires/>; Tristan Kirk, "Ex-Wife of Multi-Millionaire Stripped of 'Meal Ticket for Life' Is Denied Chance to Appeal," *Evening Standard* (27 November 2018), online: <www.standard.co.uk/news/london/exwife-of-multimillionaire-stripped-of-meal-ticket-for-life-is- denied-chance-to-appeal-a4001006.html>.
94 Cass R Sunstein, "On the Expressive Function of Law" (1996) 144:5 U Pa L Rev 2021 at 2021.
95 See *ibid* at 2028.
96 *Ibid* at 2045.
97 See Douglas, *Obligation, supra* note 3 at 36.
98 *Ibid* at 224.
99 *Miller: McFarlane, supra* note 16 at para 144.
100 See Gillian Douglas, "Sharing Financial Losses as well as Gains on Divorce" (2018) 32:1 Austl J Fam L 108.
101 See Diduck, "Sharing Loss," *supra* note 21.
102 *Ibid.*
103 See Diduck, "What Is Family Law For?," *supra* note 8 at 312.

4

The Complex Interrelationships of Financial and Child-Related Issues in Post-separation Disputes

Gender Matters

Rachel Treloar

Lawyers and allied professionals who work in the family law field are taught that, in post-separation disputes, money and child-related issues are, and should be, distinct from each other. However, the quantum of money available to a party has significant implications for their ability to access the justice system, as well as for their relative power and autonomy. Although the Canadian courts will not enforce agreements where there appears to be an "exchange" of kids for cash (or vice versa), these matters are often interconnected in the minds of lawyers and parents.[1] Even children whose parents are divorced tend to see money and love as interconnected, in part because we live in a market society where family resources are implicated in social relations.[2] While the interlinking of financial and child disputes is often seen as illegitimate (such as for vindictive purposes), the issues are not discrete; rather, they often involve complex ethical issues concerning parental responsibility, child welfare, and fairness of financial arrangements.[3] Thus, post-separation financial inequities between parents (or perceptions thereof) may contribute to ongoing conflict, constrain choices available to the less well-off party – usually the mother[4] – and may result in legitimate legal disputes going unaddressed and unheard.

This chapter presents selected findings from a qualitative study conducted in British Columbia with twenty-five parents who, at one time, experienced a high-conflict separation or divorce[5] and later came to see the experience as transformative (that is, having changed them in a positive sense despite the challenges they faced at the time). While considerable research, policy discussion, and intervention is based on outsider-expert understandings of parents enmeshed in high-conflict disputes post-separation, little is known about how parents themselves make meaning of their circumstances and how they navigate or overcome the challenges they face in the long term. Furthermore, we know little about how parents resist dominant social and professional discourses about parents in conflict regarding children's arrangements following separation. Through interviews with parents to understand how they make sense of and navigate these discourses and their difficulties over time, this study begins to fill both gaps in the research. Parents spoke about their life experiences and made meaning of their legal disputes retrospectively – in some cases looking back over periods of significant personal, social, and legal change. This work illustrates how money- and child-related issues are interconnected, both in the practical sense of parents' lived experiences and in terms of the gendered meanings of money – which include not only the ability to provide for children in a material sense but also what it means to be responsible and to care.

Overview of the Literature

Feminist legal scholars have reported extensively on how unequal financial resources, gendered power relations, and the historical exclusion of women from the public realm can result in their disadvantage in the context of child-custody disputes.[6] "Stubbornly gendered"[7] parenting arrangements and social expectations that mothers will be selfless in facilitating their children's well-being and autonomy, while also accepting significant constraints on their own autonomy, may place mothers at a disadvantage in the negotiation process. In combination, these factors pose challenges for the well-being of both mothers and their children. This chapter draws on relational autonomy theory[8] as an analytical lens for contextualizing these disputes, and for highlighting how gendered meanings of money and of autonomy intersect in participants' accounts, with particular implications for autonomy and equality.

Relational autonomy, in contrast with liberal and individualistic notions of autonomy and the individualistic self, views the individual as embedded in a broad range of social and political relations, and therefore regards people's experiences as complex.[9] Since relational autonomy theory views people as socially embedded and relationships as making autonomy possible, relational ties may enhance the autonomy of one person while posing a risk to the autonomy of another[10] and making some people more vulnerable to abuse (whether through the actions of an individual or as a result of oppressive social circumstances and institutional structures). More broadly, relational autonomy views vulnerability as a function of our interconnectedness, not simply a lack of resilience and independence that can be remedied with a particular service or resource.

A lack of empathy and support for parents involved in litigation is often justified by government on the basis of personal choice.[11] That is, if people make poor choices with respect to partners, they should face the consequences of those decisions, including paying for the services they need, rather than relying on the public purse. However, notions of choice are socially constructed and tend to ignore social contexts, power relations, and other factors that may position parents differentially. Within heterosexual partnerships, parenting generally imposes greater limitations on mothers' autonomy than on men's autonomy as fathers.[12]

In a recent study of parents involved in disputes over child support, Kristin Natalier and Belinda Hewitt found that parents both reproduced and contested gender in their accounts, as mothers stressed their authoritative position with respect to children and fathers emphasized their authority as breadwinners.[13] My study findings were quite similar in that regard, but they also highlighted the burden on parents receiving child support (usually mothers) when they were left with inadequate resources and were unable to obtain or enforce child-support orders. Mothers in my study saw this phenomenon as a significant injustice, and one that made it challenging for them to fulfill their child-related responsibilities. In Canada, breadwinning is still valued over caregiving.[14] Thus, ignoring the material difficulties mothers face when they are left to pick up the pieces in a context that does not value their care work further perpetuates injustice, and, as Natalier and Hewitt rightly pointed out, reproduces their subordination.[15]

Considerable research suggests that the primary reason that financial and child-related issues are so contentious is that these disputes tap into broader debates about gender and power, often linked to the distribution of paid work and care in family life. It was not until the 1980s that the "gender contract" was recognized by the women's movement as failing to protect women from the economic consequences when the arrangement failed.[16] Under this gendered arrangement, many women gave up their jobs after marriage to become full-time wives and mothers, while men assumed a breadwinning role and continued to advance in their careers. In my study, of the four mothers who separated during the 1980s, only one did not follow this pattern. However, my findings suggest that economic disadvantage at separation – whether in the 1980s or more recently – is more complex and nuanced in practice than previous studies that focused solely on the gendered division of work and care would have recognized. These additional nuances include fluidity in patterns of employment and care (both at the individual and parental level), complex parent- or child-health issues, and the role of family law and policy in promoting arrangements of shared responsibility and care – arrangements that are not always viable or enforceable. Thus, while clear gender patterns may result in different kinds of bargaining power at the level of the couple,[17] these same gender patterns also have implications for knowledge construction and subsequently for policy as well as law reform.[18]

Notions of involved fathering as promulgated through law, policy, and professional discourse operate in tension with women's credibility and autonomy as mothers, while also obscuring gendered inequities and patterns of care.[19] In the context of child-support disputes, Natalier and Hewitt contend that, when claims of engaged fathering are "incorporated into policy or law, they institutionalize domination and subordination by reinforcing hegemonic masculine control over money and compelling traditional feminine subservience to men's interests and financial authority."[20] In the contemporary capitalist and neoliberal context,[21] money is a significant factor in the choices (and resources) available to separating parents,[22] not only to resolve their disputes with the other parent and then move on, but also to raise their children according to mainstream notions of good parenting and with the opportunities to encourage the success of their children. Household resources have a considerable impact on parents' ability to provide for their children in terms of social networks and opportunities, in addition to having implications for children's education, health, and overall well-being. Money is also necessary for parents to obtain support and other needed services, such as counselling, for themselves and their children. Those who must access the courts and who have limited means often forego these services in order to pay legal fees.[23] Thus, resources have a considerable impact on resilience[24] as well as on maternal autonomy.[25]

This chapter will focus on two subthemes within the broader theme of the interrelationship of financial and child-related issues: the division of labour within households, both pre-separation and post-separation; and financial autonomy as a component of personal agency. The narratives of mothers who participated in the study are the primary focus of the discussion. "Relational autonomy"[26] is used as an analytic lens to contextualize these post-separation disputes and for considering the implications for mothers' autonomy and agency.

As Alison Diduck contends, legal understandings of parents' financial disputes rely on an impoverished notion of autonomy that obscures the interdependencies of family relations and their (still) gendered consequences; hence, as long as gender and gender roles have meaning in our society, they should not result in disadvantage.[27] The findings of my study, as reported here, suggest that gender roles and stereotypes still do result in disadvantage post-separation. Nevertheless, the overall study findings[28] also demonstrate that, over time, parents who are adequately supported with personal, material, and systemic resources that are appropriate for their needs do exercise their agency and move forward in their lives regardless of ongoing difficulties. This process occurs over the life course and alongside broader social, political, and legal changes.

Overview of the Study

This chapter draws from my doctoral research, which explored how parents made sense of their experiences of a high-conflict divorce process involving children, and the interpretive resources they drew on to do so. The research aimed to understand how collective meanings and norms shape personal meanings and experiences of divorce as well as how change occurs in this context. Rather than simply documenting these meanings and highlighting their appearance in participants' talk, my study aimed to understand how some individuals accommodate, resist, attempt to renegotiate, or otherwise act to transform these dominant meanings and norms, and in so doing, transform themselves. The first research question was: How do individual mothers and fathers come to make meaning of, and know themselves through, the process of a high-conflict divorce? More specifically, how are these individual interpretations influenced by social locations, relations, and discourses (such as those of motherhood, fatherhood, responsibility, rights, and care) as well as debates about gender relations and family life? The second research question asked how collective meanings drawn from extra-legal discourses (of child welfare, for example) shaped personal meanings and experiences of conflict in such situations and influenced the uptake of legal norms. Related questions included the following: How does high-conflict divorce become transformed into a positive experience? What personal and social processes and relations facilitate this process? What challenges are encountered, and how are they overcome?

In the research, I used a qualitative research design and a critical feminist framework grounded in a relational ontology[29] and social constructionist epistemological perspective.[30] My study involved in-depth, face-to-face interviews, conducted between 2012 and 2014, using a general interview guide. Interviews were semi-structured, with questions designed to address specific aspects of the research questions while also providing space for participants to cover topics of importance to them. Participants were recruited through alternative dispute resolution (ADR) practitioners, lawyers, health professionals, and nonprofit agencies,[31] as well as through newspaper ads, posters, and chain-referrals. After identifying key themes within each individual account, I noted how dominant discourses and social locations such as gender, generation, and employment status, as well as individual and interpersonal factors, shaped these accounts, and then summarized key themes within each account. I then determined common themes across interviews and developed them into subthemes. Final data analysis attended to shared meanings and experiences,[32] traced processes of constructing meaning, and situated these processes in practices of knowledge production that individuals use to make meaning of their circumstances.

Participants were parents who were residents of British Columbia and identified themselves as having experienced a high-conflict separation or divorce involving children, and who, in retrospect, regarded surviving or navigating the experience as having changed them in a positive sense. Eighteen mothers and seven fathers (aged forty-two to seventy-two years at the time of the interview) participated in the study. Between four and twenty-three years had elapsed since the separation; and all had separated between the 1980s and 2010, under the former legislation (*Family Relations Act*).[33] The age of participants' youngest children at the time of separation ranged from unborn to fourteen years old, and eighteen parents had a child less than five years of age. All participants described the relationship with their former partner as heterosexual.[34] Twenty-two of the twenty-five participants were Caucasian, one identified as Latino, and two identified as Chinese Canadian. Eight parents were born outside Canada, mainly in Europe. Beyond these demographic characteristics, parenting arrangements, socio-economic circumstances, labour force participation, occupation, education, and geographic location tended to be quite fluid over time, especially for mothers.

Although participants decided whether their post-separation process fit the description of high-conflict (as described in recruitment materials and discussed during pre-screening), most participants described complex circumstances and often multiple issues that played a role in the disputes. These circumstances included domestic violence, physical health and mental health issues (of a parent and/or child), addiction, financial issues, and child abduction. Some parents saw themselves as having lacked the personal skills or (adult) development to deal with their circumstances at the time. While I analyzed participants' narratives for common themes, there were exceptions for most findings, as participants' circumstances were individually complex and their social locations intersected and varied. Nevertheless, gender issues were central to parents' accounts. Consequently, the significance of gender in the interrelationships of financial and child-related issues in post-separation parenting disputes is the focus of this chapter. I present findings that show how these disputes are connected with broader issues of gender and power, including the implications for power and choice among those who need to use the legal process. I argue that disputes over child support also involve gendered meanings of responsibility and care, which further contribute to conflict between the parties and have implications both for settlement of their disputes and for their autonomy. As well, I make the case that gender and other social locations together influence the meanings parents assign to money and autonomy. These meanings have implications for parents' perceptions of each other, and thus can contribute to conflict. Parents' personal meanings also play a part in their legal decision making and the outcomes they seek.

Gender Work and Care: Contract and Conflict

This section addresses a subtheme of the interrelationship of financial and child-related issues – that concerning gender roles, gendered norms, and the gender contract. Participants spoke at length about the division of labour within households, both prior to separation and in terms of expectations regarding how it should (or should not) change afterwards. Even in two-parent households, the balance of paid work and family responsibilities must be organized, with roles either assumed or negotiated between spouses. The division of labour both prior to and after separation has changed slowly over time,[35] although the gendered landscape of care within the family still persists.[36] The division of labour is also subject to generational and class norms, and thus reflects both social change and change within individual households. However, as feminist scholars have noted, gendered power relations play a key role in this division of labour.[37] Many feminist scholars, especially those from Nordic countries, have used the concept of "gender contract" to describe power relations between men and women, particularly pertaining to the gendered division of paid and unpaid labour. These contracts occur broadly in the social organization of paid and unpaid work, as well as within the workplace and at the family level. Although men's participation in child care has increased,[38] family responsibilities are still largely organized by gender, and it is often mothers who exit the labour force to have and care for children. Women's lower earnings[39] and the intermittency of their labour force participation,[40] in combination with a lack of affordable quality child care,[41] play a significant role in perpetuating these gendered arrangements. Nevertheless, "often missing in discussions about post-divorce parenting is recognition of the material basis of the privatized family and responsibility for care work … Divorce can be a time when the implications of these gender gaps become particularly salient for women."[42]

Most participants described their relationships as having followed a gendered division of paid work and care, with men working full time during the marriage and women taking primary responsibility for children and domestic activities, whether or not they were in the paid labour force.

While they were married, just over a third of the mothers in the study either did not work outside the home or worked part time around the needs and schedules of their children and partner. In other words, their primary role was to care for and support their family. Most sought employment at some stage post-separation, and one started her own business. Approximately two-thirds of the women worked full time while married (with breaks to care for their infants), and most maintained or increased their work hours after separation, although one later reduced her work hours due to having a child with mental health issues. Two mothers were on long-term disability at the time of the interview (one, the result of an injury sustained during spousal assault, and the other because of a medical condition that was attributed to the stress of prolonged litigation). Overall, their employment situations were more fluid and diverse than those of the men whom I interviewed. Nevertheless, there were continuities as well as changes in the balance of paid work and domestic work among participants following separation, with men being more likely to work less, and women being likely to increase the number of hours in paid work.

Generally, fathers reported exercising their agency and choosing to work less so they could spend more time with their children, whereas mothers' choices were more often in response to the circumstances chosen by others (for example, non-payment of child support or court decisions). Thus, mothers' ability to exercise their agency or make choices regarding the balance of work and care is limited if their former spouse resists paying child support and insists on sharing care. This is not only because of their weaker financial position resulting from formerly agreed upon domestic arrangements, but also because shared work and care post-separation is now the norm, unless parents agree, or a court orders, otherwise. Although both mothers and fathers exercise agency in their choices around work-family balance, fathers seem to expect to be autonomous in their choices, whereas mothers in this study were conscious of constraints upon their choices.

To illustrate the gender contract described at the start of this section, one mother (Kathy, late fifties) described how she and her former husband "were childhood sweethearts" and, while he went to university, she "went to secretarial school," because they agreed that her role would be in the home. She said: "He had a very bright future ahead of him … and he seemed to love me a lot and vice versa and so that's where we were headed." For this reason, she did not pursue education or training with the intention of being in the labour force full time. In line with feminist literature on the public/private divide,[43] most participants described men's work as prioritized within their marriage, whereas women's work inside the family was often invisible outside of it. Furthermore, although the work of both was crucial to family functioning, the man's contribution tended to be aligned with dominant conceptions of work and was visible as work outside the home. Among the older women in my study and those in the upper-middle class (for example, married to professional men), work typically involved attending to the needs and activities of her husband and children, caring for their home and garden, and sometimes overseeing major renovations or improvements to their home.

Although they embraced motherhood and took on these responsibilities wholeheartedly, some women described how, following separation, their former spouse wanted to change the arrangement. This was particularly true among mothers who believed both that their former husbands wished to displace them from the primary caregiver role and were being dishonest about finances. Even those women who had exited the labour force when they became mothers and had no recent experience in the job market were immediately pressured to look for employment. This often occurred at a time when they were settling distressed children, dealing with litigation, and sometimes selling the family home or moving. Therefore, what was seemingly happily agreed upon during the marriage (that is, the gender contract) became contentious at separation. For instance, Doug described his former wife with thinly disguised contempt as having "never worked" during their marriage, thus portraying her as a non-contributor to the household. Two mothers also described being treated with contempt during the legal process for wishing to remain full-time caregivers. In the case of Andrea (mid-fifties), her close relationships with her children was later reconceived by her former husband and his legal team as maternal gatekeeping and parental alienation (another woman faced similar allegations).

As Carol Smart has noted in the context of child-custody disputes, fathers are often treated like the prodigal son, whereas mothers often feel a real sense of injustice when their work and loyalty evidenced over many years is minimized in comparison.[44] Moreover, they are often blamed when things go wrong, and they experience far greater scrutiny than mothers of intact families.[45] For example, Andrea described her former husband's frequent international travel, which meant that she was often alone with her children for extended periods of time. When one of their three children developed significant health problems, Andrea and her husband agreed that she would home-school the children. However, post-separation this father's poor relationship (and lack of experience) with the children became problematic, and, at the same time, Andrea was pressured to return to the paid labour force – ostensibly because she was seen as a gatekeeper to the children's relationship with their father and as interfering with his greater involvement in their lives. Despite the conduct of her former husband and his lack of caregiving history, she felt that not only was she expected to adjust or concede to his demands, but she was also criticized for her mothering activities. Thus, Andrea noted that

> when you get into court it's fault, fault, fault divorce and you are constantly blamed and there's somebody to blame. So, I felt like one of those little voodoo dolls and the whole legal system was constantly looking for the dike. Like where do we put it that she is going to completely implode. I phoned my lawyer one day and … I said, "What is the point of this?" It is not healthy. I'm a full-time caregiver and it's really hard for me to contain this all the time and to be relaxed around my children and … be effective at what I do when I have to be under this kind of pressure all the time. I'm also being told, don't poison your children. So I was working really hard to not show it in my face and body and not to say anything. I didn't see the value added for me to be spewing about what was going on in our divorce to our children. It was not going to help them, they were already stressed out enough.

In court, she perceived herself as being treated with contempt and her child-rearing efforts as being without value. Given the energy and love she had poured into her children (interlinked with her identity as a mother and strong family values), it is understandable that she would both resist and resent being portrayed in such a manner.

To a large extent, gendered generational norms played a role in the established division of labour. Older participants usually described a more traditional division of labour (that is, male breadwinner and female homemaker). Sheila described this as "the conditioning of the times." However, even those who bought into this gendered arrangement made statements that suggested occasional ambivalence about their role. Only one mother (Lisa, early fifties) described herself as having done the majority of breadwinning and most of the family care work, saying that her husband was "just like another child." Although social change is apparent in family life over time (that is, over generations), such changes do not occur distinct from broader social or policy continuities and changes. In this regard, Smart and Neale noted that it is too much to expect parents to simply start "equal parenting" at the point of separation if the pattern has not been established beforehand.[46] Such expectations, they argued, are an attempt at social engineering.[47]

Among participants who more recently separated during their thirties and forties, there was additional evidence of shifting roles, sometimes with accompanying tension. For example, a father in his forties[48] who had recently become the primary carer described the shift as presenting many challenges that had been invisible to him as a sole breadwinner. He extensively described his efforts to balance employment and child care, which left him without personal time, saying, "I often think this isn't what I signed up for and, you know, you just have to go, whoa, wait a minute, like stop feeling like the victim here; you know, suck it up."

Interestingly, two men said that their former wives had entered into relationships with men of higher income soon after separation. They expressed resentment about their obligation to pay child support to a former wife who appeared to have a higher household standard of living than they did, and whose spouse they believed was financing the litigation. Rick resented his former wife's financial dependence and referred to child support as her "paycheque." He stated:

> [A]s soon as we weren't together anymore, she wanted, what it felt like she wanted, was to maintain the lifestyle and just kind of have me out of the picture, which would be having the kids full-time … [W]hereas me saying[,] "Okay, let's forget about the money for a bit and let's focus on the kids. I'll take the kids half the time and I'll adjust my lifestyle, you adjust your lifestyle." It didn't fly at all.

Overall, five of seven men in the study wanted more time with their children post-separation (of the two others, one became the primary caregiver by default as a result of his former wife's poor health, and the other and his former wife agreed on and implemented an even time split at the outset). While Steve and his former wife also agreed to an even time split, he needed to reduce his work hours first in order to make the arrangement viable (his wife also worked full time or more throughout the marriage). All five of these men were successful in changing the balance of care to some degree, and three of the five had the primary responsibility for their children at some point. Those who sought greater involvement with their children described how this involvement changed the meaning of fatherhood for them.

Yet, as described above, some mothers are largely content with the pre-separation status quo and feel that continuity is in the interests of their children. In this study, such mothers were often those who had left the workforce by agreement and who saw their unpaid work as their contribution to the family. In fact, two mothers spoke of their former husbands' absolute insistence on their role as a homemaker. One refused to allow her to return to work, even when his business was failing. Sheila (now in her late seventies) quoted her husband, who allegedly stated, "If you're not there to make me breakfast in the morning I consider that grounds for divorce ... [T]hat's your job. There [are] no ifs, ands, and buts." Despite her description of his unwillingness to negotiate and his lack of interest in participating in domestic duties, she described how she loved to attend to the needs of others. Thus, despite some suggestion of ambivalence at his greater power in the relationship (and more broadly), she was also complicit in the arrangement. However, her lack of access to shared resources ultimately left her vulnerable to domestic violence. As set out in the then prevalent cultural norms regarding gender, work, and family life (i.e., the gender contract), women often relinquished control over certain aspects of married life in exchange for financial security and male protection. Indeed, that was particularly the case among couples who sought an upwardly mobile life plan and agreed on a traditional division of labour. This lack of access to shared financial resources became especially problematic when Sheila sought to leave her marriage as a result of domestic violence.

Gender intersects with class post-separation, with norms and expectations about family life often coming from participants' families of origin or their current social networks. In terms of pressures from their family of origin, two women described how their own mothers encouraged them to seek a family-minded man with good earnings potential. One detailed the advice her Chinese mother gave her as "Look for a good family, look for a good income, somebody who's a good hard worker, [has a] work ethic, and is going to be a good family man."

Almost half of the women described an upwardly mobile life plan (shared with their former spouse), with two speaking with considerable pride about homes that they had designed and that were later featured in magazines. In a similar vein, a third of parents (both fathers and mothers) referred to residential neighbourhoods or schools (as markers of class) when contrasting themselves with their former spouse. Indeed, post-separation, with their life plans in disarray and in the face of conflicts over money (and in the context of broader awareness of the social tension of income inequality), most participants raised issues that seemed to have a class-conflict dimension. Some spoke of their former spouse as having had a privileged upbringing (versus their own hard-working, "down-to-earth" family ethic); the wealthy new partner of their former spouse; and marked differences in income, education, and aspirations between themselves and their former spouse. For example, Josie described her family as "not really wealthy but wealthy in a lot of other ways" and as having "a culture of trust and love," while describing her former husband's family as a powerful family that was "wealthy but dysfunctional." Andrew noted that he had been internationally educated, while his former wife had grown up in state-subsidized housing. Another father described his extensive work and travel experience and stable parents, as in complete contrast to the experience and background of his former spouse. Although, on the surface, it appears that these are simply descriptions of class differences and attempts by one party to differentiate themselves from the other, it could also be that, in some cases, participants are stirring old class wounds and insecurities[49] or claiming status. Thus, what is clear from these stories is not only the relevance of gendered meanings of work and care, but also the relevance of perceptions of unequal social class in post-divorce conflicts and identities.

Work-life balance was a particular challenge mentioned by participants. Although most had ideals about family life and work-family balance, a number of participants mentioned the effect of prolonged litigation on their careers, or the challenges they faced in doing everything that needed to be done. While such juggling and stress are common for parents, with many struggling to reconcile their productive and reproductive lives,[50] the additional demands of litigation can be overwhelming. One father, formerly in full-time employment, successfully sought a change of parenting arrangements in which his former spouse was no longer involved. Consequently, he described challenges similar to those mentioned by mothers in the study and the need to reduce his paid work hours. Some participants also had children with special needs or health issues, as well as aging or ill parents to care for. Three women were hospitalized for medical issues that were likely precipitated by stress, and a number of other participants described either periods of severe emotional stress or medical conditions that were triggered or exacerbated by stress (for example, autoimmune diseases). Part-time work was sometimes seen as necessary when children had special needs. Among mothers with large families, part-time employment was preferred in order to accommodate the needs and schedules of their children. Some mothers sought new careers that would allow them to be more autonomous (in an individualistic sense) and better provide for their family (in a relational sense). However, many mothers were also aware of their derivative dependency,[51] which constrained their autonomy. It may also be said that, although they themselves needed support and care, mothers took responsibility for solving their own difficulties (in a neoliberal sense), even when it meant that they were left with a sense that the world was not a just and caring place.

As described here, labour force attachment varied among participants, largely along gender lines. While generation and class also played a role, there was considerable diversity among participants. Sometimes these variations were due to preferences and choice, but more often they were due to the unique challenges and contextual factors faced by a parent or parents, such as the chronic illness of a parent or child. For some parents, labour force participation held the seeds of agency and personal transformation; whereas, for others, either an increase in parental responsibilities or the satisfaction of superb child outcomes, achieved through hard work and personal struggle, had a similar effect.[52]

As illustrated in this section, gendered norms regarding the division of paid work and care affect the decisions parents make, both when in a relationship and post-separation. Generational and class norms also influence the decisions that parents make in this regard. That said, change is often uneven and contested, and ambivalence and resistance toward change featured in many narratives of post-separation transitions and conflicts. In reflecting on parents' response to upheaval and change, I was reminded of Ridgeway's explanation for the persistence of gender inequality in contemporary society.[53] Ridgeway held that, when faced with uncertainty and change, people draw on cultural frames (or shared expectations) to assist them in organizing new ways of doing things. By so doing, they reformulate gender stereotypes into new activities and forms of organization.[54] In the context of my own research, it seems that gender stereotypes and gendered patterns of behaviour are particularly apparent (and often stubbornly entrenched) in the context of post-separation conflicts. In the next section I will explore another subtheme, that of financial autonomy as a component of personal agency. By so doing, I intend to further illustrate how money and child-related issues are largely interconnected, and what the implications are for mothers' agency and autonomy in light of this connection.

Financial Autonomy as a Component of Personal Agency

Financial autonomy in relation to child support was largely a gendered theme in my research, linked not only to the household division of paid work and care but also to broader cultural norms. Men in the study tended to see financial autonomy as a component of individual identity (in terms of power, status, and ownership), and within their domain; whereas women were more likely to see financial responsibility in more relational terms, while also sometimes (usually later on) coming to see it as an aspect of personal agency. However, among both women and men in the study, ethnicity, generation, and other social locations also influenced understandings of the relationship between money, power, and autonomy. Although there are gendered dimensions to this subtheme, tensions and nuances exist, even within individual narratives. As described in the previous section, these differences can be at least partly attributed to broader social changes that are often in tension with each other and not clear-cut. For many parents, divorce is a time where change occurs on multiple interacting levels. As well, their ability to respond to, and cope with, these changes has a great deal to do with the personal, social, and material resources available to them. This subtheme builds on the previous section by illustrating how the distribution of financial and child-care responsibilities may have repercussions for mothers' autonomy (in a relational sense).

Among mothers in the study, issues concerning the division of paid work and unpaid care and gender roles and expectations largely overlapped. Post-separation, most were constrained in their ability to meet household expenses and struggled with the implications for their long-term financial autonomy. As well, mothers often found themselves struggling with their lesser financial power during legal negotiations, having to make ends meet with no, or limited, funds at their disposal, seeking or attempting to maintain employment, and meeting the needs of their children during the family transition – all at the same time as they were expected (by the courts and their former spouse) to step back from their role as mothers. Many also felt pressured or misled during legal negotiations, which they attributed to the other party as well as to their own lack of knowledge and/or power. In combination, these pressures often significantly impacted their view of their former spouse and contributed to the further deterioration of their relationship.

Dominant discourses of the "good divorce,"[55] which are perpetuated in policy and by professionals, promote the ideal of former spouses as parenting partners. Such an ideal is more closely aligned with the views expressed by mothers in this study, whereas fathers tended to adopt more mainstream (and masculinist) societal ideals of personal and financial autonomy.

Although all of the mothers in the study understood that financial and child-related issues should be legally separate, money and the responsibility for children became intertwined due to practical realities. Those who were pressured into shared parenting agreements during post-separation negotiations (arrangements that have significant financial implications), despite their concerns about the viability of such an arrangement and/or whether it was in the interests of their children, often found that having agreed to the parenting arrangement, important financial details of the separation went unresolved. Alternately, details were agreed to in the negotiations but were later either not adhered to or not enforceable. Shelly, a mother in her early forties, explicitly linked her former spouse's underpayment of child support with his rights and responsibilities as a father, saying, "he pays me minimally and then he pays me almost nothing and has the nerve to demand to see their report cards and to have some input into whether or not I'm doing a good enough job raising them." While Shelly recognized that refusing his input was not a position supported by law, he was not, in her view, acting like a parent. He wanted "the privileges, but not the responsibilities," of parenthood.

Regardless of whether these mothers went to court to litigate financial issues or abandoned their claims entirely, they felt that both the system and their former partners were unfair. In particular, many felt that their former partners had played the system and were not held to account for their financial responsibilities. Consequently, they found it very difficult to reconcile that someone who seemed to act in self-interest at the expense of his family (and his integrity) was a caring parent whom they could trust to put the interests of their children ahead of his own. Even the mothers who were of the view that some form of shared parenting was possible, and even desirable, found that reaching agreement about financial matters was either far more difficult than anticipated or, indeed, impossible.[56]

Despite the fact that parental decision making post-separation is supposed to be about children's best interests, mediation turns on notions of give and take; thus, parents who had conceded in one area (which was then often formalized and put into practice) often felt that they had been deceived. Mothers who had not anticipated being in the labour force while they had young children at home and had not undertaken training or education with that expectation, found the process of moving from financial dependence (at the same time as they were dealing with litigation and the needs of young children) most challenging. Those who continued to work full time, or who maintained part-time employment, were often in positions that did not provide sufficient income for them to support children alone. Mothers who were able to support their children on their own income post-separation were in the minority. One such mother (Leanne) was glad that she had established her career before starting her family: once she realized her marriage was not going to work, she was able to return to the labour force full time. She was particularly grateful to her parents for encouraging her to get a good education and for teaching her to be self-supporting. They had taught her not to depend on anyone else to support her and to live within her means. After saving carefully for a new home, she was very reluctant to answer people's questions about her marital status because "[i]n my neighbourhood, if someone asks if I'm a single parent, I know that what they are really asking me is 'If you are a single parent, how can you afford to live here?'" Furthermore, she believed that, if she told people the occupation of her former spouse, who pays only minimal child support, they would assume that she lives where she does because he is paying for it, whereas she has a beautiful home in a very nice neighbourhood thanks to her own work and financial decisions. While undoubtedly Leanne was proud of her individual accomplishments, her conception of agency is an individualistic rather than a relational one. Leanne's success was accomplished with little financial or other support from her former spouse, and without the help she needed from the family justice system. Perhaps this helps to explain her concern that others will see the fruits of her labour in relational terms, linked to assumptions about the contribution of a high-income-earning father.

Mothers who did manage to achieve financial independence took considerable pride in the outcome of their efforts, although some made significant health and personal sacrifices in order to do so. In some cases, their children also suffered. Julie described how she agreed to her child's father taking their child because she had no job, no money, and nowhere to live. Unable to see a way forward at the time, she was also suicidal. A friend suggested that she go on welfare, but "that was a trigger for [her]." She did "not [want to go] on welfare, not now, not ever." Although she did get a job and find housing, by the time she was able to find and regain custody of her child, who had been moved to another city without the father giving her information about their whereabouts, the child was suffering from significant mental health and behavioural issues.

As well, many mothers returned to school or undertook training, began businesses, and or found creative ways to earn extra income. In some cases, they worked at a second job from home while their children were in bed at night. Carol, who sold her family business after exiting an abusive marriage and then combined social assistance and low-paid jobs for several years, decided to obtain an education in order to better support her children (her ex-husband refused to pay child support). First, she got her high school diploma and then she decided to undertake a law degree. Unsure how she would pay for it, she was fortunate to find a social worker who supported her plan. She used her own experience and knowledge of the law to help others going through divorce. Another mother dropped out of university to support her husband during a post-graduate degree and then become a full-time mother. After her separation and a lengthy child-custody dispute, she could not bear to return to court to battle over financial issues. Without any financial support from her former husband, she returned to university, studied counselling, and then developed a successful mediation practice. Throughout her divorce, she had held to an ideal of a friendly and cooperative post-divorce parenting relationship with her former husband. Unable to achieve it, she went on to use what she had learned to assist others, building her financial independence in the process.

Another mother, Lisa, felt a strong sense of injustice, although she had started her own business and was beginning to make money. The following interview excerpt revealed the mixture of pride in her self-efficacy and autonomy alongside her frustration with the injustice that she was left with the majority of the financial responsibility on a lesser income.

> I was thinking I'd go back to court and try and get more money and all of that stuff, but it just sucked the life out of me ... made my life horrible. So, for the last six years, my quality of life said, okay, I'm not going to touch that arena. But now it's ridiculous not to. And financially, my business is just now starting to take off. I feel successful ... and yet I've got $1,200 in my bank account between me and my next mortgage payment and no other income, right? So, it's like I have to work my ass off to get [contracts] to be able to sustain this whole process.

Overall, unless they were already in secure full-time employment, mothers often felt vulnerable and were afraid about how they would support themselves and their children. Not only did some mothers carry the financial responsibility of both parents (a responsibility that had direct implications for their autonomy), but improving their financial circumstances also became paramount in order to reduce the vulnerability they and their children faced. As Carol disclosed,

> My biggest thing was to gain financial independence so that I would never again find myself in that situation. Because I stayed so long that I had no finances at all. And I knew that, when I left, he would make sure that I had no finances. So, I wanted to gain financial independence because I understood it would allow me to be me and not worry about how I was going to survive. Because when I was busy trying to survive, I couldn't grow, right? It was survival mode. So, I knew I had to do something else and that's what pushed me through.

Some mothers found themselves on their own with regard to supporting their children. Despite the many challenges they faced, their efforts to survive and thrive ultimately bore fruit and the seeds for their financial autonomy. All of this group felt they had been let down, not only by their children's other parent, but also by the system. Thus, while they felt pride and took great pleasure in their accomplishments and those of their children, for many parents there was also a lingering sense of betrayal and loss of trust. Not only was the father not held accountable, but, because these ex-husbands neglected their parental responsibility, a number of mothers were left with the majority of financial responsibility while on a lower income. Although some had prepared for such an eventuality, they nevertheless saw it as an injustice.

Arguably, financial matters are inevitably difficult post-separation, with both parents having to find ways to manage life on less money overall. Many of the fathers who participated in this study were keen to step back from being the primary breadwinner and sought to take a greater role in their children's lives. Mothers who were not in the labour force were at a significant disadvantage in such a situation, particularly when there had been shared expectations that their primary role would be in the home (and they had not trained in careers that would allow them to support a family). Although their former partner's priorities might have changed, theirs had not. In many cases, the division of labour and concomitant financial implications were addressed through some form of ADR – a process based on an assumption that both parties are acting with good faith and that there is full disclosure. Unfortunately, this does not always turn out to be the case. Mothers in the study saw their former partners who resisted paying child support as failing to put the needs of their children first and, therefore, as not being responsible. Although some continued to try to pursue the matter legally, others gave up and put their energy into their children and careers instead. Cindy summed this up succinctly: "We play[ed] different games. So, he play[ed] the game of the one with the most money wins and, ah, for me it's about who am I being in the world and am I fulfilling my purpose."

Cindy went on to talk about her decision to invest in herself rather than spend money on litigation after years of investment in ADR unravelled without a financial settlement. She believed that investing in her education, as well as personal counselling and coaching, was "[a] better investment," noting that she was "not a gambler" – she "might get the money or might not get the money." Cindy framed her decision as contributing to her "empowerment," as her formulating a choice for herself and not depending on someone else for money. Thus, she saw herself as making a choice and an investment in herself. Some recently divorced mothers, however, have to depend on social assistance for a period of time. Carol, for example, said that she felt that all the systems had failed her and her children. In order to achieve her goal of self-sufficiency and family well-being, she struggled to exercise agency within the constraints of social assistance and her minimal income. Similar contradictions concerning the agency and autonomy of low-income mothers have been described elsewhere in the literature.[57]

Although they had been able to express agency in small ways and overcome considerable challenges, some mothers were very apprehensive about the future. Some even blamed themselves for circumstances that were beyond their control. For example, Julie spoke about her decision not to go on welfare in a manner that reflected negative social judgments about welfare dependence. Such judgments and stereotypes are often wrapped into lone mothers' subjectivity.[58] Somewhat in contrast, but still reflective of neoliberal imperatives, another mother emphasized that all she had achieved was by careful saving prior to starting her family and her prudent decision to return to full-time employment as soon as her youngest child was in school full time. Although the former decision was made long in advance of separation, the decision to return to the labour force was made once she recognized that her marriage was not viable. Hence, although high-conflict divorce may facilitate maternal agency, this agency is often manifested in neoliberal ways. As demonstrated by studies of lone mothers on welfare,[59] as well as a seminal study of autonomous motherhood, choice and agency are enacted in a neoliberal context that may constrain or enable mothers' autonomy according to their socio-economic (and other) circumstances.[60] Even mothers who are economically privileged and who have parented autonomously from the start contend with stigmatization because of their family status.[61]

This subtheme of the interrelationship between financial and child-related issues highlights financial autonomy as a component of personal agency. Among participants, financial autonomy in relation to child support was largely a gendered theme, with men tending to see financial autonomy as an aspect of individual identity, whereas women were more likely to see it in more relational terms, in that they recognize the interdependencies that characterize family life. However, as described above, additional social locations and individual factors play a role. A common theme in men's narratives was the expectation that, after separation, their former spouse would take on a greater role in financial provision for herself and their children, whether or not she was in the labour force or had recent experience. At the same time, fathers also sought a greater parental role. Mothers more often found themselves with less financial power during negotiations, struggling to make ends meet and expected to seek or maintain employment, regardless of their perceptions of the children's needs or their own wishes.

In the context of family law, Alison Diduck contends that autonomy has become "the friendly face of individual responsibility."[62] It is ironic, then, that family relations, which involve both care and interdependencies, "are simultaneously encouraged and rendered invisible ... in the rush to promote the parties' autonomy post-separation."[63] Given contemporary notions of personal choice and responsibility, now embedded in social and legal norms, those left disadvantaged when the other parent does not, or in some cases cannot, step up to the plate find themselves abandoned by the state, and hence more vulnerable. With the push to privatize the costs – which means, among other things, differential access to legal assistance and other supports – the connection between financial and child-related issues in the context of high-conflict disputes becomes even more evident. Significantly, as Diduck points out in this volume, despite what looks like a change of norms, the burdens continue to fall on primary care providers (the majority of whom are women).[64]

Conclusion

In my research, a significant theme that recurred in both mothers' and fathers' narratives, albeit in different ways, was financial disputes with the other parent. Although financial disputes are generally viewed as disputes between parents that are, and should be, kept separate from parenting matters, mothers especially described how financial conflicts often compounded other challenges and stresses, and spilled over into most aspects of personal and family life, thus impacting not only the quality of their parenting and family life but also their personal autonomy. For example, if one parent hides or minimizes their income, the other parent might have to spend several hours each evening when the children are in bed working on a second job from home, rather than enjoying their very limited free time and some respite. Mothers also described children being subjected to complaints about child support, and their own sadness, frustration, anger, and shame when their children went without. On the other hand, some also described their pride at the opportunities they were able to resource for their children, and in their own steps toward financial autonomy. In that it helps to highlight how gendered meanings of money and of autonomy intersect in participants' accounts, the analytic lens of relational autonomy proves fruitful for contextualizing these disputes, and for understanding the gendered implications for autonomy and equality. While not addressed in this chapter, parents also raised issues concerning the cost of obtaining a just resolution of their disputes. Where there is an imbalance of power and resources, these issues were especially linked with participants' beliefs about having been failed by the justice system, and about not being heard.

Participant narratives about the division of labour, both during marriage and as contested during separation, reflect broader social tensions and the unevenness of change over time, particularly where expectations and norms in one area (for example, shared work and care) are unmatched in another (for example, family-friendly labour force policies or the availability of child care). This has implications for parental autonomy and constrains parents' real choices at separation. As well, choice and agency are enacted in a neoliberal context that may constrain or enable mothers' autonomy, according to their socio-economic (and other) circumstances. Therefore, it is not surprising that, at a time of personal and family upheaval, there is conflict and ambivalence about changing the balance of paid work and care between parents. A gendered division of labour also had implications for access to justice and support resources,[65] primarily for the women in this study. Yet, despite the many obstacles faced and often an enduring sense of having not been heard and of injustice, mothers exercised their agency and became self-authorizing in the long-term.[66]

Financial disputes have a considerable impact on mothers' perceptions of their former partner as a parent, particularly when financial constraints affect their ability to provide for children or obtain a just resolution to disputes. Gender, generation, class, and other social locations influence the meanings parents assign to money and autonomy. Such meanings not only affect perceptions of the other parent, thereby potentially contributing to conflict, they also play a role in a parent's legal decision making and the outcomes they seek. The analytic lens of relational autonomy can be usefully employed to highlight how gendered meanings of money and autonomy intersect in mothers' accounts, with particular implications for women's autonomy and equality. Reconceptualizing responsibilities and choice in a manner that is sensitive to context, social relations, and the (still) gendered consequences of responsibilities for children, provides helpful insights for advancing policy, practice, legal reforms, and research in this area.

Notes

1 Nicholas Bala & Marie Gordon, "Kids and Cash: Interconnections of Child-Related and Economic Issues in Family Proceedings" (2012) 31:3 Can Fam LQ 309.

2 See Gry Mette D Haugen, "Relations between Money and Love in Postdivorce Families: Children's Perspectives" (2005) 12:4 Childhood 507.

3 See Carol Smart & Vanessa May, "Why Can't They Agree? The Underlying Complexity of Contact and Residence Disputes" (2004) 26:4 J Social Welfare & Fam L 347 at 358.

4 Considerable research indicates that mothers are more likely than fathers to face financial disadvantage post-separation, and this pattern is apparent across national jurisdictions (as noted by Ayesha Scott in "Hidden Hurt: The Impact of Post-separation Financial Violence in Aotearoa New Zealand" (2020) 33 Austl J Fam L 282 at 295n53). However, given same-sex relationships, socio-economic advantage, and other imbalances of power, as well as welfare state and repartnering effects, it is not always the "mother" who is the less well-off party.

5 In *In the Name of the Child: A Developmental Approach to Understanding and Helping Children of Conflicted and Violent Divorce* (New York: Free Press, 1997) at 3, Janet Johnston and Vivienne Roseby define a high-conflict divorce as involving long, bitter, and protracted disputes, about 10 percent of which last throughout the offsprings' childhood.

6 See e.g. Susan B Boyd, *Challenging the Public/Private Divide: Feminism, Law, and Public Policy* (Toronto: University of Toronto Press, 1997) [Boyd, *Challenging the Divide*]; Susan B Boyd, *Child Custody, Law, and Women's Work* (Toronto: Oxford University Press, 2003) [Boyd, *Child Custody*]; Martha A Fineman, *The Illusion of Equality: The Rhetoric and Reality of Divorce Reform* (Chicago: University of Chicago Press, 1994); Carol Smart & Selma Sevenhuijsen, *Child Custody and the Politics of Gender* (New York: Routledge, 1989).

7 Susan B Boyd, "Autonomy for Mothers? Relational Theory and Parenting Apart" (2010) 18:2 Fem Leg Stud 137 [Boyd, "Autonomy for Mothers?"] at 140.

8 See e.g. *ibid*; Robert Leckey, *Contextual Subjects: Family, State, and Relational Theory* (Toronto: University of Toronto Press, 2008); Catriona Mackenzie & Natalie Stoljar, *Relational Autonomy: Feminist Perspectives on Autonomy, Agency, and the Social Self* (New York: Oxford University Press, 2000); Jennifer Nedelsky, "Reconceiving Autonomy: Sources, Thoughts and Possibilities" (1989) 1 Yale JL & Feminism 7; Jennifer Nedelesky, *Law's Relations: A Relational Theory of Self, Autonomy, and Law* (New York: Oxford University Press, 2011).

9 See Boyd, "Autonomy for Mothers?," *supra* note 7 at 137–58.

10 See Leckey, *supra* note 8 at 21.

11 See John Eekelaar, "'Not of the Highest Importance': Family Justice under Threat" (2011) 33 J Soc Welfare & Fam L 311.

12 See Susan B Boyd, "Motherhood and Autonomy in a Shared Parenting Climate" in Jackie Jones et al, eds, *Gender, Sexualities and Law* (New York: Routledge, 2011) 255.

13 See Kristin Natalier & Belinda Hewitt, "Separated Parents Reproducing and Undoing Gender through Defining Legitimate Uses of Child Support" (2014) 28:6 Gender & Society 904.

14 See Beata Caranci & Pascal Gauthier, "Career Interrupted: The Economic Impact of Motherhood" (TD Bank Financial Group, 12 October 2010), online (PDF): <www.td.com/document/PDF/economics/special/td-economics-special-bc1010-career-interrupted.pdf> at 7; Statistics Canada, *Family Caregiving: What Are the Consequences?* by Martin Turcotte, Catalogue no. 75-006-X (Ottawa: Statistics Canada, September 2013), online (PDF): <https://www150.statcan.gc.ca/n1/pub/75-006-x/2013001/article/11858-eng.pdf>.

15 See Natalier & Hewitt, *supra* note 13 at 904–6.

16 Carol Smart, "Law and Family Life: Insights from 25 Years of Empirical Research" (2014) 26:1 Child & Fam LQ 14.

17 See Katalien Bollen, Alain Verbeke & Martin Euwema, "Money or Children? Power Sources in Divorce Mediation" (2013) 19:2 J Family Studies 159 at 167–70.

18 See Kay Cook & Kristin Natalier, "Selective Hearing: The Gendered Construction and Reception of Inquiry Evidence" (2014) 34:4 Critical Social Policy 515 at 518.

19 See e.g. Susan B Boyd, "Still Gendered After all This Time? Care and Autonomy in Child Custody Debates" in Nicky Priaulx & Anthony Wrigley, eds, *Ethics, Law and Society. Vol. V: Ethics of Care, Body Politics, Theorizing the Ethical and Governance* (Aldershot, UK: Ashgate, 2013) 69.

20 Natalier & Hewitt, *supra* note 13 at 922.

21 See Brenda Cossman, "Family Feuds: Neo-Liberal and Neo-Conservative Visions of the Reprivatization Project" in Brenda Cossman & Judy Fudge, eds, *Privatization, Law, and the Challenge to Feminism* (Toronto: University of Toronto Press, 2002) 169; Rachel Treloar & Susan B Boyd, "Family Law Reform in (Neoliberal) Context: British Columbia's New Family Law Act" (2014) 28:1 Intl JL Pol'y & Fam 77 at 79–81; Rachel Treloar, "The Neoliberal Context of Family Law Reform in British Columbia, Canada: Implications for Access to (Family) Justice," in Mavis Maclean, John Eekelaar & Benoit Bastard, eds, *Delivering Family Justice in the 21st Century* (Oxford: Hart-Bloomsbury, 2015) 15 [Treloar, "Neoliberal Context"] at 18 for a discussion of family law in the context of neoliberalism.

22 See Treloar & Boyd, *supra* note 21 at 94.

23 See Rachel Treloar, "High-Conflict Divorce Involving Children: Parents' Meaning-Making and Agency" (2018) 40:3 J Soc Welfare & Fam L 340 [Treloar, "High-Conflict Divorce"] at 348.

24 See Martha A Fineman, "The Vulnerable Subject and the Responsive State" (2010) 60:2 Emory LJ 251.

25 See Susan B Boyd et al, *Autonomous Motherhood? A Socio-Legal Study of Choice and Constraint* (Toronto: University of Toronto Press, 2015).

26 See e.g. Boyd, "Autonomy for Mothers?," *supra* note 7 at 148–50.

27 Alison Diduck, "Justice by ADR in Private Family Matters: Is It Fair and Is It Possible?" (2014) Family Law 616 at 617–19.

28 See Treloar, "High-Conflict Divorce," *supra* note 23, for an overview of the study findings.

29 Ontology refers to assumptions about the nature of reality. A relational ontology holds that people are interdependent and embedded in a complex web of social relationships. These connections, which involve both responsibility and care, affect both how people understand the world and how they see themselves.

30 Epistemology refers to assumptions about the framework of knowledge. Social constructionists focus on the social process by which individuals make sense of their experience, rather than individual cognitive processes. I take the view that reality is actively constructed by individuals in interaction with others.

31 I sent information packages to these "professional gatekeepers," including an "invitation to participate," which they were asked to forward to potential participants. It was then up to that individual to decide if they met the study criteria and wished to participate.

32 In writing about the experiences of study participants, I use pseudonyms and changed minor details in order to ensure their anonymity was protected. As an additional step to protect participant privacy, I use common themes in my written findings rather than individual portraits. However, even removing identifying information and using pseudonyms involves a small risk that others could link up interview excerpts or commentary across publications. Thus, following Janice Morse, who advises researchers not to identify the participant in every quotation "unless there is a compelling reason to do so," where that is likely, I have grouped participants' comments together or employed phrases such as "a mother" or "a father." Janice Morse, "The Contracted Relationship: Ensuring Protection of Anonymity and Confidentiality" (1998) 8:3 Qualitative Health Research 301 at 302.

33 *Family Relations Act,* RSBC 1996, c 128.

34 Arguably, the absence of participants who were in same-sex relationships with the other parent (as well as individuals from a broader range of cultural backgrounds) is a limitation that affects the study findings.

35 See e.g. Carol Smart & Bren Neale, *Family Fragments?* (Cambridge, UK: Polity Press, 1999).

36 See e.g. Boyd, "Autonomy for Mothers?," *supra* note 7.

37 For a discussion of this concept in English, see e.g. Birgit Pfau-Effinger, "The Gender Contract and Part-Time Paid Work by Women – Finland and Germany Compared" (1994) 26:9 Environment and Planning A: Economy and Space 1355 at 1359.

38 See Statistics Canada, *Families, Living Arrangements and Unpaid Work*, by Anne Milan, Leslie-Anne Keown & Covadonga Robles Urquijo, Catalogue no. 89–503-X (Ottawa: Statistics Canada, December 2011) at 20.

39 See *ibid.*

40 See Caranci & Gauthier, *supra* note 14.

41 See OECD, Secretary General, *Doing Better for Children* (Paris: OECD Publishing, 2009).

42 See Treloar & Boyd, *supra* note 21 at 80.

43 See e.g. Boyd, *Challenging the Divide, supra* note 6; Martha A Fineman, *The Autonomy Myth: A Theory of Dependency* (New York: New Press, 2005) [Fineman, *Autonomy Myth*].

44 See Carol Smart, "The Legal and Moral Ordering of Child Custody" (1991) 18:4 JL & Soc'y 485 at 500.

45 See Boyd, *Child Custody, supra* note 6.

46 Smart and Neale, *supra* note 35 at 66.

47 *Ibid* at 31.

48 I have intentionally not provided a pseudonym for this father as, in combination with details published elsewhere, it is likely he would be identifiable.

49 See Diane Reay, "Beyond Consciousness? The Psychic Landscape of Social Class" (2005) 39:5 Sociology 911 at 924.

50 See Gillian Calder, "The Personal *Is* Economic: Unearthing the Rhetoric of Choice in the Canadian Maternity and Parental Leave Benefit Debates" in Sharon Cowan & Rosemary Hunter, eds, *Choice and Consent: Feminist Engagements with Law and Subjectivity* (London: Cavendish, 2007) 125.

51 See Fineman, *Autonomy Myth, supra* note 43.

52 See Treloar, "High-Conflict Divorce," *supra* note 23 at 7–8.

53 See Cecilia Ridgeway, *Framed by Gender: How Gender Inequality Persists in the Modern World* (New York: Oxford University Press, 2011).

54 See *ibid.*

55 Constance Ahrons, *The Good Divorce: Keeping Your Family Together When Your Marriage Comes Apart* (New York: HarperCollins, 1994).

56 See Rachel Treloar, "'My Problem, My Solution'? Private Ordering and Self-Help in British Columbia, Canada" in Mavis Maclean & Bregje Dijksterhuis, eds, *Digital Family Justice: From Alternative Dispute Resolution to Online Dispute Resolution?* (Oxford: Hart-Bloomsbury, 2019). The chapter discusses my research findings with respect to ADR negotiations.

57 See e.g. Jane Pulkingham, Sylvia Fuller & Paul Kershaw, "Lone Motherhood, Welfare Reform and Active Citizen Subjectivity" (2010) 30:2 Critical Social Policy 267.

58 *Ibid* at 285.

59 See Amber Gazso & Susan A McDaniel, "The Risks of Being a Lone Mother on Income Support in Canada and the USA" (2010) 30:7/8 Intl J Sociology & Social Policy 368 at 378–80; Pulkingham, Fuller & Kershaw, *supra* note 57 at 286–87.

60 See Boyd et al, *supra* note 25 at 54.

61 See Wanda Wiegers & Dorothy Chunn, "Stigma and Resistance: The Social Experience of Choosing Sole Motherhood in Canada 1965–2010" (2015) 51 Women's Studies Intl Forum 42.

62 Alison Diduck, "Autonomy and Vulnerability in Family Law: The Missing Link" in Julie Wallbank & Jonathan Herring, eds, *Vulnerabilities, Care and Family Law* (New York: Routledge, 2014) 95 at 96.

63 *Ibid.*

64 Alison Diduck, Chapter 3 in this volume.

65 See Treloar & Boyd, *supra* note 21; Treloar, "Neoliberal Context," *supra* note 21.

66 See Treloar, "High-Conflict Divorce," *supra* note 23 for a more detailed discussion.

PART 3

Norms' Stickiness

5

Familial Ideology, Privatization, and Care Arrangements for Children in the Family Law and Child Protection Systems

Wanda Wiegers

In 2016, about 98 percent (5,733,935) of children aged fourteen and under who resided in private Canadian households were living with one or both of their biological or adoptive parents.[1] About 1 percent (83,000 children) were living without a biological or adoptive parent and with grandparents, other relatives, or with foster caregivers.[2] A smaller number of children were living in institutions or group homes or outside of Canada.[3]

My objective in this chapter is to examine the impact of both familial ideology and privatization on the legal regulation of the relationship between children and their parents or alternative caregivers and on a range of different care arrangements available for children.[4] These themes are explored within and at the intersection of the family and child protection legal systems; the former system addresses the impact of general custody or guardianship and maintenance statutes, and the latter authorizes the provision of services and the removal of children from the care of their parents/custodians and their placement in other homes or facilities. While both systems are intended to protect and promote the best interests of children, child custody is generally constructed as a "'private' contest between parents" and child welfare as a "'public' contest between the parent and state when the private world of the family is seen as problematic."[5] I will examine the similarities and differences between these systems, as well as their relationship in one Canadian jurisdiction, that of British Columbia.

Specifically, three issues will be addressed. First, I will consider the extent to which familial ideology remains relevant to existing care arrangements for children across both the family law and child protection systems.

For the vast majority of children in Canada, care remains fundamentally rooted, culturally and in practice, in parentage and in conjugal definitions of family. However, at the same time, legal systems are increasingly recognizing the significance of extended family and community or cultural ties to a child's best interests. I will identify and compare the degree to which these kinship ties are recognized in terms of decision-making responsibility, contact, and support in the two legal systems.

Second, I will explore the extent to which care is being privatized and costs shifted away from the state onto private individuals. Scholars have noted the impact of privatization in the family law context, largely through an expansion and more rigorous enforcement of private support obligations, and in welfare law, through broad definitions of spousal and eligibility criteria.[6] It is not surprising, then, that privatization is, as I will argue, also visible through the off-loading of some of the costs of care onto kin and substitute care providers, although the extent to which this is occurring differs in the child protection and family law systems.

Finally, I draw attention throughout to who bears the costs of care and to how different care arrangements are compensated across both systems. Child-care labour includes the services provided to children and the emotional labour of building relationships between family members. I will argue that, across all placements, costs are externalized largely to women, whose caring labour is invisible or devalued. Child-care labour, for which women remain primarily responsible, is recognized to some extent in the family law context through private obligations of spousal support and property division, but such recognition is dependent upon having a spouse with assets or an ability to pay. In the child protection context, the labour of child care (as opposed to the coverage of direct child expenses) is quite literally invisible, except for children with complex and specialized needs. To the extent that the costs of care are off-loaded, they are borne disproportionately by working-class, impoverished, and Indigenous women.

In general, I argue in this chapter that the normative appeal of familial ideology remains highly important to both the legal regulation of and social practices related to the care of children. However, context matters, and both familial ideology and privatization agendas play out differently in different legal systems, particularly in relation to the role of non-parents. While the diversity of family forms has been recognized to varying degrees, the nuclear or two-parent family – both intact and in a fragmented form post-separation – is still largely regarded as the pre-eminent family form, as a naturally loving, safe, and private space, in which children's primary needs for connection and guidance can best be met. In terms of lived experience, the vast majority of children in Canada lived in private households in 2016 and most of these children lived with both parents or in a step-family.[7] In the family law system, parents are primarily liable for their children's support and are accorded primary authority in relation to their upbringing. Privatization, working in tandem with traditional familial norms and those of individual responsibility, is most intense in the context of parental care, as mothers disproportionately shoulder the labour, and parents, relative to substitute caregivers in the child protection system, receive less in state supports. In the family law context, privatization pressures have had little impact on the liability for child support of non-parents who are not spouses of parents, nor on claims for the support of parents by their adult children. Non-parents, such as kin, may now claim a right of contact with children notwithstanding parental opposition, but their claims to parenting responsibility and time have generally been subordinate to the claims of parents.

By contrast, non-parents and kin relations have been increasingly relied on to care for children who have been removed from parental care. Over the past century, the child protection system moved away from the institutional care of children toward family-based care in the form of foster care and, more recently, kinship care and subsidized adoption. Each of these forms of care offers cost savings relative to institutional or contracted residential care. In this context, kin in particular are playing a more significant role, with kinship still generally defined through biological ties, and, hence, naturalized, but linked also to distinctive cultural norms and practices in the relevant community. For Indigenous children, who are highly over-represented in state care and still exposed to the long-term impacts of colonization, residential schools, and the Sixties Scoop on their families and communities, kinship care can offer multiple advantages, if well supported.[8] However, the appeal of a family setting, preferably a nuclear one, of biological ties where possible, of cost savings through assumptions of altruism, and of the provision by women of caring labour at less than market cost, all reflect prominent dimensions of Western-based familial ideology.

Most common to both the family and child protection systems, then, is the reliance on the unpaid or undervalued caring labour for children that women disproportionately provide in a family setting. Working-class, impoverished, racialized, and single women are most likely to be under-compensated, owing to a lack of partners, or of partners who lack the financial means to compensate them in the family law system, and to the off-loading of costs through family-based care in the child protection system. The undervalued caring labour of women, exposed most dramatically by the COVID-19 pandemic, continues to be central to familial ideology, privatization, and women's inequality.

In what follows, I will discuss the emergence and normative content of Western familial and related ideologies in relation to the allocation of care and responsibility for children. In doing so, I rely on feminist theorists of familial ideology from as many as forty years ago to highlight how the ideology has or has not evolved into the present. I will examine care arrangements in the family law system and, then, the child protection system, including an assessment of trends and costs in each form of state care.

The findings set out in this chapter are based largely on a review of relevant statutes, regulations, policy manuals, standards, and documents as well as reports of the Provincial Representative for Children and Youth up to January 2020. I have tried to simplify what is a very complex field while attempting to be sensitive to the extent to which the language of statutes and manuals may not reflect realities on the ground.[9]

Familial Ideologies and the Allocation of Care and Responsibility for Children

In 1982, Michèle Barrett and Mary McIntosh argued that the family was not only a social and economic institution but also an ideology.[10] A dominant ideology, which emerged in the course of the Industrial Revolution in England, represented the ideal family as a private unit composed of a husband/father, who provided financial security, a mother/wife, who undertook primary responsibility for domestic labour, and their children.[11] An assumption of biological kinship rendered this nuclear family model seemingly natural and above mere social conventions, despite its correspondence largely with the practices of white, middle-class families in mid-nineteenth-century Britain and its consolidation through law and social and reform movements. Apart from appearing natural and private, and offering an opportunity for the "expression of emotional need not legitimate elsewhere,"[12] this family form was viewed as a safe, protective space and as the best site for rearing children, since their exposure to two opposite-sex parents would promote stability, gender socialization, and economic well-being. While recognizing the source of its appeal, Barrett and McIntosh argued that familial ideology (familialism) served as a primary vehicle for the transmission of class position and wealth as well as for gender inequality through its positioning of women as economic dependants both in the family and the market.

As Barrett and McIntosh recognized, familial ideology has also served as a "focal point" for a number of related ideologies that have shaped family relations in Western cultures, albeit in different ways and through varied professional discourses.[13] An ideology of childhood as a distinct life stage of natural dependency placed children at the centre of family life and cast them as innocent, vulnerable, and in need of protection.[14] Ideologies of motherhood and domesticity represented women as having an innate capacity for nurture and positioned the family as their natural domain and as the "antithesis to the cash nexus" in capitalism.[15] When embedded within the private family, women's caring labour is not only expected to be provided "for free" but is also far less visible than it would be in other contexts. Meanwhile, the process of procreation, pregnancy, and childbirth provides a material source for naturalizing this allocation of unpaid care and responsibility for children.

According to Jan Dizard and Howard Gadlin, with the shaping of the "minimal family," broader kinship bonds were weakened.[16] As an ideal, the nuclear companionate family focused on meeting the emotional and material needs of its immediate members without substantial reliance on extended kinship ties. The nuclear ideal, though never fully realized, was made more viable over the past century through industrialization, urbanization, and the expansion of markets for services, along with enhanced social programs and unionization. While households could expand to meet the needs of kin at different points, and some families remained highly dependent on kinship ties, the assistance offered to and by kin was, for many, "more and more a supplement, a gesture," rather than an obligation.

Dizard and Gadlin also note that "[w]ithin … roughly the scope of one generation, significant numbers of Americans ceased expecting their children to care for them in their old age."[17] The normative family and one's primary commitments were thus more tightly bound up in and represented by the husband-wife-child unit.

The hegemony of the nuclear family and related ideologies has since been challenged on many fronts. In terms of how families are lived and experienced, changes in material conditions such as the erosion of the family wage have rendered dual-earner households, at 69 percent in 2015, the majority of Canadian households with children.[18] The increase in common law unions has undercut the dominance of marital norms, and the legal recognition of lesbian and gay families and of reproductive technologies has challenged the normative status of biological connections along with the heterosexual two-parent model. Children are also increasingly seen as individuals having some rights.[19] Further, there is an emergent ideology of fatherhood that presents fathers as equal and vital participants in the rearing of children, and the division of labour in the family as a matter of private choice. With genetic testing, biogenetic ties within and outside of conjugal unions have become even more important to the identification of fatherhood.[20]

The importance of extended familial ties as a crucial refuge from poverty, racism, and colonization has also been increasingly recognized.[21] Too often, however, Black and Indigenous families have been experienced not as private but rather as sites of state control. For First Nations communities, the destructive impact of state involvement through residential schools and the Sixties Scoop has been well documented[22] and, according to Kline (writing in 1992), constituted a "modality of colonialist regulation."[23] In British Columbia, the numbers of First Nations children in state care increased dramatically after 1955, and they remain disproportionately represented in the child protection system as a result of colonialism, the intergenerational impact of residential schools and child welfare policies, racism, and higher rates of chronic poverty.[24] Children of racialized and immigrant parents, of poor, working-class, and/or single parents, and of parents living with physical or mental disabilities have also been more vulnerable to state removal and their families subject to greater scrutiny due to a greater dependence on social assistance, among other social services.[25] All such parents have by necessity, if not by custom, also relied to a greater extent on kinship support.

While these challenges have reshaped the content and boundaries of familial and intersecting ideologies, some features remain highly relevant and have an "enduring influence," especially under conditions of neoliberalism.[26] Material conditions still favour at least two parents as a more economically viable family unit, given sex segregation in the workforce, low wages, and the lack of affordable child care.[27] Indeed, seven out of ten children up to age fourteen in Canada in 2016 lived with both of their biological or adoptive parents.[28] Moreover, women continue to provide most of the unpaid child-care labour in almost all households,[29] and, when children are removed and enter the child protection system, it is usually mothers, rather than fathers, who are individually blamed and shamed as irresponsible parents.[30] If anything, the expectations of motherhood have intensified under neoliberal governance, even though the capacity to deliver on these expectations is increasingly undermined by precarious employment.[31] In neoliberal times, child dependency also assists in constructing adults, including caregivers, as self-reliant individuals and adult dependency as a personal pathology.[32]

As well, the nuclear family model is still reproduced and enforced by law, such as welfare law, which can, through intrusive spousal definitions that position women as economic dependants, disqualify them from receiving public support.[33] This ideal also continues to inform the legal acceptance of new family forms (such as same-sex marriage) as well as parenting outcomes after divorce or separation through an emphasis on preserving and fostering the relationship between children and both of their parents, while also privatizing responsibility.[34] The ages of children for whom support can be claimed have been extended, definitions of parenthood enlarged, and enforcement measures intensified,[35] all of which relies on the belief that families should take care of their own. In the child protection context, an expectation that mothers provide primary care has tended in the past to both devalue cultural norms of kinship care and blame neglect on individual Indigenous mothers, rather than on colonialism, racial oppression, and poverty.[36]

According to Fudge and Cossman, writing in 2002, the composition of the family may have become less important than the support function it bears.[37] Yet, as noted above, privatization has aligned with many of the core beliefs of familial ideology, some of which have proven highly resistant to change in law and social practice. As well, who constitutes family, who has parental authority, and who can be expected to bear a support obligation must still be defined, and some normative basis for the imposition of responsibility is needed. Cossman has noted tensions between neoconservatism and neoliberalism in constructions of family in the context of the legalization of same-sex marriage and the definition of spouses in welfare law.[38] In the context of family and child protection law, neoconservatives might favour the extension of responsibility to kin, given their emphasis on "community authority, social order and tradition."[39] Biologically ascriptive ties also naturalize and, as Barrett and McIntosh noted, offer "outward tokens of similarity, familiarity and belonging."[40] However, the extension of support obligations by virtue only of such ties is hard to square with both dominant familial norms and the norms of individual choice and responsibility that underpin neoliberalism.

In what follows, I will explore the relationship between individual responsibility, familial ideology, and privatization and the role of each in shaping care arrangements for children in the family and child protection systems. In both systems, the state ultimately allocates care and responsibility. Both systems are ostensibly aimed at ensuring the "best interests of children" – an apparently impartial and universal norm that confers broad discretion on judges[41] – but neither provides adequate support for family life. In the family law system, the parties are typically parents, and it is here, where the most is at stake in terms of costs (since the vast majority of children are cared for by parents), that the privatization of support is most rigorously enforced and public supports most limited. In the child protection system, by contrast, the state is responsible for the support and maintenance of children taken into state care, subject to the shifting of all or part of that responsibility onto private individuals.

The Family Law System

Parenting disputes in the family law system raise issues of decision-making responsibility and parenting time as well as financial support. Under the federal *Divorce Act*,[42] liability for child support is limited to married spouses who are parents or who, typically as step-parents, have stood in the place of a parent according to the test in *Chartier v Chartier*.[43] Under British Columbia's *Family Law Act*, parents, who are defined to include step-parents under certain circumstances, can claim or be ordered to pay child support.[44] A non-parent can claim or be liable to pay support only if they have been appointed as a guardian with parenting responsibilities that extend beyond dealing with the child's legal and financial interests.[45] One must, however, apply (that is, choose) to be appointed a guardian, and the duty of a non-parent guardian to provide support is secondary to that of a parent.[46] Reported cases dealing with claims for support from a non-parent guardian are also rare. More commonly, biological, intended, or adoptive parents seek support from each other or from step-parents, and non-parent guardians seek support from parents. Child support may also be sought from parents by ministries responsible for social assistance and child protection (before a continuing custody order is made), but few decisions have dealt with such applications.[47]

Legislation providing for support claims by parents against their adult children was introduced in British Columbia in 1922, during a period of widespread economic deprivation, but repealed in 2011.[48] Despite pressures to reduce social programs in neoliberal regimes and an increasing demographic of elderly parents, the privatization of familial support is now restricted to claims against parents or those who assume a parental role, rather than against adult children. It is thus bounded by a nuclear family model and a norm of adult independence and responsibility rather than intergenerational reciprocity.

The *Federal Child Support Guidelines* (*CSG*) govern the quantification of child support.[49] The table amounts of the *CSG* are generally intended to address the additional costs of raising children in a household, which are assumed to rise or fall relative to the payor's income. The table amounts are not intended to compensate the labour involved in nor the opportunity costs of providing care for children. These costs are explicitly addressed only through property division or support as between spouses.[50] Recognition and direct compensation for child-care labour, which is disproportionately borne by mothers, is thus contingent on spousal status and the accumulation of assets or ability to pay as well as the willingness and ability to pursue or litigate a claim.

This allocation of private responsibility for caring labour, along with a resistance to raising taxes to enhance collective responsibility, is reflected in the lack of adequate public supports for the rearing of children by parents. Parental care is shored up by public benefits such as social assistance, the Canada Child Benefit (CCB) (a tax credit that is targeted to income and payable until a child is eighteen), and a supplementary federal Child Disability Benefit (CDB) payable to families caring for children with serious disabilities. To be eligible for social assistance, applicants are generally required to seek employment, and those who qualify as workers may have claims to maternity, parental, or other forms of leave and partial wage replacement for limited time periods.[51] The CCB was intended primarily at the outset to incentivize low-wage employment, and subsequent enhancements have been aimed at "[helping] with the cost of raising children."[52] However, 9.8 percent of children and youth under eighteen in British Columbia still lived in poverty as of 2017 (as defined by the Market Basket Measure),[53] and numerous reports have indicated that parents lack access to affordable housing, quality daycare, and culturally appropriate services such as respite and mental health supports that could assist in avoiding the removal of their children by child welfare authorities.[54]

In terms of applications for parenting time and decision-making responsibility or guardianship, almost all such disputes arise between parents and spouses; extended family or unrelated parties typically become involved only when parents are in crisis. A spouse who is a parent or stands in the place of a parent can seek parenting time or decision-making responsibility under the *Divorce Act*. As a result of amendments, a non-spouse, as in the past, will require leave to apply for a parenting order, but they must now also stand, or intend to stand, in the place of a parent to the child.[55] In the past, leave has generally been granted where an opposing party could not establish that the application was frivolous or vexatious.[56] In *Chartier*, a number of factors were identified as relevant to whether one stands in the place of a parent, including the formation of a family through co-residency, financial provision, discipline, intentions, as well as the conduct of the claimant and child.[57] Non-spouses may alternatively apply for leave to obtain a contact order, which allows for visits but does not grant decision-making responsibility or expose the applicant to claims for child support.[58] Thus, applications by non-parents are constrained, to a lesser extent by the need for leave for a contact order and to a greater extent when parenting orders are sought.

Under provincial law, parents (which include biological, adoptive, or intended parents) are guardians of a child, subject to an agreement between them or a court order to the contrary.[59] A court order is generally required to transfer guardianship to a non-parent under the *FLA*; it cannot be achieved simply by agreement or with the consent of the parent.[60] Unless the director has custody of a child who has been removed from their parents under the *Child, Family and Community Service Act* (*CFCSA*), any person may apply to be appointed a child's guardian.[61] As with the *Divorce Act*, the *FLA* also allows applications for contact by non-guardians by agreement or court order, but applications can be made without leave of the court and expressly include those of grandparents.[62]

Once standing to apply has been established, the allocation of contact, parenting time, and decision-making responsibility for a child is to depend solely on an assessment of the child's best interests.[63] A child's cultural or linguistic heritage, including Indigenous upbringing and heritage, will be considered relevant to a best-interests assessment under both the *DA* and the *FLA*.[64] Any order may be varied, given a material change in circumstance (if, for example, a parent recovers stability). Few cases, however, have involved applications for custody or guardianship by relatives such as grandparents. In a contest between a mother and pre-adoptive parents in *King v Low*, the Supreme Court held that "parental claims must not be lightly set aside, and they are entitled to serious consideration in reaching any conclusion. Where it is clear that the welfare of the child requires it, however, they must be set aside."[65] There is no presumption in law favouring biological parents; however, the Court of Appeal in *Chera v Chera* identified "a common sense approach to custody disputes that provides for, all other matters being equal, a parent's right to raise his or her child."[66] Whereas psychological bonding has been significant in cases involving non-related applicants, and the focus of intense criticism in cases involving Indigenous children and non-Indigenous applicants,[67] it does not appear to carry as much weight in contests between parents and kin. In British Columbia, grandmothers have lost guardianship claims to parents even where they have been long-term primary caregivers.[68]

In contests with parents, courts are more likely to find that contact or access by kin, rather than guardianship, is in the best interests of a child, given statutory reforms that have recognized such claims to a greater extent along with the importance of a child's cultural heritage.[69] Although courts will consider the parent's views and avoid placing a child in circumstances of "real conflict and hostility,"[70] the trend in favour of access to non-parents, particularly grandparents, likely represents an effort to provide children with more emotional and potentially more voluntary financial supports and resources. The enforcement of extended family ties in some measure does represent a challenge to parental authority and a disjuncture between the imposition of financial responsibility for children and the exercise of control over them. However, non-parents remain only marginally involved in care arrangements for children within the family law system.

Apart from the above constraints, there are practical barriers to applications by non-parents for guardianship or parenting orders under the *FLA* and *DA*. Indeed, many, perhaps most, kin caregivers are raising children informally, without involvement in either the family law or child protection systems, without the security of a guardianship order, and without services or additional financial supports.[71] Guardians appointed under the *FLA* or persons with parenting orders under the *DA* are generally free of ongoing surveillance by the court or child protection workers. However, this degree of privacy or minimal surveillance through the family law system is difficult for poor and marginalized families to achieve.[72] These families may already be under heightened state surveillance due to reliance on social services, and the family law system is costly to access unless one is eligible for legal aid. Kin caregivers may also be wary of increased conflict with parents through litigation, and Indigenous parents may be distrustful of both the family law and child protection systems. Moreover, financial supports in excess of income assistance, the CCB, and other subsidies generally available to those on low incomes, are available only in the child protection system.[73] Obtaining legal guardianship has in fact disqualified guardians from receiving financial support equivalent to that available under the child protection system.[74]

In summary, the inherent value of child-care labour, provided principally by women, is explicitly recognized and compensated only as between spouses through spousal support or property division in the family law system. While the *FLA* provides an opportunity to seek financial support from non-parents who are not spouses and who seek to become and are appointed guardians, such applications appear to be rare. As well, challenges to parental control and responsibility outside of conjugal or biological relations are uncommon, require leave and/or a significant parental role, and must be found to be in the best interests of children. In somewhat of a departure from the nuclear family model, continuing contact with extended family and the express recognition of grandparents in British Columbia is now seen as having the potential to be in a child's best interests, notwithstanding parental opposition. Nonetheless, the family law system remains closely aligned with notions of individual responsibility, minimal conceptions of family (focused on parents and their conjugal partners), along with an intensification of privatized support for children and their primary caregivers. In the child protection system, as discussed in the next section, the possible care arrangements for children are not as limited.

The Child Protection System

In the child protection system, families are, by definition, subject to state coercion through removal or state supervision. In British Columbia, most children in this system are apprehended by the Ministry of Child and Family Development (MCFD) as a result of neglect that is closely correlated with poverty and intergenerational trauma.[75] The failure to provide adequate preventive supports to families living in conditions of chronic poverty has been well documented and was highlighted by the findings of a federal human rights tribunal in 2016. The tribunal held that the federal government had discriminated against First Nations children and families by way of funding formulas that favoured apprehension over prevention.[76] The BC *CFCSA*, like child protection statutes in other jurisdictions, contains language that authorizes the provision of services to support families in staying together.[77] However, parents and activists in British Columbia have complained that financial and other supports for parents are less than what is provided to foster caregivers and that assistance should be provided long before a crisis emerges.[78] In the United States, Dorothy Roberts identified a widespread failure to provide preventive supports, even though such supports were less costly than non-parental care. She attributed this failure to the belief that families should be responsible for their own children and a "refusal to see a collective responsibility for children's welfare."[79]

Children who are removed from their parents or guardians in British Columbia may be found in need of protection and, depending on what is seen to be in their best interests, can be returned to their parents with or without supervision or placed in the interim, temporary, or continuing custody of the director (a person designated by the Minister) or other persons.[80] Where the director obtains custody on a temporary or continuing basis, the Ministry must consider the child's best interests in choosing the home or facility into which the child is placed.[81] Although the BC statute sets out an array of rights for children, including input into significant decisions,[82] only an internal review of the exercise of a director's powers to determine placements is provided for under the *Act*.[83] Children may be placed in state care up to age nineteen, and those who are in care at nineteen or who have received financial assistance or services may obtain additional supports through agreements directly with the Ministry.[84]

Historically, the child protection system has relied heavily on private institutions and on families to deliver care. The dominant forms of care have changed over time from forms of apprenticeship or indentured labour, to institutional care in orphanages and residential schools, and then, over the late nineteenth and twentieth centuries, to family-based care. While institutional care has been widely associated with inferior instruction, physical and sexual abuse, cultural repression, and high levels of contagion, historians have also found examples of institutional care and boarding that were supportive of families in need and resisted adoption and fostering.[85] Institutional care is now generally viewed as a last resort, and family-based care, in the form of foster care, kinship care, or adoption, is considered the best site for child rearing.[86] More recently, given shortages of foster caregivers along with protests by Indigenous communities, placements in kinship care have increased.[87] Under the *CFCSA*, priority must be given to placements with a relative,[88] and, in the case of Indigenous children, with extended family or a child's Indigenous community.[89] Recent provincial amendments have emphasized the involvement of Indigenous communities in planning throughout the process, to ensure cultural and relational permanency.[90] The federal government has also passed legislation intended to affirm and transfer jurisdiction over the protection of First Nation, Métis, and Inuit children to Indigenous governing bodies and has defined "best interests" to include the importance of cultural continuity and family and community relationships in all child protection proceedings involving Indigenous children. How this legislation will affect care arrangements for Indigenous children is not fully known at this point.[91]

As of 31 March 2018, 6,698 children were in the care or custody of the MCFD in British Columbia.[92] The MCFD provides residential services that include foster care (regular, restricted (kinship), and specialized), non-foster kinship care, subsidized guardianship, contracted residential services (group homes and more institutionalized placements), as well as subsidized adoption.[93] Although publicly funded, these care arrangements are privatized to the extent that they are assigned or contracted out to private individuals or firms. They also operate at the intersection of the family and market, and therefore risk being seen either as only altruistic gestures or, conversely, as purely market transactions.[94]

While an assessment of the quality of different care arrangements is beyond the scope of this chapter, state care is clearly no guarantee of child safety. There have been injuries and deaths across all types of child placements in Canada, raising questions as to whether some children would have been safer or better off had they remained in parental care. In what follows, I will review the trends in different forms of child placement along with differences in terms of legal custody, compensation, and the provision of monitoring and supports. I will discuss whether caring labour has been recognized and adequately compensated, and will identify who bears these costs. This review underscores the high cost of institutional or contracted residential care of children and the ways in which such costs are reduced or contained through family-based care, provided largely by women.

Contracted Residential Services

In 2018, a total of 1,148 children or youth spent time in contracted residential facilities in British Columbia.[95] According to a 2019 report of the BC Auditor General, these placements were generally seen as appropriate for children and youth with special needs, a history of trauma or cognitive-behavioural challenges, or mental health issues, or for those at risk of self-harm or suicide. The placements were intended to provide more structured and specialized care than was available through the foster care system.[96]

As of January 2019, contracted residential service providers included thirty nonprofit and sixty-three for-profit organizations.[97] Although facilities providing care to three or more children and youth must be licensed by health authorities[98] and residential services appear to be subject to extensive standards,[99] the Auditor General found that the standards were dated and did not define clearly the quality of service or the required skills, and that training for staff was not regularly monitored.[100] In 2017, the Representative for Children and Youth described staffed residential care homes (or group homes) generally as rental homes in which children were looked after by a team of staff members who rotated through the residence and were paid on a per diem basis. Its report stated that "[m]any of these homes operate on a 'contractor' business model in which the agency has no employees, but contracts out casework to individual caregivers,"[101] raising issues as to the impact of the profit incentive on accountability, family reunification, and children's well-being.[102] This report was issued in response to the death of a Métis youth who had been placed in the care of a for-profit residential agency for seven years, with paid caregivers who had no meaningful connection to him or his culture. The Representative noted flagrant discrepancies between the prescribed standards and the care provided, since the conditions of care were never adequately or consistently monitored.

The province's Residential Service Standards set out a standardized approach to determining the price of staffed residential services.[103] Allowable costs include wages and benefits, program costs (food, transportation, phones, training), facility costs, client support costs (clothing, recreation, education, etc.), and other administrative costs. Job categories consist of night workers, clinical counsellors, behavioural therapists and interventionists, resident nurses, and activity workers. These job categories and costs highlight the broad range of services that have been traditionally provided by mothers. The BC Auditor General noted that staff "receive low pay for difficult work"[104] but also found that contracted residential services ended up being more costly than foster care, accounting in 2017–18 for 17.8 percent of the bed days purchased (units measuring the number of spaces purchased within contracted and foster residential services) and 61 percent ($151.5 million) of the total cost. Foster caregivers, by contrast, provided 82 percent of the bed days purchased, at 39 percent ($97.6 million) of that cost.[105]

Foster Care

Foster care is the most common type of placement for children under the guardianship of the BC Ministry.[106] When introduced in Ontario, foster care was believed more likely to lower the risk of disease, allow for more individualized care, and better integrate children in communities.[107]

However, the placement of children in private families also increased the vulnerability of children to abuse, distanced them to a greater extent from their parents, and, for Indigenous children in particular, exposed them to racism and cultural dislocation.[108]

According to Veronica Strong-Boag, social welfare authorities initially believed that women would step up and provide foster care without financial support. She documented how the caring labour of foster mothers has been both expected and undervalued, in part because cash was seen as a "contaminant" and inconsistent with "codes of maternal altruism."[109] Surveys of the motivations of foster caregivers consistently emphasize altruism, and participants in such surveys are overwhelmingly women.[110] All of this aligns with an ideology of motherhood and the notion that women should naturally provide nurture in a family setting. Foster care has generally been provided by women in working-class households, but Indigenous and racialized women, most often kin, have increasingly been recruited.

Traditionally, foster care has also replicated the nuclear model of family, with a full-time female caregiver and a male primary breadwinner.[111] The BC Ministry's website now notes that "[f]oster caregivers are not expected to give up their employment in order to care for children. Providing foster care is not a job – families choose to foster because of a concern for children and desire to contribute to their community."[112] This effort to appeal to dual-earner households reflects the above-noted emphasis on altruism and likely obscures or minimizes the extensive demands of caring labour, given the needs of traumatized children.[113]

Foster caregivers must meet residential space requirements and pass criminal, child abuse, or protection history checks as well as annual reviews. Additionally, they are expected to provide a "level of service" that "will ensure that children and youth in care receive services of the highest possible quality."[114] Standards include requirements to comply with rules; facilitate periodic visits between the child, social workers, and family members; keep records; practise safe child-management; and provide caring support, educational support, leisure activities, nutrition, health care, and a safe environment. Despite these substantial requirements, the basic family care rate (for regular and restricted care) does not nominally include compensation for caring labour.[115] According to the provincial *Foster Care Handbook*, this rate is intended to reimburse foster caregivers for direct expenditures such as the child's share of the cost of food, household expenses, transportation, health and personal care items, outings, clothing, equipment, a child's personal allowance, babysitting when the caregiver is away, gifts and activities, and education.[116] Problematically, caregiving labour here is not recognized as a service or as labour; however, caregivers can benefit to the extent that their compensation is not taxable nor must it be reported as income for the purposes of eligibility for social assistance.[117]

Foster caregivers caring for more than one child can also benefit to some degree from economies of scale;[118] nonetheless, the material rewards for foster care have "regularly been meagre."[119] Foster caregivers have complained of the off-loading of child expenses over time and of the failure to keep up with inflation, particularly the cost of housing in some areas of British Columbia.[120] The basic foster care rate in British Columbia had not been increased between 2009 and 2019, when the New Democratic government increased the monthly rate by about $190 (to $994.82 for children under twelve years of age and $1099.12 for children from twelve to eighteen).[121] This means that inflationary costs for over a decade were not covered and that a substantial increase in the Canada Child Benefit in 2016 paid by the federal government to the MCFD under the *Children's Special Allowances Act*[122] had not been passed on to directly benefit children in foster care.[123] Foster caregivers may be able to access Ministry supports such as respite care and resource workers, but they lack pension, health, and disability benefits. Most contracts are also short-term, offering no long-term financial stability.[124] The invisibility of their caring labour likely contributes to a perception that foster caregivers are mere volunteers or babysitters and to a lack of respect for their knowledge and skills.[125]

Not surprisingly, foster care seems to be in short supply.[126] Chronic shortages have been variously attributed to a decline in the availability of full-time homemakers (women), to the greater demands of care due to an increase in children identified as having special needs, to low pay in light of these demands, and to intrusive state supervision.[127]

Kinship Care

Available reports suggest that, over the past two to three decades, the use of foster care has declined and kinship care has increased.[128] Initial concerns regarding safety as a result of intergenerational abuse or a lack of supervision and exposure to birth parents appear to have been largely addressed by screening, regular planning sessions, and mandated safety checks. Empirical research suggests that kin placements can increase stability for children and reduce the overall number of placements children experience.[129] Placements with relatives or those having an emotional connection to children can also help to preserve cultural identity and reduce trauma, particularly for children in those Indigenous or other communities whose cultural norms favour extended conceptions of family.[130]

Increased placements with kin respond as well to the shortage of non-kin foster caregivers and fiscal pressures to contain costs. According to Strong-Boag, grandmothers and aunts have generally been at the forefront of kinship care but have "routinely received the lowest level of compensation."[131] In British Columbia, children can be placed under the Extended Family Program with persons who have been given care of the child by a parent and who have an established relationship with the child or a cultural or traditional responsibility for the child.[132] Post-apprehension, children may alternatively be placed in kinship (restricted) foster care or with other non-parents in out-of-care arrangements on an interim, temporary, or permanent basis.[133] If placed out-of-care on an interim or temporary basis, custody will still be subject to supervision under terms recommended by the director, which may include the right of workers to visits and to remove the child if the terms are not complied with.[134] Such care providers are paid at the same rate as foster caregivers, but coverage of medical, dental, and optical services for children is subject to the approval of the director.

Where a director applies for and obtains a permanent transfer of custody in favour of a non-parent, the latter becomes a guardian whose status is no longer enforceable under the *CFCSA* but rather under the *FLA*.[135] As guardians, they continue to receive maintenance payments equivalent to the foster care rate until the child is nineteen, but they themselves will be responsible for medical, dental, and optical costs unless they qualify, as with other parents, for additional subsidies or can arrange with the Ministry to meet the unique needs of a child or address extenuating circumstances.[136]

The Extended Family Program (EFP) is intended for parents who are temporarily unable to care for their children but wish to retain guardianship and work toward reunification.[137] Before April 2019, caregivers under the

EFP were paid $554.27 (for children under twelve) and $625 (for children twelve and over) per month, compared to $803.82 and $909.95, respectively, for foster caregivers or others having out-of-care placements. Since April 2019, all kinship caregivers are being paid the same basic family care rate as foster caregivers,[138] which, in the case of the EFP, amounts to an increase of 75 percent. Caregivers under the EFP, unlike foster and other out-of-home caregivers, also remain eligible for the Canada Child Benefit or the Child Disability Benefit and may receive additional medical, optical, and other supplementary benefits.[139] According to budget documents, these changes were intended to respond to the recommendations of Grand Chief Ed John, who found that differential payments to kin reflected a policy bias against permanency options for Indigenous children.[140] The changes can render the EFP the most financially supported placement option in British Columbia; however, the agreements between the Ministry and care providers must be reviewed every six months. As of March 2019, only 440 children or youth had been placed in the EFP, compared to 6,263 placed in the care of the Ministry.[141]

As with foster caregivers, initial resistance to compensation for kin care providers was linked to notions of caregiving as a private responsibility.[142] There were also concerns that payment would provide parents with an incentive to transfer care to kin and attract families into the child protection system.[143] While the United States Supreme Court in *Miller v Youakim* has required that kinship foster caregivers receive the same compensation as non-kin foster caregivers,[144] there is still a lingering expectation that biological relatives should be caring for children without the same level of support given to foster caregivers.[145] Research in the United States subsequently established that subsidized guardianship for kin "significantly elevated permanency rates above the level that probably would have been attained if only subsidized adoption were available."[146] Subsidized guardianship also reduced costs compared to formal foster care but did so largely by reducing administrative costs through file closure.[147]

To the extent that file closure resulted in reduced supports, this outcome is consistent with findings in both Canada and the United States that kin generally receive less training, less supervision and information, and fewer services than foster caregivers.[148] The low numbers in formal kinship care, particularly in the EFP, also suggest that kin care providers are either not being fully informed of existing supports or are afraid to ask for supports when agreements are negotiated, given a distrust of state agencies.[149] Kin are in fact likely to need *more* supports and services than foster caregivers; they tend to be older, more likely to live in poverty and be in poor health, and less likely to have prepared for a caregiving role.[150] Negotiating a relationship with birth parents can also be challenging; tensions with birth parents can reduce the chances of reunification, but close relationships can raise concerns about inadequate supervision. Kin are less likely to want to adopt, but some research suggests that children in kinship care, as opposed to foster care, are less likely to be reunified with parents.[151] According to Callahan et al, "grandparents and their grandchildren [have been required to] squeeze themselves into a template, the nuclear family, which hardly matches their reality."[152]

Subsidized Adoption

Where parents are unable to resume care of a child, adoption has been promoted as a way of providing a child with a sense of belonging and lifelong security, a "forever family." Adoption is a particularly attractive option for state agencies in neoliberal times, as it can potentially shift the entire cost of care onto private individuals. Under the *Adoption Act,*[153] parents generally cease to have any parental rights or obligations upon adoption, although existing access or contact orders may be maintained if in the best interests of a child, and custom adoptions may be recognized.[154]

Strong-Boag has claimed that, over the past century, "the youngsters who could generally be most readily integrated into new households" were most likely to be adopted, leaving older children, racialized children, those with disabilities, or who were members of sibling groups in foster care.[155] The subsidies now offered to enable adoptions in British Columbia are available where children have special placement or service needs. In such circumstances, adoptive families may qualify for monthly maintenance payments and special services. To be eligible for maintenance where adoptions maintain sibling groups or significant emotional or cultural ties, the adoptive family must meet an income and asset test, and agreements are reviewed every two years, or sooner if financial circumstances change.[156] A family with a net income of less than $80,000 a year can receive monthly maintenance payments of $806.78 for a child under twelve, and $926.53 for children twelve years and older, which is about $162 to $176 less than payments to other caregivers, or 82 to 85 percent of those payments. Adopters are eligible for the Canada Child Benefit and Child Disability Benefit but not generally for other medical or optical benefits, and importantly, all financial supports and special services end when the child turns nineteen.[157] Subsidized adoption can still be substantially less costly to the state than ongoing foster care.[158]

Conclusion

The above survey of care arrangements in one Canadian province illustrates that familial and related ideologies along with the impacts of privatization are relevant across the full spectrum of child placements and across both the family law and child protection systems. However, these ideologies and the pressure to privatize at present manifest differently and in complex ways within each system.

In the family law system, private child support obligations are still based largely on individual conduct or choice, and they generally arise from biological, intentional, or adoptive parentage or active parenting within the conjugal relationships of parents. Claims to parenting time or contact by grandparents or others having a significant relationship with a child can be obtained even in the face of parental opposition, and as such do challenge traditional nuclear definitions of family in the family law system. However, guardianship is difficult to obtain in contests with parents, and support obligations, at least in practice, are rarely imposed on extended family or non-parents. Also, while support for adult children has been extended over longer periods, support for parents by adult children is no longer a legal obligation in British Columbia. Support for caregivers, predominantly mothers, is also a private responsibility, available only if there is a spouse with property or the ability to pay. Thus, family law and ideology together work to concentrate care and financial responsibility in relation to children and caregiving within parental and associated conjugal relationships.

In the child protection system, family-based care is seen not only as the best site for the care of children, consistent with familial ideology, but also as a cost-effective option for the state. Relative to other placements, parents within this system receive the least financial or related supports for parenting, and, when children are removed, they can be liable to support alternative placements. Foster care is less costly than institutional or group care and presumed to be motivated in large part by altruism. Informal and formal placements with kin can, in many instances, generate further cost savings for the state relative to foster care and can also be naturalized through biological connection, which is how kinship has commonly been constructed in Anglo-Saxon cultures. Kinship care can clearly benefit children by helping to sustain their cultural communities and by promoting extended, if not lifelong, emotional and financial supports. However, in the absence of adequate funding commitments,[159] there is a risk that a cultural discourse around kin and community relationships is being, or could be, appropriated in the service of privatizing agendas.

Preventive supports for parents well in advance of crises could avoid or minimize the removal of children from their homes. Once children are in the child protection system, the financial burden of care is necessarily borne to a greater degree by the state, and caregivers are subject to some degree of state supervision. Commendably, the New Democratic government, which was first elected in British Columbia in 2017, has undertaken measures that have extended daycare subsidies and investments, increased child benefits and maintenance rates for care providers, and involved First Nations to a greater extent in permanency planning. The BC government has also committed to both developing a poverty-reduction strategy and implementing the *United Nations Declaration on the Rights of Indigenous Peoples*.[160] However, the shifts in forms of care that we have witnessed over the past century have still facilitated a substantial, though not a wholesale, off-loading of costs. Across all types of placements, the care of children is still performed disproportionately by women, and recognition of their labour is discursively absent across almost all forms of state care and benefits. While compensation has proven necessary to enable substitute care, the state continues to privatize the care of children but does so largely through familial ideology and the invisibility of domestic labour in a family setting. Across both the family and child protection systems, in the final analysis, costs are borne disproportionately by women and, of course, by children.

Notes

1 See Statistics Canada, "Portrait of Children's Family Life in Canada in 2016," Census in Brief (Ottawa: Minister of Industry, 2017), online (PDF): <www12.statcan.gc.ca/census-recensement/2016/as-sa/98-200-x/2016006/98-200-x2016006-eng.pdf> [Statistics Canada, "Portrait"] at 2.

2 See *ibid*. The number of children living with grandparents was 32,505 (0.6 percent); with other relatives 22,610 (0.4 percent); and with foster caregivers, 28,030 (0.5 percent). Note that data are missing for fourteen First Nations reserves and settlements, thirteen of which did not provide permission for enumeration.

3 See *ibid* at 2, note 2.

4 Consideration of detention facilities for young offenders, independent living arrangements and tertiary care or facilities operated by the state such as hospitals and mental health facilities, daycare and other forms of care contracted for by parents is beyond the scope of this chapter.

5 Judith Mosoff et al, "Intersecting Challenges: Mothers and Child Protection Law in BC" (2017) 50:2 UBC L Rev 435.

6 See e.g. Brenda Cossman, "Family Feuds: Neo-Liberal and Neo-Conservative Visions of the Reprivatization Project" in Judy Fudge & Brenda Cossman, eds, *Privatization, Law, and the Challenge of Feminism* (Toronto: University of Toronto Press, 2002) 169. Privatization is a recurring theme in this collection: see also, in different contexts, Chapter 1 by Allison A Tait, and Chapter 6 by Nicola Barker.

7 See Statistics Canada, "Portrait," *supra* note 1 at 2–3.

8 See *infra*, notes 129–30.

9 See Hester Lessard, "The Empire of the Lone Mother: Parental Rights, Child Welfare Law, and State Restructuring" (2001) 39:4 Osgoode Hall LJ 717. Demonstrating how the statutory language of family preservation in British Columbia and Ontario was belied in practice by funding cuts. See also West Coast LEAF, *Pathways in a Forest: Indigenous Guidance on Prevention-Based Child Welfare* (Vancouver, 2019) online (PDF): <http://www.westcoastleaf.org/wp-content/uploads/2021/03/West-Coast-LEAF-Pathways-in-a-Forest-web-Sept-17-2019-002-Online-Version-2021-compressed4.pdf > [LEAF].

10 Michèle Barrett & Mary McIntosh, *The Anti-Social Family* (London: Verso, 1982) at 21.

11 "Dominant ideology" has been identified as a belief system that arises from specific material conditions but appears natural and self-evident, necessary and legitimate. Ideology offers something *real*, which engages belief and is constructed and reconstructed through oppositional ideologies. See Marlee Kline, "Child Welfare Law, 'Best Interests of the Child' Ideology, and First Nations" (1992) 30:2 Osgoode Hall LJ 375 at 394 [Kline, "Child Welfare Law"].

12 Barrett & McIntosh, *supra* note 10 at 23.

13 *Ibid* at 29.

14 See Kline, "Child Welfare Law," *supra* note 11 at 390–95; Wanda Wiegers, "Child-Centred Advocacy and the Invisibility of Women in Poverty Discourse and Social Policy" in Dorothy Chunn, Susan B Boyd & Hester Lessard, eds, *Reaction and Resistance: Feminism, Law and Social Change* (Vancouver: UBC Press, 2007) 229 [Wiegers, "Child-Centred Advocacy"].

15 Barrett & McIntosh, *supra* note 10 at 34.

16 See generally Jan E Dizard & Howard Gadlin, *The Minimal Family* (Amherst: University of Massachusetts Press, 1990).

17 *Ibid* at 65.

18 See Statistics Canada, "The Rise of the Dual Earner Family with Children," Canadian Megatrends (Ottawa: Minister of Industry, 30 May 2016), online: Statistics Canada, <www150.statcan.gc.ca/n1/pub/11-630-x/11-630-x2016005-eng.htm>.

19 See *Convention on the Rights of the Child,* GA Res 44/25, UNGAOR, 44th Sess, Supp No 49, UN Doc A/44/49 (1989) art 20 [*CRC*].

20 See Susan B Boyd et al, *Autonomous Motherhood? A Socio-Legal Study of Choice and Constraint* (Toronto: University of Toronto Press, 2015) at 131, 220. At the same time, attention to domestic violence has revealed that many families are profoundly unsafe for women and children, who are its primary victims. In 2018, 79 percent of police-reported intimate partner violence victims were female; see *Family Violence in Canada: A Statistical Profile, 2018* (Ottawa: Statistics Canada, 2019), Table 2.1, online, Statistics Canada <https://www150.statcan.gc.ca/n1/pub/85-002-x/2019001/article/00018-eng.htm>.

21 See e.g. Carol Stack, *All Our Kin: Strategies for Survival in a Black Community* (New York: Basic Books, 1974) for an early work.

22 Patricia Monture, "A Vicious Circle: Child Welfare and the First Nations" (1989) 3:1 CJWL 1; *Honouring the Truth, Reconciling for the Future: Summary of the Final Report of the Trust and Reconciliation Commission of Canada* (Ottawa: Truth and Reconciliation Commission, 2015); LEAF, *supra* note 9.

23 Kline, "Child Welfare Law," *supra* note 11 at 388.

24 As of May 2016, less than 10 percent of the child population in British Coumbia was Indigenous, but approximately 60 percent of children in care in the province were Indigenous, and these children were less likely to obtain permanent placements than non-Indigenous children in care. See Office of the Premier, *Indigenous Resilience, Connectedness and Reunification – From Root Causes to Root Solutions: A Report on Indigenous Child Welfare in British Columbia*, by Grand Chief Ed John (Victoria: Ministry of Children and Family Development, 2016), online (PDF): <fns.bc.ca/wp- content/uploads/2017/01/Final-Report-of-Grand-Chief-Ed-John-re-Indig-Child-Welfare-in-BC-November- 2016.pdf> [John Report] at 11–12.

25 See Monture, *supra* note 22; Lessard, *supra* note 9; Mosoff et al, *supra* note 5; Dorothy E Roberts, "Kinship Care and the Price of State Support for Children" (2001) 76:3 Chicago-Kent L Rev 1619.

26 Boyd et al, *supra* note 20 at 167.

27 See Melissa Moyser, "Women and Paid Work," in Statistics Canada, *Women in Canada: A Gender-based Statistical Report,* Table 1 (last modified 9 March 2017) online: Statistics Canada, <www150.statcan.gc.ca/n1/en/pub/89-503-x/2015001/article/14694-eng.pdf?st=d1ifZtvR>, identifying employment rates and median monthly child-care fees. See also Kendra Milne, *High Stakes: The Impacts of Child Care on the Human Rights of Women and Children* (Vancouver: Westcoast LEAF, 2019) at 43–46, online (PDF): <www.westcoastleaf.org/wp-content/uploads/2016/07/High-Stakes-low-res-for-web.pdf>. This report highlights the relationship between a lack of affordable, high quality, and culturally appropriate child care and a heightened risk of child apprehensions.

28 Statistics Canada, "Portrait," *supra* note 1.

29 See Melissa Moyser & Amanda Burlock, "Time Use: Total Work Burden, Unpaid Work, and Leisure," Chart 1, July 30, 2018, online: Statistics Canada, <https://www150.statcan.gc.ca/n1/en/pub/89-503-x/2015001/article/54931-eng.pdf?st=KIiHv_Rx>.

30 See Lessard, *supra* note 9 at 718; Marlee Kline, "Complicating the Ideology of Motherhood: Child Welfare Law and First Nation Women" (1993) 18:2 Queen's LJ 306 [Kline, "Complicating the Ideology"]; Mosoff et al, *supra* note 5.

31 See Sharon Hays, *The Cultural Contradictions of Motherhood* (New Haven, CT: Yale University Press, 1996) at 8; Judy Fudge & Brenda Cossman, "Introduction: Privatization, Law, and the Challenge to Feminism" in Judy Fudge & Brenda Cossman, eds, *Privatization, Law and the Challenge of Feminism* (Toronto: University of Toronto Press, 2002) 3.

32 See Wiegers, *supra* note 14; Cossman, *supra* note 6 at 212. Public health messaging during the pandemic has also likely reinforced the image of the family home as a place of safety, comfort, and support.

33 See Shelley Gavigan, "Familial Ideology and the Limits of Difference" in Janine Brodie, ed, *Women and Canadian Public Policy* (Toronto: Harcourt Brace, 1996) 255; Cossman, *supra* note 6 at 170.

34 See Boyd et al, *supra* note 20 at 10–11.

35 See Wanda Wiegers, "Commodification and the Allocation of Care and Responsibility for Children" (2017) 67:2 UTLJ 206 at 218 [Wiegers, "Commodification"]. See also *An Act to Amend the Divorce Act, the Family Orders and Agreements Enforcement Assistance Act and the Garnishment, Attachment and Pension Diversion Act and to Make Consequential Amendments to Another Act*, SC 2019, c 16, which enhances information sharing between federal and provincial agencies and prioritizes family support obligations in garnishment proceedings.

36 See Monture, *supra* note 22; Kline, "Complicating the Ideology," *supra* note 30.

37 Fudge & Cossman, *supra* note 31 at 29.

38 Cossman, *supra* note 6.

39 *Ibid* at 177.

40 Barrett & McIntosh, *supra* note 10 at 23. They also noted that conservatives believed that families should turn to kin for help before looking to charity and the state (at 47).

41 Kline, "Child Welfare Law," *supra* note 11 at 395.

42 See *DA, supra* note 35, s 15.1.

43 See *Chartier v Chartier,* [1999] 1 SCR 242, 235 NR 1 [*Chartier*].

44 See *Family Law Act,* SBC 2011, c 25, s 146 [*FLA*]. The threshold for the liability of a step-parent is low, as support can be sought from a step-parent who has contributed to the support of the child for as little as one year, where the proceeding is commenced within one year of the last contribution. See *ibid,* ss 147(4), 149(3). However, the duty of a step-parent is more limited than that of biological, adoptive, and intended parents and court-appointed guardians. See *ibid,* s 147(5).

45 *Ibid,* s 146.

46 *Ibid,* s 147(3).

47 *Child, Family and Community Service Act,* RSBC 1996, c 46, s 97(1)(a) [*CFCSA*]. See e.g. *British Columbia (Director of Child, Family and Community Service) v GL and MH,* 2019 BCPC 20, where the child was in care under a s 8 agreement due to autism. Through involvement in conception, deliberative choice (as in adoption or the use of reproductive technologies), or participation in family life, parents and their conjugal partners are, in the vast majority of cases, responsible for child support.

48 The BC Law Institute found that the legislation did not provide effective relief; "parental support is an outdated concept that does not fit well with contemporary society." See British Columbia Law Institute, *Parental Support Obligation in Section 90 of the Family Relations Act* (Vancouver: BCLI, 2007) at i, online: British Columbia Law Institute, <www.bcli.org/project/parental-support-obligation-section-90-family-relations-act>.

49 *Federal Child Support Guidelines,* SOR/97-175.

50 See *DA, supra* note 35, s 15.2 for married spouses seeking a divorce. Those who are married or have lived in a marriage-like relationship for at least two years can claim spousal support and property division under the *FLA, supra* note 44, ss 3, 81–109, 160–69.

51 *Employment and Assistance Act,* SBC 2002, c 40. Note that British Columbia, unlike some provinces, exempts child-support payments when calculating the income of the family unit and its eligibility for assistance – *Employment and Assistance Regulation,* BC 226/2019, s 6; Schedule B, s 1(xiv). For a review of

maternity, parental, and caregiving leaves and pay in Canada, see Eric Tucker, Leah F Vosko & Sarah Marsden, "What We Owe Workers as a Matter of Common Humanity" (2020) 57:3 Osgoode Hall LJ 665. Low-income families may also be eligible for the Canada Workers Benefit, a refundable tax credit having a maximum annual value of $2,335 for families as of 2019.

52 Government of Canada, "Canada Child Benefit: Overview" (last modified 18 November 2019), online: Government of Canada, <www.canada.ca/en/revenue-agency/services/child-family-benefits/canada-child-benefit-overview.html>. As of July 2019, the maximum CCB payment per annum was $6,639 per child under six and $5,602 per child six to seventeen years of age. Other child-related benefits have included a BC early childhood tax benefit of up to $55 monthly per child under six for eligible families (replaced and enhanced in 2020 by a child opportunity benefit); and modest federal contributions for those who can afford to save for their child's post-secondary training or education through a Registered Education Savings Plan and the Canada Learning Bond (for low-income families). Both the CCB and CDB are indexed to inflation.

53 See Statistics Canada, "Low Income Statistics by Age, Sex and Economic Family Type" (last modified 22 November 2019), online: Statistics Canada, <www150.statcan.gc.ca/t1/tbl1/en/tv.action?pid=1110013501&pickMembers%5B0%5D=1.13>.

54 See LEAF, *supra* note 9 at 30, 41. See also Mark E Courtney, "The Costs of Child Protection in the Context of Welfare Reform" (1998) 8:1 The Future of Children 88 at 100, discussing the "competing demands" of workfare programs in the welfare system and the protection of children in the child protection system. Note that the New Democratic government in British Columbia has committed to developing a poverty-reduction strategy to reduce child poverty by 50 percent in five years. See British Columbia, *Together BC: British Columbia's Poverty Reduction Strategy* (Victoria: Government of British Columbia, 2019), online (PDF): <www2.gov.bc.ca/assets/gov/british-columbians-our-governments/initiatives-plans-strategies/poverty-reduction-strategy/togetherbc.pdf>. See also *Poverty Reduction Strategy Act*, SBC 2018, c 40 [*Poverty Reduction Strategy Act*]. The New Democratic government also introduced an Affordable Child Care Benefit in 2018 that allows for child-care subsidies up to an annual income of $110,000 and beyond in some cases. See British Columbia, "Affordable Child Care Benefit," online: British Columbia, <www2.gov.bc.ca/gov/content/family-social-supports/caring-for-young-children/child-care-funding/child-care-benefit>.

55 See *DA*, *supra* note 35, s 16(5), s 2(1), s 16(3). The amendments referenced in the text were passed prior to January 2020 but did not take effect until 1 March 2021.

56 See e.g. *Arnink v Arnink,* [1999] BCJ No 2712, [1999] 2 RFL (5th) 24.

57 *Chartier, supra* note 43.

58 *DA, supra* note 35, s 16(5).

59 *FLA, supra* note 44, s 40. Parents who have never resided with a child are default guardians only if agreed to by all guardians, if they have regularly cared for a child, or in some circumstances of assisted reproduction (at s 39).

60 See *ibid,* s 50. The consent of a child twelve years old and over is required. See *ibid* at s 51(4). An affidavit must also be signed identifying the relationship with the child, the plan of care, any incidents of family violence, any prior proceedings involving the children, and up-to-date checks with the protection order registry and criminal records. See *ibid,* s 51; *Provincial Court (Family) Rules,* BC Reg 417/98, rule 18.1; *Supreme Court Family Rules,* BC Reg 169/2009, rule 15–2.1.

61 *CFCSA, supra* note 47; *FLA, supra* note 44 at ss 50–51; *WN v CG,* 2012 BCCA 149; Wanda Wiegers, "Child Placement and the Legal Claims of Foster Caregivers" (2019) 52:2 UBC L Rev 631 [Wiegers, "Child Placement"]. A non-parent who obtains a transfer of permanent custody under the *CFSA* can be deemed a guardian, *FLA,* supra note 44, s 51(5); *CFSA,* supra note 47, ss 54.01(5), 54.1.

62 *FLA, supra* note 44, ss 58, 59. Under *FLA* s 59(4), access orders under ss 54.2(2.1) or (3) under the *CFCSA* are deemed contact orders under the *FLA.*

63 *FLA, supra* note 44, s 37(1); *DA,* supra note 35, s 16(1).

64 *DA, supra* note 35, s 16(3)(f); *FLA, supra* note 44, ss 37(2), 41(e), 209 (Treaty First Nation children). See e.g. *Pasco v Pasco,* 2015 BCSC 1412 at para 157.

65 *King v Low,* [1985] 1 SCR 87, 16 DLR (4th) 576 at para 27, McIntyre J. See also *British Columbia Birth Registration No 99–00733 (Re),* 2000 BCCA 109, finding that, where all else is equal, biology can be a decisive factor.

66 *Chera v Chera,* 2008 BCCA 374 at para 55, [2008] BCJ No 1807, Smith JA.

67 See e.g. *Racine v Woods,* [1983] 2 SCR 173, [1983] SCJ No. 71; Monture, *supra* note 22 at 199–202; and see Wiegers, "Child Placement," *supra* note 61.

68 See e.g. *DB v BB,* 2017 BCPC 359. The three-year-old child had always lived in the grandmother's home, but the court found that she could not fully meet the child's need for psychological and emotional security, given her troubled relationship with the child's mother. If both parents and grandparents meet a best-interests test, the parent should be preferred. See also *PGW v PFW and CVR,* 2017 BCPC 36, where guardianship was given to the father over the maternal grandmother, who had cared for the children for many years. See also *FMAC v CTF,* 2019 BCPC 19 (parents also retained guardianship).

69 See e.g. *DA, supra* note 35, s 16(5); *FLA, supra* note 44, s 41(e).

70 *FLA, supra* note 44, s 51, s.37; *DD v AC,* 2017 BCPC 5; *Fawcett v Read,* 2016 BCSC 310; *Chapman v Chapman,* [1993] BCJ No 316 (QL), [1993] WDFL 412.

71 Marilyn Callahan et al, "Catch as Catch Can: Grandmothers Raising Their Grandchildren and Kinship Care Policies" (2004) 54 Can Rev Social Policy 58. There were 55,115 children in formal and informal kinship care in Canada in 2016. See Statistics Canada, "Portrait," *supra* note 1. The BC Parents' Support Services Society estimates that there are 13,000 children in formal and informal kinship care in British Columbia. See "Update: 2019 BC Budget – What Does It Mean for Kinship Care Families?" online: Parent Support Services Society of BC <www.parentsupportbc.ca/2019-bc-budget-what-does-it-mean-for-kinship-care-families/>. The number of children in informal kinship care is unknown.

72 See also Chapter 1 by Allison A Tait in this collection.

73 See discussion below of benefits available through the child protection system.

74 Wiegers, "Commodification," *supra* note 35 at 234–39. See Justine Hunter, "Marina Miller Has Raised Five Siblings with a Little Help from Strangers, but Precious Little from Government," *Globe and Mail* (15 November 2019), online: <www.theglobeandmail.com/canada/british-columbia/article-marina-miller-has-raised-five-siblings-with-a-little-help-from/> [Hunter]. The article recounts the story of Marina Miller, who, as the legal guardian of her five siblings, did not qualify for additional financial assistance. BC Premier Horgan promised to review the Ministry's policies in this respect.

75 According to the MCFD, neglect was the basis for protective orders in 72.2 percent of all cases as of December 2018. See British Columbia, Ministry of Children and Family Development, "Permanency for Children and Youth in Care: Case Data and Trends" (Victoria: MCFD, 2018), online: British Columbia, <mcfd.gov.bc.ca/reporting/services/child-protection/permanency-for-children-and-youth/case-data-and-trends>; John Report, *supra* note 24 at 32.

76 *First Nations Child and Family Caring Society of Canada v Attorney General of Canada (Minister of Indian Affairs and Northern Development)*, 2016 CHRT 2 [*Caring Society*].

77 *CFCSA, supra* note 47, ss 5, 8. Under supervision orders if recommended by the director, see *ibid*, s 41.1. A director must consider whether less disruptive measures can protect a child prior to apprehension unless the child is in immediate danger, see *ibid* at s 30.

78 Brielle Morgan et al, "BC Supporting Foster Parents Instead of Supporting Struggling Families, Experts Say," *Mission City Record* (29 June 2019), online: <www.missioncityrecord.com/news/b-c-paying-foster-parents-instead-of-supporting-struggling-families-experts-say/>. Morgan et al reported that the MCFD could not provide a breakdown of expenditures on family preservation versus children and youth in care. See LEAF, *supra* note 9 at 5, identifying "significant gaps in the types of services" needed and "systemic and individual barriers to accessing" existing services. See also generally Leslie T Foster & Brian Wharf,

People, Politics, and Child Welfare in British Columbia (Vancouver: UBC Press, 2007).

79 Roberts, *supra* note 25 at 1640, 1633–34.

80 *CFCSA, supra* note 47, ss 30–41, 42.2(7)(c), 49(5), 54.01(5).

81 See *ibid,* s 71(1).

82 See *ibid,* s 70, including rights to be fed, clothed, nurtured, consulted, and informed of rights and procedures for enforcing rights to privacy. Children age twelve and over specifically have a right to have their views with respect to a plan of care taken into account and rights to notice of various proceedings under the *CFCSA*.

83 See *ibid,* s 93.1; *Child, Family and Community Service Regulation,* BC Reg 527/95, s 15(1) [*CFCS Reg*].

84 See *CFCSA, supra* note 47, s 12.3; *CFCS Reg, supra* note 83, ss 8.3, 8.4.

85 See Veronica Strong-Boag, *Fostering Nation? Canada Confronts Its History of Childhood Disadvantage* (Waterloo, ON: Wilfrid Laurier University Press, 2011).

86 See e.g. *CRC, supra* note 19, art 20. The *CRC* obligates states to provide alternative care for a child, including foster placement, adoption, or "if necessary placement in suitable institutions for the care of children" and with "due regard" to the "desirability of continuity in a child's upbringing and to the child's ethnic, religious, cultural and linguistic background." See also Bruce MacLaurin & Nicholas Bala, "Children in Care" in Nicholas Bala et al, eds, *Canadian Child Welfare Law: Children, Families and the State*, 2nd ed (Toronto: Thompson Educational Publishing, 2004) 111 at 122–29.

87 See MacLaurin & Bala, *supra* note 86 at 122; Rob Geen, "The Evolution of Kinship Care Policy and Practice" (2004) 14:1 Future Children 130.

88 See *CFCSA, supra* note 47, s 71(2); see also ss 2(e), 3(c), 3(e), 4(e).

89 See *ibid,* ss 71(3), 2(b.1), 2(f), 3(b), 3(c.1), 4(2).

90 See *ibid,* ss 8(3), 33.1, 34, 36(2.1), 28(1), 39(1), 48(1.1), 49(2), 50(4), 50.01, 54.01(3), 54.1(2), 60(1).

91 *An Act respecting First Nation, Inuit and Metis Children, Youth and Families,* SC 2019, c 24 [*First Nation, Inuit and Metis*]. Sections 16 and 17 prioritize placements and promote ongoing attachments with a child's extended family, community, and siblings if consistent with the best interests of the child.

92 See Office of the Auditor General of British Columbia, Oversight of Contracted Residential Services for Children and Youth in Care (Report), by Carol Bellringer (Victoria: OAGBC, 2019), online (PDF): <www.bcauditor.com/sites/default/files/publications/reports/OAGBC_OCRS_RPT.pdf> [BC Auditor General] at 7.

93 See *ibid* at 18.

94 See Wiegers, "Commodification," *supra* note 35.

95 See BC Auditor General, *supra* note 92 at 22.

96 See *ibid* at 21–23; Mélanie Doucet, Élodie Marion & Nico Trocmé, *Group Homes and Residential Treatment Placements in Child Welfare: Analyzing the 2008 Canadian Incidence Study of Reported Child Abuse and Neglect* (Can Child Welfare Research, 2018), online (PDF): <https://cwrp.ca/sites/default/files/publications/Group%20Home%20And%20Residential%20Treatment%20Placements%20In%20Child%20Welfare%20Analyzing%20The%202008%20Canadian%20Incidence%20Study%20Of%20Reported%20Child%20Abuse%20And%20Neglect_0.pdf> [Doucet, Marion & Trocmé].

97 See BC Auditor General, *supra* note 92 at 21.

98 See *Community Care and Assisted Living Act,* SBC 2002, c 75.

99 See British Columbia, Ministry of Children and Family Development, "Standards for Staffed Children's Residential Services: Provided under the Child, Family and Community Service Act 1998" (Victoria: MCFD, revised April 2019) [Residential Services Standards].

100 See BC Auditor General, *supra* note 92 at 40–47.

101 Representative for Children and Youth, *Broken Promises: Alex's Story* (Victoria: RCY, February 2017) [*Alex's Story*] at 19.

102 See Susan Vivian Mangold, "Protection, Privatization, and Profit in the Foster Care System" (1999) 60:4 Ohio St LJ 1295.

103 Residential Services Standards, *supra* note 99.

104 BC Auditor General, *supra* note 92 at 37.

105 *Ibid* at 22.

106 See Representative for Children and Youth, *Annual Report 2018–2019 and Service Plan 2019/20 to 2021/22* (Victoria: RCY, 2019) [RCY Annual Report] at 41, online (PDF): <https://rcybc.ca/wp-content/uploads/2019/10/rcy-arsp-2018-2019_final.pdf>.

107 See Xiaobei Chen, *Tending the Gardens of Citizenship: Child Saving in Toronto 1880s–1920s* (Toronto: University of Toronto Press, 2005) at 119–23.

108 *Ibid* at 123, 127.

109 Strong-Boag, *supra* note 85 at 162.

110 *Ibid* at 157.

111 Rob Twigg, "Passion for Those Who Care: What Foster Carers Need" in Sharon MacKay, Don Fuchs & Ivan Brown, eds, *Passion for Action in Child and Family Services: Voices from the Prairies* (Regina: Canadian Plains Research Center, 2009) 165 at 177–80; Strong-Boag, *supra* note 85 at 147–68, 159, 163.

112 Government of British Columbia, "Foster Care Payments in BC," online: British Columbia, <www2.gov.bc.ca/gov/content/family-social-supports/fostering/for-current-foster-parents/foster-care-payment>.

113 Child-care subsidies may be available to foster caregivers if needed to supplement the care provided or if recommended by the child's worker. See British Columbia, Ministry of Child and Family Development, *Resource Work Policies, Chapter 8* (Victoria: MCFD, 2019), online (PDF): <www2.gov.bc.ca/assets/gov/family-and-social-supports/foster-parenting/resource_work_policies.pdf> [Resource Work Policies] at 58–59.

114 British Columbia, Ministry of Children and Family Development, *Standards for Foster Homes* (Victoria: MCFD, 2019), online (PDF): <www2.gov.bc.ca/assets/gov/family-and-social-supports/foster-parenting/standards_foster_homes.pdf>.

115 See also Hannah Roman, "Foster Parenting as Work" (2016) 27:2 Yale JL & Feminism 179. Specialized foster care includes a "service payment" for children with complex needs, although this payment is also not considered income for income tax or income assistance purposes.

116 See British Columbia, Ministry of Children and Family Development, *Foster Family Handbook*, 5th ed (Victoria: MCFD, 1997) at 43–44.

117 See *Employment and Assistance Regulation*, BC Reg 263/2002. Section 11 exempts foster care payments and payments to kin under the *CFCSA*.

118 Roman, *supra* note 115 at 213.

119 Strong-Boag, *supra* note 85 at 203; Twigg, *supra* note 111 at 177.

120 According to a survey in 2017, 75 percent of 730 respondents had had to pay out of pocket for a health-related expense, and 93 percent for a non-health-related expense; the top priority for foster caregivers was increased monthly care rates. Heather Lightfoot & Jasmine Wu, *Final Report: Do the Current Care Rates Reflect the True Costs of Meeting the Needs of Foster Children in British Columbia?* (2017), on file with the author.

121 See British Columbia, Ministry of Children and Family Development, "Foster Child Placement with a Person Other Than the Parent in BC" (Victoria: MCFD, 2019), online (PDF): <www2.gov.bc.ca/assets/gov/family-and-social-supports/foster-parenting/maintenance_rate_increases_by_care_category.pdf>.

122 *Children's Special Allowances Act*, SC 1992, c 48.

123 The 2019 increase in the Canada Child Benefit as a result of indexation was passed on to caregivers, amounting to an increase of about $12 monthly.

124 Interview with a representative of the BC Federation of Foster Parent Associations, 29 July 2019 [BCFFPA Interview].

125 See Twigg, *supra* note 111 at 176.

126 BC Auditor General, *supra* note 92 at 23, 36.

127 Strong-Boag, *supra* note 85 at 164–71.

128 As of 31 March 2019, 6,263 children were in care in British Columbia, 1,214 were in the Extended Family Program and its predecessor, Children in the Home of a Relative, and 736 in the out-of-care options. See RCY Annual Report, *supra* note 106 at 41.

129 See Geen, *supra* note 87 at 143. In a meta-analysis of studies comparing outcomes in foster care and kinship care, children in the latter were found to experience fewer behavioural and mental health disorders, fewer placement moves, and higher levels of well-being. See Mark Winokur, Amy Holtan & Keri Batchelder, "Systematic Review of Kinship Care Effects on Safety, Permanency, and Well-Being Outcomes" (2018) 28:1 Research on Social Work Practice 19.

130 See e.g. Royal Commission on Aboriginal Peoples, *Report of the Royal Commission on Aboriginal Peoples, vol 3: Gathering Strength* (Ottawa, 1996) at 10–11; Pamela Gough, *Kinship Care*, CECW Information Sheet no 42E (University of Toronto Faculty of Social Work, 2006) at 3.

131 Strong-Boag, *supra* note 85 at 109. See also Richard Sullivan, Margo Nelson & Amanda Oliver, "Kinship Care in an Era of Cost Containment" (2015) 72/73 Can Rev Social Policy 95.

132 See *CFCSA, supra* note 47, Ss 2(e), 2(f), 8. Guardianship remains with the parents, but some parental responsibilities are transferred to the care provider under s 8 agreements. Family-conferencing provisions may also include extended family in developing a plan of care if parents are unavailable. See also *ibid*, ss 20(2), 21. The Child Out of the Parental Home (on-reserve) and Child in the Home of a Relative programs were discontinued in 2010, but recipients of these programs remain eligible for grandfathered benefits (which are less than that paid under the EFP) and may transition to the EFP.

133 See *CFCSA, supra* note 47, s 35(2)(d) (interim custody), s 41(1)(b) (temporary), s 54.01 (permanent transfer of custody before a continuing custody order), s 54.1 (permanent transfer after a continuing custody order) for out-of-care options. See also *ibid* s 54 (cancellation of a continuing custody order).

134 *Ibid*, s 41.1.

135 See *ibid*, s 54.2. Note that only the director can apply for a transfer of custody under ss 54.01 and 54.1. For further requirements for a permanent transfer of custody before a continuing custody order, see *ibid*, s 54.01(5)–(7). If in the child's best interests, a court may dispense with a six-month residency requirement.

136 Government of British Columbia, "Permanent Transfer of Custody of a Child to Someone Familiar in BC," online: British Columbia, <www2.gov.bc.ca/gov/

content/family-social-supports/fostering/temporary-permanent-care-options/permanent-transfer-of-custody-to-someone-familiar> and see *CFCSA, supra* note 47 at s 5. Kin caregivers under the EFP and under interim, temporary, and permanent orders are eligible for child-care subsidies and surcharges on a non-income-tested basis.

137 *CFCSA, supra* note 47, s 8. Placement within the EFP requires consent of the child's parent, prior criminal record or Ministry involvement checks, three written references, a home visit, and an assessment. Relatives with legal guardianship under the FLA are not eligible. See Government of British Columbia, "Foster Child Placement with a Person Other Than the Parent in BC: Extended Family Program," online: British Columbia, <www2.gov.bc.ca/gov/content/family-social-supports/fostering/temporary-permanent-care-options/placement-with-a-person-other-than-the-parent> [EFP].

138 British Columbia, Ministry of Children and Family Development, "Maintenance Rate Increases by Care Category," online (PDF): <www2.gov.bc.ca/assets/gov/family-and-social-supports/foster-parenting/maintenance_rate_increases_by_care_category.pdf>.

139 British Columbia, Ministry of Children and Family Development, *Out of Care Policies: Chapter 4* (April 2020) [*Out-of-Care Policies*]. Maintenance payments will count as income in assessing the child benefits. Parents can be required to contribute financially toward the child's care under the EFP and under interim or temporary out-of-care placements.

140 *Ibid.* See also John Report, *supra* note 24 at 118–19, 129.

141 RCY Annual Report, *supra* note 106 at 41. Note that 736 children were in other out-of-care options, and 774 were still in the Child in the Home of a Relative program, where rates have not increased. EFP placements are generally limited to twelve to twenty-four months, depending on the age of the child, but they may be extended under customary care arrangements for Indigenous children with a supervisor's approval. See *Out-of-Care Policies, supra* note 139 at 27.

142 Geen, *supra* note 87 at 141.

143 *Ibid.* See also Roberts, *supra* note 25.

144 *Miller v Youakim,* 440 US 125 (1979).

145 See generally Ramona Denby, *Kinship Care: Increasing Child Well-Being through Practice, Policy and Research* (New York: Springer, 2015).

146 Mark Testa, "Subsidized Guardianship: Testing an Idea Whose Time Has Finally Come" (2002) 26:3 Social Work Research 145 at 146, 157.

147 See *ibid.* In this study, adoption had to be ruled out as a possibility before private guardianship was available (to address the concern that guardianship would reduce adoptions), and children had to have been in care for two years.

148 See Geen, *supra* note 87 at 137, 139; Christine Schwartz et al, "When Relatives Are the Best Source" (2014) 8:3 Children's Mental Health Research Q 3 at 5; Susan Burke & Glen G Schmidt, "Kinship Care in Northern British Columbia" (2009) 88:6 Child Welfare 127; Representative for Children and Youth, *BC Adoption and Permanency Options Update* (Victoria: RCY, August 2019) at 9 [RCY, *Permanency Options*]. Unlike foster caregivers, kinship caregivers are not assigned a resource worker: BCFFPA Interview, *supra* note 124.

149 LEAF, *supra* note 9 at 49–51, 79, indicating workers lack the time to create plans and explore options for families. Worker shortages, heavy caseloads, problems with recruitment, retention, and supervision, along with budgetary constraints and a culture of cost containment within the Ministry can contribute to these outcomes. See Representative of Children and Youth, *The Thin Front Line: MCFD Staffing Crunch Leaves Social Sorkers Overburdened, BC Children Under-protected*, by Mary Ellen Turpel-Lafond (October 2015), online (PDF): <rcybc.ca/wp-content/uploads/2019/05/rcy-thethinfrontline-oct2015-final_revised.pdf>; Sullivan, Nelson & Oliver, *supra* note 131.

150 See Schwartz et al, *supra* note 148 at 5; Roberts, *supra* note 25 at 1634.

151 See Geen, *supra* note 87 at 141; Roberts, *supra* note 25 at 1634–5; Kimberly Brisebois & Shawna J Lee, "Foster and Kinship Care: An Examination of the Legislation That Aims to Improve Permanency and Continuity of Care in Ontario" (2012) 3:1 Can J Humanities & Social Sciences 101. See also Winokur, Holtan & Batchelder, *supra* note 129, finding similar reunification rates.

152 Callahan et al, *supra* note 71 at 74–5.

153 *Adoption Act*, RSBC 1996, c 5, ss 37(1), 38, 46.

154 While the *Act* recognizes custom adoptions, that is, adoptions "effected by the custom of an Indian band or aboriginal community" (*ibid*, s 46), the Ministry was unable to verify that any such adoptions had taken place over the twenty years the legislation has been in effect. See RCY, *Permanency Options*, *supra* note 148 at 8.

155 Strong-Boag, *supra* note 85 at 84, 81.

156 Government of British Columbia, "Post-Adoption Assistance Program," online: British Columbia, <www2.gov.bc.ca/gov/content/life-events/birth-adoption/adoptions/how-to-adopt-a-child/adopt-from-foster-care/post-adoption-assistance-program> ["Post-Adoption"]. The gross assets of families must not exceed $300,000 CAD, excluding the primary residence, vehicle, pensions, and RRSPs, and an adoption social worker must verify that the child's situation requires financial assistance. See also *Adoption Regulation*, BC Reg 291/96, ss 26–28.

157 "Post-Adoption," *supra* note 156. At higher incomes, benefits will decrease gradually based on the number of dependent children in the family.

158 See Ontario Ministry of Children, Community and Social Services, "A Message from the Expert Panel on Infertility and Adoption" (August 2009), online: Ontario, <www.children.gov.on.ca/htdocs/English/professionals/infertility/index.aspx>.

159 See e.g. *First Nation, Inuit and Metis*, *supra* note 91. See also Naiomi Walquan Metallic, Hadley Friedland & Sarah Morales, "Promise and Pitfalls of C-92: An Act respecting First Nations, Inuit, and Metis Children, Youth and Families " (Toronto: Yellowhead Institute, 2019) at 8–9, online (PDF): <yellowheadinstitute.org/wp-content/uploads/2019/07/the-promise-and-pitfalls-of-c-92-report.pdf>.

160 *Poverty Reduction Strategy Act*, *supra* note 54; *Declaration on the Rights of Indigenous Peoples Act*, SBC 2019, c 44.

6

Family, Gender, and the Public/Private Divide in the United Kingdom's *Human Rights Act 1998*

Nicola Barker

The public/private divide has long been a focus of feminist scholarship (and indeed is a prevalent theme in this book: see the chapters by Allison Tait, Brenda Cossman, and Rachel Treloar).[1] By the late 1990s, laws and policies had been introduced to protect women's equal participation in the workplace and recognize the economic penalties incurred by women as a result of the gendered division of household labour.[2] However, the division of labour in both the (heterosexual) family and paid labour force remained "largely intact" even for professional women, despite law reforms,[3] and gender inequality continued to be exacerbated by intersecting inequalities of race, class, disability, and sexuality.[4] At the same time, the privatization of public services meant that "fundamental changes" were occurring in terms of the public/private boundary between state and market.[5]

In the past ten years, during which the government of the United Kingdom has been ideologically driven toward state austerity and privatization, there has been a dramatic increase in charitable food banks filling the (deliberately created) gaps in state welfare provision,[6] individual families providing social care in the absence of accessible state provision,[7] and private companies delivering public services, including services that have historically been firmly in the public sector, such as health care and probation services.[8] The boundary between public and private spheres has continued to shift decisively in the direction of enlarging the *private* sphere at the expense of the *public*. This shift, whether it is toward the private family realm or the private sector, has a disproportionate impact on women, whose relatively secure and unionized public-sector jobs are transferred to the private sector,[9] and who perform the vast majority of unrecognized caretaking labour within the family when the state reduces its support.[10] As a result, the combination of privatization and the politics of austerity has impacted women particularly hard. Black and minority ethnic (BME) women have been "disproportionately disadvantaged," due to being more likely than white women to be employed in the public sector or subcontracted to the state via private-sector organizations, as well as more likely to have gendered caring responsibilities within the family.[11] This has been exacerbated by the COVID-19 pandemic, which is widely recognized to have increased gender inequalities in the United Kingdom and disproportionately impacted BME communities, disabled people, and those who are pregnant.[12]

In this chapter, I critically examine the *Human Rights Act 1998* (UK)[13] (*HRA 1998*) by drawing on feminist literature on the public/private divide. My focus is on the extent to which the *Act* has been able to effectively promote gender equality in a context where our human rights are at risk from the actions of private multinational corporations rather than the state, and where gender equality is arguably most at risk within the family due to the unequal power dynamics created by the privatization of care and the gendered division of labour. I argue that the *HRA 1998* overlooks the gendered impact of the public/private divide in both of these contexts – that is, in the divide between work and family, and between state and market. In doing so, it misses an opportunity to effectively address sex discrimination in the "enjoyment of rights and freedoms set forth in [the *European Convention on Human Rights*]," as per Article 14 of the ECHR,[14] and renders the *Act* ineffective at holding the Parliament of the United Kingdom to account when it creates laws that increase the vulnerability of women within the family.

The *HRA 1998* was groundbreaking because it was the first piece of legislation that codified a modern "Bill of Rights" in UK law. It did not contain any new substantive provisions of its own, but it allowed UK courts to directly implement the *European Convention on Human Rights* (*ECHR*).[15] The *ECHR* had already been binding on the UK government from the time that it came into force in 1953, but it is a long and expensive journey for an individual to enforce their rights via the European Court of Human Rights in Strasbourg [ECtHR]. A victim or potential victim of an *ECHR* violation must first exhaust their domestic remedies before being able to satisfy the admissibility requirements of the ECtHR. The *HRA 1998* sought to "bring rights home"[16] by requiring UK courts to follow Strasbourg jurisprudence.[17] It allowed UK courts "so far as it is possible to do so" to interpret legislation in a way that is compatible with the *ECHR*,[18] and, where such interpretation is not possible, to issue a declaration of incompatibility.[19] The UK courts do not have the power to strike down incompatible legislation but instead the declaration simply informs Parliament of the incompatibility of a provision with the *HRA*. The decision of whether to remedy this incompatibility remains in Parliament's hands, though, in practice, Parliament has so far responded to most declarations by legislating to remove the incompatibility.[20] Furthermore, with regard to new legislation, the Minister in charge of a bill must, before second reading, either make a statement that, in their view, the bill is compatible with the *HRA 1998*, or state that, although they are unable to make such a statement, the government nevertheless wishes to proceed with the bill.[21] The purpose of this was to "ensure that the human rights implications are debated at the earliest opportunity."[22]

In terms of the public/private divide, the key provision of the *HRA 1998* is s 6, which provides that "it is unlawful for a *public authority* to act in a way which is incompatible with a Convention right."[23] It then goes on to specifically identify that both courts and tribunals, and "any person certain of whose functions are functions of a public nature," are included in the definition of public authority for the purposes of the *Act*.[24] The language in s 6 gave rise to speculation at the time of its enactment that the *Act* may have indirect horizontal effect and that it could be extended to private companies operating public services.[25] However, the courts have adopted a restrictive interpretation of the definition of "public authority," despite the reasonably broad language in the *Act* itself, and have recently precluded the possibility of indirect horizontal effect, at least in some circumstances. This is the first aspect of the public/private divide that I will consider.

I will then draw on an example of where the *Act* has been assumed to have little or no relevance at all: the recent reforms to the family justice system, which have removed legal aid for most private law family matters, and the related push toward private resolution of family disputes. As I will demonstrate below, these reforms had significant gender equality implications in the context of access to justice, yet the legislation introducing them received a declaration of compatibility, and there were few, if any, explicit mentions of gender equality in the various committee stages and reports during the bills' passages through Parliament.

Feminist Critiques of the Public/Private Divide

A number of feminist scholars have charted the development of the public/private divide. Margaret Thornton, for example, dated the public/private divide to ancient Greek thought, where "a clear separation existed between the *polis* or public sphere, and the *oikos,* the home or the private sphere."[26] Within the *polis,* all citizens were free and equal, but citizens were only men; meanwhile, the *oikos* was "a realm of inequality and 'unfreedom,' where wife, children and slaves were not free."[27] There was, Thornton noted, a symbiosis between the inequality of the home and the equality of the political sphere: in other words, the former was necessary to allow men to participate in the latter.[28] This reliance on private inequalities to enable public participation, in its twentieth-century form, has been a recurring theme in the feminist critiques of the public/private divide. The rise of the private sphere as central to liberalism has been associated most closely with the industrialization of Western capitalist societies in the nineteenth and early twentieth centuries, when, as Susan B. Boyd described, "the spheres of family/home and paid work became physically and conceptually more separate."[29] The public/private divide remains predominantly associated with liberal theorists such as Hobbes, Locke, and Mill.[30] As Katherine O'Donovan pointed out, a "classic statement" of the liberal approach can be found in the *The Report of the Departmental Committee on Homosexual Offences and Prostitution* [*Wolfenden Report*], which famously stated that "there must remain a realm of private morality and immorality which is, in brief and crude terms, not the law's business."[31] This classic liberal notion sought to protect men from other individuals and from the state, and regarded the family as "unproblematically private and as a barely visible appendage to society."[32] With the growth of the welfare state and increasing regulation of family through the twentieth century, the emphasis, where it was on the family at all, was on preserving family privacy.[33]

This preservation of privacy is very much the approach of the *HRA 1998,* because it protects individuals from the state. For example, the focus of the right to private and family life often comes at the expense of protecting those within the family from other family members, though it does require the state to intervene in the most extreme cases of threat to life, or cases of inhuman or degrading treatment, which would violate other *ECHR* rights.[34] Nevertheless, we see evidence of the family courts prioritizing the family life of violent men over the safety of women and children. In 2016, the Women's Aid Federation of England published a report, *Nineteen Child Homicides,* which told the stories of nineteen children who had been killed by their fathers who were known perpetrators of domestic abuse.[35] In some of the cases, the mother was also killed.[36] In over half of the cases, the courts had ordered unsupervised contact with this parent.[37] The ways in which protection for victims and potential victims has been further limited by the recent reforms to the family justice system is discussed below.

In much of the feminist literature, there is an explicit acknowledgment that the dividing lines between public and private are blurred and not fixed. For example, Susan B. Boyd described the public/private divide as "an ideological marker that shifts in relation to the role of the state at particular historical moments, in particular contexts, and in relation to particular issues."[38] It is generally used to denote the separation of the state, the market, and the family, into different spheres, but in different times and different contexts each of these can either be public or private. The state, for example, is not one monolithic body, but rather a "set of diverse institutions,"[39] which can enter into private contracts, and the family, assumed by liberals to be quintessentially private, becomes "public" at specific moments such as for a marriage or divorce, or if child protection measures become necessary.[40] The boundary between public and private, then, is often "wiggly, slippery, and impossible to draw."[41] Variously described as a "fiction," "an illusion," and a "myth," the idea of separate spheres is sustainable, as Susan Moller Okin noted, only if feminist scholarship is ignored.[42] In other words, gender inequalities in the market and family are a "two-way causal cycle,"[43] each influencing the other.[44] It is not so much a dividing line between public and private as a triangle between state, market, and family. Margaret Thornton argued that there ought to be a fourth category of "social organization," which would be bodies such as unions, religious communities, academia, and community groups.[45] However, even this more "refined schemata"[46] may not lead to a more precise understanding of the divide because the boundaries of public and private within and between each of those categories remain blurred: they are not mutually exclusive.

This feminist literature has drawn on and expanded on the famous feminist slogan "the personal is political" to illustrate the ways in which public and private are overlapping and mutually reinforcing concepts. Catharine MacKinnon, for example, suggested that "[t]o see the personal as political means to see the private as public."[47] As Susan B. Boyd explained: "Social relations that hitherto were viewed as personal or private were to be politicized, analysed, exposed to scrutiny, and rendered an appropriate arena for regulation by state and law, especially where violence was concerned."[48]

This is not to suggest that there should be no private sphere. These scholars generally acknowledged the central role that privacy has played in feminist campaigns, such as those for reproductive rights.[49] There are positive values to privacy, particularly in the context where "privacy is one of the many things which women tend to lack" within the family.[50] Instead, the critiques focused on the ways in which law fails to intervene to protect women in the domestic sphere, on the basis of family privacy. To counter this failure, Susan Moller Okin suggested that, rather than eliminate privacy altogether, the protection should be focused on "privacy *within* the family," rather than family privacy, as this would protect individual family members from those who are more powerful.[51] This could potentially overcome the problem that Katherine O'Donovan famously described, a problem that sees the family being "a unit, a black box, into which the law does not purport to peer. What goes on inside the box is not perceived as the law's concern."[52]

However, as I will argue below, the general direction of law reform in the United Kingdom over the past decade in particular has been to reinforce the family's "black box."[53] The combined aims of the removal of legal aid for most family law matters through the *Legal Aid, Sentencing and Punishment of Offenders Act 2012* (UK),[54] and the reforms to the private family law justice system in the *Children and Families Act 2014* (UK),[55] ss 10 and 11, were to encourage families to resolve most disputes privately. This is an example of what Katherine O'Donovan referred to as the "privatisation of conflict."[56] The effect of these provisions has been to increase the vulnerability of women and children through decreasing access to legal assistance. As such access would fall within the ambit of the "right to a fair hearing" under Article 6 of the *ECHR*,[57] and, in some circumstances, could fall within the prohibition of inhuman and degrading treatment under Article 3, these reforms could arguably have been subject to judicial review on the basis of gender discrimination under Article 14 of the *ECHR*,[58] and there should at least have been a pause before these provisions were given a statement of compatibility with the *HRA 1998*. However, with the narrow exception of a judicial review on behalf of domestic violence survivors, such a case has not been taken, despite repeated and strong judicial criticism of the reforms in the family courts.[59] This, I argue, is illustrative of the ineffectiveness of the *HRA 1998*. I will return to this argument after considering the issue of contracting out public services to private bodies and to the private family.

Privatization of Public Services

Increasingly, with successive UK governments ideologically committed to privatization, the market has taken over activities formerly performed by the state. In Margaret Thornton's words, "the activities of mega-corporations, including multinationals ... [become virtually] indistinguishable from the exercise of public power."[60] Since the mid-1990s, the power of multinational corporations contracting previously public-sector work, such as Serco and G4S, has grown exponentially. This privatization was ostensibly taken into account in the language of s 6 of the *HRA 1998*, so there was initial optimism that the *Act* might have a broad applicability – first, through indirect horizontal effect on the basis of the specific inclusion of courts and tribunals as being bound by the *Act* in s 6(3)(a),[61] and, second, by the wording of s 6(3)(b), which suggests a broad meaning of the term "public authority" to include private bodies that have some public functions. As Morag McDermont noted, "some in the professional and academic legal community took the government's rhetoric during the debate on the Human Rights Bill seriously and assumed that the meaning of 'public function' would be interpreted broadly."[62] However, this optimism was quickly dashed by a series of cases in which the courts took a narrow approach.

In the case of *YL v Birmingham City Council*, a private care home for the elderly (in which individual places were funded by the local council in pursuance of their statutory obligations) did not satisfy the test under s 6(3)(b) of the *HRA 1998*. An elderly woman with Alzheimer's disease was to be evicted from her care home after a dispute between its staff and her daughter.[63] Though the home was private, YL's fees were paid by the local authority, which had a statutory duty to provide for her care,[64] and her daughter, who paid a small "top-up" contribution.[65] The argument on behalf of YL was that evicting her from her home would constitute a violation of her right under Article 8 of the *ECHR* to respect for her home. However, by a three-to-two majority, with Lord Bingham and Baroness Hale dissenting, the House of Lords held that the home was not providing "functions of a public nature" under s 6(3)(b), but instead was "simply carrying on its private business with a customer who happens to be a public authority."[66] In contrast, had YL been in a local authority care home, she would have had a claim against a core public authority. The question in this situation is not so much where the line between the public and private ought to be drawn, but rather whether such a line ought to be relevant at all: it is not any more acceptable for a vulnerable elderly person to lose their home if they are paying privately than if the state is paying for their place. While private residents could have a claim in contract law, private law is unlikely to provide the remedy that is most useful to the victim in cases such as YL's. She wanted to remain in her home. However, in contrast to privately funded residents, who may at least have a claim in contract, the *HRA 1998* potentially leaves state-funded residents with no legal recourse at all. The contract is between the local authority and the care home, and, in cases where the place is fully funded (that is, with no top-up fees), there may be no contractual relationship between the care home and the resident.[67] The resident becomes the subject of the contract, not a party to it. In such cases, residents may become what the Joint Committee on Human Rights has described as "stranded victims."[68]

It is worth noting that, as part of the UK feminist judgments project, Helen Carr and Caroline Hunter have demonstrated that this case could have been decided differently based on existing law.[69] Writing as Baroness Hunter-Carr, a fictional feminist judge in the House of Lords, they found that the state cannot relinquish responsibility for vulnerable groups, even if it contracts out their care to a private provider. They then held that s 6(3)(b) requires that these privatized functions such as statutory social care will always be "functions of a public nature."[70] Agreeing in this respect with Lord Bingham and Baroness Hale's dissent in *YL*, they found that, "to achieve a human rights culture, the state must always remain responsible for those entitled to [public] services. The fact that the Council are a party to the ongoing contractual arrangements underlines the persistence of their obligations."[71] They also went further to suggest in *obiter* comments that the state would remain responsible even where a vulnerable person was not directly funded by the state.[72] In their view, "[i]t would be a tragic irony if citizens gained more rights against the state only to have the state slough off its responsibilities to the most vulnerable."[73]

This specific example was rectified by legislation following a public outcry after the *YL* case, so that private care homes then were included within the definition of public authority, though this was not the case with other privatized public services where service users may be equally vulnerable.[74] However, this provision was quietly rescinded in 2015 so that once again vulnerable people in private care homes are not protected by the *HRA 1998*.[75]

The *HRA 1998* sought to create a "human rights culture" in public services, but it has arguably failed to appropriately position the public/private divide. Although it attempted to include privatized services, this attempt has been undermined by the limited interpretation adopted by the courts to the issue of "functions of a public nature." What the *YL* case demonstrates, in my view, is that a human rights culture would need to permeate beyond the public sphere into the realm of private law in order to provide an effective remedy in the context of private provision of formerly public services. In other words, it would need to have horizontal effect.

More recently, the case of *McDonald v McDonald* appears to have closed down the possibility that the inclusion of the courts as a public authority in s 6(3)(a) could lead to an indirect horizontal effect, at least in certain circumstances.[76] This was a case involving parents who had purchased a house for their adult disabled daughter. In breach of the mortgage terms, they had granted her an assured short-hold tenancy, and she paid rent from her housing benefit. However, when their business ran into financial difficulties, they defaulted on the mortgage, even though their daughter had continued to pay rent. The receivers served an eviction notice to the daughter as the mortgage term was coming to an end and there were some rent arrears, although payments were being made.[77] A possession order was granted, and the question for the Supreme Court was whether the lower court should have considered the proportionality of the eviction, taking into account the daughter's rights to her home under Article 8 of the *ECHR*, as they would have done with a public-sector landlord under the *HRA 1998*, s 6.[78] The Supreme Court, in a unanimous judgment, took a very narrow view of s 6(3)(a), finding that the purpose of the *ECHR* was to prevent human rights abuses by the *state*.[79] While the court is a state body, it is "merely the forum for the determination of the civil right in dispute between the parties."[80] The Supreme Court found that the terms of the contractual relationship between the parties took precedence at least where that was governed by domestic legislation, in which the democratically elected legislature had already balanced the competing rights of landlords and tenants.[81] To hold otherwise, they suggested, would be to allow the *ECHR* "to be directly enforceable as between private citizens so as to alter their contractual rights and obligations."[82] They also noted that landlords had *ECHR* rights under Article 1 of the First Protocol (A1P1) and that potentially allowing a tenant's Article 8 rights to be invoked could lead to a breach of those A1P1 rights, particularly if it resulted in a possession order being postponed for a significant period, leading to financial loss without compensation.[83]

Together, these two lines of case law rule out both the idea that private contractors performing a public service could be "exercising functions of a public nature" and that the *HRA 1998* could have an indirect horizontal effect, at least as between private citizens who have a relationship that is already governed by domestic legislation. The result is that those who rely on the private sector have been effectively left without the protection of the *HRA 1998*. In contrast, those who receive the same services directly from a state provider are protected. In this age of austerity and increasing privatization, the latter group is very small and shrinking rapidly. The legal separation of the public and the private has, as Judy Fudge and Brenda Cossman have argued, "created barriers to developing integrated policies that deal with the complex interconnections of our world."[84] This is perhaps most evident when thinking about these private bodies that provide public services, and it has not gone unnoticed in either Canada or the United Kingdom that, just as the public law mechanisms for holding government to account were strengthened, the "privati[z]ing impulse," as Thornton referred to it, appears to have accelerated exponentially, transferring many public services into the realm of the private.[85] On that basis alone, I would argue that we have to question the effectiveness of the *HRA 1998*. The narrow interpretation of the concept of "functions of a public nature"[86] combined with increasing privatization have rendered the *Act* toothless in some circumstances involving the most vulnerable members of society.

The *HRA*'s non-application to services contracted by the state has particular effect on women, not only as service users but also as workers. Women make up two-thirds of public-sector workers, and, compared to other groups, higher proportions of BME women are employed in the public sector.[87] The impact of transferring these jobs to the private sector, with the associated increased casualization, decreased remuneration, and weaker union influence, also has a serious impact on women's economic security. For example, BME women are over-represented in the health and social work sector, which has "made them more vulnerable to being engaged on zero-hours contracts and in other forms of temporary work," which are common in these sectors.[88] Privatization is, of course, not new: it was pushed strongly by the Thatcher government and was described at the time by Angela Coyle as possibly "the most serious threat to pay, employment protection and rights since the war."[89] In her study of the contracting out of National Health Service cleaning work, Coyle noted that, since privatization, the "already poor pay and conditions" have deteriorated further[90] in the wake of the necessity to cut costs in order to make a competitive tender and win the contract.[91] The inevitable impact of this "downward spiral of cost cutting"[92] can be seen in several recent examples of private-sector contractors in financial difficulties, unable to reduce their costs any further, with some either walking away from the contract[93] or going into liquidation.[94] The indirect effects on gendered economic inequalities caused by austerity and privatization of public services as a result of the disproportionate numbers of women, especially BME women, employed in the (formerly) public sector, are not currently taken into consideration by either the *ECHR* or the *HRA 1998*. Moreover, privatization does not take the form of transferring state responsibilities only to private sector bodies, but also to individual families.

Privatization of Care

The ideology of austerity, in which public services have suffered significant cuts since 2010, has had a disproportionate impact on the poorest families: a report by the Women's Budget Group and Runnymede Trust predicted that, by 2020, these families would lose access to services worth over £4,300 per year.[95] This research found that Black and Asian families would be impacted more than white families,[96] and female lone parents would lose access to services worth over £4,900 per year, which would account for over 10 percent of their standard of living, while single men without children would lose the least.[97] Other studies indicate that the poorest parts of the country have suffered the largest cuts to public services,[98] and poorer families are both more likely to rely on these services and less likely to be able to afford to pay for them privately when they are cut.[99] As a result, it is largely women within these families who have had to provide unpaid care to make up for the absence of public services, sometimes at a direct cost to their own paid employment.[100]

Despite increases in women's employment outside the home, the public and private spheres remain "highly gendered,"[101] in that men continue to dominate the public sphere of paid work while women generally continue to hold primary responsibility for domestic and caretaking labour, even when they also work outside the home.[102] Though there have been attempts to redress this balance through initiatives such as flexible working arrangements and shared parental leave,[103] research suggests that, as more women than men requested flexible work, this has led to "mummy track" careers with lower earnings and perceptions of less commitment on the part of the worker.[104] Research has also found that flexible work can reinforce traditional gender roles. For example, Heejung Chung has found that men work longer hours when offered flexible work, whereas women increase their care duties. She also found that flexible work "led to income premiums for men but not for women, and that mothers who use flexible working are more likely than their male colleagues to face flexibility stigma – the idea that they are less committed and less productive – as a result."[105] She found that "more than a quarter of mothers experienced negative career consequences" due to flexible working, whereas for fathers it was one in ten.[106] In terms of the public/private divide, caretaking is still very much a "private" activity, with some accommodations being made to support carers to remain in work, but still with a resulting negative impact on their careers.[107] Neither the divide itself nor the gendered division of caretaking labour seems to be particularly troubled. Similarly, while the introduction of shared parental leave sought to encourage more men to be active parents, there has been no requirement that employers who offer enhanced contractual maternity leave payments need to also extend those to employees taking shared parental leave.[108] This means that there may well be financial disincentives for non-birth parents to take parental leave over and above those of birth parents who have maternity-leave entitlement, as well as potential career risks associated with taking a long period of leave.

Writing in 1985, Katherine O'Donovan argued that the understanding of family, with its gendered division of labour, as private and "not the law's business"[109] has meant that the public/private divide "accounts for the modern legal subordination of women."[110] We might say that, now, the state is at least trying to make things better with initiatives such as shared parental leave, although it is not entirely succeeding. However, the withdrawal of access to legal aid and the resulting increase in privatization of family disputes has closed legal avenues that women might have had on divorce to redress this continuing power imbalance where there is still a gendered division of labour within the family. Instead, the emphasis is now on private negotiation between the parties and on women becoming financially self-sufficient as soon as possible after divorce. The public/private divide is stronger than ever and just as problematic for women. This divide is more difficult to challenge through existing human rights mechanisms than the privatization of public services, perhaps even impossible. It has also become even more prevalent through the operation of the politics of austerity, which has rolled back not only the welfare state but also much of the family justice system.

Family Law Reforms

In this section, I discuss two family law reforms that ought to have been seriously questioned by a human rights regime that is committed to gender equality: the *Legal Aid, Sentencing and Punishment of Offenders Act 2012*

(*LASPO*) and the *Children and Families Act 2014*. Together, they have virtually eliminated access to legal representation for private family law matters and encouraged private settlements of disputes outside of the court system, with few protections for potentially vulnerable parties such as victims and survivors of domestic abuse. In my view, these reforms should fall within the existing provisions of the *HRA 1998*, access to justice being clearly within the ambit of Article 6 of the *ECHR* and there being an arguable discriminatory effect on the grounds of sex, for the purposes of Article 14. Yet, the *HRA 1998* has played a very limited role in challenging the gender inequalities in this privatization of family conflict.

Legal Aid, Sentencing and Punishment of Offenders Act 2012

LASPO removed legal aid from all private family law matters except where there was evidence of domestic violence. The aim was to reduce the cost of legal aid to the public purse as part of the government's austerity agenda and to "encourage people to resolve their problems themselves and to use alternatives to courts where they are effective."[111] Ironically, with clients no longer consulting solicitors who had "routinely referred publicly funded clients to mediation,"[112] the number of family disputes entering mediation dropped by almost 50 percent following the withdrawal of legal aid, and the number of unrepresented litigants in private family cases has increased by 30 percent.[113] The withdrawal of legal aid was not limited to family law, but rather applied to a wide range of legal issues. The result has been that some parts of the country have become "legal aid deserts,"[114] with no legal aid solicitors available. Those who cannot afford to pay for legal representation in family cases must effectively choose between mediation and representing themselves in court.[115] This undermines one of the central tenets of mediation: that it must be voluntary.[116] What Rosemary Hunter termed the "LASPO gap" (that is, the gap between the ability to resolve a dispute through mediation and eligibility for litigation legal aid under *LASPO*) also increases pressure on mediation services to not refuse unsuitable cases, as the parties would otherwise be forced to represent themselves in court with little or no assistance.[117]

The resulting increase in unrepresented litigants has caused a number of problems, not only for access to justice but also for the court system.[118] As one Family Court judge told *The Guardian*:

> The combined effect of the cuts [to the court system] and Laspo are [*sic*] disastrous. The courts are being pared down to the bone at a time when they are filling up with [litigants-in-person] … [who] don't know a good point from a bad one; they don't understand the law; they don't understand what they have to prove and they don't know how to ask a question.[119]

Even when they can competently and confidently represent themselves, unrepresented litigants may face other financial barriers to accessing courts that could previously have been covered by legal aid. These include court fees and other related costs, such as medical reports, drug test reports, and psychiatric reports, which could be essential for evidencing a case.[120]

It is possible to get legal aid for public family law issues, such as for proceedings by a local authority seeking a care order, for example,[121] or where a child has been abducted or unlawfully removed from the United Kingdom.[122] In other cases, it may be possible to access legal aid if the means test (financial eligibility) and merits test (strengths and weaknesses of the case) are satisfied. Yet, these relate only to applications for non-molestation and occupation orders, restraining orders, forced-marriage protection orders, female genital mutilation protection orders, orders in relation to child abduction that are not made under an international convention, and mediation.[123] Otherwise, private family law matters are not eligible at all, unless the applicant can demonstrate that they meet both the means test and the merits test, and also can provide certain types of evidence of domestic abuse. This evidence includes a criminal conviction or arrest, court orders relating to domestic or sexual violence, or letters from health professionals or domestic violence agencies.[124] Where such evidence is available, legal aid is available for divorce, financial provisions on divorce, child arrangements, and child support.[125] However, as Rights of Women found, over a third of domestic abuse survivors were unable to access legal aid.[126] The strict criteria make it essentially inaccessible for many women, even those on low incomes: "I earn a low income, yet I've been assessed as having too much disposable income … and when you aren't eligible you're expected to pay full solicitors costs – there's no help anywhere in between. I've had to face my violent ex-partner in court twice now, and will have to continue to do so as I simply cannot afford costs."[127]

Rights of Women brought a judicial review challenging the requirement to provide evidence of domestic abuse within the last twenty-four months in order to access legal aid, and arguing that the evidence requirements were too restrictive, being focused on physical abuse and ignoring emotional, psychological, and financial abuse. Victims of financial abuse in particular would not have access to any of the forms of evidence required.[128] The group was successful on traditional judicial review grounds on the basis that the evidence requirements in the Regulations frustrated the statutory purpose: to ensure that legal aid is available to domestic abuse victims.

The only mention of the *HRA 1998* in the Court of Appeal judgment is a sentence explaining that Rights of Women's claim had initially included alleged breaches of the *Act* but that permission had been refused for those grounds by the lower court judge.[129] No reasons were given for this refusal in the judgment. Yet, as Shazia Choudhry and Jonathan Herring have argued, requiring a domestic abuse survivor to litigate in person against their abuser is likely to constitute a violation of their right to a fair trial under Article 6.[130] Despite its being prohibited in criminal courts, alleged abusers are permitted to cross-examine their victims in family courts,[131] and, due to lack of legal aid, victims may still have to cross-examine their abusers. This could also constitute a violation of the state's obligation to protect against inhuman and degrading treatment under Article 3, to the extent that it enables the court system to be used to continue the abuse.[132] Given this, it seems strange that an *HRA 1998* challenge was not permitted, and, although law reforms are currently under way to prevent an alleged perpetrator from cross-examining a victim, the *HRA 1998* appears to have played little or no role in bringing this about. Instead, it appears that lobbying and reports by women's organizations such as Women's Aid and Rights of Women have been key, as was the All-Party Parliamentary Group on Domestic Violence, led by Jess Phillips MP and Maria Miller MP.[133]

In general, *LASPO* has reduced women's access to justice in private family law matters. As Felicity Kaganas has argued:

> [I]t is the competent poor, the unacknowledged vulnerable and the unassertive who are most affected by the LASPO. Women, collectively, are more likely than men to fall into these categories and the result is

> that women, in particular, who benefited historically from wider and easier access to justice, are those who are most disadvantaged by its curtailment.[134]

According to the Ministry of Justice's *Equality Impact Assessment*, women are more likely than men to rely on legal aid. Indeed, 65 percent of those who will no longer receive legal aid in family law matters are women.[135] As women make up just over 40 percent of legal aid clients in civil matters, they are clearly over-represented in family law legal aid cases.[136] The Ministry of Justice also recognized a disproportionate impact on BME clients, who were "slightly more likely" to have private family legal aid funding.[137] There was, however, little recognition of the gender and race equality implications of this in the *Equality Impact Assessment*. For example, the fact that the withdrawal of legal aid for private family law matters "may" have greater impact on women and BME clients was dismissed as "an inevitable effect of the composition of the client base for civil legal aid in this category."[138] There was no acknowledgment that this means that women and BME people are, as a result, more likely to have difficulties accessing justice in private family matters. There was no recognition that some abusive men use repeated applications to continue to harass women, who, without access to legal advice, may not know how to ask the court for an order preventing further applications.[139] The legal aid reforms were also considered to be justified as a proportionate means of achieving the legitimate aims of controlling public expenditure, redressing the balance between state and individual responsibility for resolving disputes, and focusing limited legal aid resources elsewhere.

Children and Families Act 2014

The *Children and Families Act 2014* (UK) introduced further reforms to the system of private family law, designed to encourage private settlement of disputes and avoid litigation, primarily through channelling disputes toward mediation. It introduced a requirement that separating couples must consider mediation as an alternative to litigation. Unless an exemption applies, such as in a case where there is evidence of domestic abuse, they cannot litigate until they have attended a Mediation, Information and Assessment Meeting (MIAM). This replaced a Pre-Application Protocol for Mediation Information and Assessment in Practice Direction 3A, para 3.5, introduced in 2011, which "expected" litigants to first attend a MIAM.[140] During the Committee hearings on the bill, Edward Timpson MP noted that parties would not be compelled to use mediation and that an assessment as to the suitability of mediation would be conducted by the mediator.[141] Further, he asserted that "[when] a party suffers *or is at risk of* domestic violence," they would not be expected to attend a MIAM.[142] The risks associated with this statutory requirement were noted by Lisa Nandy MP, who highlighted the issue of unreported domestic violence and the likelihood that "one party might seek further mediation in order to perpetuate abuse that has not met the narrow criteria set out in the rules."[143] She also connected this policy to the withdrawal of legal aid for most private family law cases under *LASPO*, which was due to come into effect during this bill's passage through Parliament. Nonetheless, the combined gender equality implications of these reforms were not explicitly discussed in the Committee. Yet, as Hilary Sommerlad argued, these reforms together represent "the (re-)establishment of the family as a strictly private sphere,"[144] with access to family justice "re-constituted as a commodity," available only to those able to pay. Since women have been predominantly impacted, Sommerlad contended that this also represents "part of a wider misogynist turn," reversing gender equality gains made over the past thirty years, particularly for working-class and BME women.[145]

The *Act* also revised the welfare principle to introduce a statutory presumption that both parents should be involved in their child's life where this would be safe and consistent with the child's welfare. There is no explicit consideration of dangers posed by this presumption to survivors of domestic abuse and their children, and no specific mechanism for these risks to be accounted for as part of a consideration of whether involvement would be in the child's best interests. In fact, the government claimed that the family justice reforms would *enhance* human rights by reducing "unnecessary delays in the family court system and refocus decision-making on the best interests of the child."[146] It suggested that these reforms would strengthen children's rights under the *ECHR* to effective access to the courts (Article 6) and to family life (Article 8).[147] However, I would suggest that the absence of, or difficulty in accessing, legal aid, combined with an idealistic drive toward mediation and private dispute resolution, presents a clear danger that gendered power inequalities within a family could be replicated or exacerbated on separation. In fact, a recent report by Jenny Birchall and Shazia Choudhry found "clear examples of family courts prioritizing perpetrators of domestic abuse's rights to family life over survivors' and children's rights to life and to be free from degrading treatment."[148] Nevertheless, and despite a brief (and unelaborated) mention of the need for children and vulnerable adults to be safeguarded,[149] the government failed to consider such issues. Instead, the focus is on contributing to "a societal shift towards greater recognition of the value of both parents in a child's life, and to a reduction of the perception of bias in the court system" and "supporting parents to work together in the best interests of their child."[150]

Privatization of Conflict

Both of these provisions, I suggest, are part of the same process of privatizing family disputes[151] and, through presuming without evidence – and indeed with plenty of evidence to the contrary – that marriages are now equal, deliberately overlooking where the burden of caretaking falls within families. Family disputes are seen as inherently private matters,[152] access to legal advice as unnecessary in cases involving the ending of a marriage and making arrangements for children,[153] at least in all but the most "deserving" of cases.[154] There is a "received wisdom that law and lawyers should be avoided" in family disputes, in favour of mediation.[155] As Alison Diduck has argued, this "virtual delegalisation" of family disputes reinforces the boundary between public and private in a way that has serious consequences for family justice.[156] While the most obvious examples of abusive relationships should be screened out by mediation providers, research suggests that this may not always happen, and in other cases the abuse is not sufficiently evidenced for the victim to become eligible for legal aid, or it is sufficiently evidenced but the victim cannot find a legal aid lawyer.[157] It is also likely in some cases that behaviour would not fall within the definition of domestic abuse, but that the power dynamics between the couple, whether a result of gender, socio-economic background, education, or other factors, are such that neither mediation nor self-representation are likely to result in a just outcome. Those who actually perform the caretaking labour within families continue to be disadvantaged by the current construction of the private family and of family disputes as private matters. More generally, these reforms are regressive, returning the family to the "black box" described in 1985 by Katherine O'Donovan, into which the law still (or once again) does not *in fact* peer, due to difficulties accessing family courts and legal advice, even though it does now *purport* to do so. Family disputes, as Alison Diduck has argued, "must not be, as a matter of policy, buried again."[158]

The example of withdrawing legal aid for private family law disputes privatizes conflict in terms of making individuals responsible for resolving their own disputes, regardless of the power dynamics or obstacles in the way of that happening. When these reforms seek to transfer family disputes from the arena of the (public sector) court to the (often private sector) mediation company, we see another example of the privatization of formerly public services. In this case, that formerly public service is family justice. The difficulties in holding private-sector service providers to account, particularly in terms of standards such as those in the *HRA 1998* that would apply to public-sector providers, are detailed above. As Alison Diduck has noted, it is unclear who mediation companies are ultimately accountable to: the clients, the courts, or the state. We must, she argued, "be clear about whether they are providing a service or are providing justice and what the difference may be between the two."[159]

The place at which the public/private divide is drawn in the *HRA 1998* makes the "public" encompassed by the *Act* so narrow that it evidently did not occur to lawmakers that the gender equality implications of limiting access to justice in a wide range of family law matters, from divorce and child arrangements to the validity of prenuptial agreements, might make these provisions incompatible with the *Act*. It does not appear to have occurred to them that there might be gender equality implications of withdrawing legal aid and encouraging (private) mediation over (public) access to family courts, or that these implications might matter. In my view, a human rights framework that does not force these issues to at least be considered is one that does not take gender equality sufficiently seriously.

Conclusion

As it has now passed its twentieth anniversary, the *HRA 1998* appears to be in jeopardy, with frequent misrepresentations of the *Act* in the media[160] and political hostility, fuelled largely by its perceived "foreignness" and specifically its connection with the *ECHR*.[161] This has resulted in promises to repeal the *HRA 1998* and replace it with a British Bill of Rights, a process which began in 2011[162] and which has recently been revived in the form of an "Independent Review" of the *Act*.[163] The *HRA 1998* has enabled a number of important challenges to both governmental decisions and primary legislation. An Equality and Human Rights Commission study from 2009 found that the *Act* has had a positive influence on decision making in contexts such as the National Health Service, local councils, and other regulatory services.[164] There are also many high-profile judgments, from an early case in which same-sex couples were treated as spouses for the purposes of tenancy succession,[165] to the recent finding that the requirement on landlords to check immigration status (which was a key part of the government's "hostile environment" policy) is discriminatory on the basis of race.[166]

For women, the *Act* has facilitated a number of important gains, including holding the police to account for a failure to undertake an effective investigation in a series of sexual offences cases.[167] For this reason, Southall Black Sisters and the End Violence against Women Coalition have described the *HRA 1998* as "an essential tool" for women to challenge policing failures with regard to domestic abuse, sexual violence, and human trafficking offences.[168] Similarly, as women's rights activist Tania Pouwhare said in an interview with Emily Grabham in 2007, "[the *Act* is] another way of making a really big fuss." It is not "the magic bullet, but it's just another tool in your armoury."[169] However, there are many criticisms of using rights discourse to secure progressive social change in general,[170] and the *HRA 1998* itself is far from perfect. Ultimately, what I am wondering is whether a revisit, reconception, or overhaul of our approach to human rights might give rise to more progressive possibilities for securing gender equality. My argument is that, while the *HRA 1998* has clearly had some positive impact on gender equality, it has hardly lived up to its promise, particularly in terms of access to justice for women in family matters. Where it largely falls short is in its utter failure to move beyond, or even shift the borders of, the public/private divide. To the extent that the *HRA 1998* reinforces the public/private divide, it is problematic for women – both carers and those cared for, and both within the family and within paid employment. If the *Act* continues to enforce human rights only in the public sphere and not the private, and if it continues to focus on civil and political but not economic and social rights (which can recognize caretaking labour through social welfare rights),[171] it will remain of limited use in the fight for gender equality.

Notes

I would like to thank Susan B. Boyd; Kerry-Ann Barry; James Organ; the volume editors, Erez Aloni and Régine Tremblay; and the three anonymous reviewers for their insightful and constructive feedback on various drafts of this chapter.

1 See also e.g. Susan B Boyd, ed, *Challenging the Public/Private Divide: Feminism, Law, and Public Policy* (Toronto: University of Toronto Press, 1997) [Boyd, *Challenging*]; Margaret Thornton, ed, *Public and Private: Feminist Legal Debates* (Oxford: Oxford University Press, 1995); Katherine O'Donovan, *Sexual Divisions in Law* (London: Weidenfeld & Nicholson, 1985); Susan Moller Okin, "Gender, the Public and the Private" in David Held, ed, *Political Theory Today* (Stanford, CA: Stanford University Press, 1991) 67; Carole Pateman, *The Disorder of Women: Democracy, Feminism and Political Theory* (Stanford, CA: Stanford University Press, 1989); Nicola Lacey, "Theory into Practice? Pornography and the Public/Private Dichotomy" (1993) 20:1 JL & Soc'y 93 [Lacey, "Theory into Practice?"]; Brenda Cossman & Judy Fudge, eds, *Privatization, Law, and the Challenge to Feminism* (Toronto: University of Toronto Press, 2002).

2 See Boyd, *Challenging*, *supra* note 1 at 6.

3 *Ibid* at 6–7.

4 *Ibid.*

5 Susan B Boyd, "Challenging the Public/Private Divide: An Overview" in Susan B Boyd, ed, *Challenging the Public/Private Divide: Feminism, Law, and Public Policy* (Toronto: University of Toronto Press, 1997) 3.

6 See May Bulman, "Food Bank Use in the UK Reaches Highest Rate on Record as Benefits Fail to Cover Basic Costs," *The Independent* (24 April 2018), online: <www.independent.co.uk/news/uk/home-news/food-bank-uk-benefits-trussell-trust-cost-of-living-highest-rate-a8317001.html>.

7 See Sarah Marsh, "Nearly 8 Million People Providing Care for Family Members Without Pay," *The Guardian* (16 July 2018), online: <www.theguardian.com/society/2018/jul/16/nearly-8-million-people-providing-care-for-family-members-without-pay>.

8 See Hugh Pym, "NHS: How Much Does It Spend on the Private Sector?" *BBC News* (8 May 2018), online: <www.bbc.co.uk/news/health-44043959>; Mattha Busby, "Grayling Attacked over 'Disastrous' Part-Privatisation of Probation Service," *The Guardian* (16 February 2019), online: <www.theguardian.com/society/2019/feb/16/unions-condemn-chris-grayling-disastrous-part-privatisation-of-probation-working-links>.

9 See Women Count: A Resource for Gender Responsive Budgeting Groups, "Public Sector Employment" (2017), online: Women Count, <womencount.wbg.org.uk/what-gender-budget-analysis-can-show/public-services/public-sector-employment>. Statistics from 2017 show that women constitute two-thirds of public sector employees in the United Kingdom and that 34 percent of women compared to 18 percent of men are employed in the public sector. The gender pay gap is also much smaller in the public than the private sector: approximately 18 percent compared to approximately 25 percent. See also Angela Coyle, "Going Private: The Implications of Privatization for Women's Work" (1985) 21 Feminist Rev 5.

10 See Gaelle Ferrant, Luca Maria Pesando & Keiko Nowacka, "Unpaid Care Work: The Missing Link in the Analysis of Gender Gaps in Labour Outcomes" (OECD Development Centre, December 2014), online (PDF): <www.oecd.org/dev/development-gender/Unpaid_care_work.pdf>.

11 Akwugo Emejulu & Leah Bassel, "Minority Women, Austerity and Activism" (2015) 57:2 Race & Class 86.

12 See e.g. Rachel Hall, "Women Doing More Home Schooling during Covid Lockdown Than Men," *The Guardian* (19 February 2021), online: <https://www.theguardian.com/education/2021/feb/19/women-doing-more-home-schooling-during-covid-lockdown-than-men>, and the various written and oral evidence submitted to the Women and Equalities Committee Inquiry: *Unequal Impact: Coronovirus (Covid-19) and the Impact on People with Protected Characteristics* (HC 276), online: UK Parliament, <https://committees.parliament.uk/work/227/unequal-impact-coronavirus-covid19-and-the-impact-on-people-with-protected-characteristics/publications/>.

13 *Human Rights Act 1998* c 42 (UK) [*HRA 1998*].

14 *European Convention on Human Rights,* Council of Europe, CETS No 194 (entered into force 1 June 2010) [*ECHR*]; *HRA* 1998, Schedule 1.

15 *ECHR, supra* note 14.

16 UK, Secretary of State for the Home Department, *Rights Brought Home: The Human Rights Bill* (Cm 3782) (1997) [*Rights Brought Home*].

17 See *HRA 1998, supra* note 13, s 2.

18 *Ibid,* s 3.

19 *Ibid*, s 4.

20 See UK, Parliament, Human Rights Joint Committee, *Human Rights Judgments: Seventh Report of Session 2014–15* (London: Stationery Office, 2015) at para 4.13.

21 See *HRA 1998*, *supra* note 13, s 19.

22 *Rights Brought Home*, *supra* note 16 at 3.3.

23 *HRA 1998*, *supra* note 13, s 6 [emphasis added].

24 *Ibid*, s 6(3).

25 See e.g. HWR Wade, "Horizons of Horizontality" (2000) 116:2 Law Q Rev 217; Murray Hunt, "The 'Horizontal Effect' of the Human Rights Act" (1998) Pub L 423.

26 Thornton, *supra* note 1 at 2.

27 *Ibid* at 3.

28 *Ibid*.

29 Susan B Boyd, "Can Law Challenge the Public/Private Divide? Women, Work and Family" (1996) 15 Windsor YB Access Just 161 [Boyd, "Can Law Challenge"] at 163.

30 See Pateman, *supra* note 1 at 121; Thornton, *supra* note 1 at 3–6.

31 Cited in O'Donovan, *supra* note 1 at 9.

32 Thornton, *supra* note 1 at 5.

33 See Boyd, "Can Law Challenge," *supra* note 29 at 163.

34 *Opuz v Turkey*, *No 33401/02*, [2010] 50 EHRR 28, 27 BHRC 159.

35 Women's Aid, *Nineteen Child Homicides* (Bristol: Women's Aid, 2016), online (PDF): <1q7dqy2unor827bqjls0c4rn-wpengine.netdna-ssl.com/wp-content/uploads/2016/01/Child-First-Nineteen-Child-Homicides-Report.pdf> [Women's Aid].

36 See *ibid* at 15–16.

37 *Ibid*.

38 Boyd, *Challenging*, *supra* note 1 at 4.

39 Lacey, "Theory into Practice?," *supra* note 1 at 95.

40 See e.g. *ibid*.

41 Boyd, "Can Law Challenge," *supra* note 29 at 164.

42 Okin, *supra* note 1 at 67.

43 *Ibid* at 77.

44 See O'Donovan, *supra* note 1 at 160.

45 Thornton, *supra* note 1 at 6–7.

46 *Ibid* at 7.

47 Catharine A MacKinnon, quoted in O'Donovan, *supra* note 1 at 18.

48 Boyd, *Challenging*, *supra* note 1 at 10.

49 See Thornton, *supra* note 1 at 16; Lacey, "Theory into Practice?," *supra* note 1 at 100; O'Donovan, *supra* note 1 at xi; Okin, *supra* note 1 at 76.

50 Lacey, "Theory into Practice?," *supra* note 1 at 100.

51 Okin, *supra* note 1 at 86.

52 O'Donovan, *supra* note 1 at 12.

53 *Ibid.*

54 *Legal Aid, Sentencing and Punishment of Offenders Act 2012 c 10* (UK).

55 *Children and Families Act 2014 c 6* (UK).

56 *Ibid* at 199.

57 *ECHR, supra* note 14.

58 See *ibid.*

59 See *MG, JG v JF, JFG (a Child through the Guardian),* [2015] EWHC 564 (UK) at para 20 for an overview of this per Justice Mostyn. Summarizing the situation, he concluded that "in the field of private children law the principle of individual justice has had to be sacrificed on the altar of public debt."

60 Thornton, *supra* note 1 at 5.

61 See e.g. Wade, *supra* note 25; Hunt, *supra* note 25. Though this was subject of debate, see Gavin Phillipson, "The Human Rights Act, Horizontal Effect and the Common Law: A Bang or a Whimper" (1999) 62:6 Mod L Rev 824; Nicholas Bamforth, "The True 'Horizontal Effect' of the Human Rights Act 1998" (2001) 34 Law Q Rev 117.

62 Morag McDermont, "Commentary on YL v Birmingham City Council and Others" in Rosemary Hunter, Clare McGlynn, & Erika Rackley, eds, *Feminist Judgments: From Theory to Practice* (Oxford: Hart Publishing, 2010) 311.

63 See *YL v Birmingham City Council,* [2007] UKHL 27 (UK) [*YL*] at para 45.

64 The *National Assistance Act 1948* (UK), 11 & 12 Geo VI, c 29, s 21(1)(a) provides that local authorities must "make arrangements for providing residential accommodation for persons who by reason of age, infirmity or any other circumstances are in need of care and attention which is not otherwise available to them."

65 *YL, supra* note 63 at para 43.

66 *Ibid* at para 27.

67 See Stephanie Palmer, "Public, Private and the Human Rights Act 1998: An Ideological Divide" (2007) 66 Cambridge LJ 559 at 572.

68 *Ibid.*

69 Helen Carr & Caroline Hunter, "YL v Birmingham City Council and Others" in Rosemary Hunter, Clare McGlynn, & Erika Rackley, eds, *Feminist Judgments: From Theory to Practice* (Oxford: Hart Publishing, 2010) 318.

70 *Ibid* at 326.

71 *Ibid.*

72 *Ibid.*

73 *Ibid* at 325–26.

74 See *Health and Social Care Act 2008* (UK), c 14 s 145.

75 *The Care Act 2014 and Children and Families Act 2014* (Consequential Amendments) Order 2015 (S.I. 2015/914), art 1(2), Sch. para 90 (with arts 1(3), 3).

76 *McDonald v McDonald*, [2016] UKSC 28 (UK) [*McDonald*].

77 *Ibid* at paras 2–5.

78 *Ibid* at paras 32–39.

79 *Ibid* at para 41.

80 *Ibid* at para 44, quoting Lord Millett in *Harrow London Borough Council v Qazi*, [2003] UKHL 43 (UK).

81 See *Protection from Eviction Act 1977* (UK), c 43; *Housing Act 1980* (UK), c 51, s 89; *Housing Act 1988* (UK), c 50.

82 *McDonald, supra* note 76 at para 41.

83 *Ibid.*

84 Judy Fudge & Brenda Cossman, "Conclusion: Privatization, Polarization, and Policy: Feminism and the Future" in Brenda Cossman & Judy Fudge, eds, *Privatization, Law and the Challenge to Feminism* (Toronto: University of Toronto Press, 2002) 403 at 416.

85 See e.g. Palmer, *supra* note 67; Judy Fudge, "The Public/Private Distinction: The Possibilities of and the Limits to the Use of Charter Litigation to Further Feminist Struggles" (1987) 25:3 Osgoode Hall LJ 485 at 490. See also Thornton, *supra* note 1 in relation to Australia.

86 *HRA 1998, supra* note 13, s 6(3)(b).

87 Women's Budget Group and Runnymede Trust, *Intersecting Inequalities: The Impact of Austerity on Black and Minority Ethnic Women in the UK*, by Sarah-Marie Hall et al (17 October 2017) online (PDF): <www.runnymedetrust.org/uploads/PressReleases/Correct%20WBG%20report%20for%20Microsite.pdf> [Hall et al] at 45.

88 *Ibid* at 47.

89 Coyle, *supra* note 9 at 21.

90 See e.g. *ibid* at 5.

91 See *ibid* at 16.

92 *Ibid.*

93 For example, Stagecoach and Virgin Trains East Coast both exited their franchise to run trains on the East Coast mainline between London and Edinburgh three years early after financial losses resulting from Stagecoach's having "got its numbers wrong" and overbidding on the contract. See "Legal Threat over Virgin Trains East Coast Rail Franchise," *BBC News* (19 April 2018), online: <www.bbc.co.uk/news/uk-england-43821044>.

94 The most high-profile example of this is Carillion, which was "one of the largest suppliers of services to the public sector" in the United Kingdom and held a wide range of government contracts from construction to building management. See Daniel Thomas "Where Did It Go Wrong for Carillion?" *BBC News* (15 January 2018), online: <www.bbc.co.uk/news/business-42666275>.

95 See Hall et al, *supra* note 87 at 27.

96 The research finds that of the poorest 20 percent of households, Black and Asian households will have their living standards reduced by approximately 11 percent, and white households by approximately 9 percent. See *ibid* at 28.

97 *Ibid* at 27–28.

98 "Within each class of authority, there is a clear tendency for the percentage cuts to be greatest in the most deprived category and least in the most affluent." Annette Hastings et al, *The Cost of the Cuts: The Impact on Local Government and Poorer Communities* (Joseph Rowntree Foundation, 10 March 2015) at 11, online: Joseph Rowntree Foundation, <www.jrf.org.uk/report/cost-cuts-impact-local-government-and-poorer-communities>.

99 See Hall et al, *supra* note 87 at 27.

100 See *ibid.*

101 Boyd, "Can the Law Challenge," *supra* note 29 at 163.

102 For example, the United Kingdom's gender pay gap remains at close to 20 percent and is worse as women age. For women aged 50–59, it is approximately 27 percent. The pay gap for women who work full time is approximately 9 percent. This gender pay gap has been attributed largely to women continuing to be responsible for unpaid caring. See UK, House of Commons, Women and Equalities Committee, *Gender Pay Gap: Second Report of Session 2015–16* (No 584) (2016), online (PDF): <https://publications.parliament.uk/pa/cm201516/cmselect/cmwomeq/584/584.pdf>.

103 The right to request flexible work hours was introduced initially for parents and carers in 2002 by amendment to the *Employment Rights Act 1996* (UK), c 18 s 47E and Part 8, but later extended to all workers after twenty-six weeks' continuous employment by the *Children and Families Act 2014* (UK), c 6, Part 9, s 131.

104 UK, Equality and Human Rights Commission, *Working Better: Meeting the Changing Needs of Families, Workers and Employers in the 21st Century* (Equality and Human Rights Commission, March 2009) at 57, online (PDF): <webarchive.nationalarchives.gov.uk/20141013170704/http:/www.equalityhumanrights.com/sites/default/files/documents/working_better_final_pdf_250309.pdf>.

105 Heejung Chung, "Opinion: Flexible Working Can Reinforce Gender Stereotypes," (28 January 2019), *Chartered Management Institute* (blog), online: <www.managers.

org.uk/insights/news/2019/january/opinion-flexible-working-can-reinforce-gender-stereotypes>.

106 *Ibid.*

107 See Chapter 5 by Wanda Wiegers in this volume.

108 See *Ali v Capita Customer Management Ltd,* [2019] EWCA Civ 900.

109 O'Donovan, *supra* note 1 at 11.

110 *Ibid* at x.

111 M of J, *Legal Aid Reform: Scope Changes, Equality Impact Assessment (EIA)* (n.d.) at para 8, online (PDF): <webarchive.nationalarchives.gov.uk/20120215135709/http://www.justice.gov.uk/downloads/consultations/eia-scope-changes.pdf>. For critiques of this, see Jess Mant, "Neoliberalism, Family Law and the Cost of Access to Justice" (2017) 39:2 J Soc Welfare & Fam L 246; Felicity Kaganas, "Justifying the LASPO Act: Authenticity, Necessity, Suitability, Responsibility and Autonomy" (2017) 39:2 J Soc Welfare & Fam L 168.

112 Rosemary Hunter, "Inducing Demand for Family Mediation: Before and After LASPO" (2017) 39:2 J Soc Welfare & Fam L 189 [Hunter, "Inducing Demand"] at 192.

113 Anne Barlow, "Rising to the Post-LASPO Challenge: How Should Mediation Respond?" (2017) 39:2 J Soc Welfare & Fam L 203.

114 UK, HL/HC, Joint Committee on Human Rights, *Enforcing Human Rights: Tenth Report of Session 2017–19* (HC 669; HL Paper 171) (July 2018), online (PDF): <https://publications.parliament.uk/pa/jt201719/jtselect/jtrights/669/669.pdf>.

115 Barlow, *supra* note 113 at 204.

116 See *ibid.*

117 Rosemary Hunter, "Exploring the LASPO Gap" (2014) 44 Family Law 660 [Hunter, "Exploring the LASPO Gap"] at 661.

118 See Amelia Hill, "How Legal Aid Cuts Filled Family Courts with Bewildered Litigants" *The Guardian* (26 December 2018), online: <www.theguardian.com/law/2018/dec/26/how-legal-aid-cuts-filled-family-courts-with-bewildered-litigants>.

119 *Ibid.*

120 See James Organ & Jennifer Sigafoos, *The Impact of LASPO on Routes to Justice,* Research Report 118 (Manchester: Equality and Human Rights Commission, 2018) at 21, online (PDF): <www.equalityhumanrights.com/sites/default/files/the-impact-of-laspo-on-routes-to-justice-september-2018.pdf>.

121 Also a supervision order, child protection order, or child assessment order.

122 See "A Guide to Family Law Legal Aid" (last modified January 2018), online: Rights of Women <rightsofwomen.org.uk/get-information/family-law/family-law-legal-aid/>.

123 See *ibid.*

124 See *ibid.*

125 See *ibid.*

126 See Owen Bowcott, "Third of Domestic Violence Victims Cannot Provide Evidence for Legal Aid," *The Guardian* (12 March 2015), online: <www.theguardian.com/society/2015/mar/12/third-of-domestic-violence-victims-cannot-provide-evidence-for-legal-aid>.

127 UK, "Written Evidence from the Rights of Women," AET0023 (9 February 2018), online: <data.parliament.uk/writtenevidence/committeeevidence.svc/evidencedocument/human-rights-committee/enforcing-human-rights/written/78212.html>.

128 See *R (Rights of Women) v Lord Chancellor and Secretary of State for Justice*, [2016] EWCA Civ 91 at para 43.

129 See *ibid* at para 6.

130 Shazia Choudhry & Jonathan Herring, "A Human Right to Legal Aid? The Implications of Changes to the Legal Aid Scheme for Victims of Domestic Abuse" (2017) 39:2 J Soc Welfare & Fam L 152. For judicial discussion of the *ECHR* implications of this, see *Q v Q; Re B (A Child); Re C (A Child)*, [2014] EWFC 31, [2015] 1 WLR 2040, [2015] 3 All ER 759, per Munby J.

131 This will change when the *Domestic Abuse Act 2021* (UK), c 17, s 65 comes into effect in Spring 2022.

132 Choudhry and Herring, *supra* note 130 at 159. See also UK, All Party Parliamentary Group on Domestic Violence, *Domestic Abuse, Child Contact and the Family Courts* (April 2016) online: <https://www.womensaid.org.uk/wp-content/uploads/2015/11/APPG-Inquiry-report-domestic-abuse-child-contact-and-the-family-courts.pdf> [All Party Parliamentary Group on Domestic Violence]. The President of the Family Division has also recognized that this happens. See James Munby, "Unheard Voices: The Involvement of Children and Vulnerable People in the Family Justice System" (Annual Lecture of the Wales Observatory on Human Rights of Children and Young People, Swansea University, 25 June 2015), online: <https://www.swansea.ac.uk/media/Sir-James-Munby-Annual-lecture-2015.pdf>.

133 See All Party Parliamentary Group on Domestic Violence, *supra* note 132.

134 Kaganas, *supra* note 111 at 169.

135 See M of J, *Legal Aid Reform: Scope Changes, Equality Impact Assessment (EIA)* (n.d.) at para 9.26, online (PDF): <https://webarchive.nationalarchives.gov.uk/ukgwa/20111013060733/http://www.justice.gov.uk/downloads/consultations/eia-scope-changes.pdf>.

136 See *ibid.*

137 *Ibid* at para 9.30.

138 *Ibid* at para 9.18.

139 See Liz Trinder et al, *Litigants in Person in Private Family Law Cases,* Ministry of Justice Analytical Series (2014) at 32, online (PDF): Assets Publishing Service, <assets.publishing.service.gov.uk/government/uploads/system/uploads/attachment_data/file/380479/litigants-in-person-in-private-family-law-cases.pdf>.

140 Hunter, "Inducing Demand," *supra* note 112 at 191.

141 See UK, HC, Public Bill Committee, Children and Families Bill, 2012–13 Sess, No 7 at 262.

142 *Ibid* [emphasis added].

143 *Ibid.*

144 Hilary Sommerlad, "Access to Justice in Hard Times" in Mavis Maclean, John Eekelaar & Benoit Bastard, eds, *Delivering Family Justice in the 21st Century* (Oxford: Hart Publishing, 2015) 243 at 247.

145 *Ibid* at 248.

146 Joint Committee on Human Rights, *Legislative Scrutiny: Children and Families Bill; Energy Bill.* Third Report of Session 2013-14, HL Paper 29, HC 452 (June 2013) at 14, online (PDF): <https://publications.parliament.uk/pa/jt201314/jtselect/jtrights/29/29.pdf>.

147 See *ibid.*

148 Jenny Birchall & Shazia Choudhry, "*What About My Right Not to Be Abused?" Domestic Abuse, Human Rights and the Family Courts* (Bristol: Women's Aid, 2018), online (PDF): <https://1q7dqy2unor827bqjls0c4rn-wpengine.netdna-ssl.com/wp-content/uploads/2018/05/Domestic-abuse-human-rights-and-the-family-courts-report.pdf>.

149 See Secretary of State for Education, *Children and Families Bill Contextual Information and Responses to Pre-Legislative Scrutiny.* Annex 1, "Government Response to the Recommendations Made in the Justice Select Committee's Report on Family Justice Provisions," at 44 (para 38), online (PDF): <https://assets.publishing.service.gov.uk/government/uploads/system/uploads/attachment_data/file/219658/Children_20and_20Families_20Bill_202013.pdf>.

150 *Ibid* at 51 (para 63).

151 See also Eekelaar and Maclean's characterization of the LASPO reforms as "privatised justice" in John Eekelaar & Mavis Maclean, *Family Justice: The Work of Family Judges in Uncertain Times* (Oxford: Hart Publishing, 2013) 201.

152 See John Eekelaar "'Not of the Highest Importance': Family Justice under Threat" (2011) 33:4 J Soc Welfare & Fam L 311.

153 See Kaganas, *supra* note 111 at 175.

154 See Nicola Lacey, "Justice Redefined: Or Justice Diluted?" (2014) Family Law 593.

155 Kaganas, *supra* note 111 at 175.

156 Alison Diduck, "Justice by ADR in Private Family Matters: Is It Fair and Is It Possible?" (2014) Family Law 616 at 617.

157 See Hunter, "Exploring the LASPO Gap," *supra* note 117 at 660.

158 Diduck, *supra* note 156 at 619.

159 *Ibid* at 617.

160 See e.g. Michelle Farrell, Eleanor Drywood & Edel Hughes, eds, *Human Rights in the Media: Fear and Fetish* (Abingdon, Oxon: Routledge, 2019).

161 Michelle Farrell & Edel Hughes, "Magna Carta and the Invention of 'British Rights'" in *ibid* at 274.

162 The Commission on a Bill of Rights was established shortly after the Conservative/Liberal Democrat Coalition government took office in 2010. Their Discussion Paper was published in August 2011. See UK, Commission on a Bill of Rights, *Do We Need a UK Bill of Rights?* (Discussion Paper) (London: National Archives, 2011); Rob Merrick, "Theresa May to Consider Axing Human Rights Act after Brexit, Minister Reveals," *The Independent* (18 January 2019), online: <www.independent.co.uk/news/uk/politics/theresa-may-human-rights-act-repeal-brexit-echr-commons-parliament-conservatives-a8734886.html>.

163 Robert Buckland, "The Human Rights Act Is Not Infallible," *Daily Telegraph* (7 December 2020), online: <https://www.telegraph.co.uk/politics/2020/12/07/human-rights-act-not-infallible/>.

164 See UK Equality and Human Rights Commission, *Human Rights Inquiry: Report of the Equality and Human Rights Commission* (London: Equality and Human Rights Commission, 2009).

165 *Ghaidan v Godin-Mendoza,* [2004] UKHL 30.

166 *R (on the application of Joint Council for the Welfare of Immigrants) v Secretary of State for the Home Department,* [2019] EWHC 452 (Admin).

167 *Commissioner of Police of the Metropolis v DSD and another,* [2018] UKSC 11.

168 Nogah Ofer, *Violence against Women and Girls: Protecting Women's Human Rights and Holding the State to Account* (End Violence against Women Coalition, 2017), online (PDF): <www.endviolenceagainstwomen.org.uk/wp-content/uploads/Human-Rights-Act-report-Oct-2017.pdf>.

169 Tania Pouwhare & Emily Grabham, "'It's Another Way of Making a Really Big Fuss': Human Rights and Women's Activism in the United Kingdom. An Interview with Tania Pouwhare" (2008) 16:1 Fem Leg Stud 97 at 107.

170 See e.g. Carol Smart, *Feminism and the Power of Law* (London: Routledge, 1989); Patricia Williams, *The Alchemy of Race and Rights* (Cambridge, MA: Harvard University Press, 1991); Didi Herman, *Rights of Passage: Struggles for Lesbian and Gay Legal Equality* (Toronto: University of Toronto Press, 1994).

171 See Beth Goldblatt & Lucie Lamarche, eds, *Women's Rights to Social Security and Social Protection* (Oxford: Hart, 2014); Beth Goldblatt, *Developing the Right to Social Security: A Gender Perspective* (London: Routledge, 2016). See also Robin West, "The Right to Care" in Eva Feder Kittay & Ellen K Feder, eds, *The Subject of Care: Feminist Perspectives on Dependency* (Lanham, MD: Rowman & Littlefield, 2002) for an argument that there should be a "right to care" and, more specifically, a right to material support for caretaking from the state.

PART 4

Measuring Norms

7

One Myth Leads to Another

From Ignorance of the Laws to the Presumption of Informed Choice among de Facto Spouses

Hélène Belleau

Since 1970, we have seen significant growth in common law unions and in births outside marriage in North America and in several European countries, including Norway, France, Austria, the United Kingdom, and the Netherlands.[1] De facto union has become a real alternative to marriage.[2] In Quebec, in particular, where, historically, almost all couples were married, 40 percent of couples are presently living in de facto unions, the largest proportion of unmarried spouses in Canada.[3] Moreover, the majority of children in Quebec are born of unmarried parents.[4]

Governments have responded in a variety of ways to this significant increase in de facto unions – both within the Canadian federation and internationally. Some jurisdictions have chosen to grant de facto spouses the same rights and obligations as married spouses, while others have implemented a variety of measures (registration, opportunity to draft a contract, etc.) and policies to give them all or part of the rights previously reserved to married spouses.[5] Although it is not possible to take all these measures and policies into account, the legal frameworks of the various countries are set in a variety of contexts in terms of the social safety net, the welfare state, the relative economic autonomy of the spouses, and so on. Their impact on cohabitants is therefore also variable from one country to another.

In several countries, the presumption that de facto spouses are well-informed about the rights and responsibilities affecting them, and that they make an informed decision about the type of union they choose is undermined by findings about their ignorance of the laws in this area. The purpose of this chapter is to examine this presumption by dealing with three underlying assumptions: that couples take legal issues into account in the decision to marry or not; that couples have at least some knowledge of the rights and responsibilities that apply to them; and that a better knowledge of the laws would lead spouses to anticipate the possibility of a breakup and, if necessary, to protect themselves legally and/or economically from the negative consequences of this eventuality.

The aim of this chapter is to bring together a consistent international literature that undermines the idea that the vast majority of spouses make choices and modify or adapt their matrimonial behaviour on the basis of legal knowledge. As we will see, de facto spouses, who often believe that they are protected as if they are married, can make decisions about various aspects of their personal, family, and work lives without measuring the impact of separation or the death of a spouse.[6] Further, this chapter will shed light on the foundations of the legal intuition of our fellow citizens by highlighting the prevailing social norms surrounding de facto unions. In some respects, these norms seem out of step with those conveyed by the law. Finally, by highlighting certain specifics of conjugal relations, this chapter will show the limits of the potential benefits of information campaigns in this area.

Despite the importance of unmarried unions in Quebec, this province is the only one in Canada that has not yet implemented a legal framework for de facto relationships.[7] The perils of this situation were illustrated in 2013, when the highest court in the country looked at the case of Lola and Eric,[8] de facto spouses in Quebec. This case mounted a constitutional challenge where the question of proper regulation of de facto spouses was raised in terms of discrimination and right to equality. In a split decision, four Supreme Court of Canada judges rejected the allegation of discrimination because, according to them, it had not been shown that the idea that de facto spouses choose not to be subject to marriage rules perpetuated prejudice or stereotypes.[9] Although former Chief Justice McLachlin concluded that Quebec's current approach was discriminatory, she nevertheless considered that this discrimination was reasonable and proportionate with respect to the objective of promoting spousal choice and autonomy.[10] In short, at the heart of this decision is a presumption of a consensus on the part of both spouses to live in a de facto union in order to evade the rights and obligations of marriage and possibly to structure their relationship according to their needs.[11] The debates aroused by this case constitute the starting point of our study. That is why, as a first step, we will give some details about the legal situation in Quebec.

Quebec's Legal Context of Conjugality

In Quebec, the evolution of the law over the past forty years has produced a significant difference in the treatment of couples by private law, on the one hand, and public law (social and fiscal), on the other.[12] Private law, which is found in the *Civil Code of Québec*,[13] governs the patrimonial and extra-patrimonial rights and obligations of individuals in a horizontal relationship – between members of a married couple or between parents and children. In 1980 and 1991, the legislature had the opportunity to question the relevance of providing civil consequences for de facto unions – but it abstained from doing so, purportedly for the purpose of preserving the freedom of choice of individuals.[14] The underlying reasoning was that individuals were choosing not to marry in order to avoid the legal framework of marriage. Presently, de facto spouses in Quebec have no rights or obligations toward each other when the relationship breaks down or one of them dies. No sharing rule is required with respect to patrimony. Thus, regardless of the number of years of cohabitation or whether the couple has children, each de facto spouse leaves the union with what he or she has paid for. It should be noted, however, that the legislature made certain provisions that may require a parent to provide support for their child.[15] In short, de facto union under Quebec civil law has almost no automatic effect, except vis-à-vis third parties. As for the legal obligations between the unmarried spouses, the norm is one of imprecision.[16]

While private law concerns horizontal relations, public law refers to vertical relationships between the state and citizens. In recent decades, Quebec has extended certain rights and responsibilities previously reserved for married spouses to de facto couples. For the provincial government, the aim was to recognize the equal rights of all spouses, regardless of their marital status, rights enshrined in the provincial constitution. The adoption of the *Charter of Human Rights and Freedoms*[17] in 1975 had the effect of accentuating the assimilation of de facto spouses to the status of married spouses by prohibiting discrimination on the basis of marital status.[18] Thus, several social and fiscal laws (both federal and provincial) now treat de facto spouses and married spouses similarly.[19]

Since 1993, the consequences of a common law union are modelled on those of marriage in the realms of taxation and social programs.[20] The rights and obligations of de facto spouses generally relate to the length of their cohabitation.[21] For example, after a year of cohabitation or at the birth of a child, unmarried couples are required by tax law to identify themselves as "common law spouses" in their tax return and are treated as if they were married.[22] Following this logic, the calculation of benefits (for legal aid, social assistance, etc.) is based not on individual income, but rather on family income, thus imposing on de facto couples an economic solidarity that they did not necessarily choose.

The dual position of the government, in private and public law, vis-à-vis individuals living in de facto unions has created a certain confusion within the population. Nevertheless, the debate on whether it is relevant to impose a legal framework, which is found elsewhere in the world, on de facto unions in Quebec is currently polarized between two positions: one that advocates respect for "free choice" of de facto partners not to live in the legal framework of marriage and another that advocates for protections of the most vulnerable spouse.[23] The argument of free choice and neutrality of the state in relation to conjugal unions outside of the law is based on the idea that spouses make an informed choice and that they at least minimally know the laws that concern them.[24] The sociological analysis that follows will, by the questions it raises, feed the debate that is currently unfolding in legal circles in Quebec and abroad.

In light of these general considerations, it is important to first identify what spouses consider in their decision to marry or not. The following section reviews empirical surveys in order to address this issue.

Why Marry or Not?

In four studies conducted in Quebec between 2005 and 2011, as well as in 2015, we systematically explored the reasonings that led couples to marry or to live in de facto relationships.[25] Contrary to a certain legal and political discourse claiming that de facto spouses do not wish to marry because they reject marriage's restrictive legal framework, we have repeatedly observed that spouses making such decisions rarely take the legal dimension into account. On the contrary, they considered the decision, first and foremost, within an emotional and relational logic and referred to the symbolism of marriage (religious or not) in the reasons given to marry or to remain in de facto relationships.[26] People who married said they did so out of love, for family tradition, for religious reasons, to publicly express their love, or for the festive side of the wedding.

De facto spouses, on the other hand, said they did not marry for a multitude of reasons, including the high cost of a wedding and the prospect of incurring debt at a time of their lives when they had other priorities.[27] While it is possible to get married at little cost in Quebec, many couple pointed out that a very intimate wedding would not be acceptable for family or friends. Some referred to the fact that 50 percent of marriages end in divorce, which seems perilous for those who do not know the separation rates of unmarried cohabitants. Many said they reject marriage, which they associated with a traditional vision of gender relations or sometimes saw as an economic trap for women. Other referenced divorce-related conflicts as a concern. Finally, many expressed the idea that love was private and that their relationships did not concern the church or the state, which is entirely in the rhetoric of the second modernity, as discussed by Ulrich Beck.[28]

These rationales for de facto union, evoked during in-depth interviews with more than 150 Quebec respondents and in a large survey (*N*=3,250) conducted in the province, reflect in all respects those of other studies conducted elsewhere in the world. Barlow et al, for example, discovered similar patterns in the British context. In their analysis of the British Social Attitudes Survey 2000 (*N*=3,101) and a series of qualitative interviews with forty-eight respondents, they concluded that

> [r]easons for cohabiting rather than marrying included – avoidance of stereotyped gender roles associated with marriage, disillusionment with marriage, trial marriage, avoiding divorce, the emotional security of living together, unexpected pregnancy, and the cost of a "proper" wedding being outweighed by other priorities. The perceived legal position is *not* normally directly related to the decision to marry or cohabit for interviewees in the in-depth study.[29]

In a recent Dutch study (*N*=1,800), Poortman and Mills[30] posited the hypothesis of a direct link between the legal framework of the union chosen by the spouses and their degree of commitment. Yet, by the end of the study, they questioned this hypothesis and concluded, "In light of these findings, we doubt the validity of our theoretical assumption that legal security leads people to invest more in their relationship. Our doubts are substantiated by research demonstrating that people are poorly informed about legal arrangements in general or [with respect to] their own arrangements, making it unlikely that such considerations would guide their behavior."[31]

If a significant portion of today's spouses base their choice to marry or not on non-legal reasons, it does not exclude the fact that they may have a good knowledge of their rights and responsibilities. However, some recent studies reveal that such a level of understanding is not always the case.

From Legal Intuition to the Myth of Automatic Marriage

Since the 1960s, a growing number of studies have focused on identifying how private citizens understand law.[32] Although generally poorly understood by citizens,[33] the law often converges with people's practical intuitions – at least, this is the case when the laws are adapted to their historical and social situation. As Jean Carbonnier, eminent jurist and sociologist of law, wrote:

> Often lawyers are delighted to discover that the man in the street, even the law student in the throes of the exam, can find the answers – even if he cannot develop them – to questions of the law. It is not that the law is known to them – far from it. But it is because they intuitively reconstitute the reasoning that led the legislator to his decision. This legal conscience is an embryo of legislative capacity. If the knowledge of the law is rare – and more and more rare – the legal conscience, thus understood, remains rather divided, insofar as the law continues to coincide, if not always with morality, at least with a certain good practical sense.[34]

Thus, the gap between social norms and values, on the one hand, and those enacted by the law, on the other, risks compromising the effectiveness of laws.[35]

For example, laws may be ignored or disrespected by a large part of the population, and their implementation and enforcement would therefore be difficult. As we see it, "the effects of the law are not the fruit of 'the force of law' by itself, but also of the force of other normative orders which law combines, on which it takes support, or of which it meets resistance or opposition."[36]

In this respect, the case of marriage appears particularly interesting, since its normative system strongly interacts with other normative systems such as religion, the economy, and, more generally, the customs of particular cultures and societies.

The Myth of Automatic Marriage

The "common law marriage myth"[37] has been the subject of several recent studies in England.[38] When an unmarried couple separates in England, the spouses do not benefit from measures providing for the division of property or maintenance obligation, as is the case for married couples, and judges do not have the power to intervene in this matter.[39] From 1970 onwards, several rights and responsibilities previously reserved for married spouses were extended to de facto couples in that country.[40] Over the years, there has been a great deal of confusion among the English population because of the plurality of legal rules applying to de facto spouses. Sometimes these rules treated couples as if they were married; at other times, as if they were mere strangers.[41] Relying on the British Social Attitudes Survey, Barlow et al have documented the extent of the misbeliefs in this area from a representative sample of the British population. The conclusions of their empirical investigations are summarized as follows:

> Over half of those interviewed in the national survey believed, incorrectly, that cohabitants have a "common law marriage" giving them the same rights as married couples ... Whatever their knowledge of the law, only a small number of cohabitants had made any provision regarding the legal consequences of their relationship. There is strong support among cohabitants and others for treating married and cohabiting couples the same in law.[42]

In a 2011 study,[43] we highlighted the importance of the "myth of automatic marriage" among Quebec's French-speaking population. We defined this myth as the belief that de facto partners have the same rights and obligations as married people after one-to-three years of cohabitation or upon them having children. It became clear that the majority of the sixty people we interviewed had little-to-no knowledge of the rights and obligations surrounding marriage and common law relationship.

In our more recent survey, conducted in 2015 with 3,250 Quebec residents, we explored respondents' legal knowledge. Analysis of this survey showed that 45 percent of Quebec de facto spouses believed they had the same legal status as married people; only 4 percent stated that they could not answer the question. This means that nearly half of Quebec de facto spouses do not know the state of the law on this issue. The survey also showed that 49 percent of de facto partners believed that their assets would be shared equally in the event of a breakup, while 8 percent said they were unable to answer the question on this issue. In other words, 57 percent of de facto spouses in Quebec did not know the law on this issue. Finally, 39 percent of unmarried cohabitants believed that the financially weaker spouse would be entitled to spousal support at the time of the breakup, while 16 percent said they were unaware of the law with respect to this question. Thus, 55 percent of Quebec de facto spouses did not know the law on this issue.[44]

Over the past twenty years, several writings by Quebec jurists have shown a similar confusion to the one among the general population on the question of the legal framework of de facto unions in Quebec.[45] The observation of such confusion among the population is pointing in the direction of a need for a legal framework for de facto unions. This subject is not new or unique to the province of Quebec.

Based on analysis of data from the 2004 Scottish Social Attitudes Survey of 1,637 respondents, Fran Wasoff and Claudia Martin have emphasized the significance of the public's ignorance of the laws surrounding conjugality in Scotland.[46] These researchers showed that half of the respondents believed that common law couples who had lived together for a number of years had the same rights as married people, which is untrue.[47] This study also revealed that 22 percent of respondents believed that unmarried cohabitants who had lived together for ten years without having children could claim financial compensation from their life partners at the end of the union, which is also false. To this last group was added the 10 percent of respondents who admittedly that they did not know the laws in this area.[48]

Although less detailed than the aforementioned studies, other writings mention legal misbeliefs in Sweden, Germany, the United States, and the Netherlands.[49] For example, following a legislative change concerning de facto couples in Sweden in 1987, Ulla Bjornberg wrote:

> A Swedish investigation in the 1980s suggests that a large majority of cohabiting partners believe that there is no reason to get married for economic or legal reasons. They have a vague knowledge about rules and their legal status in cases of separation. Very few have made separate agreements on property since they thought that the same rules as for marriage applied also to them. They resisted marriage for ideological or emotional reasons and declared that there was no need for a formal document making their wish to have a union explicit.[50]

Finally, there is the classic research of Lynn Baker and Robert Emery[51] on the legal knowledge of married spouses in Virginia, in the United States, with respect to divorce. In the first study of 137 married respondents, the authors concluded that the majority of participants correctly answered about 60 percent of questions about legal knowledge surrounding a separation. The results were about the same for child care (61 percent), spousal support (64 percent), and child support (61 percent); the exception was goods-sharing questions, where the correct answer score was lower (53 percent).[52]

In short, it is important to consider the reasons to marry or not within the context of the limits of couples' understanding of legal knowledge and also within the context of social norms. Changing norms reveal social acceptance of de facto unions and the decline in popularity of the institution of marriage as a necessary passage to conjugality.[53] We also observe that a significant proportion of respondents in several countries attach more importance to affective and symbolic reasons than to the legal dimension of marriage, while believing, mistakenly, in a similarity of rights and obligations between marital and de facto unions.

Explaining the Findings

The social scientific literature offers at least two lines of explanation for understanding the nature of misunderstanding in this area. First, legal intuition is usually based on people's "good practical sense." Second, the anticipation of a breakup entails a financial cost, but also potentially a relational cost.

Legal Intuition and "Good Practical Sense"

According to Pascoe Pleasence and Nigel Balmer,[54] Anne Barlow et al,[55] and Belleau and Pascale Cornut St-Pierre,[56] many survey respondents believed that laws reflected the social and family reality they lived and that legislators should legitimize the factual situations that they believed to represent the majority. Their understanding of the law seems to be based on their own values and sense of justice rather than formal knowledge of the actual laws. These conclusions extend those of John Darley et al in criminal law and Pauline Kim's in labour law.[57] Moreover, Lee Ross[58] shows that people generally believe that the state sets up just rules and that its conception of justice is the same as theirs. Indeed, in a survey of more than 3,000 British respondents, Pleasence and Balmer showed, on the one hand, the similarity of the erroneous beliefs of married people and non-married spouses and, on the other hand, the proximity of these false beliefs with certain social values regarding marital life and conceptions of moral justness. According to the authors, "in the absence of clear understanding of the law, it would appear that people tend to assume it concurs with what they think it ought to be."[59]

There are also surprising similarities in misconceptions and errors by surveys' respondents living in very different legal and national contexts. Beyond being married, interviewees cited the length of the union, the presence of a child in common, and the exercise of parenthood to justify assigning rights and responsibilities.[60] It is interesting to note that, for respondents, the presence of children seems to be more important than the notion of duration. When a couple had a child, survey respondents both in Quebec and in England very often equated this union with that of a married couple or a long-term union.[61]

This additional weight that respondents give to parenthood in relation to marital status is also evident in the rights and responsibilities they postulate regarding children. In England, a significant portion of the population believed that the rights and responsibilities of the father to his children did not derive from marital status, as is the case today, but rather from the exercise of parenthood.[62] About half of respondents to the British Social

Attitudes Survey mistakenly believed that an unmarried father had the same rights and responsibilities with respect to children as a married father. The proportion of respondents was similar (47 percent) in the Pleasence and Balmer study based on the Civil and Social Justice Panel Survey.[63] In the 2007 Quebec survey, only 48 percent of unmarried cohabitants knew that a male de facto partner had no right or obligation to children born to his spouse, even if they lived together.[64] In our survey conducted in 2015, the proportion of respondents with the same misbelief had grown slightly, to 51 percent.[65]

The respondents' errors generally tended to assign rights and responsibilities to spouses who did not have them, rather than the opposite. For example, the myth of automatic marriage in Quebec and England suggests that, after a few years together or with the arrival of a child, the state treats de facto spouses as if they are married, which is false. It is remarkable to note the synchronicity of the changes that have taken place in the social laws, which, from 1970, in both Quebec and England, equated de facto couples with married couples, alongside the emergence of the myth of automatic marriage.[66] Here the effects of the law on morals is visible in the sense that citizen ignorance stems, in part, from the perverse effects of the dual discourse that governments hold with regard to spouses and financial industry, particularly in the field of insurance, which treats common law spouses as married people.[67]

In sum, the legal intuition of citizens seems to be based on what they believe to be right and what they believe reflects lived reality. These false beliefs are, in turn, reinforced by states in certain social and/or tax laws, which treat de facto spouses as if they were married.

Do Not Anticipate Breakdown: It Might Prevent It

National statistics on divorce rates are generally well known to spouses. Nevertheless, with regard to the future of their own union, survey respondents most often displayed disproportionate optimism. According to Williams, marriage is "the quintessential context in which people are unrealistically optimistic."[68] This optimism adds to a bias called "the above average effect,"[69] which consists of thinking oneself as less likely than the average to experience certain events. Thus, even when couples are led to imagine how their separation would take place, most people remain very optimistic about the rules of law that would apply to their situation as well as the attitude of their spouse in which they have full confidence. This optimism is all the more marked as it allows people to feel they have some control over the negative events that could happen in their lives, such as a divorce.[70]

This optimism does not reflect a blindness attributable solely to the feeling of love. It refers to a very real social function in the process of conjugal construction. According to Reece:

> With regard to romantic relationships, people are optimistic but not mindlessly so ... [A] dose of realism would not necessarily enhance lovers' predictive accuracy, because the optimism bias significantly enhances outcomes (Armor and Taylor 2002: 341), functioning as a powerful self-fulfilling prophecy (Sharot, 2012: 44). Although people's overly optimistic expectancies are only rarely completely fulfilled, they generally get closer to their goal than if they had not been unrealistically optimistic. This is partly because the optimism bias enhances motivation and persistence (Armor and Taylor, 1998: 354).[71]

In other words, optimism about the union leads spouses to invest more in the relationship, from a long-term perspective. Conversely, the anticipation of a breakdown and noting of the risks inherent to contemporary unions may also have a real emotional cost, such as undermining optimism bias in couples.[72] In fact, the event of separation implies that the spouses address various scenarios and deal with topics that may raise important disagreements between them. These "negotiations" introduce a reasoning where the defence of personal interests (you against me) comes before the norm of altruism that characterizes love relations (the idea that the other partner and the couple must come before personal interests).[73] Spouses often prefer to silence this eventuality or postpone these discussions indefinitely. The years of cohabitation often allow spouses to build a relationship of trust that is strong enough to address the unspeakable, as well as to negotiate and argue for their personal interests without questioning the relationship and its sustainability.[74]

Finally, beyond the relational costs that these negotiations can induce between spouses, the preparation of a contract can have a significant financial cost. The law is complex, and professionals are typically needed to help people draw up contracts, wills, or living arrangements. The fees of lawyers and notaries, but also the technical language of law and its complexity, are not within everyone's capacity.[75]

Some Solutions

Improving the legal literacy of stakeholders, although necessary, does not seem very promising. Indeed, the idea that a better knowledge of rights and responsibilities would necessarily lead spouses to take measures to reduce the risks associated with a relationship breakdown, is not unanimously held in the scientific community.[76] First, several studies mentioned above show that the erroneous knowledge in this field is very resistant to change.[77] As we have pointed out, the failure to consider the laws may have adverse economic consequences for those living on the margins of the law. However, negotiations to reach an agreement or a cohabitation contract are also not neutral for spouses, because they can lead to important financial and relationship costs. This probably explains in part why so few spouses, married or not, anticipate a relationship breakdown and why even fewer take concrete measures (legal and financial) with regard to this eventuality.[78]

In response the common law marriage myth, the British government has tried to improve the knowledge of common law spouses with respect to the rights and responsibilities that particularly concern them. After an extensive media campaign to inform the public of important differences in the legal framework of married and common law unions, the national survey that had revealed the existence of the automatic wedding myth was revived in 2006. Anne Barlow et al concluded that there was an increase in uncertainty in the responses and that the extent of belief in the myth had decreased by only four percentage points in six years. While 35 percent of common law spouses answered questions correctly in 2000, in 2006 this number was 39 percent.[79] Although it is not possible for us to evaluate the quality of this media campaign, this attempt by the British government does not seem to have been very effective.

In this context, another solution to explore (and one certainly more expensive and difficult to achieve) is to standardize social laws, tax laws, and private laws, either by clearly distinguishing the statuses in all laws, or by granting all couples the same rights and responsibilities, with some adjustments. This solution obviously requires rethinking the law as a whole in order to give it a coherence from the point of view of individuals and families, but also of prevailing views with respect to social norms and values.

Conclusion

To understand the behaviour of today's spouses with regard to marriage and, more specifically, to legal norms, we cannot limit ourselves to studying the effectiveness of the law in the strict sense of the term – namely, the way in which the law achieves legislators' objectives. All of a law's social effects – whether they are symbolic, current, deferred, expected or not – should be taken into account by drafters. The finding of a lack of knowledge of marital rights and obligations calls for legislative work aimed at limiting the ambiguity of messages sent by the state, particularly in the area of tax, social, and private laws. It also suggests the need for clear information campaigns. Yet, in light of the studies listed here, it is doubtful that the latter measure is sufficient.

Spousal negotiations, particularly around money issues, are an important source of stress and misunderstanding within households. The instrumental use of legal rules, especially through the drafting of cohabitation agreements, applies to only a very small portion of the population. A significant number of citizens think that the state defines general rules consistent with their point of view, which, they believe, reflects the realities of couples and families today. As Carbonnier has pointed out, to be known to the public and to claim some effectiveness, laws must coincide in good part with morality and good practical sense.[80] At present, however, there seems to be a real gap between the norms conveyed by law and those shared by Quebec spouses in particular. Given the ineffectiveness of information campaigns in an economic context where the state is trying to reduce expenses, another avenue for law reform should be privileged in our view. The state should impose a minimum framework for all couples (for example, after three years or five years of cohabitation) with the possibility of drafting agreements that reflect their particular family situation (for example, blended households) or possibly allow couple to avoid a framework altogether (the solution of opting out). In the latter case, the burden to prove to the other partner that it is in their interest to have no protection should fall to the economically stronger spouse. With such an approach, the law no longer evokes the binding rules that impose and forbid, but rather provides access to justice by creating a framework that alleviates conflict during a relationship breakdown while preserving autonomy, freedom, and equality.

Notes

I would like to warmly thank Martina Chumova, Annabelle Seery, Robert Leckey, and Marie-Claire Belleau for their valuable comments and suggestions. This study would not have been possible without the financial support of the Social Sciences and Humanities Research Council of Canada.

1 See Andrew J Cherlin, “Demographic Trends in the United States: A Review of Research in the 2000s” (2010) 72:3 J Marriage & Fam 403 [Cherlin, “Demographic Trends”]; Kathleen Kiernan, “Unmarried Cohabitation and Parenthood in Britain and Europe” (2004) 26:1 Law & Pol’y 33; Brienna Perelli-Harris et al, “The Educational Gradient of Childbearing within Cohabitation in Europe” (2010) 36:4 Population & Development Rev 775.

2 In Quebec, unmarried cohabitants are known as de facto spouses. See Cherlin, “Demographic Trends,” *supra* note 1; Kiernan, *supra* note 1. The process of individualization peculiar to modern societies has brought to the fore the quest for autonomy, the enhancement of personal fulfillment, authenticity, and the “pure relationship,” but also for relationships outside traditional institutional constraints. This transition has led to the weakening of social norms defining the behaviour of individuals while valorizing personal choices. See generally Irène Théry, *Le démariage: justice et vie privée* (Paris: Odile Jacob, 1993); Andrew J Cherlin, “The Deinstitutionalization of American Marriage” (2004) 66:4 J Marriage & Fam 848; Johan Surkyn & Ron Lesthaeghe, “Value Orientations and the Second Demographic Transition (SDT) in Northern, Western, and Southern Europe: An Update” (2004) 3:1 Demographic Research 45; Tomas Sobotka, “Overview Chapter 6: The Diverse Faces of the Second Demographic Transition in Europe” (2008) 19:1 Demographic Research 171; Pamela Smock, “Cohabitation in the United States: An Appraisal of Research Themes, Findings, and Implications” (2000) 26:1 Annual Rev Sociology 1; Julie Brines & Kara Joyner, “The Ties that Bind: Principles of Cohesion in Cohabitation and Marriage” (1999) 64:3 Am Sociological Rev 333.

3 See Statistics Canada, “Families, Households and Marital Status: Key Results from the 2016 Census of Canada,” Catalogue no. 11-001-X (2 August 2017), online: Statistics Canada, <www150.statcan.gc.ca/n1/daily-quotidien/170802/dq170802a-eng.htm>. According to this publication:

> The proportion [of couples living common law] in Canada [21.3%] was ... slightly higher than in the United Kingdom (20.0% in 2015), but lower than in France (22.6% in 2011), Norway (23.9% in 2011) and Sweden (29.0% in 2010) ... In 2016, Quebec (39.9%) and the three territories – Nunavut (50.3%), Northwest Territories (36.6%) and Yukon (31.9%) – had the highest proportions of common-law unions, considerably above the average for the rest of Canada (15.7%, excluding Quebec and the three territories). The proportions in Quebec and the territories were also higher than those in countries with high shares of common-law couples, such as Sweden.

Not only is the share of common law unions high in Quebec, but it has also risen faster in Quebec than elsewhere in the past few decades. The share of common law unions in Quebec was only slightly higher than the national average in 1981 (8.2% versus 6.3%), but was nearly twice as high in 2016 (39.9% versus 21.3%).

4 See Institut de la Statistique du Québec, *Le bilan démographique du Québec. Édition 2016*, by Chantal Girard et al (Quebec: Institut de la Statistique du Québec, 2016) at 10, online (PDF): <https://collections.banq.qc.ca/ark:/52327/bs2739506>. Almost two babies out of three were born to unmarried parents in Quebec in 2015.

5 See generally Cynthia Grant Bowman, *Unmarried Couples, Law, and Public Policy* (New York: Oxford University Press, 2010).

6 See Sean H Williams, "Sticky Expectations: Responses to Persistent Over-Optimism in Marriage, Employment Contracts, and Credit Card Use" (2009) 84:2 Notre Dame L Rev 733; Lynn A Baker & Robert E Emery, "When Every Relationship Is Above Average: Perceptions and Expectations of Divorce at the Time of Marriage" (1993) 17:4 Law & Human Behavior 439; Bowman, *supra* note 5.

7 See generally Robert Leckey, "Families in the Eyes of the Law" (2009) 15:8 Institute for Research on Public Policy Choices 42.

8 *Quebec (Attorney General) v A*, 2013 SCC 5, [2013] 1 SCR 61 [*Quebec (Attorney General)*], quashing *Droit de la famille – 102866*, 2010 QCCA 1978, [2010] RJQ 2259 [*Droit de la famille – 102866*].

9 See Carmen Lavallée, Hélène Belleau & Édith Guilhermont, "La situation juridique des conjoints de fait québécois" (2017) 73:1 Droit et cultures 69.

10 *Ibid.*

11 See *Quebec (Attorney General)*, *supra* note 8. In this judgment, five out of nine judges concluded that the treatment of de facto spouses in Quebec was discriminatory and violated the right to equality defined in the *Canadian Charter of Rights and Freedoms*, Part I of the *Constitution Act, 1982*, being Schedule B to the *Canada Act 1982* (UK), c 11 s 15. Of these, four considered it to be an acceptable discrimination in a free and democratic society (s 1) with respect to the

division of property, but only one, McLachlin CJ, concluded that this was also acceptable discrimination with regard to the maintenance obligation. A majority of the Court thus confirmed the constitutionality of the contested measures, and the decision leaned in favour of Eric. In 1995, the couple known as Lola and Eric decided to live together in Quebec, which was Eric's place of residence. They lived together for seven years and had three children before they separated in 2002. Lola wanted to get married, but Eric did not, saying he did not believe in the institution of marriage. Lola applied for custody of her children, and also challenged the provisions of the *Civil Code of Québec* that give married couples the right to divide family property and receive spousal support. She argued that because these laws do not apply to unmarried couples, the law discriminates against her based on her marital status, which was unconstitutional. Eric's position was in line with Quebec's law, which denies spousal support and property division rights to de facto spouses. It seems appropriate to explore the path of legislative reform because it would introduce, within the legal logic, some elements that are external but necessary. A real democratic debate is needed on this issue in Quebec, and the social sciences can and must contribute to such an enterprise in an informed manner.

12 For a similar finding in French law, see Jacques Commaille, "D'une sociologie de la famille à une sociologie du droit. D'une sociologie du droit à une sociologie des régulations sociales" (1986) 18:1 Sociologie et sociétés 113.

13 *Civil Code of Quebéc* [*CCQ-1991*].

14 Alain Roy, *L'évolution de la politique législative de l'union de fait au Québec. Analyse de l'approche autonomiste du législateur québécois sous l'éclairage du droit comparé*. Rapport d'expertise. (Quebec: Ministère de la Justice du Québec, 2008) [Roy, *L'évolution de la politique législative*].

15 See art 585, *CCQ*. See Dominique Goubau, Ghyslain Otis & David Robitaille, "La spécificité patrimoniale de l'union de fait: le libre choix et ses dommages collatéraux" (2003) 44:1 Revue générale de droit 3.

16 See Mireille D Castelli & Dominique Goubau, *Le droit de la famille au Québec*, 5th ed (Quebec: Les Presses de l'Université Laval, 2005).

17 *Charter of Human Rights and Freedoms,* CQLR 1975, c C-12, s 1.1.10:

> Every person has a right to full and equal recognition and exercise of his human rights and freedoms, without distinction, exclusion or preference based on race, colour, sex, gender identity or expression, pregnancy, sexual orientation, civil status, age except as provided by law, religion, political convictions, language, ethnic or national origin, social condition, a handicap or the use of any means to palliate a handicap. Discrimination exists where such a distinction, exclusion or preference has the effect of nullifying or impairing such right.

18 According to Benoît Moore:

> This recognition of de facto spouses in statutory or social law was accentuated in the 1980s and 1990s, this time through the application of section 15 of the *Canadian Charter of Rights and Freedoms*. The courts have repeatedly held that limiting the effects of these laws to marriage alone is discriminatory under the Charter, on the ground that these effects are not based on the legal relationship between the spouses, but on their "factual dependence."

Benoît Moore, "Variations chromatiques: l'union de fait entre noir et blanc" in Générosa Bras Miranda & Benoît Moore, eds, *Mélanges Adrian Popovici: les couleurs du droit* (Montreal: Thémis, 2010) 97 [my translation] [Moore, "Variations chromatiques"]. Roy, *L'évolution de la politique législative, supra* note 14 at 13.

19 See *An Act to amend various legislative provisions concerning de facto spouses,* SQ 1999, c 14 for the provincial law. See *Modernization of Benefits and Obligations Act* SC 2000, c 12 for the federal law. See also Alain Roy, "L'évolution de la politique législative de l'union de fait au Québec" in *Conférences des juristes de l'État* (Cowansville, QC: Yvon Blais, 2013) at 145 for a detailed analysis of Quebec's legislative history on the subject.

20 We could have added civil union here. This institution, little known to the Quebec populace, was created in 2002 to allow the union of same-sex spouses, then impossible under federal law. In its form and legal effects, civil union is almost similar to marriage.

21 See *Workers' Compensation Act,* CQLRc A-3 (replaced); *Act respecting financial assistance for education expenses,* CQLR c A-13.3; *Act respecting legal aid and the provision of certain other legal services,* CQLR c A-14; *Automobile Insurance Act,* CQLR c A-25; *Act respecting insurance,* CQLR c A-32 (replaced); *Taxation Act,* CQLR c I-3; *Act respecting the Québec Pension Plan,* CQLR c R-9; *Act respecting income support, employment assistance and social solidarity,* RSQ c S-32.001 (replaced). For a more complete list, see Castelli & Goubau, *supra* note 16 at 172.

22 Government of Quebec, "Loi sur les impôts," online: Quebec, <www4.gouv.qc.ca/fr/Portail/citoyens/programme-service/Pages/Info.aspx?sqctype=sujet&sqcid=613>.

23 Although income gaps between men and women have narrowed over the years in Quebec, statistics still show significant differences, especially after the birth of children in a household. In 2006, 75 percent of women aged twenty-five to fifty-four with children under the age of fifteen were employed. Their salary was approximately 69 percent of men's. See Quebec, *Conseil du statut de la femme. Portrait statistique égalité femmes/hommes: ou en sommes-nous au Québec?* (Quebec: CSF, 2010). Also, men work more outside the home after the arrival of a child, while women tend to reduce their paid working hours. See Institut de la

Statistique du Québec, *Le marché du travail et les parents,* by Sandra Gagnon (Quebec: Institut de la Statistique du Québec, 2009) at 14. The economic consequences of a relationship breakdown when spouses live in a de facto relationship in Quebec affect mothers, but also their children, who sometimes have very different living standards than they did before the breakup. *Droit de la famille – 102866, supra* note 8 at 145.

24 See Hélène Belleau & Pascale Cornut St-Pierre, "La question du 'choix' dans la décision de se marier ou non au Québec" (2011) 66:1 Lien social et politiques 65 [Belleau & Cornut St-Pierre, "La question du 'choix'"].

25 The present chapter is based on a quantitative study representative of Quebec's population (*N*=3,250). See Hélène Belleau, Carmen Lavallée & Annabelle Seery, *Unions et désunions conjugales au Québec: rapport de recherche. Première partie: le couple, l'argent et le droit* (Montreal: INRS Centre Urbanisation Culture Société, 2017), online (PDF): <espace.inrs.ca/5763/1/belleau-2017-unionsA.pdf> for an outline of the methodologies of the study. This chapter is also based on four qualitative empirical research studies carried out in Quebec between 2005 and 2012, with 180 respondents. The semi-directed interviews, each lasting approximately two hours, focused on the economic dynamics between spouses in relation to legal issues. The methodological aspects of these studies can be found in other publications. See e.g. Hélène Belleau, "Entre le partage des dépenses et le partage des avoirs: les comptes conjugaux des ménages québécois" in Hélène Belleau & Caroline Henchoz, eds, *L'usage de l'argent dans le couple: pratiques et perceptions des comptes amoureux: perspective internationale* (Paris: Harmattan, 2008) 113; Hélène Belleau, *Quand l'amour et l'Etat rendent aveugle: le mythe du mariage automatique* (Quebec: Presses de l'Université du Québec, 2011) [Belleau, *Quand l'amour*]; Hélène Belleau & Pascale Cornut St-Pierre, "Conjugal Interdependence in Quebec: From Legal Rules to Social Representations on Spousal Support and Property Division on Conjugal Breakdown" (2014) 29:1 CJLS 43.

26 In this text, we use the terms "de facto spouses" and "unmarried cohabitants" as synonyms.

27 See Belleau, Lavallée & Seery, *supra* note 25.

28 See Ulrich Beck, *La société du risque: sur la voie d'une autre modernité*, translated by L Bernardi (Paris: Aubier, 2001).

29 Anne Barlow et al, *Family Affairs: Cohabitation, Marriage and the Law* (London: Nuffield Foundation, 2002) [Barlow et al, *Family Affairs*]. See also Pamela J Smock, Wendy Manning & Meredith Porter, "'Everything's There Except Money': How Money Shapes Decisions to Marry among Cohabitors" (2005) 67:3 J Marriage & Family 680; Elaine E Sutherland, "From 'Bidie-in' to 'Cohabitant' in Scotland: The Perils of Legislative Compromise" (2013) 27:2 Intl JL Pol'y & Fam 143; see Bowman, *supra* note 5, regarding the reasons spouses are giving for not getting married.

30 Anne-Rigt Poortman & Melinda Mills, "Investments in Marriage and Cohabitation: The Role of Legal and Interpersonal Commitment" (2012) 74:2 J Marriage & Family 357.

31 *Ibid* at 373. See also Lynn Baker & Robert Emory, "When Every Relationship Is Above Average: Perceptions and Expectations of Divorce at the Time of Marriage" (1993) 17 L & Human Behavior 439.

32 See e.g. Pascoe Pleasence & Nigel J Balmer, "Ignorance in Bliss: Modeling Knowledge of Rights in Marriage and Cohabitation" (2012) 46:2 Law & Soc'y Rev 297; Patricia Ewick & Susan S Silbey, *The Common Place of Law: Stories from Everyday Life* (Chicago: University of Chicago Press, 1998).

33 See generally Andrew Ashworth, "Ignorance of the Criminal Law and Duties to Avoid It" (2011) 74:1 Mod L Rev 1; Lynn A Baker, "Promulgating the Marriage Contract" (1990) 23:2 U Mich JLR Ref 217.

34 Jean Carbonnier, *Droit civil,* vol 1 (Paris: Presses universitaires de France, 2004) at 233 [my translation].

35 Harrell R Rodgers & Charles S Bullock, *Law and Social Change: Civil Rights Laws and Their Consequences* (New York: McGraw-Hill, 1972).

36 Guy Rocher, "L'effectivité du droit" in Andrée Lajoie et al, eds, *Théories et émergence du droit: pluralisme, surdétermination et effectivité* (Montreal: Thémis Publishing, 1998) 133 at 144 [my translation].

37 In English, the expression "common law marriage myth" refers to at least two distinct meanings: the existence of a marriage after a simple exchange of consents between the parties, or the idea that common law spouses have the same rights and obligations as married spouses. In this text, we are referring only to the second definition. See Rebecca Probert, "Common-Law Marriage: Myths and Misunderstandings" (2008) 20:1 Child & Family LQ 1 for a thorough analysis of the origin and uses of this expression. See Göran Lind, *Common Law Marriage: A Legal Institution for Cohabitation* (New York: Oxford University Press, 2008) for information on the United States.

38 Anne Barlow & Simon Duncan, "New Labour's Communitarianism, Supporting Families and the 'Rationality Mistake': Part II" (2000) 22:2 J Soc Welfare & Fam L 129; Anne Barlow et al, *Cohabitation, Marriage and the Law: Social Change and Legal Reform in the 21st Century* (Oxford: Hart Publishing, 2005) [Barlow et al, *Cohabitation*]; Mary Hibbs, Chris Barton & Joanne Beswick, "Why Marry? Perceptions of the Affianced" (2001) 31 Family 197; Rosa Panades et al, *Informing Unmarried Parents about Their Legal Rights at Birth Registration* (London: One Plus One, 2007); Pleasence and Balmer, *supra* note 32.

39 See Probert, *supra* note 37.

40 *Ibid.*

41 See Anne Barlow et al, "Just a Piece of Paper? Marriage and Cohabitation" in Alison Park et al, eds, *British Social Attitudes: The 18th Report. Public Policy, Social Ties* (London: Sage Publications, 2001) at 29. It is interesting to note that, among the administrative categories used by the state was "common law marriage." See Panades et al, *supra* note 38. The parallel with the use made in Quebec of the concept of "spouse" (*conjoint*) as an administrative category, despite highly variable definitions from one program to another, is remarkable. See also Roy, *L'évolution de la politique législative*, *supra* note 14.

42 Barlow et al, *Family Affairs*, *supra* note 29.

43 Belleau & Cornut St-Pierre, "La question du 'choix,'" *supra* note 24.

44 Belleau, Lavallée & Seery, *supra* note 25. In 2007, a survey conducted for the Chambre des Notaires with 805 residents of Quebec showed that only 40 percent of people living in de facto unions knew that they would never have the same legal status as married couples, even after several years of cohabitation. It also revealed that only 36 percent of de facto spouses knew that, in the event of a breakup, property acquired during the union would not necessarily be split in equal parts. Finally, it should be noted that only 23 percent of people in an unmarried cohabitation knew that, at the time of a breakup, the poorest partner would not be entitled to alimony. Chamber of Notaries of Quebec, *Perception du mariage et de l'union libre*, by Ipsos Descarie (Quebec: Chambre des notaires du Québec, 2007) [Ipsos Descarie] at 42.

45 See e.g. Alain Roy, "Partenariat civil et couple de même sexe: la réponse du Québec" (2001) 35:3 RJT 663; Michelle Giroux & Anouk Laurent, "Portrait critique de l'union de fait en droit Québécois" (1989) 20:1 RGD 129; Christianne Dubreuil, "L'union de fait au Québec: inexistence dans le Code civil" (1999) 28:1–2 Cahiers québécois de démographie 229; Jocelyne Jarry, *Les conjoints de fait au Québec: vers un encadrement légal* (Cowansville, QC: Yvon Blais, 2008); Denis Lapierre, "Les contrats de la vie commune" in *Développements récents sur l'union de fait* vol 140 (Cowansville, QC: Yvon Blais, 2000); Jacques Beaulne, "Aperçu de la situation juridique des conjoints de fait au Québec: aspects civils, sociaux et fiscaux" in Jacques Beaulne & Michel Verwilghen, eds, *Points de droit familial: rencontres universitaires notariales belgo-québécoises* (Montreal: Wilson & Lafleur, 1997) 236; Moore, "Variations chromatiques," *supra* note 18; Alain Roy & Violaine Lemay, *Le contrat conjugal: pour l'amour ou pour la guerre? Étude empirique des représentations professionnelles du contrat conjugal chez les juristes et les psychothérapeutes* (Montreal: Éditions Thémis, 2009). See also Benoît Moore, "Les enfants du nouveau siècle (Libres propos sur la réforme de la filiation)" in *Développements récents en droit familial* vol 176 (Cowansville, QC: Yvon Blais, 2002) 75; Brigitte Lefebvre, "L'évolution de la notion de conjoint en droit

Québécois" in Pierre-Claude Lafond & Brigitte Lefebvre, eds, *L'union civile: nouveaux modèles de conjugalité et de parentalité au 21e siècle* (Cowansville, QC: Editions Yvon Blais, 2003) 3 at 20.

46 Scottish Executive Social Research, *Scottish Social Attitudes Survey 2004: Family Module Report*, by Fran Wasoff & Claudia Martin (Edinburgh: Scottish Executive Social Research, 2005). See also Sutherland, *supra* note 29 at 143.

47 See Wasoff & Martin, *supra* note 46 at 42.

48 *Ibid* at 16.

49 The authors of a report published by the Law Commission in England pointed out: "It would seem that failure to appreciate the legal distinctions between marriage and cohabitation is not unique to this jurisdiction. Evidence from Germany and the Netherlands suggests that there is a similar problem there." See UK, Law Commission, *Cohabitation: The Financial Consequences of Relationship Breakdown* (Law Com No 307) (London: Her Majesty's Stationery Office, 2007) at 149. For Holland, see Katharina Boele-Woelki et al, eds, *Huwelijk of geregistreerd partnerschap? Een evaluatie van de Wet openstelling huwelijk en de Wet geregistreerd partnerschap in opdracht van het Ministerie van Justitie* (Molengraaff instituut, Universiteit Utrecht, 2006) at 187. For the Netherlands, see Ministry of Justice, *Registered Partnership in the Netherlands: A Quick Scan*, by Bram van Dijk & Yvonne Scherf (Amsterdam: DSP-groep BV, 1999). See Bowman, *supra* note 5 at 21 for the United States. For France, two surveys dealing specifically with spouses' legal knowledge were identified. A representative survey of the population carried out by the Chambre des notaires de Paris in 2010, with 955 respondents, concluded that the rights and obligations of the *pacsés* (i.e., civil partnership) in certain respects are less known than those de facto couples. For example, while 75 percent of respondents know that common law spouses do not inherit automatically in the absence of a will, only 45 percent of them know about *pacsé* spouses. See BVA Group & Chambre des notaires de Paris, "Les Français et les notaires " (2010), online (PDF): <https://www.bva-group.com/wp-content/uploads/2017/02/fichier_tp365-_20_minutes_-_notairesa1ea5.pdf>.

50 Ulla Bjornberg, "Cohabitation and Marriage in Sweden – Does Family Form Matter?" (2001) 15:3 Intl JL Pol'y & Fam 350 at 354–55. The study mentioned by Bjornberg is E Callenmyr, "Sambolagen (Joint Homes Act)," an essay in Civil Law 20, Juridiska Fakulteten, Uppsala Universitat, 1989. Callenmyr's comments were based on two surveys: first, the Gavle study, completed in 1974 by the Ministerial Committee, in preparation for new legislation to provide guidance to common law couples. Both partners within 101 married couples and 111 cohabiting couples were interviewed. The second was the Tidaholm Study,

conducted in 1989 with 117 respondents. In 2013, a qualitative study of about fifteen Swedish respondents showed that they believed that marriage had advantages over common law unions, although they were unable to explain what those might be. The author sees such attitudes as reflecting a positive prescriptive presumption with regard to marriage. See Jacob Strandell, *We're One, but We're Not the Same: Individualization and Increasing Marriage Rates Unraveled* (master's of science thesis, Lund University Department of Sociology, 2013) [unpublished] at 21.

51 Baker & Emery, *supra* note 6. Baker and Emery submitted two populations to their questionnaires: 137 married spouses and 92 students enrolled in a family law course. The latter group of respondents answered the questionnaire before (*n*=92) and after (*n*=80) taking the family law course.

52 *Ibid* at 441.

53 See Belleau, Lavallée & Seery, *supra* note 25.

54 Pleasence & Balmer, *supra* note 32.

55 Barlow et al, *Cohabitation, supra* note 38.

56 Hélène Belleau & Pascale Cornut St-Pierre, "Pour que droit et familles fassent bon ménage: étude sur la conscience du droit en matière conjugale" (2012) 25:1 Nouvelles pratiques sociales 62 [Belleau & Cornut St-Pierre, "Pour que droit"].

57 John M Darley, Kevin M Carlsmith & Paul H Robinson, "The Ex Ante Function of the Criminal Law" (2001) 35:1 Law & Soc'y Rev 165; Pauline T Kim, "Norms, Learning, and Law: Exploring the Influences on Worker's Legal Knowledge" (1999) 2 U Ill L Rev 447.

58 Lee Ross, David Greene & Pamela House, "The False Consensus Effect: An Egocentric Bias in Social Perception and Attribution Processes" (1977) 13:3 J Experimental Social Psychology 279. See also Ira Mark Ellman & Sanford L Braver, "Should Marriage Matter?" in Marsha Garrison & Elizabeth S Scott, eds, *Marriage at the Crossroads: Law, Policy, and the Brave New World of Twenty-First-Century Families* (New York: Cambridge University Press, 2012) 170.

59 Pleasence & Balmer, *supra* note 32 at 323.

60 See Barlow et al, *Cohabitation, supra* note 38 at 45; Wasoff & Martin, *supra* note 46; Kim, *supra* note 57; Pleasence & Balmer, *supra* note 32 at 302. For the United States, see Ellman & Braver, *supra* note 58 at 196.

61 See Pleasence & Balmer, *supra* note 32; Belleau & Cornut St-Pierre, "La question du 'choix,'" *supra* note 24; Belleau & Cornut St-Pierre, "Pour que droit," *supra* note 56; Barlow et al, *Cohabitation, supra* note 38.

62 See Barlow et al, *Cohabitation, supra* note 38.

63 *Ibid* at 50; Pleasence & Balmer, *supra* note 32 at 322.

64 See Ipsos Decarie, *supra* note 44 at 33.

65 *Ibid*; Belleau, Lavallée & Seery, *supra* note 25 at 69.

66 See Anne Barlow & Grace James, "Regulating Marriage and Cohabitation in 21st Century Britain" (2004) 67:2 Mod L Rev 143; Barlow et al, *Cohabitation, supra* note 38; Belleau, *Quand l'amour, supra* note 25.

67 See Benoît Moore, "L'union homosexuelle et le Code civil du Québec: de l'ignorance à la reconnaissance?" (2002) 81:1 Can Bar Rev 121.

68 Williams, *supra* note 6 at 757.

69 This phenomenon is widely documented in scientific literature and in many disciplines such as economics, psychology, health, and law, albeit under sometimes different terms, such as "comparative optimism." See Gerd Gigerenzer, "How to Make Cognitive Illusions Disappear: Beyond Heuristics and Biases" (1991) 2:1 European Rev Social Psychology 83; NC Higgins, Michelle D St Amand & Gary D Poole, "The Controllability of Negative Life Experiences Mediates Unrealistic Optimism" (1997) 42:3 Social Indicators Research 299; Jeffrey J Rachlinski, "The Uncertain Psychological Case for Paternalism" (2003) 97:3 Nw UL Rev 1172.

70 David Dunning, Chip Heath & Jerry M Suls, "Flawed Self-Assessment: Implication for Health, Education and the Workplace" (2004) 5:3 Psychological Science in the Public Interest 69.

71 Helen Reece, "Leaping without Looking" in Robert Leckey, ed, *After Legal Equality: Family, Sex, Kinship* (London: Routledge, 2015) at 122 citing David A Armor & Shelley E Taylor, "When Predictions Fail: The Dilemma of Unrealistic Optimism" in Thomas Gilovich, Dale Griffin & Daniel Kahneman, eds, *Heuristics and Biases: The Psychology of Intuitive Judgment* (Cambridge: Cambridge University Press, 2002) at 341; Tali Sharot, *The Optimism Bias: Why We're Wired to Look on the Bright Side* (London: Constable and Robinson, 2012) at 44; David A Armor & Shelley E Taylor, "Situated Optimism: Specific Outcome Expectancies and Self-Regulation" (1998) 30 Advances in Experimental Social Psychology 309.

72 Rachlinski, *supra* note 69; Reece, *supra* note 71.

73 Hélène Belleau, Chiara Piazzesi & Annabelle Seery, "Conjugal Love from a Sociological Perspective: Theorizing from Observed Practices" (2020) 45:1 Can J Sociology 23.

74 Barlow et al, *Cohabitation, supra* note 38.

75 Reece, *supra* note 71.

76 Barlow et al, *Cohabitation, supra* note 38; Panades et al, *supra* note 38; Baker & Emery, *supra* note 6 at 439; Williams, *supra* note 6 at 737. According to Williams, "[e]ven providing personalized risk information has only fleeting and inconsistent effects on the strength of the above-average effect."

77 Williams, *supra* note 6; Baker & Emery, *supra* note 6; Barlow et al, *Cohabitation, supra* note 38. For the hardship and consequences of negotiating divorce agreements, see Chapter 4 by Rachel Treloar in this volume.

78 Several authors show that few de facto spouses enter into agreements about what happens in the event of a breakup. See e.g. Nina Dethloff, "New Models of Partnership: The Financial Consequences of Separation" (2011) 12:1 ERA Forum 89 at 96. See Wasoff & Martin, *supra* note 46; Sutherland, *supra* note 29 for Scotland. In England, among common law spouses where only one spouse owns the family home, less than 10 percent have signed a contract. See Bowman, *supra* note 5 at 177. According to our 2015 survey conducted in Quebec, about 5 percent of de facto spouses have signed a cohabitation agreement. See Belleau, Lavallée & Seery, *supra* note 25 at 59. See also Baker & Emery, *supra* note 6 at 446; Barlow et al, *Cohabitation, supra* note 38 at 5; Panades et al, *supra* note 38 at 32, Williams, *supra* note 6; Pleasence & Balmer, *supra* note 32.

79 Barlow et al, *Cohabitation, supra* note 38 at 41.

80 See Carbonnier, *supra* note 34 at 233.

8

"WAR" and Other Reasons People Move In Together

Analyzing Cohabitating Relationship Progressions in British Columbia

Erez Aloni and Adam Vanzella-Yang

> Well, honestly, things in Whistler are kind of, sometimes, we call it a "WAR," a Whistler Accelerated Relationship, so sometimes you're moving in together because it's way cheaper and stuff.[1]

A column entitled "13 Signs You're Ready to Move In Together" in the magazine *Glamour* – which styles itself as the "source for what matters to women now" – advises readers that "the end of your lease doesn't automatically equal move-in time."[2] Quoting from a self-help book, the column warns: "You have to say with 100 percent confidence that moving in together has nothing to do with your finances."[3] The column further adds, "If you feel pressure to move in from anyone (your parents, your friends, your partner – even yourself), you may not be ready."[4]

Are cohabitants in British Columbia following this advice, or do they mostly move in together because of housing constraints and other financial matters? Or do they do so because of love or a desire to spend more time together? More generally, what is the process that cohabitants in British Columbia go through when they decide to move in together? And why is it important that we learn more about this? Using interviews with thirty couples who live in unmarried cohabitation in British Columbia, this chapter provides some answers to these questions.

The number of romantically involved couples in Canada who live in informal intimate relationships – that is, they are not married or registered in another partnership scheme – has grown dramatically over the past two decades. This trend has an impact on numerous aspects of public policy:

from crafting modernized family law to features of urban design. Yet, surprisingly, compared with the United States and other similar countries, the data on the lives of unmarried couples in Canada are scanty, especially outside Quebec. In 2000, Professor Zheng Wu, Canada's primary demographer of cohabitation, stated that there are insufficient data about the lives of cohabitants in Canada.[5] Not much has changed since then in terms of the availability of such data. This chapter aims to shed light on couples' decision making about moving in together and is based on a qualitative study that we conducted in British Columbia in 2018–19.

Canada, like other nations around the world, has experienced a skyrocketing number of intimate couples who live in informal relationships.[6] In 2019, the number of Canadians who lived in "common law" partnership – defined by Statistics Canada as living in "conjugal" relationships for at least one year – reached over 3.7 million individuals, compared with 14 million married individuals.[7] In 2016, over 20 percent of all Canadian couples were in common law relationship – more than three times the proportion in 1981.[8]

The constant growth in the number of unmarried cohabitants has numerous implications. Understanding the progressions and functions of these relationships is therefore essential to inform scholarship and policy. The most obvious implication is with respect to law: how should the law, which was traditionally predicated on the model of the nuclear marital family, react to the proliferation of unmarried cohabitants? In particular, living together has become a fundamental element of legal doctrines that recognize informal cohabitants as equal to spouses in terms of financial obligations the partners have to one another, as well as in terms of eligibility to state benefits.[9] From a sociological perspective, understanding the lives of cohabitants and incorporating them into academic accounts "is crucial for evaluating family patterns, the life course of individuals, children's well-being, and social change more broadly."[10] From an economic perspective, the length of time during which couples move from cohabitation to marriage (if at all), the role of cohabitation (for example, as a precursor or alternative to marriage), and unmarried couples' behaviours in terms of household finances have effects on wealth distribution, employment patterns, poverty, economic inequality, and reproductive patterns.[11] Relationship patterns matter even for urban-planning studies, as the availability of housing might affect the progression of couples' relationships, which might, in turn, affect the housing market. This is far from an exhaustive list, but the idea is clear: understanding conjugal informal cohabitation is important across various areas of public policy.

In Canada, more research is needed on couples' decision-making processes and timelines for moving in together. While we know a little about the sociodemographic characteristics of cohabiting couples, the length and stability of their relationships, and their economic behaviour, there are important gaps in knowledge that remain to be addressed. In fact, most studies are from Quebec, where legal treatment of cohabitants' obligations to one another is different from that the rest of Canada.[12] Related research from Quebec is often incommensurate with the rest of Canada because the cultural contexts of cohabitation in Quebec – the functions it fulfills for couples and societal views on it – are unique.[13] Further, most studies in Canada are quantitative; but *qualitative* studies in this area are critically important because they can "provide the sort of in-depth data important for nuanced assessments of recent and possible future changes in family patterns."[14] This chapter's intentions are modest – this study does not purport to, nor can it possibly, fill the many gaps in this area. Nonetheless, we believe that it provides important initial insights on the progression into shared living among young adults in British Columbia.

Methods

We interviewed thirty cohabiting couples living in British Columbia: twenty-seven different-sex couples and three same-sex couples.[15] We recruited participants through ads on Facebook and posted in coffee shops across the city of Vancouver. We conducted face-to-face interviews with couples residing in Vancouver (n=18). Most frequently, participants set the interview at a coffee shop; occasionally, we met in people's homes. We held interviews on Skype with couples living in other parts of British Columbia (n=12). The interviews ranged from approximately thirty to ninety minutes, and we offered each couple a sixty-dollar Amazon gift card as an honorarium.

Although there are methodological benefits to interviewing partners separately, we opted to interview them together.[16] When it comes to the issues discussed in this chapter, this choice did not matter much – since many of the topics are not controversial but rather involve straightforward information on the couples, such as how they met, how long they have known each other, and how they decided to move in together. Our initial intention was to switch to interviewing individuals separately after a few pilot rounds, but we noticed that people frequently relied on their partner for recollection of events and corrected each other when one partner mentioned something that did not correspond with the other person's perspective. Importantly, we realized that people were often surprisingly blunt in their responses and that the presence of a partner in the interview tended to function as an accuracy check. We thus concluded this strategy had more merits than drawbacks.

Though the sample is diverse in several ways, most respondents are highly educated, middle-income, young professionals between the ages of twenty-one and forty-three. The majority have at least a bachelor's degree (or are in the process of obtaining one) and are not religious. Only three of the couples we interviewed had children living in the household. In sum, our sample reflects the conventional notion of cohabitants as more prone to uphold liberal values and to not have religious reasons to get married, but it likely overrepresents well-educated cohabitants.[17] Table 8.1 provides the ages and occupations of participating couples.

We used a semi-structured, open-ended format for the interviews. These interviews addressed a variety of topics, from how individuals understand the law to how they divide their housework chores. In this chapter, we focus on participants' responses to questions on their transition from dating to moving in together. More specifically, we analyze their answers to the following questions: When did you move in together? How long had you dated before moving in together? Where did you live before you moved in together? When did you decide to move in together (i.e., how long after beginning dating and before the actual move-in date)? What made you decide to move in together? Were there any specific issues you were concerned with in the process of moving in together? How did you decide on where to live? (Who moved in with whom, or did you find a new place together?) Overall, how would you describe the transition period? We report on and analyze some of the results below.

TABLE 8.1
Overview of participating couples

#	Pseudonyms	Ages	Occupations
1	Veronica/Howard	21 and 21	Student and worker at a nonprofit/Student and software developer
2	Andrea/Fabian	27 and 26	Bike workshop coordinator/Carpenter
3	Tim/William	32 and 31	Chemistry instructor/Unemployed
4	Lori/Konan	28 and 29	Graduate student/Hotel manager
5	Kelley/Megan	43 and 48	Midwife/Accountant
6	Rachel/Nathan	36 and 35	Legal assistant/Software engineer
7	Anita/Jared	27 and 29	Dietician blogger/Computer engineer
8	Olivia/Dave	37 and 40	Software sales rep/Chiropractor
9	Vanessa/Martin	30 and 42	Unemployed/Entrepreneur
10	Lindsey/Bode	29 and 30	Small business owners (both)
11	Abigail/Barak	23 and 25	Urban farmer/Recent graduate
12	Kate/Robert	29 and 33	Engineer/Engineer
13	Amelia/Asher	31 and 31	Mortgage broker/General manager
14	Lily/Liam	28 and 33	Marketing/Technician
15	Maya/Zachary	32 and 35	Student/Service manager
16	Seana/Tobias	28 and 30	High school teacher/Social worker assistant
17	Priscilla/Don	30 and 29	Events coordinator/e-Commerce employee
18	Kemala/Ethan	30 and 31	Counsellor/Medical writer
19	Naomi/Axel	32 and 38	Electrician/Sprinkler fitter
20	Kathleen/Lucas	32 and 27	Art teacher/Unemployed
21	Irina/Kevin	36 and 43	PhD student/Communications
22	Stella/Otis	48 and 31	Provincial government/Security guard
23	Elsie/Samuel	27 and 28	Visual artist/Applications support engineer
24	Julian/Oscar	28 and 27	Property manager/Project coordinator
25	Ruth/Rupert	29 and 28	Lawyer/Teacher
26	Mila/Hugo	33 and 35	Occupational therapist/Labour contract negotiator
27	Christy/Jacob	26 and 29	Banker/Executive
28	Mabel/James	30 and 31	Brewery worker/Landscaper
29	Adrienne/Hunter	30 and 29	Actor/Writer
30	Valorie/Lulu	33 and 44	Social worker/Data manager

How Long Did They Date before Moving In Together?

Understanding how long, on average, couples date before moving in together is significant for various reasons. Sociological studies have hypothesized that breaking up from a cohabiting relationship is more difficult than from a non-cohabitating relationship.[18] Basically, cohabitation adds another layer of constraints that could impel couples to stay together despite lack of compatibility. Hence, moving in together without appropriate deliberation or an adequate dating period potentially increases the risk of remaining in an unstable relationship and of lowering the relationship's quality.[19] In general, a moderate pace of progression in a relationship corresponds to better relationship quality. As Sassler and Miller explain, "numerous studies have found that slowly developing relationships, at least among marrieds, are often of higher quality than those that developed rapidly. Such may be the case for cohabiting relationships, as well."[20] Importantly, studies in the United States found that "the pace of entry into coresidence is slower [for women from more advantaged backgrounds] than for less-advantaged women."[21] This means that a longer dating period – important for stabilizing a relationship – is a privilege of those who are better off.

Moving in together too slowly, on the other hand, might raise some policy concerns as well. For example, if many people live in relationships of interdependency but in separate households for long duration before they move in together, then the law might reconsider the factor of cohabitation as a proxy for interdependency.[22] Or, as we see below, sometimes there are external reasons, such as risk of loss of public benefits, that might deter couples from moving in together. Hence, an unusually slow-moving process might suggest that we ought to consider policies related to the issues behind couples' reluctance to share a residence. Finally, to the extent that many of the choices couples make regarding the timing of cohabiting are related to financial considerations, then we should ponder how economic inequality is connected to important relationship transitions.

Overall, the median time that interviewees dated before moving in together was 12 months, and the average was 19.3 months. The average should be taken with a grain of salt, however, because one couple dated ten years before taking up shared residence, and two couples dated five and six years, respectively. We will discuss their stories below, but they are outliers: eighteen couples out of thirty dated a year or less before moving in together.

The shortest periods – ten couples who dated less than half a year before beginning cohabitation – provide interesting anecdotes on how a tight housing market affects decisions about relationships. One couple we interviewed formed their relationship in reverse order – that is, after they had already lived together. Don and Priscilla (twenty-nine and thirty) met while they were living in a shared house with eight or nine other people. They explain that the main reason for living in such a setting was money. But further, Don shares that a "lot of people that approached that house were doing it for the experimental purpose and to share things in the greater community context." They dated for six months before they decided to move into a shared yet bigger room within the same household. The decision to move in together was easy, as Don states: "Practicality. It's so much easier to make that decision when you're already living in the same house, but then on top of that just sharing a rent."[23]

Naomi (thirty-two) and Axel (thirty-eight) are another couple who first lived together then started a romantic engagement. They have been best friends for over a decade. When Naomi bought a house (because rent was too expensive, she put a small down payment on an inexpensive property in the suburbs), she invited Axel to join her as a platonic roommate to assist with paying the mortgage. Later, their relationship started to change because Naomi wanted to have an intimate relationship with Axel; eventually, they became a couple. This is another instance, then, in which an unaffordable real estate market served a matchmaking role – it created the conditions that allow people to meet or to transition into intimate partners.

On the other side of the scale, we find those who waited more than five years before moving in together. Interestingly, two of these three couples are of the same sex and are also relatively older than the others in our sample. Kelley and Megan, forty-three and forty-eight, dated for six years before they started sharing a residence. They waited impatiently for this moment, as living separately had become very difficult. In Kelley's words, "It was just so annoying to not live together; it was like really very hard. I mean we spent probably three and four nights together a week … back and forth, back and forth, back and forth, and it just became so unbearable. So as soon as we possibly could we did [move in together]." The reasons they avoided living together earlier is that Kelley, at the time, was studying to be a midwife. She is also a single parent. As such, she was eligible for tuition assistance and a housing subsidy. If she moved in with Megan, the result would have been the elimination of her entire assistance because their two incomes would be combined for purposes of determining eligibility. Kelley says the consequences were so dire that "I would have lost a lot of financial aid and a lot of access to ... well, all of everything that I got, basically." Megan adds that moving in together and losing all assistance "would have suddenly thrown us both into poverty and no education." So, they decided to wait until Kelley graduated before they could cohabit.

Lulu and Valorie, forty-four and thirty-three, dated for five years before moving in together because they thought that moving earlier "might be pressure on the relationship." In particular, since they are a non-monogamous couple, cohabitation could create awkward situations. Lulu puts it in the following terms: "For the first three years of our relationship I had another significant relationship and, obviously, people have multiple partners and live with one of their partners, but for me I always found that a bit hard to imagine, like trying to have dates with the other person, when I was dating, with my partner like in the next room or something." However, at year four of their relationship, "it started to get a bit tiring going back and forth between two different places."

It might be that the fact that two of the three couples being of the same sex is a mere coincidence. But we can also speculate that since LGBTQ2S+ people in Canada and elsewhere, on average, still earn less than their heterosexual and cisgender counterparts, they might be more exposed to the set of considerations and pressures that Kelley and Megan experienced.[24] Hence, couples of sexual minorities might need to think more about the possible elimination or reduction of their social assistance (welfare) than their counterparts. Likewise, because same-sex couples are more likely than others to be in open relationships or other versions of non-monogamous partnerships, the story of Lulu and Valorie might be reflective of a common narrative of LGBTQ2S+ folks.[25] Of course, our sample is too small to make any argument about this, and we only raise this as a possible research question for future studies.

The third couple who dated for long time, ten years, has a different account. Mabel and James, thirty and thirty-one years old, were high-school sweethearts. After high school, they chose to live in different cities for a period to find out what it was like to be apart from each other. Subsequently, Mabel moved to Vancouver for university while James remained in Toronto.

They kept up a long-distance relationship during this time and were happy to finally share a residence when James moved to Vancouver.

In summary, most of the couples we interviewed moved in together within a year of starting to date. Those who moved in together in less than six months often did so because of housing reasons. Those who moved after long-term dating did so out of personal choices about relationship structure (for example, non-monogamous), although one couple in particular delayed moving in together for the detrimental financial consequences cohabitation could have.

When we analyze these data, a few observations immediately present themselves. First, the tight housing market in Canadian cities induces shared housing arrangements – a trend that becomes common across the Global North[26] – in which people co-reside with multiple strangers and/or friends. Some recent studies have begun exploring this way of living as a form of non-kin intimacy that serves as an alternative to the nuclear family, as well as other sociological and psychological dimensions of the relational dynamics in these households.[27] Adding to this emerging strand of research, this chapter suggests that another underexplored aspect of this model is shared housing as a site for *meeting* intimate partners. The model's uniqueness, as Don and Priscilla's story suggests, is that it presents the opportunity to cohabit without intimate relationships before beginning the romantic phase. Moving into the same room within shared housing might be simpler and a gradual move compared with moving in after an intimate relationship has begun. Further, moving into a shared room provides an opportunity to test the relationship while taking smaller risk in case the relationship ends with a breakup. Future sociological research can explore how relationships that progress in this "reverse order" – first cohabiting, then dating – change our perception of the conventional process of dating, the quality of such relationships, and the impact on other housemates who might be less interested in living with a non-platonic couple.

Second, waiting to move into a shared residence as a means to avoid termination of benefits raises significant policy questions. This study calls for rethinking the use of cohabitation both as a marker for financial interdependency and for purposes of delimiting eligibility in various areas of social assistance. Using the fact of cohabitation as a marker for partnership – that is, as a marker that can result in termination or reduction of assistance – is common in the Global North.[28] The government of British Columbia, for example, employs a rigorous functional test to detect who is considered a "spouse" for this purpose, and as little as twelve months' cohabitation could suffice for partners to be considered as spouses.[29] Although we discussed only Kelley and Megan's experience, another couple we interviewed was highly concerned about losing disability benefits. They found a clever way to overcome the problem, and hence quickly jumped over this barrier, but not all couples can use their solution. In any event, maintaining two households is a waste of resources and of time if a committed couple avoids living together *only* because they think it will throw them into poverty. This policy obviously has the strongest effect on couples in lower socio-economic positions and on people with disabilities (which qualifies them for governmental assistance). The point is not that living together is always good, but that avoiding it only in order to maintain benefits – for those who *want* to share residency – is most harmful to people who are already having a hard time financially. In general, moving in with a partner can be beneficial in terms of emotional and monetary support, and people should not be motivated to live alone out of fear of losing financial help; this applies even more strongly in regard to people with low incomes, those living with disabilities, single parents, and so on.

Third, polyamory and other non-monogamous relationships are becoming increasingly popular, and raise many new legal questions.[30] These relationships' progression and legal implications remain underexplored topics. The decision to move in with more than one partner – and the timing of doing so – might have different financial and social meanings than those intended by monogamous couples. From legal and sociological standpoints, there is a need for more research about common patterns of and rationales for such a decision. For example, under British Columbia's *Family Law Act,* the date that the relationship is deemed to have begun is "the date on which [the partners] began to live together in a marriage-like relationship."[31] This means that when measuring what assets are subject to equal division among the partners, and how much they have appreciated, the point that matters is the time of moving in, not the time that the partners qualified as "spouses," which is after two years of living together in a marriage-like relationships. For instance, if a couple broke up after five years of living together, and lived in a marriage-like relationship right away, they are considered "spouses" for purposes of property and spousal support division only after two years. But upon breakup, the valuation time is backdated to the time the couple moved in initially, therefore the entire five years will matter for property appreciation. From that moment, any increase in value of property (even "excluded property" – property that is not part of the divisible pool) is equally divided upon breakup. The same is true with regard to spousal support – the calculation of spousal support entitlement and quantum includes the initial time of moving in together. There is a question whether this indicator – the time they "began to live together in a marriage-like relationship" – operates in the same way for monogamous and non-monogamous relationships. Backdating to the initial point of cohabitation might be unfair to all, but seems to be particularly unfit in the case of non-monogamous people, who might take longer to qualify as married-like than monogamous couples. From the very small sample of polyamorous couples we had (n=3), the answer appears complicated and requires some additional research. A larger-scale study of the transitioning process among non-monogamous individuals will add clarity and nuance to these issues.

These are just initial observations about couples' timing in residing together. In the next part, we look more closely – and more systematically – at the reasons for and the processes of entry into co-residence.

Why Did They Move In Together?

We organized the stated reasons to move in together in four main categories: practical, external catalyst, emotional, and relationship consideration. Most interviewees gave more than one reason for the move, and we coded all their reasons. Some accounts fall under more than one category. For example, difficulty in maintaining cross-border relationships could fall under "practical" but also under "external catalyst" – such as a decision to immigrate to a partner's country of residence; a roommate who is about to leave the apartment is an example of a move due to a financial (practical) reason as well as an external catalyst. When these issues arose, we tried to remain consistent as to which *one* category we used. Sometimes, however, the interviewees directly addressed dual issues in their responses; for example, mentioning practicality and external catalyst together. In cases where the answers showed complexities and intersection between the categories, we have included them in both. We also coded each category into subcategories as follows:[32]

- Practical reasons: "financial," "convenience" (for example, always together, too much back and forth), and "other" practical reasons
- External catalyst: "housing" issues (for example, end of lease), and "life events" (for example, pregnancy)
- Emotional: including affection and romantic reasons (no subcategories)
- Relationship considerations: moving to the "next level" and "other" relationship reasons

We present the results of reasons for moving in together in Table 8.2. Because a couple could have provided more than one reason, the total number of couples in subcategories exceeds the total number of couples in the main categories.

TABLE 8.2
Reasons for moving in together

Category/Subcategory	Number of couples
Total couples who named practical reasons	21
Number who cited financial reasons	11
Number who cited convenience reasons	13
Number who cited other practical reasons	10
Total couples who named external catalysts	10
Number who cited housing reasons	8
Number who cited other "life events"	7
Total couples who named emotional reasons	10
Total couples who named relationship considerations	15
Number who cited testing relationships and/or next stage	11
Number who cited other relationship considerations	4

Practical Reasons

Interviewees mentioned "practical" considerations most commonly. At the outset, it is interesting to point out that many couples used language that incorporates an efficacy orientation. They discussed the move using terms such as "efficient," "logical," "practical," "pragmatic," and, often, "just made sense."

The most-cited subcategory for a practical reason was "convenience." Interviewees often expressed the position that at the time they decided to move in together, they already essentially shared a residence. Hence, it was practical to join forces. They often found themselves spending much of their time in their partner's home, with the other unit sitting unused. One interviewee said that he spent so much time at his partner's home that he went back to his home "just to water my plants." Often, one partner's belongings were already in the other partner's place. When we asked Kemala (thirty) at what point in the relationship they decided to move in together, her answer was illustrative: "When I started to stay here [in her partner's apartment] five nights in a week." And she adds later, "I was never staying in my place in New West at that point." In typical fashion, her belongings were mostly placed in her partner's apartment. Tim (thirty-two) describes one situation in which "we went travelling together and on the way back we realized that if I was to leave my suitcase there I could easily move in because everything was already there." Some couples stated that it was too much of a hassle to move their stuff from one place to the other, or to commute between the two places.

For Ruth (twenty-nine), the practical considerations related not merely to belongings and price of property. A cat lover and a cat's human, she had to bring her cat to her partner's space every visit, which meant having to deal with double sets of litter boxes, food, and other logistics. She describes this as an annoyance: "I think I was getting a little frustrated with going back and forth cause I used to bring my cat over cause I didn't have a cat sitter, so I would like bring the cat back and forth." As she tells it, this situation served as a catalyst for her to pressure Rupert (twenty-eight) into moving in together: "I had two litter boxes and it was just a lot like logistically for me; it was more difficult to go, go back and forth to his place, so I think I was like, 'come on.'"

Another subcategory that came up frequently was financial reasons, in particular, the costs of maintaining two households. As one interviewee puts it: "She was here most of the time and I was like, 'this is silly, why are you spending your money on rent elsewhere?'" Another, different couple, uses a similar rationale: "Of course splitting rent is always cheaper than not splitting rent, yeah."

Christy (twenty-six) explains how saving on housing was a major consideration in their decision to move in together:

> I did not think [moving in] was such a big deal in the beginning, but I had a huge discussion with him just to decide whether we should move in together to save more money; and the place that I was renting at that time was [very] expensive. So we were discussing whether to move in together and he was a little bit hesitant, but ... I really don't care, I just need a place to stay and crash, really. I guess he eventually saw, well, it's better; we can save some money by staying together.

For Christy, then, cost of housing is not only an inducement to move in together, but also a leverage, a way for her to convince her partner to jump into common living.

One couple's story so sharply illustrated the impact that the tight housing market had on incentives to share residency that we chose to use it as the title of this chapter. Bode (thirty) and Lindsey (twenty-nine) are, respectively, Australian and English immigrants who live in Whistler. They have been together for 4.5 years, and moved in together after a year and a half of dating. They seemed to be still hesitant about their relationship – whether it is serious and permanent. It sounds like these same reservations about their relationship existed when they first began cohabitation. It is clear that housing prices were a key incentive in their taking this step. Lindsey portrays the effect of the housing market on couples' relationship progression as a known phenomenon in their town, one that has the name "Whistler Accelerated Relationship." Bode adds: "It's hard to afford rent and all that jazz in maybe BC generally, but especially Whistler. So maybe that was like what started it." Lindsey emphasizes how housing considerations can trump other considerations in decision making: "We talk about basically how outside Whistler ... couples take a bit more time sometimes, they're like, 'okay, so are we really serious about this relationship? Do we see it going a long way? Blah, blah, blah,' you know, they do that whole thing, and then they're like, 'okay, we're ready.' And here we're [focused on housing]." Bode shares that they were rushed to settle down because of the cost of housing: "It's probably a fraction sooner than we may have ideally wanted to." Lindsey agrees with this statement.

Moreover, housing prices serve not only as a major cause to cohabiting but also might set up a barrier to separating. As Bode admits honestly, "[a]t times when the relationship has been troubled, we're like, well, where do we actually go, like I don't know where else to go and, and maybe having a place together has helped us stick around together a bit."

Still under the subcategory of practical financial reasons, a few couples mentioned economies of scale as a reason they started cohabiting. Howard and Veronica, both twenty-one years old and both students, report that, beyond saving on housing, "[we] have to buy like half the groceries on some things, like have to buy bread for one apartment, not two."

Under the subcategory of "other," we coded responses that are of a practical nature – most of them related to housing and convenience but with a particular variation that distinguishes them from the other subcategories, and that we thought merited a separate coding. In a few cases, the practical aspects included an opportunity to change one's housing arrangement. Howard and Veronica, for example, finished their first year of university and felt that it did not make sense for them to keep living in expensive university dorms. Hence, ending their dormitory living arrangement was their catalyst to move forward. Others saw the move as an opportunity to stop living with housemates. For instance, Tobias (thirty) and Seana (twenty-eight) moved in together because, among other reasons, Tobias's roommate had just left, and he "was going to get a place with another roommate but then when we started our relationship I [thought]: do I want to live with a roommate and have him around all the time when I'm in this relationship? And I thought okay, well, maybe I'll get my own place and then [Seana could move in]."

In a few cases, the practical consideration stemmed from, or was related to, immigration. Interestingly, the couples motivated by immigration considerations were also the couples who moved in together after less than half a year of dating. Vanessa (thirty) and Martin (forty-two) are avid mountain climbers who live in a mid-size town in British Columbia. Vanessa moved into Martin's home because she found it hard to keep commuting from the state of Washington. A different variation on immigration and cohabitation was presented by Rachel (thirty-six) and Nathan (thirty-five). Nathan, originally from France, moved to Vancouver for work purposes and met Rachel. He then returned to France and came back to Canada a few months later. When he returned to Vancouver, he explains, "well, I didn't really want to find an apartment by myself." As Rachel puts it, "So, yeah, well, part 'wanted to' and part like it was a practical reason, I guess." Immigration then serves as another catalyst into sharing a place.

External Catalyst

Responses in this category resemble the reasons stated in the previous category: they are based on practical considerations (most often housing considerations). Yet, we think they deserve their own separate category because the primary incentive to share a home – or, at least, regarding the timing of the decision – was based on an external event. We include two subcategories here: "housing" and "life events." The first subcategory embraces mainly issues related to housing – most typically, the end of the current living arrangement (for example, end of a lease) – that accelerated the time that couples had to decide about the next step. The second subcategory, "life events," comprises factors from pregnancy to taking employment in a different location. Overall, in the subcategory "housing" we coded eight responses, and we coded an additional seven responses in the "life events" category.

Kevin (forty-three) and Irina's (thirty-six) story of their decision to share a home is representative of the "housing" subcategory. Kevin is divorced twice, and Irina is a PhD student in the final stages of her degree. Being of an older age relative to other interviewees, they do not plan on getting married and originally did not want to rush into moving in together. Yet, the external housing situation accelerated their move. They had been dating for a year when Kevin's living arrangement came to an end. He lived with housemates, who all got along very well together, but then they received notice that the owner had decided to move into the house himself. The housemates tried to find a different place to live together but encountered Vancouver's "crazy" housing market, as Kevin describes it. Thus, Kevin's plan to move with his housemates did not work out. At the same time, Irina's housemate decided to move out, and Kevin's opportunity to move into her place became reality. Kevin, speaking with Irina's affirmation, states that "initially because we had only been dating a year we were like, well, maybe it's not quite the time to move in together." Yet, Vancouver's housing market catalyzed their move. Kevin and Irina's story is far from unique. Most couples in this category recount how the end of a lease was the stimulus to cohabitation, often prior to the time they would have wanted based on the organic progression of their relationships.

In the "life event" category, we find partners whose decision to move in was triggered by occurrences that gave rise to the decision. As instances, a few participants mentioned the end of a job or graduating from university as events that made settling down a logical next step. Olivia (thirty-seven) comments on her decision to move in with Dave (forty) because of her pregnancy. She shares that three or four months after they met "we found out I was pregnant and we're like, oh we should probably live together [chuckle] because, because we're going to have a baby."

Emotional

Emotional and romantic considerations – love, affection, the wish to spend more time together – were expressed, surprisingly, only by ten couples. It might be that the personal feelings were too obvious to mention, or that we may inadvertently have asked the questions in a way that steered the interviews toward the practical. Yet, the number might correctly reflect that emotional considerations are secondary compared with practicality, or that they are reserved to a small group. Indeed, Sassler and Miller's study found that only 12.6 percent of the reasons that couples mentioned were related to emotional causes for beginning cohabitation.[33] Further, in Sassler and Miller's study, "service class" cohabitants (people with an educational level of less than two years of college and with jobs in the service sector) were more likely than middle-class couples (defined mainly by educational attainment of at least bachelor degree) to discuss emotional and romantic aspects of their relationships. In that study, almost 20 percent of service-class respondents' reasons fell into this category, compared with 6.5 percent of reasons given by middle-class respondents.[34] Since our sample is predominantly well educated, our numbers are consistent with Sassler and Miller's findings.

When asked about the reasons they moved in together, Olivia first mentioned her pregnancy and then disclosed that Dave always stayed at her place. Dave then interjected with his reason: "Just true love." Olivia then returned to discuss practical reasons. Vanessa and Martin, the mountain climbers, had a similar dynamic in which one discussed practical reasons and the second invoked romantic reasons. As Martin explained cost-saving reasons, Vanessa asserted, "[a]nd I loved him [chuckle]." These discussions of emotions are, then, not only relatively infrequent, but are made in passing – sometimes in a type of bold statement, or as if it is external to other considerations. A few couples further connected their emotions to being able to spend more time together. Lucas (twenty-seven) clarifies that he and Kathleen (thirty-two) entered into shared living because "we both liked each other and we figured it would be a bummer when school started again because we realized that since we're very high-output workers we wouldn't really have time to see each other, so we just figured we'd move in together [chuckle]."

Relationship Considerations

In this category, we also deal with couples' emotional aspects vis-à-vis the move; however, here we code responses that pertain to moving in together as signifying a new stage in the relationship. Our initial intention was to categorize responses into two subcategories. The first was moving in to test the relationship – typically, as a precursor to marriage but sometimes simply as a test, regardless of any future interest in marriage. The second, related to the first, was couples who saw the move as taking their relationships to the next level in terms of commitment (with or without any connection to testing the relationships). However, as we worked on the coding, we observed that overlap between these two subcategories was frequent. In many cases of testing their relationships, couples expressed also, sometimes explicitly and sometimes implicitly, an intention to transition into more commitment. Hence, we decided to have just one subcategory that includes couples in both situations. We then added a second subcategory of "other" that covers relationship considerations that were more complex and nuanced than those of the first subcategory. Typically, "other" includes couples in which at least one partner was reluctant to enter this new stage and described the process of moving in together as an attempt to overcome this trepidation.

Overall, half of our interviewees named some type of relationship consideration as a reason for starting cohabitation. Eleven couples expressed an idea about testing the relationships and/or concepts of progressing to the next level. We categorized responses by four couples as "other" – typically reflecting that one partner or both were worried about entering into greater commitment.

Anita (twenty-seven) and Jared (twenty-nine), a dietician blogger and computer engineer, respectively, transitioned into shared living after dating for three years. They waited until Anita graduated from university and completed a subsequent internship, and then started to look into buying a house together. Anita speaks about her decision to settle down in classic trial-relationship language: "I think we knew that we would want to move in together before getting married, just because it's being realistic, like we didn't know how we would work or fit together by living together cause we knew that our personalities were probably very different in a living circumstance. So we wanted to live together before thinking about settling down further." Jared confirms: "It had to do with the fact that we wanted to live together before we decided to get married." Although more implicit in their discussion, the move was also a signal of a stronger commitment – as evidenced by the fact that they bought a house together. Jared conveys that Anita "wanted to buy, so that in itself was a big commitment."

Testing relationships does not have to serve as a precursor to marriage. Mila (thirty-three) and Hugo (thirty-five), respectively an occupational therapist and a labour contract negotiator, live in a long-term committed relationship. They are also ideological cohabitants. As Mila puts it: "Both of us are pretty committed to *not* getting married." Yet, they both verbalize the idea that they moved together in order to test the relationship. As Hugo remarks: "I had a sense that part of deciding if a long-term relationship was going to work out for us was also seeing how we live together."

Entering into a shared living arrangement might be the only practical option to test a relationship when partners live far from one another. It is also a vehicle to test the individual partners' relationships with other members of the new households, in addition to that with the intimate partner, in case there are other members in the household. Vanessa, who moved from the state of Washington to live with Martin and his child, also speaks about testing the relationships and moving to the next stage. Living long-distance from each other restricted them from testing the relationship appropriately, "so if we wanted to get to know each other and be around each other, it kind of required a little bit of proximity," she reports. She was also concerned about "living together and making a blended family."

The partners in the "other" category also moved in together as a way to increase commitment. However, it seems like at least one of the partners had some reservations about the transition. Kate and Robert are both engineers who met at their workplace. They dated 3.5 years before Kate (twenty-nine) moved into Robert's (thirty-three) apartment. For Kate, moving in was both the next level of commitment and a trial period. However, Robert was reluctant. He reveals that he agreed to the move "because Kate wanted to move in together." Kate confesses that she "peer-pressured him into it" and flags that it "was really hard to pressure him into it, it took a while for me to pressure him into it."

What's Love Got to Do with It? Reflecting on the Evidence

Remember the advice from *Glamour* that encourages couples not to move in with a partner due to practical economic reasons such as the end of their lease? Our study finds that at least one-third of our interviewees did indeed move for such reasons. Unsurprisingly, housing considerations have been central to couples' decision to begin cohabitation, especially for couples in Metro Vancouver and Whistler. One-quarter of the interviewees cited housing considerations as a major motive to settle down, and almost half cited economic reasons as their main motivation for entering into a shared living arrangement. We observed how frequently and effortlessly couples employed the language of convenience and practicality when discussing their move.

Only one-third of our interviewees cited emotional and romantic considerations as a reason for living together. Another third discussed cohabitation as a way to move forward or take the next step. Noticeably, those couples who cited trial relationships or the next stage tended to be relatively older (beginning of their thirties) and also more established in terms of economic status. In any event, the fact that relationship progress or emotions were discussed among only one-third of participants surprised us. Although we were familiar with another study in the United States with similar findings, we still assumed that relationships considerations would have a bigger role in the progression of relationships. Yet our sample was fairly limited; it will be helpful to see results from a larger pool and among people from a greater range of socio-economic positions.

The prominence of external events among interviewees implies that at least one-third of the couples were "sliding" into their relationships rather than being more deliberative about their decision. While we did not ask about the process and negotiations explicitly (for example, we did not ask who started the conversation or how much they discussed the issue), the answers to our questions were extensive enough for us to obtain a good sense of couples' decision-making processes. Approximately one-third of our interviewees found themselves in the position of living together without much discussion about the consequences of their move, often due to an external event. Scholarship has generally advanced the position that "although sliding transitions are not necessarily risky, we believe that they hold more potential for risk than ones based on explicit decisions."[35]

Returning to the strong connection between housing and relationship progression, the idea that the two are linked might seem obvious. However, if so, it has not been reflected in scholarship and policymaking in the area of housing. Clearly, the housing crisis in Canada has been a key area of concern for policymakers. Yet, the effect that the housing market has on people's relationships – including the fact that it may rush people into settling down before they are ready to do so, often resulting in unstable relationships – is an area that requires more research and policy considerations. It is also another reason for policymakers to incentivize the availability of cheaper, temporary, small housing units for younger adults.[36]

Another area that requires more attention – of scholars and policymakers alike – is the dimension of inequality. It is a fair hypothesis that individuals who are better off economically enjoy an advantage in their ability to screen for compatibility with partners before moving forward in an intimate relationship. If this is the case, it might provide another explanation for a Canadian study that found that "the experience of cohabitation leads to higher rates of union dissolution."[37] It is particularly instructive to examine whether dissolution of unmarried relationships is different among couples from different socio-economic backgrounds, and whether the timing of cohabitation has any correlation to the length of time that couples dated before moving in together. The bottom line is that the policy conversations about housing should include findings from family studies and considerations of how inequality in access to housing affects the stability of relationships.

Understanding accelerated transition into cohabitation becomes even more important after the lockdowns that accompanied the policies concerning COVID-19. During the pandemic, a phenomenon that was described as "turbo relationships" became common. As reported in many media outlets, the pandemic catalyzed many couples to move in together after short relationships to avoid loneliness of living as a single under lockdown rules, or as a way to have romantic and sexual relationships.[38]

Legal Meaning of Beginning Cohabitation

In considering whether unmarried couples qualify as spouses for various legal rights and duties, moving in together plays an important legal role in different legal systems. As a start, cohabitation is typically a threshold requirement in order to be accounted as spouse-equivalent. For instance, in British Columbia, partners need to live with another person in a marriage-like situation for at least two years to be considered spouses. Likewise, in Australia, in order to apply for support and division of property, couples need to cohabit in de facto relationships.[39] Couples in Australia are deemed to be in de facto relationships if they live together on a "genuine domestic basis" for two years.[40]

Cohabitation alone is not sufficient to hold a couple as equivalent to spouses. There is always a standard, such as "conjugal," "marriage-like," and "genuine domestic basis," attached to the definition. Yet cohabitation plays a big role in decisions about whether unmarried couples qualify as spouses, as well as in decisions about when the relationships began. One of the reasons is that standards regarding conjugality (marriage-like, etc.) are open to many interpretations. Terminologies like "marriage-like" do not provide much specificity, as marriage has many configurations nowadays. The result is that, in the process of deciding about the quality of relationships, judges are "applying a model of functional recognition [that] seems a plainly normative process."[41]

Often, then, judges need an objective marker as a sign for committed relationships. Cohabitation serves this purpose exactly. Therefore, moving in becomes a proxy for living in a married-like relationship. Hence, judges often use the move-in date as the time in which the couples have started living in spousal-like relationships. Some courts are well aware of this "attribution" problem – that moving in does not mean the commitment that spousal relationships have. In an oft-cited case in Canada, one judge explained that "relationships outside marriage are much more difficult to ascertain ... Often people begin cohabiting with little forethought or planning. Their motivation is often nothing more than wanting to 'be together.'"[42] But even this court's assertion – that moving in denotes little – does not capture the fact that the sentiment of "wanting to be together" is not as common as considerations of economics and of housing, in particular.

In any event, although courts are aware of diversity of relationships, commencing cohabitation remains a strong proxy for the quality of relationships. The following case is a typical example. In *Chapman v Cuthbert,* both parties agreed that they were in a marriage-like relationship but disagreed about the beginning date – which matters both for determining what is in the divisible pool (family property) and for calculating the gains from the appreciation of property. The claimant in this case argued that the couple began living in a marriage-like relationship in October 2014. Her main assertion was that, even when they had lived in separate homes, she had spent most of the time in her partner's apartment. Her partner asserted that the relationship did not become marriage-like until June 2015, when they moved into a shared apartment. The court sided with the respondent, finding that, upon moving, "their relationship saw a fundamental shift in other ways." Although their financial independence remained the same after they moved in together (they still kept separate bank accounts, etc.), moving in was a signal, for the court, that from that time forward they "operated like one family unit."[43]

Since moving in together is motivated by various considerations – and does not say enough about the parties' commitment, intentions, and interdependency – we believe that courts should attach less importance to the cohabitation itself in cases with dispute about the nature of relationships. The time of moving in, particularly, should be devalued as a proxy for relationship quality in light of the housing market's effect on people's decisions to cohabit, which appears to be more compelling than partners' emotional needs or their desire to move to the next relationship stage.

Using the move-in date as an indication of the start date of a recognized relationship is even more of a problem in cases of eligibility for income assistance, disability assistance, and other types of social welfare. In most jurisdictions, the test to qualify as spouses (and thus to lose eligibility or have it reduced) requires a minimum duration of cohabitation along with a functional test about the nature of relationships. In Ontario, for example, a short period of three months of cohabitation could be enough for a couple to be considered spouses, and therefore, to lose their eligilbity.[44] Although three months of cohabitation alone is insufficient – there must also be a showing that "social and family-like aspects of their relationship are marriage-like" – the fact that three months of cohabitation can invoke an inquiry is already concerning. Likewise, in British Columbia, a couple should cohabit for twelve months and show that "[t]he relationship demonstrates financial dependence or interdependence consistent with a marriage-like relationship" in order to qualify.[45] Presumably, proving that a couple has lived together for twelve consecutive months is likely to require government questioning and investigation.

The fact that one of the main criteria is twelve months of cohabitation, or even three months, raises concerns about unfair ascriptive recognition – or, at the least, about the hassle and invasion of privacy that people have to face in applying for benefits. This is an example of the mechanism that Allison Tait describes in Chapter 1 in this volume, by which families with low incomes are subject to invasion of privacy that families with higher wealth-holding can shield themselves from. People with lower incomes have strong incentives to move in together as a way to make living arrangements affordable. As one commentator noted, "This heavily accelerated process allows for far less individual freedom for both partners and creates a level of dependence that can result in real harm. The impact that this class-based legal distinction inflicts on the less fortunate and marginalized people of B.C. (predominantly female citizens and their children) is chilling."[46] As we saw, given that couples who move in are often motivated by practical concerns, there is no reason to believe that they are a fully interdependent unit after a short term of cohabitation. Further, given that couples move in for various reasons that are not necessarily connected to interdependency or commitment, the short term of cohabitation marker seems misguided and particularly harmful for people with low income and those who need governmental assistance.

Conclusion

Knowledge of relationship progression patterns in Canada is important for policymaking in various areas. Norms concerning moving in together are diverse and seem to differ according to socio-economic position, among other factors. Policymakers should take the diversity of these norms seriously in assigning consequences to relationship progression. Our study calls for new research on how inequality shapes couples' decision making, as well as for more policymaking involvement from family studies experts. Conversations about housing, laws recognizing unmarried couples, and eligibility criteria for public assistance should consider research on diverse types of relationships and how their development intersects with social, economic, and legal aspects of public policy.

Notes

1 Lindsey (pseudonym), an interviewee for this research, describing the process of moving in together.

2 Meredith Turits, "13 Signs You're Ready to Move In Together," *Glamour* (29 March 2019), online: <www.glamour.com/gallery/13-signs-youre-ready-to-move-in-together>.

3 *Ibid*, quoting Jessica Massa, *The Gaggle: How the Guys You Know Will Help You Find the Love You Want* (New York: Simon & Schuster, 2012).

4 Turits, *supra* note 2.

5 Zheng Wu, *Cohabitation: An Alternative Form of Family Living* (Don Mills, ON: Oxford University Press, 2000) at 73.

6 See generally Tiziana Nazio, *Cohabitation, Family and Society* (New York: Routledge, 2008) at 3–4 for discussion of patterns of cohabitation in Europe.

7 Statistics Canada, Table 17-10-0060-01, "Estimates of Population as of July 1st, by Marital Status or Legal Marital Status, Age and Sex" (5 November 2020), online: Statistics Canada <www150.statcan.gc.ca/t1/tbl1/en/tv.action?pid=1710006001>.

8 Statistics Canada, *Families, Households, and Marital Status: Key Results from the 2016 Census* (2 August 2017), online: Statistics Canada <www150.statcan.gc.ca/n1/daily-quotidien/170802/dq170802a-eng.htm>.

9 See Chapter 7 by Hélène Belleau in this volume.

10 Pamela J Smock, "Cohabitation in the United States: An Appraisal of Research Themes, Findings, and Implications" (2000) 26:1 Annual Rev Sociology 1.

11 Nazio, *supra* note 6 at 2.

12 See Chapter 7 by Belleau in this volume. Benoît Laplante & Ana Laura Fostik, "Cohabitation and Marriage in Canada. The Geography, Law and Politics of Competing Views on Gender Equality" in Albert Esteve & Ron J Lesthaeghe, eds, *Cohabitation and Marriage in the Americas: Geo-Historical Legacies and New Trends* (New York: Springer, 2016) at 59–60. They state that "[a] substantial part of the research on unmarried cohabitation in Canada has actually focused on Quebec."

13 Laplante & Fostik, *supra* note 12 at 63–64.

14 Smock, *supra* note 10 at 13–14 ("virtually all sociological knowledge about cohabitation in the United States has been based on quantitative analysis of survey or census data. Certainly, this approach has taught us a great deal about cohabitation in a very short time. Yet the broader question of the meaning of cohabitation remains difficult to address.").

15 We hesitated about whether to include the same-sex couples within this sample. In Canada, same-sex marriage has been legal since 2005 in all jurisdictions. Same-sex couples, then, do not have a specific legal reason to behave differently than different-sex couples when it comes to incentives for moving in together (that is, they are not compelled to cohabit informally, as they might be in places where same-sex marriage is unavailable). In any event, even if we had excluded the same-sex couples from our data, it would not have made a significant change in our findings.

16 See e.g. Sharon Sassler & Amanda Miller, *Cohabitation Nation: Gender, Class, and the Remaking of Relationships* (Berkeley and Los Angeles: University of California Press, 2017).

17 See e.g. Marin Clarkberg, Ross M. Stolzenberg & Linda J. Waite, "Attitudes, Values, and Entrance into Cohabitational versus Marital Unions" (1995) 74:2 Social Forces 609; Timothy A Ortyl, "Long-Term Heterosexual Cohabiters and Attitudes toward Marriage" (2013) 54:4 Sociological Q 584; Arland Thornton, William G Axinn, & Daniel H Hill, "Reciprocal Effects of Religiosity, Cohabitation, and Marriage" (1992) 98:3 American J Sociology 628.

18 See Scott M Stanley, Galena K Rhoades & Frank D Fincham, "Understanding Romantic Relationships among Emerging Adults: The Significant Roles of Cohabitation and Ambiguity" in Frank D Fincham & Ming Cui, eds, *Romantic Relationships in Emerging Adulthood* (New York: Cambridge University Press, 2010) at 243–44.

19 See *ibid* at 245.

20 Sassler & Miller, *supra* note 16, at 41.

21 Pamela J Smock & Christine R Schwartz, "The Demography of Families: A Review of Patterns and Change" (2020) 82:1 J Marriage & Family 9 at 15.

22 While married couples do not have to cohabit in order to enjoy marital protections, cohabitation is central to the recognition of unmarried couples as equivalent to spouses. See e.g. *Family Law Act,* SBC 2011, c 25, s 3(1)(b)(i). One definition for "spouse" in the *Act* is someone who has "lived with another person in a marriage-like relationship" for at least two years.

23 On the proliferation of shared housing experiences in Vancouver, see e.g. Frances Bula, "All in Together Now" *Globe and Mail* (19 January 2017), online: <www.theglobeandmail.com/life/relationships/living-with-roommates-not-just-for-studentsanymore/article33670019/>.

24 Audrey Appiahet et al, "Building the Evidence Base about Economic, Health, and Social Inequities Faced by LGBTQ2S+ Individuals in Canada" (2021), online: Social Research and Demonstration Corporation <https://www.srdc.org/media/553177/wage-phase-2-final-report.pdf>.

25 Ethan Czuy Levine et al, "Open Relationships, Nonconsensual Nonmonogamy, and Monogamy Among U.S. Adults: Findings from the 2012 National Survey of Sexual Health and Behavior" (2018) 47:5 Archives of Sexual Behavior 1439, DOI:10.1007/s10508-018-1178-7, online: <https://www.ncbi.nlm.nih.gov/pmc/articles/PMC5958351/>.

26 V Clark et al, "Shared Housing among Young Adults: Avoiding Complications in Domestic Relationships" (2017) 20:9 J Youth Studies 1191–1207.

27 *Ibid*; Zahra Nasreen & Kristian J Ruming, "Shared Room Housing and Home: Unpacking the Home-making Practices of Shared Room Tenants in Sydney, Australia, Housing" (2021) 38:2 Theory and Society 152, DOI: <10.1080/14036096.2020.1717597>.

28 For examples of termination and reduction of eligibility due to living in informal relationships, see Erez Aloni, "Deprivative Recognition" (2014) 61 UCLA L Rev 1276 at 1312, 1321.

29 Government of British Columbia, "Family Composition," *BC Employment and Assistance Policy and Procedure Manual,* online: <https://www2.gov.bc.ca/gov/content/governments/policies-for-government/bcea-policy-and-procedure-manual/support-and-shelter/family-composition>.

30 Recently, scholars and commentators have discussed legal recognition of plural partners as well as of parents. See e.g. Edward Stein, "How US Family Law Might Deal with Spousal Relationships of Three (or More) People" (2019) 51 Ariz St LJ 1395 at 1395; John-Paul E Boyd, "Polyamorous Relationships and Family Law in Canada" (Calgary: Canadian Research Institute for Law and the Family, 2017),

online (PDF): <https://prism.ucalgary.ca/bitstream/handle/1880/107213/Polyamorous_Relationships_and_Family_Law_-_Apr_2017.pdf?sequence=1>.

31 *Family Law Act,* SBC 2011 c 25 s 3.

32 Sassler and Miller divided their answers into "seven broad categories: convenience, housing needs, economic rationality, choosing to spend more time together because of mutual enjoyment, as a 'next step' in the relationship to demonstrate deepening commitment, in response to a family situation, or as a result of financial necessity." See Sassler & Miller, *supra* note 16 at 43.

33 *Ibid* at 43, Table 2, 51–52.

34 *Ibid* at 43, Table 2.

35 Stanley, Rhoades & Fincham, *supra* note 18 at 245.

36 See *Housing Vancouver Strategy* (Vancouver: City of Vancouver, 2017), online (PDF): <council.vancouver.ca/20171128/documents/rr1appendixa.pdf>. The report discusses the barriers young people face when it comes to housing, including leaving the city or living with parents longer (3, 15). It further discusses the "comprehensive approach will help us maintain Vancouver's diversity and vibrancy, and create more affordable housing options," including for young people, and moving toward a goal of accessible housing that includes "the *right type* to be suitable for households with specific needs – including younger households" [emphasis in original] (3, 36).

37 France-Pascale Ménard, "What Makes It Fall Apart? The Determinants of the Dissolution of Marriages and Common-Law Unions in Canada" (2011) 2 McGill Sociological Rev 59.

38 Brittany Wong, "Turbo Relationships Are a Big COVID-19 Dating Trend. Here's What to Know," *HuffPost* (13 October 2020), online: <https://www.huffpost.com/entry/turbo-relationships-covid-19-dating-trend_l_5f84b1fcc5b6e6d033a635fc>; Ashley Fetters, "Move In? Get Divorced? The Pandemic Forces Couples to Decide," *New York Times* (17 July 2020), online: <https://www.nytimes.com/2020/07/17/opinion/coronavirus-relationships-decisions.html>.

39 *Family Law Act 1975* (Cth), s 90SB (Australia).

40 *Ibid*, pt VIIIAB.

41 Robert Leckey, "Judging in Marriage's Shadow" (2017) 26:1 Fem Leg Stud 25.

42 *Yakiwchuk v Oaks,* 2003 SKQB 124.

43 *Chapman v Cuthbert,* 2021 BCSC 1, 2021 CarswellBC 9, 328 ACWS (3d) 85.

44 "Ontario Disability Support Program – Income Support Directives" (March 2009), online: <https://www.mcss.gov.on.ca/documents/en/mcss/social/directives/odsp/income_Support/2_3.pdf>.

45 Government of British Columbia, *supra* note 29.

46 Stephen Portman, "TAPS Valentines Day Letter to the Legislature," February 14, 2017, https://www.tapsbc.ca/post/taps-valentines-day-letter-to-the-legislature.

PART 5
Reforming Norms

9

Measuring Success of (Family) Law Reforms

Julianna Ivanyi and Régine Tremblay

To say that, in the past three decades, Canadian family law has been subject to the winds of change is an understatement. In 2002, Quebec modified its *Civil Code*'s book on the family to, among other things, include same-sex couples;[1] with its *Family Law Act* (*FLA*), British Columbia reformed the entirety of its family law regime in 2011;[2] Ontario enacted a new framework for parent-child relationships in 2017;[3] Alberta's division-of-property regime changed as of January 2020 to include adult relationships other than marriage;[4] and in October 2021, the Quebec government presented *Bill 2 – An Act respecting family law reform with regard to filiation and amending the Civil Code in relation to personality rights and civil status*.[5] Even the federal Parliament joined in the dance, using its power over marriage and divorce to modify the *Divorce Act*,[6] a rare occurrence in Canadian family law.[7] Courts have also been busy, with numerous landmark decisions rendered in the past few decades. Law has been transformed or, sometimes, stagnated by the courts: from *AA v BB*,[8] dealing with multiple parentage; to the *Reference re Same-Sex Marriage*,[9] expanding the definition of marriage at common law; and to *Attorney General v A*,[10] reaffirming the privileged status of marriage in Quebec civil law. By its very nature, family law is bound to be constantly shifting, and may or may not be in line with social norms and expectations.

This chapter considers family law as a discipline in flux. More specifically, it is concerned with law reform, as an example of changes to norms that are affecting families. Law reform and norms go hand in hand: when norms transform, law needs to adjust, and vice versa. Given these constant movements, it is somewhat surprising that more research has not been conducted on family law reform processes and their efficiency. To be clear, much has been written on the substance of specific family law reforms[11] and success in law reform generally, especially with respect to law reform commissions.[12] Yet, little of the literature seems to be tailored to family law reforms as processes or to assessing their success, or at least their efficiency. In this chapter, we engage with various questions related to family law reform: What makes a family law reform successful? How can one measure the impacts of legislative action in the realm of family law? We propose ways to evaluate what makes a law reform a success or a failure, and we put forward a framework to assess its success. We ask the important and often overlooked question of what makes a reform successful, and propose indicators for assessing success in terms of process, content, and effects. We also consider to what extent there may be a need to adjust these metrics to the unique nature of family law.

This chapter, which is part of a broader project, offers the beginning of a theoretical framework to assess success in law reform, specifically in family law. Elsewhere, we will apply this framework to specific case studies. By doing so, we hope that the broader project contributes to scholarship on both law reform processes and recent changes in family law. In addition, we hope that the information provided will influence future family law reforms in Canada, and abroad.

The questions we examine connect to fundamental aspects about the law, its content, and its role in responding to or igniting social change. The chapter is built around some assumptions. First, we see law reforms as leading to progressive change in law, but not necessarily in society. We acknowledge that there are instances in which legal changes may not be progressive enough and in which they do not necessarily lead to social change. Second, law reform is often tied to political will – or even political gain – while social change is not. Third, we decided to focus our chapter for the most part on provincial law – more specificially, family law reform in British Columbia. This is not because law reform is not happening at the federal level,[13] but rather because we share the view of Peter Hogg that the fragmentation of jurisdiction in family law is the result of "a series of accidents of history."[14] Jurisdiction should be coherent and logical, not the result of a series of accidents, and we believe provinces should have most, if not all, legislative powers when it comes to private family law.

Success in Law Reform

Law reforms take many forms and can be defined in many ways. The same can be said of success in law reform. Yet, it is crucial to engage with how to assess success when it comes to law reforms, given their social relevance, their potentially transformative nature, and the amount of human and economic resources invested in making them happen. Later in this chapter, we present a framework that can be used to assess the success of law reforms. Before presenting this framework, however, we engage in two background inquiries. The first is to understand what a law reform is. To fulfill this task, we discuss different definitions of law reform and of reform more generally. We then analyze different types of possible reforms and delineate them. The second inquiry focuses on the nature of success and the different ways to measure it in the context of law reform. To determine what makes a law reform successful, we survey the scholarship for indicators that should be considered when assessing how successful a law reform is, has been, or will be.

Law Reform and Law Reform Processes

What is a reform? General dictionaries provide definitions of "reform" as a noun, verb (transitive and intransitive), and adjective. For example, the *Merriam-Webster Dictionary* defines the transitive verb "reform" as "to put or change into an improved form or condition."[15] As a noun, it is an "amendment of what is defective, vicious, corrupt, or depraved."[16] The word comes with a certain gravitas. As Michael Kirby has written in the Australian context, "[t]he word 'reform' is a word of approbation. In our history, it is a word which has been used to describe movement that restored peace, improved the religious order and changed the system or parliament representation."[17] When it comes to defining reform in legal dictionaries or encyclopedias, *The New Oxford Companion to Law* has entries on "law reform commissions" and "law reform movements,"[18] but not on "reform" or "law reform" *per se*. Similarly, the *Private Law Dictionary*[19] and the *Canadian Online Legal Dictionary*[20] do not define "reform" or "law reform." Other sources take the risk to define these terms. Hubert Reid, in his

Dictionnaire de droit québécois et canadien, defines "réforme" : "[un] terme pour désigner des modifications d'une certaine importance visant à améliorer le droit existant."[21] *Black's Law Dictionary* proposes this definition of "law reform": "The process of, or a movement dedicated to, streamlining, modernizing, or otherwise improving a body of law generally or the code governing a particular branch of the law."[22] We can take from these common and legal dictionary definitions that a law reform requires some form of change or modification to the law and a sense that improvements will ensue.

Realistically, what constitutes a law reform is more complicated and depends on one's conception of law. In this context, according to Macdonald and Kong, law can be instrumental or symbolic.[23] An instrumental conception of law is rooted in the understanding that the law is a form of state authority and that its purpose is to "contro[l] human behaviour."[24] In contrast, a symbolic conception of law focuses "on the implicit forms of law, arising in myriad everyday relationships, and aimed at facilitating human interaction."[25] For the tenants of the first perspective – instrumentalism – "law reform means correction."[26] It is about changing rules that are not working. The authors further suggest that, within this understanding, law reform is seen as something practical "that should not expressly concern itself with theory."[27] For the second school of thought, what constitutes a law reform is slightly more complicated, given the plurality and fluidity of interactions between the rule givers and the rule recipients.[28] Further, legal rules are seen as constitutive,[29] and "[t]he constitutive and symbolic mission of law reform is consciously understood and self-consciously undertaken."[30] Law reform has almost an expressive function, but how it actually unfolds is unclear. There is, however, a sense that law can achieve broader purposes, that it can be policy oriented, and that it emanates from the ground up as much as from the top down. Law reform can generate rules within communities and create self-generated normative orders.[31] A law reform, then, is what rules mean for people operating under them and how they engender new norms that may or may not be in line with formal rules. We share Macdonald and Kong's view that, in the context of law reform, law cannot be conceived as purely symbolic or instrumental – it operates in both dimensions.[32] Similarly, a change aimed at altering behaviour could have a symbolic goal of facilitating human interaction.

A survey of the scholarship gives a sense of the scale of the task of defining "law reform," this apparently simple concept that is an integral part of law and life and that affects countless fields. In a classic book on law reform commissions, William H. Hurlburt examines what a law reform is, recognizing that different people and contexts have provided for plural – and sometimes opposite – definitions. In other words, "law reform" has no fixed or universal meaning.[33] For example, he notes that Lord Devlin suggested that, "when the law is changed in order to reach out for a different social or political objective, it is not law reform; but when the social and political objectives are agreed and it is found that the law is defective in carrying them out, the changes necessary are properly described as law reform."[34] Further, Hurlburt highlights Lawrence M. Friedman's proposition that "law reform" means "some program for changing the law."[35] However, as Hurlburt further explains, "the term is generally applied to one of two kinds of legal change. The first is a more or less general revision of the laws or of some branch of the law in the direction of consistency or systematic arrangement, i.e., codification. The second is a procedural 'housekeeping' improvement."[36]

Hurlburt ultimately settles for the following definition: "the alteration of the law in some respect with a view as to its improvement."[37] But not all changes constitute law reform. As Rollie Thompson wrote, "[g]overnments love to pass legislation, as if legislative change were the equivalent of law reform."[38] Similarly, Peter Handford warns us that most of these legislative changes are "not 'law reform.'"[39] Finally, some scholars define "law reform" based on its functions: "the point of law reform is to produce a regime that will work not just in practice but also in theory; not just instrumentally, but also symbolically."[40] For a reform to be a reform, some *envergure,* some fundamental shift in paradigm, some vision of law, and a vast knowledge of one's own law and the law of others are required. Process, content, and an anticipation of the potential effects are important.

The scholarly and dictionary definitions of "reform" and "law reform" frequently include the deceptive idea of betterment – that is, reforming means changing for the better – while acknowledging that there are plural views as to "what 'better' implies."[41] What is "better"? Is the fact that a change went through in itself a sign of change for the better? In addition to different views, the idea of betterment is complex and introduces a temporal element to evaluating success in law reform: only time can tell if changes in the law were for the better. It is also utopian to think that changes in the law could be good for all parties involved. For example, reform to achieve gender neutrality benefits certain groups but negatively impacts others.[42] Thus, we need to ask whose perspective should be considered when evaluating success in law reform.

To add another layer of complexity to the task of defining law reform, there are also different types of law reform and law reform processes. Further, the line between types of law reform and types of law reform *processes* is blurry. When it comes to law reform processes, Laura Barnett identifies three that are common in the Commonwealth: "permanently established law reform commissions, parliamentary committees and ad hoc commissions of inquiry."[43] The first type can also be called institutional law reform. Institutional law reform, as its name suggests, refers to the idea that it is possible to put in place institutions for law reform processes, but not to reform law *per se*. A significant amount of scholarship on these entities – such as law reform commissions – is available.[44] While it is beyond the scope of this chapter to provide an in-depth analysis of these entities, the topic is relevant, as it is one of the key means to implement, launch, or think about reforming the law. Most importantly, when it comes to law reform agencies or law commissions, there is scholarship on the assessment of success for these institutions that is transferable to other contexts, including the present one.

In addition to Barnett's three types, judicial law reform is another form to consider. "Judicial law reform" alludes to transformations in the law that are made through court challenges and activism. In Canada, this type of law reform has been transformative for family law. An example of this can be seen with the development of the functional approach to family law. Court challenges and judgments have been influential in shifting this area of law toward serving the functions families perform.[45] In the context of Canada, cases such as *Halpern*,[46] *Barbeau*,[47] *Rypkema*,[48] and *Gill*[49] significantly changed the law and could likely be characterized as reforming family law. The significance of this reform toward the functional family approach is – as highlighted by Millbank – that it aligns with actual experiences of family, and that it is progressive and performative.[50] The functional approach to the family has also been extensively studied, and has been used as an important tool or strategy in breaking down earlier normative conceptions of the family.[51] While one may argue that judicial reform created this approach, we also see it actively being used in judicial decision making, with judges adopting it as an interpretative method to achieve certain purposes in family law.[52]

What we refer to as judicial law reform – the change in law stemming from judicial decisions – is only half of this law reform mechanism, or half of a perspective on what is involved in this type of law reform. Indeed, judges who make these decisions are influenced by years of social movements, political pressures, and litigation. While the result is the transformation of the law through one – or sometimes a few – judicial decisions, the work is done on the ground for years, and often over decades. In the context of the United States, this phenomenon, which is referred to as law and social movements, is well documented.[53] The involvement of social movements is less documented when it comes to other types of law reforms, for example, institutional law reform or legislative law reform.[54] This way of transforming the law raises important questions about the role of the courts,[55] the definition of "rights,"[56] who has those rights, and, more generally, who holds power when it comes to effecting changes.

Like all other modes of transforming the law, this strategy has caveats. Changes initiated by particular groups tend to affect only specific stakeholders and "normalize" identities rather than celebrate differences,[57] and they may not benefit people at the margins of the law.[58] This approach also challenges the boundary between law and politics.[59] Although this type of law reform needs to be kept in mind, it tends to be absent from the scholarship that we surveyed in Canada, Australia, and the United Kingdom.

It is likely that success indicators for all these types of law reform could be different. Yet we are of the view that these diverse processes and outcomes share enough similarities to allow us to devise indicators that can be used to evaluate their success, despite their disparities in nature, scope, and so on. We are of the view that what law reform is cannot be easily confined. Still, for the purposes of this chapter, we can define the term as follows: law reform is about changing a significant aspect of the law in one field, hoping to improve it, using one or many of the strategies described above.

Measures of Success in Law Reform

With this general understanding of law reform in mind – but also with a renewed awareness of how complex the concept actually is – how can we measure *success* in law reform? Are there metrics allowing for the evaluation of whether a law reform has been successful? Before we dive into this analysis, we might ask why it is relevant to engage in such an enterprise. Why should we theorize ways to engage with law reforms and success? The first reason is accountability. Law reform mobilizes significant financial, human, and political resources. It generally occurs at times when changes are overdue and required in a specific society. This combination of social need and public resources underscores the need for accountability for governments and for actors participating in law reform. As Laura Barnett writes, a key question is what kind of law reform "is the most effective and responsive to today's changing and diverse society?"[60] The second reason to engage with success in law reform is to improve the process and avoid reproducing mistakes of the past. Sadly, in the context of family law reform, it seems that, in Canada at least, we have been reproducing the same mistakes in recent decades: law reform that is not based on empirical data, that is not supported by public education, that lacks assessment as to effects on vulnerable populations, that results in privatization and/or cuts in services, and so on. By engaging with what makes a law reform successful, our hope is to increase accountability of law reformers, to improve processes, and to avoid preventable errors. Ultimately, law reform is one of the many tools that can lead to change, but it should be done right.

Despite the importance of engaging with ways to measure success in law reform, it is crucial to be realistic and to acknowledge the pitfalls and difficulties of such an exercise. For example, what one stakeholder could see as an indicator of success could be a failure for another; some effects are direct while others are unintended; and so on. The very idea of "success" is highly challengeable. From a theoretical standpoint, we adopt a broad understanding of success, one that goes beyond the enactment of a law or a modification. Indeed, as Robert Leckey writes "[g]roups seeking equality sometimes take a legal victory as the end of the line. Once a judgment is granted, or a law is passed, coalition disband, and life goes on."[61] He goes further, adding that "[t]he 'options' that legal reforms make available ... do not benefit or appeal to all groups or subgroups equally."[62] Not only is it important to address the unintended consequences and effects of law reform beyond the legislation's enactment, it is imperative to engage with what makes a law reform successful in the first place. That being said, we are also of the view that, for some types of law reforms to be successful – for example, institutional law reform or law reform emanating from government committees – legislation must ensue. A law reform leading to no changes in law cannot be characterized as successful. Yet it is not the change itself that makes a law reform a success. To assess success, aims, processes, and effects, intended or not, must be scrutinized. While law reforms have been around for a significant period, in most countries and contexts, "we have not yet developed ... a method of assessing the effectiveness of law reforms whether made by Parliament, the Executive Government or the judiciary."[63] This statement was made about Australia, but it applies to Canada as well, and it definitely applies to family law, especially given its ever-changing nature.

Numerous indicators of success in law reform can be extracted from scholarship, while others are just common sense. According to Justice Antonio Lamer, former president of the Law Reform Commission of Canada, "every measure of law reform must focus on social problems, never on legal problems as such."[64] And, indeed, there is an undeniable social component to reforming the law. In a speech to the Law Reform Commission of Ireland, Justice Michael Kirby, who was the Chairman of the Australian Law Reform Commission from 1975 to 1985, proposed ten attributes for success in law reform, especially for law commissions:

- awareness of the fundamentals;
- consultation;
- empiricality;
- awareness of the international context;
- realism and flexibility;
- independence;
- usefulness;
- patience;
- luck; and
- confidence and boldness.[65]

While it is unclear whether these attributes apply to law reform generally, or only to institutional law reform, they offer food for thought. It's not difficult to understand what Kirby meant when he advised law reform to be consultative, empirical, or international. While most of these attributes seem self-explanatory, they take various meanings in the context of law reform. Independence is more relevant for institutional law reform, but it is likely a consideration that should be present in any law reform process. The balance with respect to independence is hard to strike, given the scrutiny, funding, and collaboration required from different levels of government. In non-institutional law reform processes, we believe this translates into non-partisan law making and the involvement of all political parties in the different steps of the process. Consultation is another successful attribute and should be part of the methodology of all law reform processes. Its purpose is "to secure information and perspectives from those who are potentially affected by any reform proposals."[66] A broad understanding of who is actually affected is required. Similarly, law reformers must be mindful that the nature of the proposed changes has an impact on the ways in which consultation needs to be conducted.

In the realm of family law, one must bear in mind that law reform is potentially socially transformative and expressive[67] and could affect everybody. Given the fundamental nature of the family and family law in society, the number of stakeholders is likely larger than a reform of the transportation of wooden goods by sea or of securities, for example. We would go further than Justice Michael Kirby here and suggest that law reform processes need to engage with the nature of the proposed change and delve deep into identifying the persons and groups affected. In certain circumstances, this will mean that positive actions are required by law reformers to reach stakeholders. For example, if we know that a specific community will be affected, but foresee that this community, for various reasons, will not, or will be unable to, participate in consultation via regular channels, we need to have mechanisms to ensure that these voices are heard. Yet mere public consultation is not enough: expert consultation should be happening in parallel. Law reform processes need to be inclusive of a variety of perspectives.

Law reform must also be empirically based. Data need to be gathered before and during the process to ensure that the law reform reflects current realities, not merely doctrinal or theoretical conceptions of family and family law. Given the duration of law reform processes, missing empirical data can be commissioned during the process. With the broad variety of empirical data–collecting resources available today, there is no reason why family law reform should be conducted based solely on doctrinal understandings of what a family should be in the twenty-first century, or of promoting unproblematized concepts such as freedom, choice, and autonomy to inform law making.[68] Empirical data and an understanding of everyday life are crucial when engaging in law reform. Scholars have been collecting data that needs to be taken seriously by reformers.[69]

Other attributes of success include being international, realistic, flexible, useful, and patient.[70] A law reform is international when it "take[s] advantage of work done elsewhere."[71] It is realistic and flexible when it "undertake[s] a mix of projects,"[72] urgent or not, long or short term. Law reform's usefulness is tailored to the context of law reform agencies, and so is its patience – its ability to be implemented over a longer period to effect more stable and longer-lasting change. All five attributes apply to other types of law reform, not only to law reform agencies, with required adjustments. For example, a useful law reform produces results, and a patient law reform is implemented over time, even when governments and political preoccupations shift. Kirby also speaks of the requirement for awareness of fundamentals, and of the importance of being lucky as well as confident and bold. While being lucky helps, it is unclear that such a condition can be a measure of success, as luck is not something one controls – instead, it highlights that, while a law reform may look successful both theoretically and practically, there are always other, uncontrollable factors that may limit its successful implementation. Attributes of success do not necessarily measure success because they assess *ex ante* rather than *ex post*. However, good *ex ante* measures are necessary for success in law reform, given that law reform operates on a continuum of process, content, and effects.

Outside of these ten factors, other scholars have commented on the conditions and criteria necessary for successful law reform. For example, Barnett, writing on the process of law reform, identified several conditions for success. For law reform to be effective and responsive – and, hence, successful – it should have a level of independence; have appropriate triggers; engage with real consultation; focus on the facts; be timely; and offer recommendations or, more precisely, practical recommendations.[73] Outside the legal sphere, Gary Banks proposes that there are two key conditions that must be satisfied for a reform to be "successful" (while he talks about reforms in general, his points are transferable to the context of law reform). The first key condition is "that the outcomes of the reform broadly accord with its objectives and what was anticipated when it was introduced."[74] This condition has two aspects: meeting the announced objectives and producing the results that were expected. These results should be achieved "without major collateral damage or unintended consequences."[75] The first component is likely easier to assess than the latter, since time and data are required to properly engage with the second component. In addition, it is hard to analyze unintended consequences as a whole, since their effects are going to differ depending on one's standpoint. Banks' second key condition of a successful reform is that it is "*sustainable*; that it is not vulnerable to being reversed, or substantially amended in ways that negates its objectives."[76] This condition is connected to the *content* of the reform as much as to its reception. The solutions must be relatively consensual and mainstream, and, correlatively, must not meet "much ongoing organised resistance."[77] In family law, this balance is hard to strike. In addition to these two key conditions, Banks adds that a reform could be good and yet not be successful. Indeed, "[r]eform will often fail if its effects have not been sufficiently thought through or it does not win acceptance as being beneficial."[78] Here again, a certain period of time must elapse in the assessment of a reform's success, since the effects and the acceptance will materialize and be analyzable only as time passes. In addition to this key condition, Banks engages with certain elements in the process of reform that assist in making a reform potentially successful: prioritizing, time, leadership, and public discussion.[79]

Other scholars have identified further elements relevant to the assessment of the successful of reforms or law reforms. According to Sir Peter North, "practicable and workable solutions are what the law reformers must produce."[80] He adds, "[i]t is no good looking for theoretical or ivory tower solutions to a problem if they cannot be clearly understood in the community at large by the people who have to operate the law."[81] Despite North's assessment, we believe that, for a reform to be successful, it should be informed by strong theory. Macdonald and Kong have examined in depth "the necessary role of theory in the effective practice of law reform."[82] In opposition to the common saying "your idea is good in theory, but it won't work in practice," they remind us that a reform that works in practice but not in theory is not likely to be successful.[83] A delicate balance must be struck, and, sometimes, the theory must take precedence but be accompanied by specific actions – such as training, education, providing information, and more – to make it well received in practice. Absent this balance of a cohesive theory coupled with practical application, the law reform will be disjointed and ineffective. This danger can be seen in the expansion of marriage's definition to include same-sex couples without altering the concept of parentage. As parentage often follows marriage, failing to think through the theory of family law and alter the rules of parentage to accord with marriage's expansion created a dissonant legal theory, resulting in a clunky, ineffective regime. The significance of theory in legal reform can be summarized as follows: there is no use in producing undertheorized law for the sake of making it "easier" for the legal community.

In the context of evaluating institutional law reform in Canada, Gavin Murphy adds other elements, including the "quality and soundness" of recommendations, in addition to an understanding that "a balance must be struck between what is desirable and what is feasible."[84] A law reform that strives for unattainable results and does not consider the practicality of its implementation will most definitely and obviously fail. At the same time, Murphy reports the words of Justice Antonio Lamer, writing that the Law Commission of Canada "made the country think about – and discuss – fundamental legal issues. That was its true success."[85] The importance of law reform's intellectual value in terms of generating informed debates and producing knowledge, regardless of the actual tangible results, must not be overlooked.

In a practical context, while she is critical of our previously noted scholars' incomplete and non-contextual metrics, Rachel Treloar suggests that "the 'success' and 'impact' of the new *FLA* [in British Columbia] are likely to be officially measured by reduced court costs and backlogs, as well as fewer families accessing the courts."[86] Indeed, empirical data on specific aspects of a law reform can provide for good assessments of success, but we have to be careful with these numbers. Another practical aspect that can be used to measure success relates to the costs of the implementation of specific measures. How much did it cost to implement change, and was the impact of the reform sufficient to justify the use of public resources? *Ex post* critiques and apparent failures following the enactment of a reform are also useful in evaluating the success of a specific reform. They are limited, as they become available only after the reform has gone through, but nonetheless are an interesting indicator. All these elements can contribute to the development of a framework for evaluating whether a law reform can be deemed successful.

Assessing Success in Law Reform: A Framework

In this section, we propose a general framework to assess success in law reform, identifying various indicators of success in three categories – process, content, and effects. While all indicators of success within these categories are important, it is beyond the scope of this chapter to explain and discuss them all; however, we do discuss those that are not self-explanatory or were not addressed in the preceding discussion. We then discuss whether this general framework can be used to measure success in family law reform, or if family law's nature poses specific challenges to measuring success.

General Framework: Success Indicators

Any framework for assessing success in law reform will have limits, but this does not mean that we should not try to establish one. Our framework builds on existing scholarship and personal insights, and should be seen not as a fixed scheme, but rather as a starting point for thinking about these issues. Table 9.1 lays out a framework that can be used to analyze whether a specific law reform can be characterized as successful; alternatively, the framework could be used to help ensure that a law reform process is successful. It should be noted that this framework applies better to some types of law reform than others. For example, it is possible to apply our framework to what Barnett calls institutional law reform, but less so to what we have termed judicial law reform. The building blocks (i.e., process, content, and effects) and the success indicators (listed under each building block) are discussed in more detail in the next three subsections. The framework could be used to analyze a specific law reform as a whole or specific aspects of a broader law reform. While it is beyond the scope of

TABLE 9.1
Success indicators

PROCESS
Extensive, effective consultation
Effective use of financial resources and resource allocation
Follows a realistic timeline
Research and collection of empirical data
Process is independent, open, and transparent
Produces results (e.g., a change in the law)
CONTENT
Issues the reform needs to address are clearly and explicitly identified
Theoretical consistency with other laws
Effective use of empirical data
Addresses reasons for reform, including criticisms from stakeholders
Practicable and workable solutions
Achievable, multifaceted, and realistic outcomes
Consensus among stakeholders as to the expected outcomes
EFFECTS
Adequate solutions to the identified issues and concerns raised in consultation
Lasting and sustainable law reform
Inspirational law reform
Limited criticisms of the stakeholders *ex post*
Enhanced social policy and initiation of key normative shifts
No creation of uncertainty beyond what is tenable in a given legal system
Absence of major collateral damage or unexpected consequence
Education and accessibility
Other statistical indicators or classic indicators of success

this chapter to apply the framework to family law reform, we will provide some concrete examples to illustrate success indicators stemming from the reform of the *FLA* in British Columbia.[87]

Table 9.1 highlights that a solid foundation is necessary for a law reform to be successful. Absent sufficient care, time, and resources being devoted to the initial stages of the law reform, it becomes more likely that the reform will fail. By "care," we mean the thought process behind the reform, including the theory behind the reform, its practical effects, and the input of the public via consultation.

The foundation must also include ample supports, both financial and administrative. While it is obvious that a reform must have the financial backing to implement the required changes, it is not sufficient to merely have such funding. There must also be institutional support to ensure the mechanisms inherent in the law reform are put into effect.

The Process of Law Reform

"Process" refers to the initial stages of the reform and to everything that is more procedural than substantive. It comprises the behind-the-scenes procedures that are necessary to develop a law reform that will be lasting and effective. While this stage is largely procedural in nature, focusing on the steps law reformers need to take, it is intertwined with substance, as it represents a way to gather information in different forms and to involve stakeholders in the crafting of the law reform. As shown in Table 9.1, a good process will rely on the following indicators: extensive and inclusive consultation; effective use of financial resources; following a realistic timeline; producing results; and an independent, transparent, and open process.

In general, for a law reform to be effective, it cannot occur in a vacuum. Consultation with experts, but also with the public, should be incorporated at every stage of the law reform process – from the beginning stages of developing a working agenda and plan, and up through the law's implementation. Such extensive consultation ensures that the law reform is actually attuned to at least some of its potential social impacts.[88] The implementation of the *FLA* was developed through extensive consultations, including through online discussion papers, meetings with key stakeholders, and a White Paper. Another example is the process that led to the enactment of the book on the family in the *Civil Code of Québec* in 1980. The report submitted as part of this reform was the result of a long and rigorous process, which included analyzing hundreds of research papers, numerous initiatives to reach out the public and experts around the world, and more than two hundred meetings in plenary committee.[89]

Regarding its financial aspects, the law reform should ensure that ample financial resources are allocated toward developing the reform and its subsequent implementation. However, it should not be a money pit. The reformer should allocate adequate resources to fund a rigorous process as well as to help ensure the success of the reform following its implementation – for example, funds for educating the public about the reform and its application to and impact on their lives. It is hard to identify a clear standard for what constitutes adequate financial resources, but, in general, the reform's budget should consider who the law reform affects and what resources will be needed to ensure smooth a transition from the old regime to the new. Any law reform not including transitional provisions[90] – and a budget for them – appears suspicious.

Timelines tie into the allocation of financial resources in that the reform-makers must ensure that ample time is devoted to implementing the law reform. Like financial resources, the key will be finding the right balance between what is not enough and what is too much. Although there may be circumstances that call for a hasty reform process, the temptation to rush through a law reform should, in general, be avoided. This is particularly true when the reform fundamentally affects the day-to-day life of members of the public. Sufficient time should be allocated to research and understand the issue to be resolved, to gather empirical data, and to develop the best strategies to tackle these issues legislatively. Of course, other strategies or processes in addition to legislative law reform could operate simultaneously and affect the timeline.

The process should meet specific requirements of independence[91] or political consensus, and of openness and transparency. As highlighted by Roderick A. Macdonald, independence relates largely to the potential for political motivations to seep into law reform: differing governments have differing agendas, which could result in different law reform agendas being pushed or abandoned to suit those goals, as opposed to improving the law for the betterment of the public.[92] To ensure that the independence of the law reform process is maintained, governments should, ideally, appoint independent reform committees to invite more open and honest public discourse and reduce the political nature of the reform.[93] In instances where a full independent committee cannot be established, lawmakers should attempt to bolster independence by focusing more heavily on the consultation process or working with external experts or researchers in that area. Political agreement across party lines can also be an indicator of a successful reform in cases where it is not possible to have an independent committee. In the context of British Columbia, an illustration of this would be the collaboration beyond party lines to enact the *FLA*.

Lastly, in terms of process, the process should have results. The idea is simple: a reform should lead to changes in the law. In British Columbia, the reform of family law led to the enactment of a comprehensive statute in a relatively short time (February 2006–March 2013).[94]

The Content of a Law Reform

"Content" refers to the substance of the reform and includes elements from the past, the present, and the future, the latter comprising the reform's expected outcomes. Unlike the past and present, the future can hardly be assessed beforehand, but a reform with strong foresight – as evidenced through thoughtful processes and content – will likely generate positive effects, or at least will be justified and could be judged a successful regardless of some unexpected outcomes. The indicators of success under this aspect of the framework are the clear and explicit: identification of issues the reform needs to address; theoretical consistency with other laws; the effective use of empirical data; a clear indication of the reasons for change, including consideration of criticisms from stakeholders; practicable and workable solutions; achievable, multifaceted, and realistic outcomes; and consensus among stakeholders as to the expected outcomes. These items are largely self-explanatory, but a few warrant further discussion.

Regarding the indicator "theoretical consistency," a law reform cannot be effective only in practice – it must also be effective in theory. As highlighted previously, law reformers must understand that individual laws do not operate separately from other legal areas – instead, multiple areas of law interact and feed off each other in a symbiotic fashion. When creating a law reform, one must be cognizant of whether there will be confusion or disparity in how the reformed law affects other areas of legal practice, or individual lives. For example, the common practice of simply transplanting law from other jurisdictions and introducing it into local legal systems is often problematic, as it disrupts the underlying harmony and cohesion among various areas of law.[95] Law reformers must account for how this reform will impact other areas and develop strategies to create consistency in the underlying theory of law.

In developing the content of the law reform, lawmakers should look to finding concrete reasons for why the law reform is necessary (indicator: criticisms of stakeholders and reasons for change). Law reform for the sake of law reform must be avoided – lawmakers should identify legitimate criticisms and concerns surrounding the current law. They may find these criticisms in a variety of sources – public consultation, court challenges, scholarship, empirical data, and reforms of similar issues in other jurisdictions. Limited criticism is not sufficient – lawmakers should look for patterns and repeated concerns raised by a variety of critical sources.

The two indicators "practicable and workable solutions" and "achievable, multifaceted, and realistic outcomes" both speak largely to the goal that the law reform must be practical and achievable. While there are slight differences between the two, they both speak to creating a regime that is realistic and functional in society. "Practicable and workable solutions" refers more to the initial stages of the law reform. Once the lawmakers are confronted with one or more reformable issues, the solutions they develop must be ones capable of being achieved. The solutions must reflect the realities surrounding the practice of law in that area, so as not to implement a change that complicates and upends an already established area of law. Solutions must be simple and can often be built on already existing concepts. "Achievable, multifaceted, and realistic outcomes" refers more to whether the anticipated law reform's outcomes will actually be achievable. It is one thing to develop a workable solution, but it is another to actually achieve the goals that the reform sought. A realistic outcome is one that is cognizant of existing realities in that legal regime, including the level of resources available to achieve the reform. For example, one of the important expected outcomes in the reform of the *FLA* was that family disputes would be settled out of court using dispute resolution (DR).[96] However, no resources were allocated to potential users of such an approach. It was not realistic to believe that, without allocating resources, people would resort to DR, which can be costly. A low-conflict dispute is estimated to cost \$12,328 to solve through arbitration and \$12,395 through litigation.[97] While mediation cuts that figure in half,[98] it still represents significant costs for a household, and not all DR options are less expensive than the courtroom.

Lastly, "consensus among stakeholders as to the expected outcomes" refers to the idea that the content of the reform will lead to specific outcomes that stakeholders forsee and agree on. If different stakeholders think the reform will lead to dissimilar results, the reform can hardly be qualified as successful.

The Effects of a Law Reform

Besides considerations of process and content, our framework suggests analyzing the effects of law reform to assess whether the reform can be deemed successful. The indicators of success when it comes to effects are: adequate solutions to the identified issues and concerns raised in consultation; lasting and sustainable law reform; inspirational law reform; limited riticisms of the stakeholders *ex post*; enhanced social policy and initiation of key normative shifts; no creation of uncertainty beyond what is tenable in a given legal system; absence of major collateral damage or unexpected consequence; and other statistical indicators or classic indicators of success. The framework's section on effects is largely self-explanatory and addresses the question of whether the reform actually accomplished what it set out to do. This area of analysis will be capable of completion only after the reform has been in effect for a while. In essence, the crucial aspects of evaluating success in this area will be whether the goals of the reform have been adopted and are sustainable in society, and whether the reform has avoided significant negative, unintended effects. A successful law reform should evaluate whether the selected solutions for the issues being tackled actually proved effective in ameliorating these issues, or whether additional or alternative solutions should have been considered. All aspects of a law reform's effects are largely dependent on the preparation done for the law reform – a reform will only be as successful as the amount of effort put into its process and content.

An interesting area where we may evaluate a law reform's success on a more theoretical level is whether it is inspirational. This refers largely to whether the reform sparked conversations and considerations of implementation in other jurisdictions. For example, when British Columbia introduced the *FLA* in 2013, it was considered groundbreaking for its progressive approach to legal parenting through the multiple-parent scheme.[99] This element of the law not only prompted discussion among family law scholars, but also moved other governments to consider introducing similar schemes to recognize more than two parents. Although this regime has been criticized,[100] it is undeniable that it was successful in moving forward discussions on our conceptions of what constitutes legal parenting. Since 2013, several other jurisdictions, including Ontario, Saskatchewan, and California, have followed British Columbia's lead in implementing similar regimes. The importance of inspirational law reform is that it highlights that the law reform effectively addressed an important societal issue that was not adequately handled under existing law. We believe that seeing other jurisdictions discuss[101] and follow suit indicates that the resources devoted to the reform were not used in vain, but moved the law closer to societal realities.

Similarly, we should be cognizant of the criticisms of stakeholders after the law has been implemented. These stakeholders often must live the reality created through the law reform and therefore may have crucial insights into whether the reform was actually effective.[102] It would be beneficial for lawmakers to seek *ex post facto* consultations with the public to assess whether the reform has addressed the concerns that they identified in the initial consultation, and whether there are areas of the reform that are simply not proving effective. Limited criticisms *ex post* indicate success. Despite the length of time needed to evaluate the effects of a law reform, this aspect of our framework likely provides the simplest metrics for determining success.

The Specificities of Family Law and the Law Reform Framework

Family law is said to be a unique legal system. It stands apart from other legal regimes, given both its centrality in every person's life and the heightened emotional state typically accompanying these matters. With these apparent differences in mind, how can the above framework apply in the context of family law? Are there specific aspects of family law that should be given consideration when determining a law reform's success? Does our framework require additional criteria to handle the so-called uniqueness of family law?

We might first ask whether family law truly stand apart. As John Dewar highlights, "family law engages with areas of social life and feeling – namely love, passion, intimacy, commitment and betrayal – that are themselves riven with contradiction or paradox."[103] It is a legal regime that straddles the line between social context and legal principle more closely than many others, resulting in heavy reliance on the lived experience of society and the family as opposed to ethereal legal principles.[104] This emotional, fact-specific, contextual arena gives family law its place outside of the norm as a "chaotic, contradictory, or incoherent"[105] legal form. Scholars, judges, and others tend to view family law as exempt from, or allowed to bend, common legal rules.[106] This bending means that normative aspects of society, such as the market, are viewed as incompatible with, or inapplicable to, family law.[107] Family law is viewed as an island in a sea of legal rationality. Some question whether it may even be characterized as law at all, given these differences from other law fields, while others suggest that it is time to abolish family law as we know it.[108]

But is family law truly that anomalous vis-à-vis other legal regimes? Does the heightened emotional state associated with it and its generally universal applicability truly separate it so significantly from other legal regimes? In reality, while family law does have unique aspects that distinguish it from other forms of law, it cannot be defined as truly exceptional.[109] Parsing family law out as exceptional ignores the reality that family law does not exist in a vacuum – instead, it touches and interweaves with many different areas of the law. Tax and immigration law, for example, both necessarily assimilate and function with family law – in so doing, these areas of law do not suddenly lose all reason and function.[110] The exceptionality argument also overlooks the emotional aspect of other fields, such as labour law, wills and estates, and property. These areas of law work collaboratively with family law and also pose their inherent emotional and irrational challenges. Further, conceptions that family law lies outside of certain norms are being unsettled – the idea that family law is incompatible with the market, for example, ignores the fact that family law routinely allows spouses to engage in market-like behaviour.[111] For example, the *FLA* permits spouses in British Columbia to enter into economic agreements with each other to modify its application at any point.[112] The law still safeguards against the vulnerabilities that may arise in family law by granting courts authority to set aside these agreements,[113] but to say general contract law does not apply oversimplifies the problem. While it is more controversial, a similar argument could be made about the contractualization of certain types of parent-child relationships.[114] Ultimately, even if there are differences between family law and other areas, it seems unwise to classify family law as being an exception to the norm. Thus, while our law reform framework does require some adjusting to address specificities in family law, the framework does not require major reworking to apply in the family law context.

Two areas of our framework have special implications for applications in the context of family law: the processes of resource allocation (particularly with respect to public education and general consultation) and consultation. Although other areas of this framework may have unique applications to family law, we view these two as the most crucial. We would argue, given our view that family law is not exceptional, that most indicators of success apply as they would to general law reforms – or, more realistically, that every legal discipline will make specific adjustment to the framework to accommodate its own uniqueness.

In the context of family law, general consultation with the public and laypeople will be especially significant. In recent decades, law's conception of the family has slowly moved away from the heteronormative nuclear family and toward a more functional approach – one where the family is defined by the functions it serves as opposed to a specific normative content. This move brings with it a need for increased consultation when considering any family law reform: the law is rarely in sync with all the varieties of intimate arrangements. A legislative body needs to be cognizant of the realities facing families, including, but not limited to, structures, needs, and interactions. The most appropriate way to obtain this feedback will be through adequate research, including surveying and consultation with the public and with interdisciplinary experts, among others. In doing so, the legislature will be able to attain the most relevant and recent information pertaining to family function, but will also better understand people's expectations. Furthermore, the legislature will be able to obtain feedback on the feasibility of the reform from those who will need to live with its implementation. Extensive consultation will also assist with other success indicators, in that it may catch areas of inconsistency or confusion, allowing these to be corrected early and thereby improving the effectiveness of the law reform. There is no one preferred method for consultation, but it is important that sufficient time, active measures, and resources be put into the consultation process to ensure the reform serves different stakeholders and creates an effective regime.

As family law issues will eventually arise with most people, regardless of age, education level, or background, it is essential that law reform in this area brings coherent change that is understandable and applicable to those in the most common contexts. Yet it also needs to recognize specific challenges and be inclusive of people whose situations may not reflect mainstream norms. As such, the success indicators about education and accessibility are especially important when measuring the success of a family law reform. This requirement to educate people and put forward comprehensive reforms becomes even more salient when we consider the state of family law and issues related to access to justice in many Canadian provinces, including British Columbia. According to a 2012 study, between 40 and 57 percent of parties are self-represented in family law matters in Canada, the proportion varying by province and territory.[115] These self-represented litigants often have no formal legal training, and they are left to navigate the legal system with minimal knowledge, damaging their case and resulting in overuse of court resources.[116] In order to create an effective family law reform, the reform must be sensible to the reality that the average user of family law lacks formal legal training. Self-represented litigants must be able to apply and understand the law, or resources must be available to help them navigate the legal system. Evaluating a reform's success on this front can be measured in two ways: directly, through the extent of education on the reform, and indirectly, through the allocation of government resources to education or legal aid services (accessibility).

Directly, family law reform will generally be considered successful where evidence demonstrates that action has been taken to educate the public regarding the reform. For example, in 2013, the *FLA* created a normalizing legal avenue for multiple-parent families in British Columbia. However, based on recent data, very few families in the province have made use of this legal avenue since its inception,[117] and case law demonstrates that the stakeholders are unaware of the requirements of the law.[118] This lack of application and the fact that families end up in court despite rules that were enacted specifically to avoid this situation may be due to a variety of factors. One of them is a lack of public education. Even though the provincial government published material explaining the new statute,[119] it launched no widespread initiatives for public education.

Indirectly, all family law reforms could be considered more successful with increased funding for legal aid and education. Providing these resources will improve the functioning of all such reform, as it will assist potential self-represented litigants in obtaining proper counsel to better represent them in complex matters, or will provide them with more opportunities for education so they can appropriately understand and apply the law. While British Columbia cut funding for legal aid significantly in 2002, largely curtailing family law services,[120] there have been motions to increase access to justice in the province for family law and other matters. In 2019, Attorney General David Eby pledged $2 million to open eight legal aid clinics across the province and reached an agreement with the city of Victoria to properly pay legal aid lawyers.[121] A large gap still needs to be filled in order to ameliorate the access to justice crisis, but it is not difficult to see how measures such as this will make family law reform more effective by decreasing confusion and use of court resources. It is essential that increased resource allocation continue, both in terms of time and funding, in order to ensure the success of future family law reforms.

Conclusion

The question of what makes a law reform successful is complicated, yet crucial. Law reform processes are recurrent and necessary, mobilize all forms of resources, and should be scrutinized. The many forms they take – and the different understandings of law and success – render the task of assessment complex. Our chapter has sought to create a uniformly applicable method of evaluating the success of law reform through various indicators of success. Our framework focuses on assessing not only the effects of a law reform (i.e., that the reform must actually accomplish what it set out to do), but also factors affecting the effectiveness of the process and content of the reform. A law reform should involve adequate consultation and allocation of resources in the development processes to ensure a smooth road map to reform and the tools necessary to effectively implement the new regime. It must respond to perceived deficiencies in the current legal system and develop practicable, workable solutions that have realistic and achievable outcomes. A law reform should achieves its goals without adverse effects, and ideally will inspire other jurisdictions to do the same. While there are certain aspects in which measuring the success of a family law reform may differ from the general framework we offered, this should not propagate the idea that family law reform is fundamentally different from other law reforms.

In this chapter, we have provided a guide for those seeking to assess a law reform. We do not offer concrete mechanisms for assessing success, acknowledging that every law reform will be unique and contextual, and will have its own elements to consider. However, we seek to provide an objective framework, composed of various indicators, that can assist in determining not only whether particular reforms were successful, but, more importantly, how to undertake better law reform processes in the future. Reforming family law will not necessarily lead to positive transformations in society, or even in law.[122] In fact, familial norms are rooted in societal, religious, and cultural expectations that the law can seldom modify. Family law can also be used to build political capital, with mitigated results. Nevertheless, law reform is one of the avenues to alter limiting norms and effect changes for families. To be effective, law reforms must be done well, with attention given to process, content, and effects.

Notes

This research is part of a larger project funded by the Law Foundation of British Columbia and the Hampton Fund (UBC). We would like to thank the participants of *Shifting Normativities* (Vancouver, 9–10 May 2019) for their constructive feedback on an earlier version of this chapter.

1 See *An Act instituting civil unions and establishing new rules of filiation*, SQ 2002, c 6.

2 See *Family Law Act*, SBC 2011, c 25 [*FLA*].

3 See *All Families Are Equal Act (Parentage and Related Registrations Statute Law Amendment)*, SO 2016, c 23.

4 As of 1 January 2020, the *Matrimonial Property Act* (RSA 2000, c F-4.7) has been renamed the *Family Property Act* (RSA 2000, c F-4.7) and now applies to adult interdependent partners (common law spouses) too. See Government of Alberta, "Dividing Property between Unmarried Partners," online: Alberta, <www.alberta.ca/dividing-property-between-unmarried-partners.aspx>.

5 Bill 2, *An Act respecting family law reform with regard to filiation and amending the Civil Code in relation to personality rights and civil status*, 2nd Sess, 42nd Leg, Quebec <http://m.assnat.qc.ca/en/travaux-parlementaires/projets-loi/projet-loi-2-42-2.html>.

6 *An Act to amend the Divorce Act, the Family Orders and Agreements Enforcement Assistance Act and the Garnishment, Attachment and Pension Diversion Act and to make consequential amendments to another Act*, SC 2019, c 16.

7 A scholar identified only eight pieces of legislation passed by the Parliament of Canada during the first century after Confederation. See S Ian Bushnell, "Family Law and the Constitution" (1978) 1 Can J Fam L 202 at 212. Since 1978, less than ten interventions have happened.

8 *AA v BB,* 2007 ONCA 2.

9 *Reference re Same-Sex Marriage,* 2004 SCC 79.

10 *Quebec (Attorney General) v A,* 2013 SCC 5.

11 See e.g. Susan B Boyd & Rachel Treloar, "Family Law Reform in (Neoliberal) Context: British Columbia's New Family Law Act," (2014) 28:1 Intl JL Pol'y & Fam 77; Susan B Boyd & Claire Young, "Who Influences Family Law Reform? Discourses on Motherhood and Fatherhood in Legislative Reform Debates in Canada" (2002) 26 Stud L Pol & Soc 43; Julien D Payne, "Family Law Reform and the Law Reform Commission of Canada" (1985) 4:4 Can J Fam L 355; Rollie Thomson, "Family Law Reform and Social Change" (1986) 5:1 Can J Fam L 11; Nicholas Bala, "Judicial Discretion and Family Law Reform in Canada" (1986) 5:1 Can J Fam L 15; Ian FG Baxter, "Family Law Reform: A Historical Perspective of the Ontario Experience" (1987) 6:2 Can J of Fam L 247; Mary Jane Mossman, "Running Hard to Stand Still: The Paradox of Family Law Reform" (1994) 17:1 Dalhousie LJ 5; Mary Ann Glendon, "Family Law Reform in the 1980's" (1984) 44:6 La L Rev 1553; Ian FG Baxter, "Family Law Reform in Canada – Comment" (1987) 35:4 Am J Comp L 801; Brenda Hoggett, "Family Courts of Family Law Reform: Which Should Come First" (1986) 6:1 LS 1.

12 See *infra*, note 33.

13 Think of the *Spousal Support Advisory Guidelines,* which have an asymmetrical weight in the country: Canada, Department of Justice, *Spousal Support Advisory Guidelines,* by Carol Rogerson & Rollie Thompson (Ottawa: Department of Justice, July 2008). A new and improved user's guide was published in 2010, and a revised user's guide in 2016.

14 Peter Hogg, *Constitutional Law of Canada,* 5th ed Supplemented, vol 1 (Toronto: Thomson Reuters, 2018) at 27.9(a).

15 *Merriam-Webster Dictionary*, online, *sub verbo* "reform."

16 *Ibid.*

17 Michael Kirby, *Reform the Law: Essays on the Renewal of the Australian Legal System* (Oxford: Oxford University Press, 1983) at 7 [Kirby, *Reform the Law*].

18 *The New Oxford Companion to Law* (Oxford: Oxford University Press, 2008) at 683–85.

19 *Private Law Dictionary,* 2nd ed (Cowansville, QC: Yvon Blais, 2016).

20 *Canadian Online Legal Dictionary,* online: Irwin Law, <https://irwinlaw.com/cold/>.

21 *Dictionnaire de droit québécois et canadien*, rev ed, 2016, online: Jurisource, <https://www.jurisource.ca/ressource/dictionnaire-de-droit-quebecois-et-canadien/>.
22 *Black's Law Dictionary*, 10th ed, *sub verbo* "law reform."
23 Roderick A Macdonald & Hoi Kong, "Patchwork Law Reform: Your Idea Is Good in Practice, but Not in Theory" (2006) 44:1 Osgoode LJ 11 at 17.
24 *Ibid.*
25 *Ibid.*
26 *Ibid* at 18.
27 *Ibid* at 20.
28 *Ibid* at 22.
29 *Ibid* at 25.
30 *Ibid* at 26.
31 Thanks to Hoi Kong for a generous conversation on the matter.
32 Macdonald & Kong, *supra* note 23 at 25.
33 William H Hurlburt, *Law Reform Commissions in the United Kingdom, Canada and Australia* (Edmonton: Juriliber, 1986) at 3.
34 Lord Devlin, "The Process of Law Reform" (1966) 63 L Soc Gaz 453 at 454, as cited in Hurlburt, *supra* note 33 at 3.
35 Lawrence M Friedman, "Law Reform in Historical Perspective" (1969) 13 Saint Louis ULJ 351 at 351, as cited in Hurlburt, *supra* note 33 at 4–5.
36 *Ibid.*
37 Hurlburt, *supra* note 33 at 6. Anyone interested in understanding better what is a law reform should read pages 3–14.
38 Rollie Thompson, "Editorial – Family Law Reform and Social Change" (1986) 5 Can J Fam L 11 at 11.
39 Peter Handford, "The Changing Face of Law Reform" (1999) 73:7 Austl LJ 503 at 507.
40 Macdonald & Kong, *supra* note 23 at 52.
41 *Ibid;* Gary Banks, *Successful Reform: Past Lessons, Future Challenges (Annual Forecasting Conference of the Australian Business Economists, 8 December 2010)*, Productivity Commission, Canberra at 5; Kirby, *Reform the Law, supra* note 17 at 10; Hurlburt, *supra* note 33 at 6.
42 See Susan B Boyd, "Equality: An Uncomfortable Fit in Parenting Law" in Robert Leckey, ed, *After Legal Equality: Family, Sex, Kinship* (New York: Routledge, 2015) 42 [Boyd, "Equality"]. One can also think of Michael Warner's well-known critique of marriage equality for segments of the queer community in *The Trouble with Normal: Sex, Politics and the Ethics of Queer Life* (New York: Free Press, 1999).

43 Laura Barnett, "The Process of Law Reform: Conditions for Success" (2011) 39 Fed L Rev 161 at 191.

44 See Ronald Sackville, "The Role of Law Reform Agencies in Australia" (1985) 59 Austl LJ 151; Roderick A Macdonald, "Recommissioning Law Reform" (1997) 35:4 Alta L Rev 831; Hurlburt, *supra* note 33; Handford, *supra* note 39; Canada, Department of Justice, *Law Reform Agencies*, by Gavin Murphy (Ottawa: Department of Justice, 2004); Barnett, *supra* note 43; Banks, *supra* note 41.

45 Jenni Millbank, "The Role of 'Functional Family' in Same-Sex Family Recognition Trends" (2008) 20:2 Child Fam LQ 155.

46 *Halpern v Canada (Attorney General)* (2003), 225 DLR (4th) 529 (ONCA).

47 *Barbeau v British Columbia*, 2003 BCCA 406.

48 *Rypkema v HMTQ et al*, 2003 BCSC 1784.

49 *Gill and Maher, Murray and Popoff v Ministry of Health*, 2001 BCHRT 34.

50 Millbank, *supra* note 45.

51 See William C Duncan, "'Don't Ever Take a Fence Down': The 'Functional' Definition of Family – Displacing Marriage in Family Law" (2001) 3 JL Fam Stud 57; Kris Franklin, "'A Family Like Any Other Family:' Alternative Methods of Defining the Family in Law" (1990) 18 NYU Rev L & Soc Change 1027.

52 In the Canadian context, the functional account is generally associated with *Charter* litigation, especially with respect to s 15.

53 See e.g. Joel Handler, *Social Movements and the Legal System: A Theory of Law Reform and Social Change* (New York: Academic Press, 1978); Michael McCann, *Law and Social Movements* (New York: Routledge, 2006); Sandra R Levitsky, "Law and Social Movements: Old Debates and New Directions" in Austin Sarat & Patricia Ewick, eds, *The Handbook of Law and Society* (West Sussex: John Wiley & Sons, 2015) at 382; Scott L Cummings, "Law and Social Movements: Reimagining the Progressive Canon" (2018) Wis L Rev 441 [Cummings, "Law and Social Movements"].

54 For an example of the influence of groups on legislative law reform, see Boyd & Young, *supra* note 11.

55 Gerald N Rosenberg, *The Hollow Hope: Can Courts Bring About Social Change?* (Chicago: University of Chicago Press, 1991).

56 Levitsky, *supra* note 53 at 384.

57 Warner, *supra* note 42.

58 See Dean Spade, "Intersectional Resistance and Law Reform" (2013) 38:4 Signs: Journal of Women in Culture and Society 1031; Kimberlé Williams Crenshaw, "Race, Reform, and Retrenchment: Transformation and Legitimation in

Antidiscrimination Law" (1988) 101:7 Harv L Rev 1331; Cummings, "Law and Social Movements," *supra* note 53 at 451ff.

59 See Scott L Cummings, "The Social Movement Turn in Law" (2018) 43:2 L & Social Inquiry 360.

60 Barnett, *supra* note 43 at 161.

61 Robert Leckey, "Introduction" in Robert Leckey, ed, *After Equality: Family, Sex, Kinship* (New York: Routledge, 2015) 1 [Leckey, "Introduction"] at 1. See also Murphy, *supra* note 44 at 59 and ff on this simplistic standard of success assessment.

62 Leckey, "Introduction," *supra* note 61 at 4.

63 Kirby, *Reform the Law, supra* note 17 at 19.

64 This quote was first used by Hurlburt. See Hurlburt, *supra* note 33 at 5. The original source is Antonio Lamer, "What We Are Doing, or the Business of Law Reform" (1977) [unpublished]. Unfortunately, we could not access this source.

65 Law Reform Commission of Ireland, *Law Reform: Ten Attributes for Success*, by the Honorable Justice Michael Kirby, 17 July 2007 (Dublin: Law Reform Commission of Ireland, 2007) [Kirby, *Ten Attributes*].

66 *Ibid* at 7.

67 On family law as expression, see Alison Diduck, "Family Law as Expression: Financial Relief in the English Courts" in this collection. See also, generally, Carl E Schneider, "The Channelling Function in Family Law" (1992) 20 Hofstra L Rev 495.

68 Autonomy and choice have been constructed and deconstructed a thousand times in the context of family law, most famously by Martha A Fineman and Jennifer Nedelsky. See Martha A Fineman, *The Autonomy Myth: A Theory of Dependency* (New York: New Press, 2004); Jennifer Nedelsky, *Law's Relations: A Relational Theory of Self, Autonomy, and Law* (New York: Oxford University Press, 2011). See also Hélène Belleau & Pascale Cornut St-Pierre, "La question du 'choix' dans la décision de se marier ou non au Québec" (2011) 66 Lien social et politiques 65. It is distressing to see that some initiatives to reform family law still conceptualize autonomy as the cornerstone of family law. See Comité consultatif sur le droit de la famille, Alain Roy (pres.), *Pour un droit de la famille adapté aux nouvelles réalités conjugales et familiales* (Quebec: Ministère de la Justice du Québec, 2015).

69 See for example, in Quebec's context, Chapter 7 by Hélène Belleau in this collection, but also Belleau's work generally.

70 See generally Kirby, *Ten Attributes, supra* note 65.

71 *Ibid* at 11.

72 *Ibid* at 12.

73 Barnett, *supra* note 43 at 170 and ff.

74 Banks, *supra* note 41 at 5.

75 *Ibid.*

76 *Ibid.*

77 *Ibid.*

78 *Ibid* at 6.

79 See Banks, *supra* note 41.

80 Peter North, "Law Reform: Problems and Pitfalls" (1999) 33:1 UBC L Rev 37 at 43.

81 *Ibid.*

82 Macdonald & Kong, *supra* note 23 at 15.

83 *Ibid.*

84 Murphy, *supra* note 44 at 60.

85 *Ibid* at 61.

86 Rachel Treloar, "The Neoliberal Context of Family Law Reform in British Columbia, Canada: Implications for Access to (Family) Justice" in Mavis Maclean, John Eekelaar & Benoit Bastard, eds, *Delivering Family Justice in the 21st Century* (London: Hart Publishing, 2015) 15 at 16.

87 *FLA, supra* note 2.

88 See Roderick A Macdonald, "Law Reform for Dummies (3rd Edition)", 51:3 Osgoode LJ (2014) 859 [Macdonald, "Law Reform for Dummies"] at 883.

89 See John EC Brierley & Roderick A Macdonald, eds, *Quebec Civil Law: An Introduction to Quebec Private Law* (Toronto: Emond Montgomery Publications, 1993) at 90–91. See also Civil Code Revision Office, Committee on the Law on Persons and on the Family, *Report on the Family, Part One* (Montreal, 1974).

90 On the importance of transitional provisions in family law reform, see Robert Leckey, "One Parent, Three Parents: Judges and Ontario's All Families Are Equal Act, 2016" (2019) 33:3 Int JL Pol'y & Fam 298.

91 When this factor applies. For example, a social movement law reform is unlikely to be independent.

92 Macdonald, "Law Reform for Dummies," *supra* note 88 at 882.

93 *Ibid.*

94 February 2006 is the date of the official announcement by the government, but we could have used an earlier date, when the Law Society of British Columbia established a Justice Review Task Force (March 2002). Similarly, the end date could have been 24 November 2011, when the *FLA* received royal assent, but we decided to use the date of its coming into force.

95 See Macdonald & Kong, *supra* note 23 at 46.

96 See Ministry of Attorney General, Justice Services Branch Civil Policy and Legislation Office, *White Paper on Family Relations Act Reform: Proposals for a New Family Law Act* (July 2010) at 2, 3, 12, 30, etc.

97 See Joanne J Paetsch, Lorne D Bertrand & JP Boyd, "An Evaluation of the Cost of Family Law Disputes: Measuring the Cost Implication of Various Dispute Resolution Methods" (Paper submitted to the Canadian Forum on Civil Justice, Toronto 2018) at 30, online (PDF): <www.cfcj-fcjc.org/sites/default/files/docs/Cost-Implication-of-Family-Law-Disputes.pdf>.

98 *Ibid.*

99 See e.g. Boyd, "Equality," *supra* note 42 at 42; Karen Busby, "Of Surrogate Mother Born: Parentage Determinations in Canada and Elsewhere" (2013) 25:2 CJWL 284; Manitoba Law Reform Commission, "Assisted Reproduction: Legal Parentage and Birth Registration" (April 2014), online (PDF): <www.manitobalawreform.ca/pubs/pdf/additional/assisted_reproduction-legal_parentage_and_birth_registration.pdf>.

100 See, e.g., Fiona Kelly, "Multiple-Parent Families under British Columbia's New Family Law Act: A Challenge to the Supremacy of the Nuclear Family or a Method by which to Preserve Biological Ties and Opposite-Sex Parenting?" (2014) 47:2 UBC L Rev 565.

101 See e.g. Paula Gerber & Phoebe Irving Lindner, "Modern Families: Should Children Be Able to Have More Than Two Parents Recorded on Their Birth Certificates?" (2015) 5 Victoria UL & Just J 34; Tricia Kazinetz, "You Can't Have One Without the Other: Why the Legalization of Same Sex Marriage Created a Need for Courts to Have Discretion in Granting Legal Parentage to More than Two Individuals" (2018) 24 Widener L Rev 179; Heather Kolinsky, "The Intended Parent: The Power and Problems Inherent in Designating and Determining Intent in the Context of Parental Rights" (2015) 119:4 Penn St L Rev 801.

102 See e.g. Susan B Boyd & Matt Ledger, "British Columbia's New Family Law on Guardianship, Relocation, and Family Violence: The First Year of Judicial Interpretation" (2013) 33 Can Fam LQ 317; Susan B Boyd & Catherine Whitehead, "Spousal Support under British Columbia's New Family Law Act: A Preliminary Analysis" (2015) 73:1 Advocate 21; Boyd & Treloar, *supra* note 11; Pivot Legal Society, "BC Takes One Step Forward and One Step Back on Protecting Women and Children" (28 March 2013), online: Pivot, <www.pivotlegal.org/bc_takes_one_step_forward_and_one_back_on_violence_against_women>; Battered Women Support Services, "The New Family Law Act and Its Implications for Battered Women" (20 December 2012), online (PDF): <www.bwss.org/wp-content/uploads/Family-Law-Act-GUIDE.pdf>.

103 John Dewar, "The Normal Chaos of Family Law" (1998) 61:4 Mod L Rev 467 at 468.

104 See *ibid* at 469.

105 *Ibid* at 468.

106 See Jill Hasday, *Family Law Reimagined* (Cambridge, MA: Harvard University Press, 2014) at 15.

107 See *ibid.*

108 See e.g. Chapter 10 by Brenda Cossman in this volume.

109 See Janet Halley & Kerry Rittich, "Critical Directions in Comparative Family Law: Genealogies and Contemporary Studies of Family Law Exceptionalism" (2010) 58 Am J Comp L 753 on family law exceptionalism.

110 See Kelly McGee, "What's So Exceptional about Immigration and Family Law Exceptionalism? An Analysis of Canonical Family and Immigration Law as Reflective of American Nationalism" (2019) 20 Geo J Gender & L 699 at 707.

111 See Hasday, *supra* note 106 at 75.

112 *FLA, supra* note 2, ss 6(5).

113 *Ibid,* s 93.

114 See for example, *ibid,* ss 28, 29, or 30.

115 See Department of Justice, Research and Statistics Division, *Self-Represented Litigants in Family Law* (Ottawa: Department of Justice, June 2004), online: Government of Canada, Department of Justice, <www.justice.gc.ca/eng/rp-pr/fl-lf/divorce/jf-pf/srl-pnr.html>.

116 See *ibid.*

117 See Régine Tremblay, "Diversité familiale en Colombie-Britannique: quels sont les impacts de la réforme de 2013?" in Paul Mongenais, Régine Tremblay & Rénald Rémillard, *Legislative Changes in Family Law* (Centre for Continuing Development of the Faculty of Law, University of Ottawa, 31 May 2019).

118 When it comes to multiple-parent families, see *Cabianca v British Columbia (Registrar General of Vital Statistics),* 2019 BCSC 2010 (CanLII). Surrogacy is another example where this also happens: see *Family Law Act (Re),* 2016 BCSC 598 (CanLII).

119 See British Columbia, Ministry of Justice, "The Family Law Act: Explained," online: Government of British Columbia, <www2.gov.bc.ca/gov/content/justice/about-bcs-justice-system/legislation-policy/legislation-updates/family-law-act/the-family-law-act-explained>.

120 Legal Aid Task Force, "A Vision for Publicly Funded Legal Aid in British Columbia" (Law Society of British Columbia, 3 March 2017) at para 7, online (PDF): <www.lawsociety.bc.ca/Website/media/Shared/docs/initiatives/LegalAidVision2017.pdf>.

121 "Province to Invest $2 Million in Eight New Legal Clinics," *Times Colonist* (4 November 2019), online: <timescolonist.com>; Canadian Press, "New Deal Gives Stability to Legal Aid Lawyers, Clients: BC Attorney General," *CTV News* (15 October 2019), online: <bc.ctvnews.ca/new-deal-gives-stability-to-legal-aid-lawyers-clients-b-c-attorney-general-1.4639438>.

122 See e.g. Chapter 3 by Alison Diduck in this volume.

10

Abolishing Family Law (as We Know It)

Brenda Cossman

> I do not believe [the changes required to the family law system] can be achieved by tinkering at the edges of the existing family law system or by grafting new procedures and services onto the existing system. The reforms I am advocating can best be achieved by undergoing a fundamental overhaul of the current system.[1]
>
> – Chief Justice Warren K. Winkler

> Ontario's family law system requires a drastic change if it is to be truly effective and responsive.[2]
>
> – Law Commission of Ontario

This chapter is a provocation and a thought experiment around the following question: What if we abolished family law? It is not a libertarian argument. I am not suggesting that the relationships that we now consider to be covered by family law be returned to some laissez-faire market-style regulation. But, what if the realm of law known as family law (marriage, divorce, property, spousal and child support) were abolished? More specifically, what if each of these areas were removed from the scope of private law? What could we build in their place?

Why would we even want to entertain this seemingly preposterous thought experiment? Primarily because family law is not working. As the quotes from Chief Justice Winkler and the Law Commission of Ontario state unequivocally, the family justice system needs radical change. Study after study have shown that the family justice system is failing Canadian families.[3] Dramatic increases in separations and divorces, the increasingly inaccessible cost of legal representation, the inadequacy of legal aid, and the protracted nature of many family law disputes have combined to produce a crisis of unmet legal needs. Notwithstanding significant substantive and procedural reforms over the past several decades, the family justice system is in a state of crisis and chaos. With individuals unable to afford lawyers and availability of legal aid being limited, the proportion of self-represented litigants in the family justice system continues to grow by leaps and bounds. The best substantive family laws are, of course, only as good as the ability of individuals to access these rights. In recent years, considerable time and effort have been directed to the questions of access to justice – to family courts, duty counsel, early front-end services, mandatory information programs, informal and consensual dispute resolution, simplified procedures, legal aid, and greater use of paralegals. Solutions have been recited over and again, by lawyers, academics, and policymakers, but political will is lacking. Vested interests, institutional inertia, and an absence of government funding leave the reports and recommendations to gather dust. The inertia has itself become the focus of study, with the Cromwell report referring to it as the "implementation gap."[4] One need look no further than the debates – and opposition of much of the family law bar – around the use of paralegals in family law to see the obstacles to change from within the family justice system and its practitioners.[5]

A main obstacle to redesigning institutional and legal structures is often a form of inertia that comes from path dependency. "Path dependency" refers to the ways in which present and future decisions are limited by decisions made in the past, even though past circumstances may no longer be relevant. In the context of public policy, once a particular policy direction has been chosen, the costs of reversal can be high. As Margaret Levi described it, "once a country or region has started down a track, the costs of reversal are very high. There will be other choice points, but the entrenchment of certain institutional arrangements obstruct an easy reversal of the initial choice."[6] Family law is, of course, deeply entrenched in institutional structures and arrangements: the brick and mortar of family courts, the substantive and procedural rules of family law, the practices of family lawyers, law school curriculums, and textbooks, casebooks, and journals, all dedicated to and constituting the discipline. Change seems nearly impossible, even inconceivable.

Despite claims as to the need for a fundamental transformation of the family justice system, the solutions have, unsurprisingly, been largely in relation to access to justice – to procedural and institutional changes that might facilitate a more efficient family justice system. What if we thought beyond the existing system? Admittedly, path dependency, vested interests, institutional inertia, and the absence of government funding would be the death knell to any attempt at radical legal and institutional reform. But what if we thought about it anyway? What if we take the Chief Justice and the Law Commission of Ontario's words seriously, albeit beyond the kind of change that they may have had in mind? What if we thought about a different way of resolving the disputes currently known as family law? What if we disarticulated the conflicts from the private civil justice system?

From an institutional-design perspective, the family justice system no longer makes sense. If we were to design an institutional approach to a problem that affects 40 percent of the population, we would not root it in private civil law. When modern family law emerged – that is, divorce and its ancillary consequences in the mid-nineteenth century – divorce was highly restricted and rare. With each wave of divorce reform and the transformations in contemporary family life, the divorce rate has risen, holding steady now at approximately 38 percent of all marriages.[7] Divorce and its financial consequences are now a pervasive part of the Canadian landscape. Yet, the idea that divorce is *private* continues to structure the substance and process of family law. While family law is subject to extensive regulation, based on a recognition of the broader public interest in ensuring the equitable resolution of disputes that arise when relationships break-down, the dispute remains one between the parties to be resolved by the parties within the civil justice system. We should not be surprised that the civil justice system is no longer capable of adequately dealing the problem: it was simply not designed for problems that affect over one-third of the Canadian population.

This chapter is part of a larger project on re-envisioning the legal regulation of family breakdown, beyond the private and civil law framework. I am interested in exploring the idea that family law should be revised as a form of social law. This new idea suggests that a system of private law is ill equipped to deal with the volume, social costs, and nature of family law disputes. Family law disputes present unique problems that require a unique form of dispute resolution. The chapter also argues that it may be time to leave Tolstoy's concept of family behind. While the clichéd words that "each unhappy family is unhappy in its own way" from *Anna Karenina* no doubt remains a truism,[8] there is a way in which family law has for too long sought to provide highly individualized solutions to the unique situations of individual families. While this individualist approach may still work for higher-income families, who are able to afford full legal representation, it fails miserably for the vast majority of Canadian families going through separation and divorce.[9] In this chapter, I try to imagine how separation and divorce could be regulated differently.

Family Law: Public/Private/Social

The public versus private nature of family law has long been the site of contestation. Family law has been seen as quintessentially private law, regulating horizontal relationships between private parties, as opposed to public law, which regulates vertical relationships between the state and private parties.[10] Yet feminist and critical family law scholarship has long interrogated in multiple ways the given nature of family law as a distinctive private law discipline. Feminists have sought to demonstrate the ways in which the public/private division has been deeply implicated in the subordination of women.[11] Critical legal scholars have challenged the public/private distinction on which family law is predicated.[12] Many have argued that modern family law does not sit neatly within a public/private distinction, as more and more elements of family life and its breakdown have become the subject of extensive government regulation. Others have pointed out the public functions of family law, as its serves to privatize support obligations for dependent individuals, a function only heightened in the post-welfare era.[13]

While many criticize the public/private distinction within family law, Anne Alstott has used such critiques to specifically challenge the idea of family law as private law. In the traditional private law view, family law "exists primarily to foster private order. On this view, family law should implement individuals' intentions – and should not redistribute risk and resources according to some public ideal. As private law, then, family law's core mission is to resolve disputes among family members when private order breaks down."[14] Alstott argued instead that family law "is more than a mechanism for implementing private preferences and resolving disputes when private order breaks down. Instead, family law forms part of a larger system of public law – a social insurance system that allocates the risk of life events like disability, family breakup, mental illness, substance abuse, and parental poverty."[15] The distributive rules of family law provide for a form of social insurance when the relationship breaks down. Alstott argued that family law operated not unlike TANF (Temporary Assistance for Needy Families, a form of US social welfare assistance) and Social Security, redressing major life risk. While family law and social insurance law have addressed different risks – family law addressing the disruptions of affective life and social insurance the disruptions of working life – she argued that the distinctions between care and work and between family and market are themselves problematic. Alstott has tried to show the many points of intersection and overlap between these regimes and, breaking from the public/private law distinction, has argued that family law should be understood as social insurance. Other scholars have sought to show family law's relationship with a multiplicity of other legal regimes. Janet Halley and Kerry Rittich have explored the genealogy of family law exceptionalism – that is, the emergence of family law as a distinctive field of legal regulation.[16] Much of what we have come to identity as "family law" refers to areas of legal regulation that Halley and Rittich call "Family Law 1" (FL1) – that is, the rules of marriage, divorce, property, support, and custody. These foregrounded rules of family law are important, but, according to Halley and Rittich, they have been "artificially segregated from other rules, lying in the background, that could, and often did, play an equally important distributive role in particular settings."[17] Family law as a distinctive area of legal regulation does not include the multiplicity of ways in which law regulates family law. Halley and Rittich identified other regimes, which they call "Family Law 2" (FL2) and "Family Law 3" (FL3). According to Halley and Rittich, FL2 entails "explicit family-targeted provisions peppered throughout substantive legal regimes that seem to have no primary commitment to maintaining the distinctiveness of the family – regimes ranging from tax law to immigration law to bankruptcy law."[18] FL3 regimes relate to "the myriad legal regimes that contribute structurally but silently to the ways in which family life is lived and the household structured."[19] The objective of Halley and Rittich was to bring FL1, FL2, and FL3 back together, to better understand the distributional impact of the multiple rules that regulate the family. Their work, and the scholarship that it has inspired, demonstrates the extent to which the legal regulation of the family lies at many interstices of public and private law. While FL1 might be framed as more traditionally private, regulating the horizontal relationship between private parties, the multiple legal regimes of FL2 and FL3 bring together a range of so-called public and private law, all impacting the distribution of "the burdens and the benefits of production, the servitudes and the securities of dependency, the labor and satisfactions of consumption."[20]

Yet none of these debates appear to have had any bearing on the unstated assumption that family law as a practice remains a private law dispute between private parties to be resolved within the civil justice system. Generally, family disputes are between two adults, with limited standing for minors in the proceedings. An individual with a family law dispute initiates a proceeding against another private individual – spouse, partner, co-parent – and courts are called upon to adjudicate the disputes that cannot be privately resolved. The argument that family law disputes are not suited for an adversarial system is well rehearsed. There has been a push and a shift to the use of various alternative or consensual dispute resolution mechanisms for family law disputes. Nevertheless, consensual dispute resolution occurs within a private law framework. While the practice of family law now calls upon a broader array of consensual dispute resolution processes, the disputes remain framed as private ones where individuals have carriage of the case and bear the legal costs of resolution, as well as bargain in the shadows of family law's rules. My contention is that this model, based on an understanding of family law as private law to be resolved within the civil justice system and its newer consensual offshoots, may no longer be the best way to think about the resolution of family disputes.

What if we began to move in a direction of reunifying the multiple domains of the legal regulation of the family? If the family were disarticulated from its private law, policy, and ideological moorings, how might we think differently about dispute resolution when the adult relationship breaks down? This moment of dispute resolution is in many respects the epitome of private family law – resolving disputes between two private parties. However, if we recognize the public and social dimensions of traditional family law – so-called FL1 – how might the resolution of this dispute be framed beyond or beside the private realm? How might the restructuring of the financial relationship between the parties, envisioned through the frame of its social dimension, be better linked with other social insurance legal regimes? In the sections that follow, I will imagine different ways of regulating this moment of family transition.

Alternative Models of Regulation

What might the legal regulation of separation and divorce look like if it were disarticulated from its private, civil law moorings? What institutional structures, procedural mechanisms, and substantive rules might be imagined or reimagined? A more radical revision might take on a restructuring of the legal order, along the lines exposed by Halley and Rittich's critique, bringing together, for example, FL1 and FL2 into a more synthetic family law as social policy. In such a model, family law would no longer solely be what Alstott describes as "a zero-sum game" of allocating market earnings within private families.[21] Instead, the allocation of risk and burdens between the parties on family breakdown would form part and parcel of a more comprehensive regime of social risk allocation including taxation, social welfare, employment insurance, and the like. Revisioning family law as social law would require major transformation in our legal categories and regimes.

My project in this chapter will be somewhat narrower in scope. Or, perhaps, it can be conceived of as a first step toward a more radical revision. In the sections that follow, I will think about ways in which the area currently called family law might be disarticulated from its grounding in private, civil law. How might the dissolution of marriage and adult personal relationships be resolved differently? This section will not be a blueprint, but will rather be highly speculative, part of the thought experiment on doing things differently. Some of the suggestions will verge on tinkering; others will be more radical. And some of the tinkering, if coupled with other suggestions, might produce a very different type of legal regime that moves beyond the private, civil regime of current family law. The purpose of the discussion is to encourage further thinking, both sweeping and narrow. How might we think about regulating family breakdown differently? With what regulatory tools could we accomplish this? The discussion that will follow will ultimately raise more questions than answers.

Forums

Many areas that were once private law have transformed to a form of public law, which has included the development of specialized tribunals to resolve disputes. Labour law (once known as a blend of employment and contract law) and landlord-tenant law (once viewed as a mix of property and contract law) emerged as distinct legal regimes, with decision-making authority allocated to administrative tribunals. Unlike more traditional areas of public law involving the individual and state, these are areas of law that continue to involve disputes between private parties: landlords and tenants, employers and unions. But a broader public – or, I would argue, social – interest was recognized, leading not only to specialized rules but also to specialized tribunals. Family law has not gone down this road. Instead, family law in Canada has debated and moved toward specialized family courts. These specialized courts – and, given the divided constitutional jurisdiction that haunts family law, unified family courts – are repeatedly cited as part of the solution to the crisis in access to family justice. Yet these courts remain rooted within the civil justice system. Might there be a role for alternative forums, such as tribunals, in reimagining the way in which family law disputes are resolved?

The advantages and disadvantages of courts versus tribunals have been much discussed. The general claim in favour of tribunals is that they are less formal, less costly, and more expedient in resolving disputes. Tribunal members are selected for their expert knowledge, in contrast to courts, where the judges are often generalists. There is a reason to interrogate these advantages in relation to family courts in particular. Family courts have been designed to address the limitations of generalist courts in resolving family law disputes: the judges are family law specialists, and the procedures are less formal. In other words, there are ways in which family courts resemble the tribunal structure. Conversely, administrative tribunals have also grown in complexity, and hearings before many tribunals can be costly and time consuming. Yet, the family courts remain rooted within a private, civil law regime, where the parties continue to bear the costs – financial and otherwise – of the proceedings.

Unified family courts retain the structure of private law – that is, of individual and private disputes. Simply moving existing family law to a tribunal structure may do little to change or improve the ways in which family law disputes are currently resolved within family courts. Transformations in other areas of law, such as labour law and landlord tenant law, did not simply involve a change in legal forums. These shifts were a fundamental rewriting of the substantive law, recognizing broader social interests. Labour law and landlord-tenant law were shifted from the realm of traditional private law (contract) to a form of social law, and both relocated to the the realm of administrative law. A shift to a different regime outside of the courts, accompanied by a broader shift in the understanding of family law as social law (as involving a social allocation of risks and costs) alongside some of the other changes I will canvass below, might be worth exploring.

To what extent, for example, might some dimensions of family law become more akin to a licensing regime? Just as marriages licences are issued by a provincially delegated body, so could divorce be approached in a similar way. Below, I will canvass the substantive law changes that might facilitate such an approach. In addition, we might ask to what extent additional family law matters might be similarly resolved administratively. Could individuals, jointly or individually, apply to a government body for their property, child, and spousal support by imputing their financial information? We might reconceptualize the process as one akin to filing taxes. Indeed, in a more radical revising of family law that incorporated other areas of law (that is, FL2), a regime could integrate taxation with separation and divorce. The taxation and family law regimes currently interact in modest ways, such as in the use of taxation information to establish income for the purposes of child support. A regime that recognized family law as social law, as a form of social insurance integrated with other regimes, could allocate the costs and burdens of separation and divorce in a manner that was no longer simply a zero-sum allocation of market earnings within the private family. Recognizing the social dimension of family law might help us reimagine new ways of allocating and regulating the costs of family breakdown that move beyond the private.

New Digital Technologies

Legal services generally have moved toward greater experimentation with new digital technologies, from electronic filings to the use of artificial intelligence in predicting and managing legal outcomes. Some legal scholars have explored how these new technologies may play a role in improving access to justice.[22] This digital revolution has had a somewhat limited impact on the structure of family law and dispute resolution. Legal information about divorce and separation is available to Canadians online, through government and legal advice sites. Legal forms are also widely available online. Lawyers have incorporated technologies into their practices, some in ways unique to the challenges of family law.[23] From digital forensics to financial disclosure, digital technologies continue to be integrated into the existing practice of family law. Courts have adopted electronic filings for divorce applications. The United Kingdom recently announced with considerable fanfare that "digital divorces" have come online, although the terms refers simply to the ability of people to now file for divorce online.[24]

In the United States, a number of internet legal providers (ILPs) offer divorce-specific services. Wevorce, for example, is a divorce platform, established in 2012, that provides what it describes as a self-guided divorce solution.[25] For a fee, Wevorce provides step-by-step assistance with divorce planning to assist couples in developing parenting and financial agreements.[26] Recommended for "amicable divorces," the service provides self-guided instruction, document generation, and access to online mediators to assist people in reaching a divorce settlement. Other ILPs assist with document generation, service, and court filings.[27] Like ILPs more generally, these divorce services have evolved relatively quickly "from standardized forms to automated assembly … [where] users can now enter relevant information in intuitive and user friendly prompts, and the Internet software converts user submissions into court ready documents."[28]

Similar ILP divorce services are more limited in Canada. DivorceOnline operates a Canadian site, which assists in generating divorce applications, provided there are no contested custody, access, support, or property issues.[29] A digital service that sought to use artificial intelligence technologies to guide couples through the divorce process was briefly available in Canada. Thistoo, available through Miralaw, provided digital divorces and digital separation agreements for a modest fee.[30] Thistoo founder Samuel Witherspoon spoke optimistically about the potential for the service to address the access-to-justice crisis in family law.[31] But the service closed after two years.[32] More common Canadian informational family law hubs are government and public service websites that make legal forms and legal information available.[33]

Divorce-focused ILPs, like ILPs more generally, face many challenges within the existing family law profession and regime. The more extensive the service, the more the ILP faces challenge around the unauthorized practice of law.[34] At what point do the documents generated and/or the information provided cross the line into legal advice and run the risk of violating professional standards of conduct? The tight regulation of the legal profession in Canada, alongside the customary opposition of lawyers to challenges to their monopoly over the provision of legal services, will no doubt present many an obstacle to the expansion of digital divorce services.

None of the ILPs have fundamentally transformed the ways in which individuals resolve their disputes related to separation and divorce. The technologies are largely add-ons to facilitate the existing private civil law regime. The more ambitious ones, like Wevorce, aim to facilitate private divorce settlements, thereby avoiding the need for contentious legal proceedings. Others seek to reduce legal fees for divorce applications by assisting in these applications. This use of digital technologies may be very helpful to separating and divorcing couples within the existing private law regime. Might there be more transformative uses of new technologies in support of institutional redesign? More specifically, how might these technologies allow us to imagine a different world of dispute resolution uncoupled from the civil justice system? A move to more digital divorce could be implemented alongside an institutional redesign of the forum, moving away from court judgments to more administrative resolutions, alongside a simplification of the rules governing family breakdown. Below, I will consider ways of simplifying some family law rules and argue that removing wide-ranging discretion from family law might help ease access-to-justice problems by rendering outcomes more predictable. The simpler the rules, the easier the rules would be to apply through digital technologies. Could we imagine a regime in which most of the issues could be addressed and resolved online? Child and spousal support could be calculated based on table amounts or formulas. Property division could similarly be determined by entering financial information online. What if all relevant information could simply be entered online, and the division of assets and support amounts could be calculated, not unlike the individual calculation of income tax? One online divorce entrepreneur stated that "[c]ouples today date online and bank online. They don't mind putting in their assets and liabilities into a computer ... If they can buy an espresso maker online, they get divorced online."[35] While somewhat facetious (it hardly needs stating that there are some rather significant differences between purchasing an espresso maker and getting a divorce), her comment does address the increasing ease of and expectations associated with conducting one's life online.

Insurance

Some scholars have sought to more explicitly connect family law with social insurance. Alstott's work has explored how social insurance might be able to do more to recognize and address the disruptions of emotional life that come with divorce and separation.[36] While I wholeheartedly endorse this idea, these are existing public policies, like social welfare and employment insurance, that address social risk. In this section, I explore the possibility of insurance more specifically tied to affective life. What if the costs of financial restructuring on separation and divorce were covered by insurance? What if individuals had to take out insurance policies before they were issued marriage licences? Because of society's recognition of the extraordinary costs associated with motor vehicle insurance, we do not let individuals drive motor vehicles without accident insurance. Why, then, do we allow individuals to enter into relationships with a 38 percent failure rate, the costs of which are increasingly recognized, without some form of insurance? There are, of course, many objections. Mandatory insurance would interfere with people's intimate choices, imposing costs on the decision to marry. The costs might produce a disincentive to marrying, leading more individuals to cohabit outside of marriage, a situation where legal protections are all the more precarious. Non-mandatory insurance would likely be ineffective – individuals do not generally enter into marriage with a view to the marriage failing. Indeed, such an attitude similarly contributes to the low rate of marriage contracts. Individuals *could* choose marriage insurance, but they likely would not.

Taking the idea of insurance seriously would require addressing a series of difficult policy questions around institutional design. Challenging actuarial and underwriting questions would need to be addressed. Would those entering into a second marriage be subject to higher premiums? Or would they be subject to lower premiums, given the statistics on the relative stability of second marriages? Would insurance premiums change after the the birth of children? Would insurance companies treat family units with stay-at-home parents differently than dual-income families? Would the insurance regime be public or private? We could imagine public insurance regimes, where the risk of divorce is pooled, with government regulation. But, given current attitudes toward government insurance regimes, of increasing costs and inefficiencies as seen with health care and public pension plans, it is hard to imagine a public policy appetite for the creation of a new regime. In contrast, advocating private insurance solutions to the problem of family breakdown might be seen as a further privatization of family dispute resolution, putting individuals' well-being into the hands of for-profit insurance companies. Is there a way of revising insurance as social? Of collectively pooling risks through nonprofit organizations?

The idea of marriage insurance is not unprecedented. In 2005, Safeguard Guaranty Corporation was founded for the specific purpose of developing divorce insurance. In 2010, the first divorce insurance policy was sold in the United States, underwritten by the Prime Insurance Company.[37] The insurance – called WedLock Divorce Insurance – was sold for a year, until the company cancelled the program. The insurance was designed to provide financial assistance for costs associated with divorce, such as legal fees or setting up a new home. Upon proof of divorce, the insured would receive a lump sum equivalent to the amount of coverage they had purchased.[38] The insurance was also designed to reward those couples whose marriages lasted – after twenty-five years, they would receive a payout larger than they would have been entitled to if they had divorced. Founder John Logan described the benefit to long-term marriages: "You could look at it as a forced savings plan that's not affected by anything in the economy."[39] According to the Safeguard website, the product is not currently available, as the company continues to search for an underwriter.[40] A limited form of divorce insurance has also been available in the United Kingdom.[41]

I am not advocating in favour of this private model of insurance, but rather simply pointing out that the idea of marriage insurance is not unimaginable. Nor am I advocating that the legal regulation of family breakdown should be reframed entirely as a matter of private risk management. Taking the idea of marriage insurance seriously would require grappling with risk management and broader interrogations of risk governance – that is, the ways in which risk is increasingly deployed as a form of governance. There is a multivalent literature interrogating the normative and analytic implications of risk governance; yet, by and large, the regulation of the family is missing from this literature. It is perhaps yet another oversight produced by family law exceptionalism – that, due to the normative assumption of family being a private concept, family is just *different*. Given the enormous incursion of risk governance into private realms, such a view ought not to be enough to immunize the family; yet, so far, it has been. Nonetheless, given the costs – both private and public – of the family justice system, a case can be made for thinking about socializing the risks and costs of marriage breakdown. Insurance provides a way of socializing burdens, so that the costs do not simply lie where they fall. Marriage insurance might provide a way of moving beyond the zero-sum allocation of market earnings within families, providing instead a potential way of socializing the economic costs of affective life. Marriage insurance is one thought experiment of doing so.

Substantive and Procedural Law Reform

There is a long history of substantive and procedural reform within the existing private, civil family law regime. Family law in Canada has been subject to several waves of major substantive reform. At the federal level, from the 1968 *Divorce Act*[42] to the 1985 *Divorce Act* [*Divorce Act* 1985],[43] grounds for divorce were narrowed. At the provincial and territorial levels, waves of reform have clarified division of property rules. At both levels, spousal- and child-support objectives, and then guidelines, have been set out to structure the obligations.[44] From the perspective of the equitable resolution of family breakdown, the substantive rights and responsibilities in Canadian law are exemplary. The problem is one of accessing these rights and responsibilities.

Recommendations for further reform, then, may sound like tinkering within the existing private, civil legal system. Nonetheless, my intention is to think more deeply about how substantive reform might support a more radical rethinking of the resolution of financial disputes during relationship breakdown. There may be a case for further substantive reform linked to a decoupling of family law from private civil law.

Divorce Reform

One concrete suggestion would be to further reform the grounds and procedure for divorce. Under the *Divorce Act* 1985, divorce is available at marital breakdown, which can be established on the basis of three grounds: adultery, cruelty, or living separately and apart for one year.[45] The overwhelming majority of divorces proceed on the basis of living separate and apart. Yet, a significant number of divorces are still sought on the basis of adultery and cruelty.[46] Divorce is within the jurisdiction of the superior courts of a province. Most divorces proceed by way of affidavit, not by trial.[47] But, even in the absence of a trial, the grounds for divorce must be established. The petitioner must establish, on a balance of probabilities, that the couple have been living separate and apart for one year, or that adultery or cruelty was committed. Each of these grounds, in turn, have tests to meet. If the grounds are not met, the divorce must be denied.

Divorce could be reformed in a number of ways. Substantively, the grounds based on fault could be eliminated. Divorces based on fault no longer provide a more immediate dissolution of the marriage. There are serious questions about whether the resources of a tightly stretched family justice system should be used to provide divorces on a fault-based ground. The defence of fault-based divorce has been that the acts in question constitute a fundamental breach of the marital relationship and ought to allow the innocent party to exit the marriage. Individuals who, for moral or religious reasons, would prefer a divorce on the basis of a fault-based ground, should be allowed to obtain such a divorce. However, the end result is the same: the marriage is dissolved, and there is no longer any implication for financial or parental rights and responsibilities. Adultery- and cruelty-based divorces take up more court resources, since the threshold of proof must be established. If it fails to be met, the court must deny the divorce. In the twenty-first century, denying divorces no longer seems like a viable use of judicial resources.

Divorce law could be further reformed by away from a grounds-based model. In the United Kingdom, an attempt was made to transform divorce from a grounds-based model to a process-based model. Irreconcilable marital breakdown would have remained the sole basis for divorce. However, the ground did not have to be established through fact, but solely through the expiry of a minimum period of one year, to allow for a consideration of the practical consequences of divorce and reflection on whether the breakdown was irreparable. Married couples petitioning for divorce would have been required to attend information sessionsto address a range of the practical considerations, including the availability of marriage counselling, the use of mediation, the welfare of children, and the financial consequences of marital breakdown (including the division of financial assets). The law was ultimately repealed. Following a series of pilot projects involving the information sessions, the government concluded that the new law was "unworkable" – more specifically, that it "would not achieve the objectives of saving savable marriages and reducing distress and conflict."[48] Currently, debates are under way to further reform divorce law in the United Kingdom.[49]

Notwithstanding the failure of divorce law reform in the United Kingdom, which remained mired in the politics of saving the institution of marriage as well as the logistical difficulties of establishing accessible information sessions, reform that eschews a grounds-based model is worthy of further interrogation. Such a reform would complete the transformation of the status of divorce to an individualized decision. No resources – private or public – would be expended on adjudicating whether a particular couple ought to remain within a marriage. In some ways, such an approach sounds like classic private law, allowing two private individuals to implement their individual intentions absent a public ideal. But I suggest that the parallel to private law would end there. The focus on family law would then be on the allocation of risks and resources on the basis of a more public (or social) ideal, namely, the financial and parenting consequences of the marital breakdown. Presently, the only financial restriction on the granting of a divorce is whether reasonable arrangements have been made for the support of the children. The application for divorce could continue to have this restriction.

Given that the majority of divorces already proceed on the basis of living separately and apart, and proceed by way of affidavit, the change would not be that dramatic, but it could focus attention and resources toward the financial and parenting dimensions of marital breakdown. And, within a more radical rethinking of family law, this kind of reform could also be coupled with a shift away from courts and toward a tribunal and/or digital model of family breakdown. What if divorce, rather like marriage, became more akin to a system of licensing? Individuals would apply for a divorce, as a kind of revocation of the marriage licence. After a given time period, the divorce would be granted, subject only to any financial requirements having been met. It could be achieved – like marriage – in an entirely administrative matter.

Objections would no doubt be multiple. As with many of the suggestions in this chapter, vested interests and path dependencies will tell us that this is impossible and/or undesirable. Some (though likely not the mainstream of the family law bar) will lament the loss of the sanctity of marriage and the importance of its preservation. Others will raise more incisive critiques about the impact on the resolution of financial and parenting disputes. Might a shift to the entirely procedural realm undermine the incentive to resolve these disputes? How might an administrative licensing system become bogged down in bureaucratic entanglements? These questions and others are important ones that need to be interrogated. Regardless, they need not stop the thought experiment in its tracks.

Reducing Discretion

Much family law reform has struggled with the tension between structured and predictable rules and individualized fairness, whether it be in court doctrine or legislative reform. Reducing the discretion that once plagued family law has been a consistent theme over the most recent decades of reform.[50] Yet tensions regarding the continued need for discretion persist. Child-support guidelines, for example, have sought to provide consistent and predictable outcomes through a formula that generates an amount of child support based on the income of the payor and the number of children. Although, as Justice Abella has opined with a resonance that goes beyond child support, "[f]airness is the Holy Grail in family law. Certainty and predictability of child support amounts do not justify a retreat from the primacy of a child's rights to a fair amount of support."[51] The child-support guidelines include various adjustments, such as provisions dealing with high-income earners, provisions dealing with children over the age of majority, and shared custody, each give the courts broad discretion to adjust the table amounts. Such discretion remains largely unstructured by the courts, providing broad latitude to trial courts to adjust child-support orders. These adjustments are required to provide for a range of quite different circumstances (shared custody is very different from sole custody; children over the age of majority may have financial circumstances very different from those under the age the majority). However, the discretion afforded to courts in the name of fairness runs the risk of undermining the objectives of consistency and predictability.

A similar tension is seen in the *Spousal Support Advisory Guidelines* (*SSAGs*).[52] The guidelines, intended to give some structure to spousal-support negotiations and orders, provide two formulas that produce a range of possible support amounts and duration. Their adoption by lawyers as a starting place for negotiation, as well as their use by courts, has brought some critical structure to an area of family law that was discretionary in the extreme. Yet, the *SSAGs* are infused with discretionary factors. The formulas first produce ranges, and then a series of factors are used to move the amount and durations within these ranges. There are also a broad range of exceptions to the formula amounts – that is, situations where the formulas would not be appropriate. The authors of the *SSAGs*, Carol Rogerson and Rollie Thompson, have emphasized that the application of the guidelines must not be mechanical, but rather must take into account specific factual situations.[53]

As with so many family law rules, the challenge is to find the balance between structure and discretion in order to tailor the outcome to the particular needs of the particular family. Some areas of family law have less discretion. For example, the division of property regimes in many provinces have limited judicial discretion to vary the equalization of property to the relatively high threshold of unconscionability.[54] The result has been to limit the extent to which exceptions to equalization are granted. The underlying idea is that marriage is an economic partnership that makes equalization a fair division for all families, subject only to unconscionability. It is an area of law where the claims around the unique situations of each unique family have less purchase.

What if we took a similar stance in the areas of family law that continued to have high levels of discretion, namely, child and spousal support? In the context of child support, there are a few relatively simple targets for reform. Section 9 of the *Federal Child Support Guidelines* (*CSG*)[55] sets out the special rules for shared custody. A controversial provision, the section provides that, if a child spends no less than 40 percent of their time with a parent, the guidelines no longer automatically apply. Instead, s 9 provides that the child support order is to be determined in accordance with:

> (a) the amounts set out in the applicable tables for each of the spouses;
> (b) the increased costs of shared parenting time arrangements; and
> (c) the conditions, means, needs and other circumstances of each spouse and of any child for whom support is sought.[56]

This is a provision with enormous discretion, and the Supreme Court of Canada has done little to structure this discretion. In *Contino v Leonelli-Contino,* the Supreme Court expressly rejected any presumptions of set-off or multiplier formulas.[57] Nonetheless, shared custody provisions could be rendered far less discretionary. They could simply stipulate that the default would be a set-off, with a multiplier to address the set costs of child care.[58] This rule could be subject to an exception based on unconscionability or the lower threshold of inequity. It could be a strong starting place to establish the child-support obligation and reduce the discretion.

Section 4 of the *CSG*, dealing with incomes over $150,000, could also be subject to some simple reforms.[59] First, the income level should be increased. The current amount of $150,000, as established in 1997, is currently valued at approximately $234,000. Given that the concern with high-income earners seems to start at higher income levels, where child-support orders might come to be seen as inappropriate, the current income level for the discretionary provision should be reconsidered, and potentially increased.[60] While high-income parents are the ones who can most afford to litigate, this ability is not always shared between the two parents in a relationship. Nor should the limited judicial resources of the family justice system be deployed to adjudicate in cases at the lower end of high incomes. The threshold should be significantly increased, thereby decreasing the number of Canadian families who would be subject to this discretion.

The suggestion of reducing discretion is somewhat sacrilegious in family law. For many, discretion is the *sine qua non* of modern family law. I have long empathized with this view, precisely because family life is so important and varied. I worry, however, that we can no longer afford a customized resolution of family breakdown. Fairness can no longer reside only in designing substantive rights and responsibilities. There needs to be a trade-off in the ability to access these rights and responsibilities. Years of demanding more legal aid, duty counsels, and other supplements to the existing system may no longer be enough, particularly in the face of declining public funding. It may be time to reconsider some of the sacred pillars of family law or to at least ponder the possibility of reconceptualizing them.

Limiting discretion within substantive family law is a type of reform that could be done within the existing regime of family law. Moreover, this type of reforms might be necessary if the process of restructuring financial relationships on separation and divorce were to be disaggregated from the private, civil justice system. The simpler the rules, the easier they are to apply. Reducing discretion could make the resolution of disputes more compatible with alternative mechanisms, such as digital artificial intelligence predictors, social tribunals, or insurance regimes.

Toward More Rethinking

The suggestions I have explored are not ones in which I am invested. I am offering them only as part of an experiment in thinking about family law differently – as part of a rethinking of the restructuring of financial and parenting relationships when the adult personal relationship breaks down. If we allow ourselves the freedom to abandon the current model and think anew, many other possibilities would no doubt spring up. It is a utopian exercise, yet one located within the current modalities of legal regulation and family life. We might also reimagine family law along entirely differently lines, from abolishing marriage to restructuring family law to decentre the conjugal in favour of the filial. Even more broadly, we could reimagine the entirety of family law and policy bringing together welfare, health, education, housing, and taxation to rethink a policy and legal regime of supporting families. My thought experiment here is narrower (and not in any way staking a claim to being better). It is to reimagine the family justice system, away from the private law model that has dominated it, in favour of a more social distribution of the costs of family breakdown. I have no doubt that other, smarter scholars and policymakers equipped with institutional design expertise could come up with better proposals. My objective here is to do little more than simply open the possibility of such rethinking.

Notes

1 Chief Justice Warren K Winkler, "Family Law and Access to Justice: Time for Change," 5th Annual Family Law Summit (17 June 2011), cited in Law Commission of Ontario, *Towards a More Efficient and Responsive Family Justice System: Interim Report* (Toronto: Law Commission of Ontario, 2012), online (PDF): <www.lco-cdo.org/wp-content/uploads/2012/02/family-law-reform-interim-report.pdf)> [Law Commission of Ontario] at 81.

2 Law Commission of Ontario, *supra* note 1.

3 See e.g. Canada, Action Committee on Access to Justice in Civil and Family Matters, *Family Justice Reform: A Review of Reports and Initiatives*, by Erin Shaw (Ottawa: Action Committee on Access to Justice in Civil and Family Matters, 2012) [Shaw]; Law Commission of Ontario, *supra* note 1.

4 See Action Committee on Access to Justice in Civil and Family Matters, *Access to Civil and Family Justice: A Roadmap for Change* (Ottawa: Action Committee on Access to Justice in Civil and Family Matters, 2013).

5 See Alex Robinson, "Debate Heats Up on Paralegals in Family Law," *Law Times* (15 May 2017), online: <www.lawtimesnews.com/news/general/debate-heats-up-on-paralegals-in-family-law/262555>; Michael McKiernan, "Paralegals in Family Law," *Canadian Lawyer* (19 March 2018), online: <www.canadianlawyermag.com/practice-areas/family/paralegals-in-family-law/274950>. For a general discussion of lawyers' resistance to challenges of their exclusive practice in family law and beyond, see Lisa Trabucco, "Lawyers' Monopoly? Think Again: The Reality of Non-Lawyer Legal Service Provision in Canada" (2018) 96:3 Can Bar Rev 460.

6 Paul Pierson, "Increasing Returns, Path Dependence and the Study of Politics" (2000) 94:2 Am Pol Sci Rev 251 at 251–52 (defining "path dependency") citing Margaret Levi, "A Model, a Method and a Map: Rationale Choice in Comparative and Historical Analysis" in Mark Lichbach & Alan Zuckerman, eds, *Comparative*

Politics: Rationality, Culture and Structure (Cambridge: Cambridge University Press, 1997) 19 at 28.

7 Vanier Institute of the Family, *Families Count: Profiling Canada's Families IV* (Ottawa: Vanier Institute of the Family, 2010) at 44. However, in 2011, Statistics Canada stopped publishing annual data on marriage and divorce rates, with the last available data based on 2008 statistics.

8 Leo Tolstoy, *Anna Karenina*, translated by Richard Pevear & Larissa Volokhonsky (New York: Penguin Classics, 2000) at 1.

9 A crucial caveat is in order here. I am not including child custody and access, or what is now increasingly referred to as the allocation of parenting responsibility, in terms of a child's residential schedule and decision-making authority. I will focus only on the financial component of separation and divorce. This includes child support, which is, of course, dependent on parenting arrangements. This narrow focus is no doubt a serious limitation of my thought experiment. But I have no proposals around rethinking the facilitation of custody and access disputes.

10 See Michael Rosenfeld, "Rethinking the Boundaries between Public Law and Private Law for the Twenty First Century: An Introduction" (2013) 11:1 Intl J Constitutional L 125.

11 See e.g. Susan Moller Okin, *Justice, Gender and the Family* (New York: Basic Books, 1989).

12 See e.g. Frances Olsen, "The Family and the Market: A Study of Ideology and Legal Reform" (1983) 96:7 Harv L Rev 1497; Frances Olsen, "The Myth of State Intervention in the Family" (1985) 18:4 U Mich JL Ref 835.

13 See e.g. Susan B Boyd, ed, *Challenging the Public/Private Divide: Feminism, Law and Public Policy* (Toronto: University of Toronto Press, 1997); Brenda Cossman & Judy Fudge, eds, *Privatization, Law and the Challenge of Feminism* (Toronto: University of Toronto Press, 2002).

14 Anne Alstott, "Private Tragedies? Family Law as Social Insurance" (2010) 4:1 Harvard L & Policy Rev 3 at 3.

15 *Ibid.*

16 Janet Halley & Kerry Rittich, "Critical Directions in Comparative Family Law: Genealogies and Contemporary Studies of Family Law Exceptionalism" (2010) 58:4 Am J Comp L 753 at 754. They described family law exceptionalism as follows: "We start with the observation that family and family law are often treated as occupying a unique and autonomous domain – as exceptional – and for a wide variety of reasons: they are unique because (unlike the market) they house intimate, private, emotional, and vulnerable relationships; they are unique because they preserve (against modernity and/or the global or foreign) the

traditional, the national, the indigenous; they are unique because (as against the secular) they derive from sacred command."

17 *Ibid* at 761.

18 *Ibid*.

19 *Ibid* at 762. They further write: "For simple examples of FL3, imagine occupancy limits in landlord/tenant law that give more or less protection to incumbents; employment rules that permit dismissal on the part of the employer 'at will' or, by contrast, require employers to give notice to employees who are dismissed without cause; rules that exclude household employees from the protective legislation governing workplaces or that craft special regimes governing such employees" (*ibid* at 762).

20 See *ibid* at 766.

21 Alstott, *supra* note 14 at 3.

22 See Jena McGill et al, "Emerging Technological Solutions to Access to Justice Problems: Opportunities and Risks of Mobile and Web-based Apps" (Knowledge Synthesis Report submitted to Social Sciences and Humanities Research Council, 13 October 2016), online (PDF): <commonlaw.uottawa.ca/sites/commonlaw.uottawa.ca/files/ksg_report_-_mcgill_et_al_oct_13_final_to_send_to_sshrc.pdf>. McGill et al explore technology "as a means of creating new pathways to justice. To that end, mobile and web-based apps intended to assist individuals with legal tasks are now being deployed in the legal services environment" (*ibid* at 2). See also Jane Bailey, Jacquelyn Burkell & Graham Reynolds, "Access to Justice for All: Toward an 'Expansive Vision' of Justice and Technology" (2013) 31:2 Windsor YB Access Just 181; James E Cabral et al, "Using Technology to Enhance Access to Justice" (2012) 26:1 Harv JL & Tech 241.

23 See "Seven Family Law Technology Tips and Tricks," *Family Lawyer Magazine* (19 February 2016), online: <familylawyermagazine.com/articles/7-family-law-technology-tips-and-tricks/>.

24 See Her Majesty's Courts & Tribunals Service, Ministry of Justice & Lucy Frazer QC MP, Press Release, "Fully Digital Divorce Application Launched to the Public" (6 May 2018), online: GOV.UK, <www.gov.uk/government/news/fully-digital-divorce-application-launched-to-the-public>.

25 "Wevorce: Changing Divorce for Good" (last modified 2017), online: Wevorce <www.wevorce.com/home>. There are many other ILPs with divorce-specific services. See e.g. "My Divorce Papers" (last modified 2017), online: My Divorce Papers <www.mydivorcepapers.com/>; "3 Step Divorce: The Original Online Divorce" (last modified 2019), online: 3 Step Divorce <www.3stepdivorce.com/>; "DivorceOnline" (last modified 2015), online: DivorceOnline <divorceonline.ca/>. Other ILP giants offer family law–specific services as well. See e.g. "LegalZoom," online: LegalZoom <www.legalzoom.com/>.

26 "Wevorce," *supra* note 25.

27 Mathew Rotenberg, "Stifled Justice: The Unauthorized Practice of Law and Internet Legal Resources" (2012) 97:2 Minn L Rev 709.

28 *Ibid* at 719.

29 "DivorceOnline," *supra* note 25.

30 See Samuel Witherspoon, "Artificial Intelligence and the Family Law Crisis" (6 June 2016), online (podcast): *Building New Law* <www.countertax.ca/bnlpodcast/s01e07-sam-witherspoon>.

31 *Ibid.*

32 *Ibid.*

33 See e.g. "Steps to Justice: Your Guide to Law in Ontario, Family Law" (last modified 2018), online: Steps to Justice <stepstojustice.ca/legal-topic/family-law>.

34 See Rotenberg, *supra* note 27.

35 See Laura Wasser, quoted in Amy Sohn, "Angelina Jolie's Lawyer Now Offers Quickie Divorces Online," *New York Times* (3 February 2018), online: <www.nytimes.com/2018/02/03/style/can-you-get-divorced-online.html>.

36 Alstott, *supra* note 14.

37 See "Safeguard: Guaranty Corporation" (last modified 2017), online: Safeguard Guaranty <www.safeguardguaranty.com/>.

38 Jennifer Saranow Schultz, "Divorce Insurance (Yes, Divorce Insurance)" (6 August 2010), online (blog): *Bucks* <bucks.blogs.nytimes.com/2010/08/06/divorce-insurance-yes-divorce-insurance/?_r=1>.

39 See "Marriage Insurance Being Pitched in U.S., Canada," *CBC News* (30 April 2012), online: <www.cbc.ca/news/canada/manitoba/marriage-insurance-being-pitched-in-u-s-canada-1.1219262>.

40 "Safeguard," *supra* note 37. According to a 2017 news story, Logan was still planning to bring the product to market, anticipating a 2018 launch. Aaron Broverman, "Could Marriage Insurance Take the Sting Out of Divorce?" *Yahoo Finance* (6 November 2017), online: <ca.finance.yahoo.com/news/marriage-insurance-take-sting-divorce-174714877.html>. At the time of writing, the service is still unavailable.

41 Catherine Baksi, "London Firm Offers Divorce Insurance," *Law Gazette* (3 August 2011), online: <www.lawgazette.co.uk/news/london-firm-offers-divorce-insurance/61692.article>.

42 *Divorce Act,* RSC 1968, c 24.

43 *Divorce Act,* RSC 1985, c 3 (2nd Supp).

44 See Federal Child Support Guidelines (SOR/97-175), which have similarly been adopted by all provinces and territories with the exception of Quebec.

45 *Divorce Act, supra* note 43, s 8.

46 In 2008, 93.6 percent of divorces were granted on the basis of living separate and apart; 3.7 percent on the basis of adultery, 1.6 percent on the basis of mental cruelty, and 1.2 percent for physical cruelty. See Anne Milan, "Marital Status Overview, 2011" (July 2013), online: Statistics Canada <www150.statcan.gc.ca/n1/en/pub/91-209-x/2013001/article/11788-eng.pdf?st=6OUdn_E5>.

47 Mary Bess Kelly "Divorce Cases in Civil Court, 2010/2011" (28 March 2012), online: Statistics Canada <www150.statcan.gc.ca/n1/pub/85–002-x/2012001/article/11634-eng.htm>.

48 See Lord McNally, Justice Minister, 2001, cited in UK, House of Commons Library, "No Fault Divorce" (Briefing Paper No 01409) by Catherine Fairbairn (London: House of Commons Library, 2019) at 14.

49 UK, Ministry of Justice, Press Release, "New Legislation to Overhaul Divorce Law and Reduce Family Conflict" (9 April 2019), online: GOV.UK, <www.gov.uk/government/news/new-divorce-law-to-end-the-blame-game>.

50 See e.g. Nicholas Bala, "Judicial Discretion and Family Law Reform in Canada" (1986) 5:1 Can J Fam L 15.

51 *DBS v SRG*, 2006 SCC 37 at para 167.

52 See Ottawa, Department of Justice, Family, Children and Youth Section, *Spousal Support Advisory Guidelines*, by Carol Rogerson & Rollie Thompson (Ottawa: Department of Justice, July 2008).

53 Ottawa, Department of Justice: Family, Children and Youth Section, *Spousal Support Advisory Guidelines: A User's Guide to the Final Version*, by Carol Rogerson & Rollie Thompson (Ottawa: Department of Justice, July 2018).

54 The *Ontario Family Law Act* RSO 1990, c F.3, s 5(6) uses the standard of unconscionabililty for a deviation from equal sharing. Other provinces use the standard of unfairness. See also e.g. the British Columbia *Family Law Act*, SBC 2011, c 25, s 95(1), which states that, under specific circumstances, "[t]he Supreme Court may order an unequal division of family property or family debt, or both."

55 *Federal Child Support Guidelines*, SOR/97-175, s 9 [*CSG*].

56 *Ibid.*

57 See *Contino v Leonelli-Contino*, 2005 SCC 63.

58 In a set-off, as used as a first step in s 9(a) of the *CSG*, child support is calculated by determining the table amount for each parent as though the other parent were seeking support. The child-support amount would be the difference between the two. In a multiplier set-off, a factor (often 1.5) is used to adjust the child support upward, recognizing the increased costs of shared custody arrangements, and approximating the savings for the recipient parent. The advantages and disadvantages have been summarized by the Department of Justice, in its review of the *CSG*, *Children Come First: A Report to Parliament Reviewing the Provisions and*

Operation of the Federal Child Support Guidelines, vol 2 (Ottawa: Department of Justice, 2002) at 70: The method is objective, relatively easy to calculate, and offers certainty and predictability, in keeping with many of the objectives of the *Federal Child Support Guidelines*. As with any formula, when the set-off formula is used with a multiplier, courts and parent do not have to calculate the details of the costs and savings associated with shared custody, thereby significantly simplifying court procedures. However, a strict formula is inflexible and may be unfair to some families. In addition, many people note that there isn't yet enough research to prove that any given multiplier will accurately reflect the increased costs of shared custody. A 1.5 multiplier assumes that 50 percent of the costs of child rearing, such as housing and transportation, are fixed.

59 *CSG*, *supra* note 55 at s 4.

60 The Department of Justice's *Children Come First* review of the Child Support Guidelines, *supra* note 58 at 43, noted that "[t]he $150,000 threshold was selected because in the mid-1990s incomes of $150,000 were regarded as being at the high end of the income spectrum. At that time, only a small percentage of Canadians earned this amount or more each year. As a result, the vast majority of cases would involve lower incomes, to which the table amounts would apply." A cursory review of the case law would suggest that departures from the guideline amount occur only at considerably higher income levels. While, in 2002, the review did not recommend any changes to s 4, I would suggest that a systemic review of high-income cases be undertaken, to determine the average income where departures are ordered, and to consider an upward adjustment of the threshold amount.

Contributors

Erez Aloni is an associate professor in the Peter A. Allard School of Law at the University of British Columbia. He has published widely on legal regulation of adult relationships and complex family structures. Aloni's work has appeared in leading publications across the world, and he is a frequent speaker at diverse forums. With Régine Tremblay, he is faculty coeditor of the *Canadian Journal of Family Law*.

Nicola Barker is a professor of law at the University of Liverpool, United Kingdom. Her research takes a feminist approach to the broad areas of constitutional and family law. Her past publications include the Hart/SLSA prize-winning monograph *Not the Marrying Kind: A Feminist Critique of Same-Sex Marriage*, as well as two edited collections and numerous articles and book chapters on the topics of marriage and conjugality, the Bermuda Constitution, and LGBT rights in the British Overseas Territories. Barker was awarded a British Academy Fellowship in 2018–19 to undertake a feminist critique of the United Kingdom's Human Rights Act.

Hélène Belleau is a sociologist and full professor at INRS – Centre Urbanisation, Culture et Société. She has been interested for several years in conjugal relations, the social use of money, and the legal framework of de facto unions. She is the scientific director of the research team Familles en mouvance and founded the Observatoire des realités familiales du Québec. She is the author of several books, including *Amour et argent: Guide de survie en 60 questions* with Delphine Lobet, and *Quand l'amour et l'État rendent aveugle: Le mythe du mariage automatique*.

Chao-ju Chen is a distinguished professor of law and director of the women's and gender studies program at National Taiwan University. She has published extensively in the intersecting fields of feminist jurisprudence, socio-legal studies, and Taiwan's legal history. Her research combines theoretical analysis with social inquiry and historical insight to examine the transformation of male dominance, the myth of liberal feminist legal reform, and the consolidation of marital supremacy under the shadow of legal Orientalism, focusing on interrogating choice, consent, and inequality. She practises engaged scholarship and is committed to advocacy on feminism and constitutional democracy through NGO participation and public writing.

Brenda Cossman is the Goodman-Schipper Chair and professor of law at the University of Toronto. She is a Fellow of the Royal Society of Canada, and has been awarded the Mundell Medal by the Attorney General of Ontario for contributions to letters and law, and the Ontario Bar Association Award of Excellence for the Promotion of Women's Equality. Her teaching and scholarly interests focus on the legal regulation of gender, sexuality, and family.

Alison Diduck has taught and researched family and child law, feminist legal theory, and current issues in law and gender for many years. She now teaches these subjects at LLB and LLM levels at UCL in London. She is the author of over forty-five publications including articles, monographs, and edited collections. She is a professor of law and was vice dean of the UCL Faculty of Laws from 2017 to 2021.

Julianna Ivanyi was called to the bar in 2021 and is a lawyer practising in Vancouver. She graduated from the Peter A. Allard School of Law at the University of British Columbia in 2020, where she was on the Board of Directors of the *UBC Law Review*. She also worked as a research assistant to Régine Tremblay, assisting in several research projects surrounding family law reform in both British Columbia and Alberta.

Allison Anna Tait is a professor of law at the University of Richmond where she teaches trusts and estates, family law, estate planning, critical theory, and feminist legal theory. Tait's research addresses the regulation of family and household economies and takes up questions of entitlement and dispossession, examining the ways that family wealth rules help to embed difference along the axes of gender, race, and class. She is currently working on a project that pairs the governance of high-wealth families with that of families living in poverty and explicates how these polar economies of excess and extraction replicate colonialist formations.

Rachel Treloar is a lecturer in law at Keele University, United Kingdom, where she teaches family law and is program director for the master's in child care law and practice. Her research involves the intersections of family law, social policy, and lived experiences. She holds an interdisciplinary PhD (sociology, public policy, and law) from Simon Fraser University. Her doctoral research, "The Construction and Transformation of High-Conflict Divorce Involving Children," was funded by a SSHRC Doctoral Fellowship and a Graduate Fellowship from the Law Foundation of British Columbia. Prior to undertaking doctoral studies, Rachel worked as a family counsellor and ran a community agency program for separating/divorcing parents and their children.

Régine Tremblay is an assistant professor and the director of the Centre for Feminist Legal Studies at the Peter A. Allard School of Law at the University of British Columbia. She is a member of the Quebec Bar and her work has appeared in English and French in publications such as the *Supreme Court Law Review*, the *Canadian Journal of Family Law*, and the *Canadian Journal of Women and the Law*. She coauthored the second edition of the *Private Law Dictionary and Bilingual Lexicon – Family/Dictionnaire de droit privé et lexiques bilingues – Les familles* and coedited *Les intraduisibles en droit civil*. With Erez Aloni, she is faculty coeditor of the *Canadian Journal of Family Law*.

Adam Vanzella-Yang is a PhD candidate in sociology and holder of a Joseph-Armand Bombardier Scholarship (SSHRC) at the University of British Columbia. He specializes in the areas of health, culture, and social inequality. His dissertation examines the role of different socio-economic resources in shaping the mental health of Canadian adults. His work has been published in leading journals such as the *Canadian Review of Sociology*, *City and Community*, and *BMC Public Health*.

Wanda Wiegers, LLB (Saskatchewan), BC (Saskatchewan), and LLM (University of Toronto), is a professor at the College of Law, University of Saskatchewan. Her research and teaching interests are in the areas of economic analysis of law, feminist and critical legal theory, family law, children and the law, domestic violence, autonomous motherhood, women and the welfare state, child welfare reform, economic inequality, and poverty law.

Index

Printed and bound in Canada by Friesens
Set in Zurich, Univers, and Minion by Apex CoVantage, LLC
Copy editor: Barbara Tessman
Proofreader: Alison Strobel
Indexer: Noeline Bridge
Cover designer: David Drummond